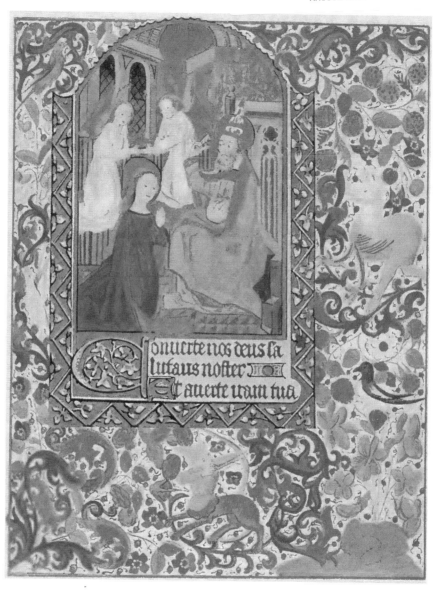

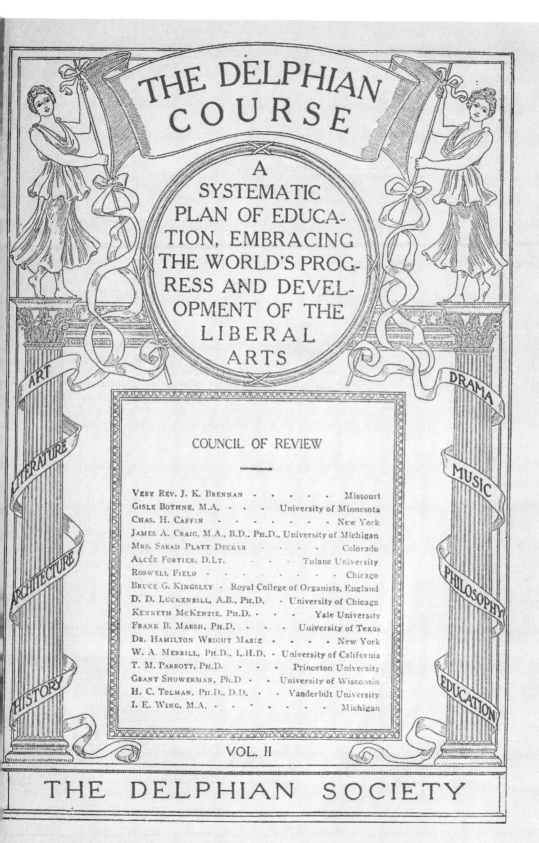

THE DELPHIAN COURSE

A SYSTEMATIC PLAN OF EDUCATION, EMBRACING THE WORLD'S PROGRESS AND DEVELOPMENT OF THE LIBERAL ARTS

ART

DRAMA

LITERATURE

MUSIC

ARCHITECTURE

PHILOSOPHY

HISTORY

EDUCATION

COUNCIL OF REVIEW

VOL. II

THE DELPHIAN SOCIETY

Hebrew Literature, Greek Mythology, Life and Art
Delphian Reading Course
Part Two
Plus Study Guide

Compiled from:
The Delphian Course, by the Delphian Society, Chicago:The Delphian Society, (1913).

Study Guide, by the Delphian Society, Chicago:The Delphian Society, (1911).

Cover Image: Orpheus Leading Eurydice from the Underworld by Jean-Baptiste-Camille-Corot (1861), from Wikimedia Commons

Libraries of Hope, Inc. Appomattox, Virginia 24522

Website: www.librariesofhope.com
Email: support@librariesofhope.com

Printed in the United States of America

TABLE OF CONTENTS
PART II.

CHAPTER XIII.

From the Captivity to the Final Disposition of the Jews............ PAGE 1

CHAPTER XIV.

Industries and Arts among the Israelites......................... 7

CHAPTER XV.

Hebrew Literature; Poetry 12

CHAPTER XVI.

Hebrew Drama; The Book of Job. Hebrew Fiction................. 23

CHAPTER XVII.

Wisdom Literature; The Prophets 39

CHAPTER XVIII.

Explorations in Palestine....................................... 45

HEBREW LITERATURE.

The Book of Ruth... 48
The Praise of Famous Men....................................... 54
King Solomon's Betrothal....................................... 55
Palestine of Today... 58

GREEK MYTHOLOGY.

Prefatory Chapter.. 69

CHAPTER I.

The Meaning of Mythology and Why We Study it.. 78

CHAPTER II.

Greek Explanation of the Origin of the World.................... 86

CHAPTER III.

Titans and Battle of the Giants. Prometheus.................... 91

CHAPTER IV.

Hera; Narcissus; Iris; Hebe.................................... 100

CHAPTER V.

Athena   115

CHAPTER VI.   PAGE

Apollo 123

CHAPTER VII.

Artemis   130

CHAPTER VIII.

Ares 135

CHAPTER IX.

Aphrodite; Cupid; Psyche; The Marriage of Cupid and Psyche.......140

CHAPTER X.

Hermes 148

CHAPTER XI.

Hestia; The Muses; The Fates 154

CHAPTER XII.

Demeter; Persephone; Bacchus; Dionysus......................... 158

CHAPTER XIII.

Pan; Oreads 169

CHAPTER XIV.

Poseidon; The Syrens; The Gorgons; Atlas; Medusa.............. 173

CHAPTER XV.

Aeolus; The Harpies   182

CHAPTER XVI.

Pluto; Tantalus; Isles of the Blest............................. 188

CHAPTER XVII.

Orpheus; Cave of Sleep; Morpheus................................ 195

CHAPTER XVIII.

Hecate; Nemesis 202

CHAPTER XIX.

Hercules; His Labors 206

CHAPTER XX.

The Remaining Labors 217

THE STORY OF GREECE.

CHAPTER I.

Relative Importance of Greek History; Physical Geography of Greece 227

CHAPTER II.

Discovery Made by Dr. Schliemann; Mycenaean Life and Culture... 236

CHAPTER III.

PAGE

Homeric Poems; Homeric Life.................................... 247

CHAPTER IV.

Sources of Greek History 262

CHAPTER V.

Early History of Sparta   269

CHAPTER VI.

Athens; Reforms of Solon.. 275

CHAPTER VII.

From Age of Solon to Persian Wars.............................. 284

CHAPTER VIII.

Struggle with Persia 292

CHAPTER IX.

Athenian Empire; Pericles   302

CHAPTER X.

Athenian Statesmen; Aristides; Themistocles 309

CHAPTER XI.

Prosperity of Athens   318

CHAPTER XII.

Causes of the Peloponnesian War.................................. 322

CHAPTER XIII.

Peloponnesian War to Death of Pericles........................... 331

CHAPTER XIV.

To the Fall of Athens. The Sicilian Expedition................... 337

CHAPTER XV.

Supremacy of Sparta; Ascendency of Thebes; The Founding of
Thebes 345

CHAPTER XVI.

Rise of Macedonia; Philip of Macedon............................ 354

CHAPTER XVII.

Alexander the Great; Effects of His Conquests.................... 366

SOCIAL LIFE IN GREECE.

CHAPTER I.

Hellenic Cities; The Agora; Houses.............................. 375

CHAPTER II.

PAGE

Wearing Apparel of the Hellenes.................................... 382

CHAPTER III.

Food in Ancient Greece... 387

CHAPTER IV.

Women in Ancient Greece... 394

CHAPTER V.

Childhood and Early Education...................................... 401

CHAPTER VI.

The Citizen's Career   406

CHAPTER VII.

Amusements and Pastimes   410

CHAPTER VIII.

Labor and Trade   414

CHAPTER IX.

Worship and Religious Festivals 421

CHAPTER X.

Spartan Life   426

GREEK LITERATURE.

CHAPTER XI.

Beginnings of Greek Literature 429
The Greek Epic 437
The Odyssey 454
Hesiod 464

CHAPTER XII.

The Greek Lyric 469
Description of Illustrations 481

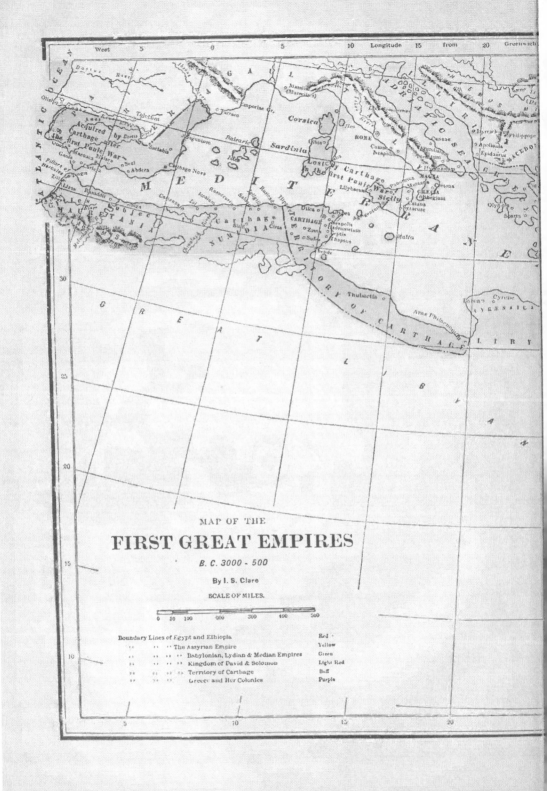

MAP OF THE

FIRST GREAT EMPIRES

B. C. 3000 - 500

By I. S. Clare

SCALE OF MILES.

0   50   100   200   300   400   500

Boundary Lines of Egypt and Ethiopia					Red
"	"	"	The Assyrian Empire		Yellow
"	"	"	"	Babylonian, Lydian & Median Empires	Green
"	"	"	"	Kingdom of David & Solomon	Light Red
"	"	"	"	Territory of Carthage	Buff
"	"	"		Greece and Her Colonies	Purple

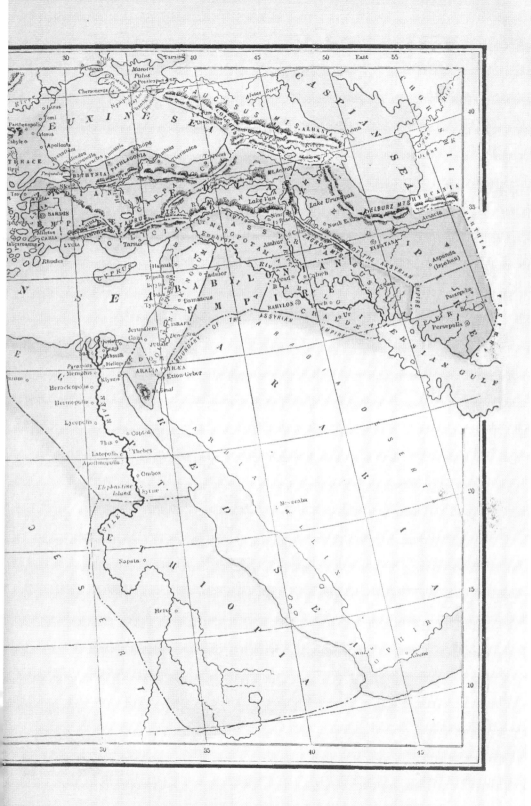

FULL PAGE ILLUSTRATIONS

PART II.

PAGE

ILLUMINATED MISSAL ....Frontispiece

JOPPA GATE, JERUSALEM... 24

CHRISTIAN STREET, JERUSALEM (BAZAAR DISTRICT)................... 40

JERUSALEM FROM THE MOUNT OF OLIVES........................... 56

SEA OF GALILEE... 72

DEAD SEA 104

HERA 136

POSEIDON 184

ATHENA 232

NIOBE 272

VENUS DE MILO... 328

ACROPOLIS AND TEMPLE OF JUPITER................................ 408

NERO AT THE CIRCUS (Photogravure)............................. 412

MAP OF THE FIRST GREAT EMPIRES................................. VI

PALESTINE.

Blest land of Judaea! thrice hallowed of song,
Where the holiest of memories pilgrimlike throng;
In the shade of thy palms, by the shores of thy sea,
On the hills of thy beauty, my heart is with thee.

With the eye of a spirit I look on that shore,
Where pilgrim and prophet have lingered before;
With the glide of a spirit I traverse the sod
Made bright by the steps of the angels of God.

Blue sea of the hills!—in my spirit I hear
Thy waters, Genesaret, chime on my ear;
Where the Lowly and Just with the people sat down,
And thy spray on the dust of his sandals was thrown.

. . . .

I tread where the TWELVE in their way-faring trod;
I stand where they stood with the Chosen of God—
Where his blessing was heard, and his lessons were taught,
Where the blind were restored and the healing was wrought.

And what if my feet may not tread where He stood,
Nor my ears hear the dashing of Galilee's flood,
Nor my eyes see the cross which He bowed him to bear,
Nor my knees press Gethsemane's garden of prayer.

Yet, Loved of the Father, thy Spirit is near
To the meek and the lowly, and penitent here;
And the voice of thy love is the same even now
As at Bethany's tomb or on Olivet's brow.

O, the outward hath gone!—but in glory and power,
The SPIRIT surviveth the things of an hour;
Unchanged, undecaying, its Pentecost flame
On the heart's secret altar is burning the same!

—Whittier.

THE STORY OF THE HEBREWS

CHAPTER XIII.

From the Captivity to the Final Disposition of the Jews.

Many of the Hebrews had fallen in the wars with Nebuch-adnezzar; the humblest were left to cultivate the desolate land, some were sold into slavery, others drifted about and were engulfed in foreign populations. The greater portion, however, settled on one of the canals of the Euphrates. Here they were kindly treated and allowed to observe their own customs. At first the exiles, coming from the hills of Palestine, were stupe-fied by the glories of Babylon—at that time the most attractive city of the ancient world. Its spacious palaces and hanging gardens surpassed anything they had known. Gradually they regained possession of their faculties and adapted themselves to their new home.

"Many a people had been swallowed up in the advance of Assyrian and Babylonian power and forever lost. Even empires once distinguished for power and civilization had so thoroughly disappeared in the vortex as to leave scarcely a distinguishable sign of their former existence. This was not to be true in the case of Judah. The Hebrew had ideas that could not be quenched, and these carried his person into a life that would not die among men. The Chaldean had destroyed the state, but the people lived on in activity. The songs of Zion might not be sung, but the words of Zion might be spoken. The Hebrew would not now pay tribute in the land of Judah, but would take tribute even of his captors, as he passed successfully forward into business in his new home. His wise leader, Jeremiah, had counselled him to make the new land his home in the fullest sense: 'Build ye houses, and dwell in them; and plant gardens, and eat the fruit of them; take

1

ye wives, and beget sons and daughters; and take wives for
your sons, and give your daughters to husbands, that they
may bear sons and daughters; and multiply ye there, and be
not diminished. And seek the peace of the city whither I
have caused you to be carried away in captivity, and pray unto
the Lord for it: for in the peace thereof shall ye have peace.'
The advice was followed. Nebuchadnezzar had gained a new
factor in his composite population, though he had lost a rich
province."[1]

Loss of their temple seemed most deplorable to the Hebrews.
Having no established place of worship, they congregated on
the banks of the river for prayer and readings from their
sacred books. Ezekial was the prophet of the captivity. He
exhorted his brethren to be strong under misfortune and cour-
ageous in their exile. He was a writer as well as a priest and
prophet. The years spent in Babylon were marked by diligent
effort to collect and give permanent form to existing Hebrew
literature.

Ezekial foretold a return to Jerusalem, and disappointment
grew into despondency as time elapsed and brought no prospect
of such good fortune. Finally the startling successes of Cyrus
came as welcome news to the ears of the captives, inspiring
hope that he might prove the long-awaited deliverer. It is
probable that the Hebrews were among the factions within
Babylon that assisted Cyrus to gain possession of the city.
Either in gratitude for such aid, or because he wished to have
a nation friendly to him in the west, Cyrus gave the captives
permission to return to their own land and to rebuild their
temple. Some forty-two thousand set out at once and it is
likely that others joined their kinsmen for several years after.
Certain it is that Ezra came to their aid with sixteen hundred
followers, and Nehemiah journeyed to them later.

Temporary homes were constructed and then attention
turned to the building of a temple which should replace the
more elaborate one built by Solomon and destroyed in the
siege of Jerusalem. After some delays, the second temple was
finished in 515 B. C., and was dedicated by religious worship
and festival.

So far as its government was concerned, Judah was now

[1] Hist. of Baby. and Assy.: Rogers, Vol. II. 335.

a Persian province, paying a yearly tax or tribute into the Persian treasury. Then Syria grew strong enough to wrest the land from Persian rule, and strife between the two countries, struggling for possession, continued some considerable time. In 334 B. C. Alexander the Great set out from Greece on his campaign of conquest. Western Asia was first invaded, and the Hebrews, wearied with tumult and burdensome taxes, opened their gates to the young general. His brilliant career had an untimely end and the vast empire he had acquired was divided among his generals. The one to whose share Palestine fell failed to hold it long. Ptolomy, the general who inherited Egypt, tried to increase his territory and marched against Judah. The Hebrews refused to submit to his rule and he waged a battle against them on the Sabbath, knowing that they would not fight on that day. One hundred thousand were taken captives to Alexandria, where already Hebrews had settled, and where they were welcomed as citizens. Because they might be depended upon to keep their word, to abide by contracts and respect agreements, they were looked upon with favor by the Greeks.

When Ptolomy II. succeeded as ruler, he sent to Jerusalem for seventy wise men who should come to Alexandria for the purpose of preparing a Greek translation of Hebrew literature. The result was the first version of the Bible, and is known as the Septuagint (from the word seventy) translation.

After a century of peace, a rising dynasty of Syria struggled with Egypt for Palestine. These were troublous times indeed. It is not possible to go into the combats that were waged back and forth, nor to describe the oppressions that befell the Jews—known after the exile by the name of the kingdom last to fall.

At length, under the Maccabees, Judah rose from her deep humiliation and succeeded in shaking herself free from foreign rule. When division of opinion occurred within the state, Rome was asked to mediate. Pompey was sent into the land and in addition to acting as mediator, exacted tribute for Rome. Crassus was subsequently sent thither as governor of the Roman province, and hesitated not to desecrate the temple by robbing it of its remaining treasure to swell the coffers of Rome. Julius Caesar was friendly to the Hebrews and his death was sincerely mourned by them. Herod the Great, at

first a provincial governor, declared his independence, and
made himself king. He shortly incurred the intense hatred
of the people, to atone for which he announced that he would
repair the temple, now practically destroyed. This was completed about the time that Christ was born.

Long years before, Hebrew prophets had foretold the coming of a great king who would restore this people to the
prosperity they had enjoyed during the united kingdom; one
who would rule them justly and make them comparable with
other nations around them. Burdensome taxes, cruel treatment, and persecution led the nation to fix its hopes always
on the future, and to especially anticipate this coming king.
When Christ was born in Bethlehem, humble shepherds and
certain wise men hailed him as the one sent in fulfillment of
the prophecy. Herod, then ruler of Palestine, naturally felt
keenly jealous of anyone who might endanger his administration, and ordered the massacre of young children so familiar
to us. When it was plain that Christ came not to establish
an earthly kingdom, the Hebrews saw, and saw with full
justice, that he was not the kind of deliverer which their
prophets had led them to expect. Therefore they repudiated
him as the one so long foretold, and continued to look for
another.

After some years of freedom from Roman tribute, taxes
were again exacted. When payment was refused, trouble with
Rome ensued. The legions sent to quell the rebellion were
roughly treated and war broke out in earnest. Vespasian was
the Roman general in command, and Josephus, the writer
and historian of later years, commanded the Hebrew defence.

The scene of warfare was one of the many heights of
Judah. When at last the Romans carried the hill, Josephus
was taken prisoner. Prophecying that his conqueror should
one day become emperor of Rome, the life of the crafty Jew
was spared. Difficulties at home prevented further subjuga-
tion of Palestine. In time Vespasian did become emperor,
and dispatched his son to complete the conquest of the sturdy
Hebrews. Carrying war into Palestine, Jerusalem was soon
besieged. This attack called forth great bravery and resource-
ful effort on the part of the Jews, who proved as formidable
enemies according to their strength as any with whom Rome
ever contended.

Jerusalem was fortunate in her position, being protected on three sides by deep gorges or ravines. The assault was accordingly made on the fourth side, guarded by four successive walls. The defense was so strong that several days elapsed before the first wall was taken; the third fell on the fifteenth day. Now the Romans made overtures of peace, displaying their strength before the eyes of the stricken people.

"Resting for a few days from toil, and strengthened by the distribution of an abundance of provisions, the Romans marched before the first wall in magnificent review. First went the infantry, clad in breastplates, and with arms uncovered; the cavalry appeared with horses and splendidly caparisoned; the whole space near glittered with warlike pomp. Josephus, now the friend of Titus, approached to advise his countrymen to yield, declaring that the invaders would now show mercy, but upon further resistance would become implacable. Many of the Jews began to regard their position as desperate, and were moved by the words of Josephus. But the leaders never wavered; they rejected all overtures, and relentlessly slew all who could be suspected of entertaining the design to submit.

"Very appalling was now the situation of the defenders. The hot summer sun beat upon the crowds in the city, still immense in number, though war had swept them off in troops. From the Mount of Olives, across the narrow Kidron, hurled day and night the projectiles which crushed houses and their inmates. Through the ravines surrounding the city prowled the hostile parties, on the watch to secure any unguarded footpath, or to scale the precipices, if there was any negligence in the watch. But worse than these outer dangers, a dreadful famine began to prevail. The fighting men, ravenous, sought for food within the houses, and put to torture the wretched inmates, to make them disclose their hidden stores. The battlements of the Antonia frowned, the Temple front flashed white from Moriah far over the hills. Beneath them what scenes of pain and death in the city like an amphitheatre that had once been so proud! It was now an arena for the rioting of terror."[2]

[2] The Jews: Hosmer, 114.

When the fourth wall fell, it was found that the Jews had constructed a fifth. A Roman soldier hurled a torch against the temple, and fire raging within the city, added to the horrors. When the final breach was made, 1,100,000 had either fallen or were slain by the Roman soldiers. The remainder, about 97,000, were taken into captivity.

Very splendid was the triumphal march of Titus through the streets of Rome. Great treasure of gold, silver and ivory was shown; numberless captives swelled his train; huge structures, built several stories high, were covered with pictures depicting the campaign and rolled along on wheels in the procession. The golden appointments of the temple and the tablets upon which were inscribed the Hebrew laws,—always guarded in the innermost part of the temple, were now paraded before the eyes of the multitude. A triumphal arch was erected above the Via Sacra in honor of Titus, the conquering hero, and still it stands today in silent testimony of the final destruction of Jerusalem. Well has the occasion been called one of the most momentous events in the world's history, since it resulted in driving forever from its home an entire race.

Here we reach the end of the political history of the Hebrew state, yet the destruction of Jerusalem did not end the history of the Jews. Henceforth their history was to be interwoven with that of Europe. During the Middle Ages and in modern times the Hebrews have played an important *role* in the affairs of men, but through these centuries their influence has been exerted individually or by detached groups—never since the fall of their city in the hills of Judah, in 70 A. D., have they been united as a nation, having their own distinct political life.

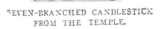

SEVEN-BRANCHED CANDLESTICK
FROM THE TEMPLE.

CHAPTER XIV.

INDUSTRIES AND ARTS.

Before the Hebrews spread over the rich plateaus to the east of Jordan, their occupations had been merely herding and grazing. On the eastern tablelands they first began to cultivate the soil, keeping still their herds and flocks, but depending less upon them.

When we find the Israelites settled in Canaan, they had already become an agricultural people. Since farm implements could nowhere be obtained, such primitive tools as were used had to be made on the farms. Knowing nothing of metal, the Hebrews were at first obliged to go to the Philistines for such simple service as the sharpening of plough-shares, but as hostilities between the two peoples increased, they no doubt learned to perform such duties for themselves.

For protection, the farmers built their houses together in little groups, while their lands reached away on every side. Thus life among them was not isolated, as it so often is among those dwelling in agricultural communities today, where machines have replaced hand labor, and large areas compose single farms. The families making up each clan would locate near one another in small settlements; these grew at length into villages, then into walled cities.

It is a mistake to suppose that contact with the Canaanites was wholly injurious. On the contrary, these earlier dwellers in Palestine had reached a higher stage of civilization than the Israelites and unconsciously the invaders learned many useful arts from them.

"The Hebrews learned many of the arts of life of the Canaanites after they settled among them. The original sources of the period mention manufactures of various kinds which have to do, not alone with a nomadic and an agricultural stage, but also with a social state considerably advanced. Mention is made of bowstrings and war-horns, of shields and spears, of shepherd's pipes and ox-goads, of doors and locks, of chairs and tables, of razors or shears, of cords and ropes, of dyed stuffs and embroidery, of the vine and barley, of wine and strong drink. But one conclusion is possible; it is that the Israelites were quick to learn of their neighbors, and that they were for the most part on such friendly terms with them that the civilization of the one people easily became, with slight modifications, the civilization of the other people."[1]

There were no efforts put forth for the maintenance of good roads for trade and caravan, yet the nature of the land was such that footpaths were easily worn down and early travel was either on foot or on the backs of asses. Indeed trade at first was mere barter and exchange, and even so, of slight account. The spirit of hospitality was so strong that travellers might find shelter in any community, with refreshment for themselves and beasts of burden.

Notwithstanding the primitive condition of labor during the years of settlement in Canaan, trade and industry of later ages had then their beginnings. We cannot now estimate the extent of progress made, but it is important to note that the transition from nomadic to agricultural life was completed before the dawn of the monarchy.

Affairs underwent great changes during the united kingdom. Commerce sprang up with surrounding countries and with others more remote, and current ideas of culture and civilization permeated Palestine. Increase of wealth brought new needs to be satisfied; comfortable homes replaced the huts of ruder times. As the requirements of a nation and a court made taxes heavier, farming was abandoned by many who saw in trade the possibility of more rapid accumulation of riches. Solomon multiplied personal wealth by commercial dealings, and later kings followed his example. The Hebrew as a rule did not himself produce articles but acted rather as a middleman, or commission merchant, with the products of other nations.

As trade became more extensive, so the interests of the farm became diversified. In place of barley and corn, a wide variety of produce was demanded. The wine-press and threshing-floor were needed on all large farms.

Fewer articles were produced at home. The caravan brought dress stuffs to the very door of the house-wife, al-

[1] Social Life of the Hebrews: Day, 71.

though coarse fabrics were still woven at home, as were all
materials used by the poorer classes. Food materials had still
to be prepared in the home. Even meal was ground in the
household. " Two shall be grinding at the mill; one shall be
taken and the other left." In such figures and illustrations
the student of economic history finds valuable materials.

With changed conditions, the general tone of city life was
not accordingly elevated. " Unwonted national prosperity
aroused among the rich and powerful in Israel a passion for
show and luxury which was the more striking because of the
contrast with the simplicity of the earlier days and the want
and penury which were still the lot of the masses. Great
estates took the place of small holdings; palaces of hewn stone
furnished with beds of ivory and silken couches, rose on the
land once held by the families of those who now were serfs.
Their idle masters sought far and wide for the choicest morsels
with which to gratify their appetites, as they stretched themselves upon their ivory couches, singing idle songs to the sound
of the viol, anointing themselves with expensive oils and engaging in shameful carousals. It was a selfish luxury which led
those who thus indulged themselves to disregard entirely the
sacred duty which they owed to their poorer brethren. A poor
debtor, even though he was a righteous man and his indebted-
ness a mere trifle, received not the slightest mercy at their
hands; indeed they exulted in the misery which they brought
upon him."

The religion of the Hebrews tended to foster simplicity.
Art among contemporaneous nations found its expression in
images of the gods—forbidden by the law of Moses and
abhorred by faithful worshippers. Consequently we find art
undeveloped among the Israelites.

As builders they never reached great skill. Solomon's
temple, while beautifully adorned, was but a chapel when compared with the great temples of its age, and it was largely the
work of Phœnician artisans. Since it was the gem of Hebrew
architecture, and dearest of all possessions of the Hebrews. we
shall stop to learn something of its style and character.

Solomon's temple was but one, and that not the largest nor
most important, of the court buildings. Approaching the
court from the south, the House of Lebanon rose first in view.

This building contained a large audience room for public assemblies, and the upper story probably was used as an armory—
a store-house for military supplies; it was called the House of
Lebanon because it stood on pillars hewn from the tall cedars
which grew upon the Lebanon mountains. Beyond was the
Judgment Hall, with its waiting hall in front. "There Solomon's throne of judgment was set up, and thither the people
brought their cases before the supreme tribunal of the kingdom."

Still farther beyond the House of Lebanon was the king's
palace, with apartments for the harem, and nearby, the Palace
of Pharaoh's daughter. Surrounding the Temple, which stood
furthest from the Audience Hall and Arsenal, was the temple
court. Within it, the Temple consisted of two chambers: the
audience chamber, and shut off from this by closed doors, the
Oracle, or Holy of Holies. Within this dark room was re-
posited the ark of the covenant—the symbol of Jehovah's
presence.

" The walls of the Temple were of hewn stone, and according to Ezekial about ten feet in thickness on the ground, and
on the outside a cubit[2] less for each higher story. The walls
on the interior were ceiled with boards of cedar, so that they
were completely covered; elaborate mural decorations gave
them an added splendor. The floors were of cypress-wood.
Light was admitted into the outer sanctuary by windows on
both sides, placed close under the ceiling; the roof was probably flat, and projected so as to keep the rain from beating
in through these apertures. Immediately in front of the entrance to the Oracle stood the little altar of cedar-wood, on
which was placed the shewbread. Great square doors, with
olive-wood posts and cypress panels, led from the large audi-
ence-room to the porch, which was of the same width as the
Temple, and about sixteen feet in length. At the entrance
stood two huge, hollow bronze pillars about thirty feet high
and nearly six feet in diameter.

" Immediately in front of the Temple, which faced the
east, was placed the large bronze altar, which was used for
the sacrifices. Near by, to supply the water needful for purification, stood the great brazen sea, which was nearly nine

[2]A cubit was about 20¼ inches.

feet high and over fifty feet in circumference; it was supported
by twelve bronze oxen." [3]

It has been possible to find traces of several styles of architecture in Solomon's Temple. As we have seen, it was built
largely by Phœnician workmen whose acquaintance with contemporary temples was probably wide. Phœnicians came in
contact with all nations in connection with their commerce,
and quite naturally whatever was in favor for building and
decoration would have been known to them.

There is no better proof of the total lack among the
Hebrews of skill in architecture and ornamentation, than that
their Temple, most sacred of all their possessions, should have
been left to the ingenuity of foreign workmen, and hence to
bear a closer relation to the religious symbols of neighboring
peoples than to their own.

The fact that wood entered so largely into the construction
of their buildings, accounts no doubt for the few remains which
have rewarded the efforts of the modern excavator in Palestine.

[3] Hist. of the Hebrew People: Vol. I, 193.

CHAPTER XV.

Hebrew Literature.—Poetry.

No other of the earliest nations left so rich a literature as did the Hebrews. We are not able to estimate how extensive it originally was, but in addition to the books at present included in the Old Testament, there were fourteen other books once included therein but subsequently eliminated by church councils, and twelve additional books are mentioned in the Old Testament, but have been lost during the flight of centuries. How many others similarly disappeared there is no means of ascertaining.

The Old Testament writings are available to all, and it is therefore best to confine our attention to them. However, it may be noted that the fourteen productions once included in the Bible and later eliminated from Bibles used by Protestants at least, are now known as the apocryphal books. They were given place in the Septuagint version, but from time to time, ecclesiastical bodies have been called together to revise the Scriptures, and they have discarded from them whatever writings, or portions of writings, seemed in their opinions to be out of keeping with their general sacred character. Nevertheless, many critics of recent time have declared certain of these apocryphal books to possess as great literary merit and as high a moral tone as others which have been retained. Whether bound in the same volume—as they are still in some editions of the Bible,—or bound separately, the apocryphal books are easily accessible to those who wish to read them.

Of the missing books, mentioned in the Scriptures but otherwise lost sight of, we will cite three cases: the editor or compiler of the Book of Joshua, having mentioned Joshua's famous command to the heavenly bodies,

" Sun, stand thou still upon Gibeon;
　And thou, Moon, in the valley of Ajalon.
　And the sun stood still,
　And the moon stayed,
　　Until the nation had avenged themselves of their enemies."

adds, " Is not this written in the book of *Jasher?* " The book of Jasher is believed to have been a collection of war ballads and songs of popular heroes.

In Second Chronicles, we are told that Manasseh's prayer, his sins and transgressions, are written among the *Sayings of the Seers;* and in Numbers (21, 14) " Wherefore it is said in the book of *The Wars of Jehovah.*"

In some instances it is probable that portions of these lost books were incorporated in compilations that remain to us, but more concerning them is not likely to be discovered.

Within the Old Testament are to be found nearly all types of literary production. " We find in this volume an illustration of almost every type of literature—ancient legend, constitutional law, political statutes, ecclesiastical law, history, epic, lyric, and gnomic poetry, drama, folklore, fiction, ethical culture, oratory, biography, philosophy and dream literature." [1]

In our study of Hebrew political history we have already discovered several of these types; ancient legends and folklore are preserved to us in the book of Genesis and furnish material for the legendary period of Hebrew history; constitutional law and political statutes may be found in Deuteronomy; ecclesiastical law in Leviticus; while history—social, religious, ecclesiastical and economic—is to be found in nearly all Old Testament writings. Biography, brief, it is true, is given concerning many of Israel's kings and leaders.

We shall consider those writings which are of a more purely literary character—poetry, drama, fiction, ethical culture and philosophy.

Hebrew poetry may be classified as (1) epic, and (2) lyric,—the latter class falling into several sub-divisions, according to its content. Pastoral poetry, elegiac songs, odes, and didactic or gnomic, may all belong to the general class of *lyric* poetry.

An epic poem is one which by narration and description sets forth a past action or event. With other peoples, the epic falls into verses as, for example, Homer's Iliad, Virgil's Aeneid, or Milton's Paradise Lost. There are no verse epics in Hebrew literature, although in some instances, the prose

[1] Life and Letters of the Ancient Hebrews: Abbott.

narrative drops into verse occasionally. The Hebrew epics
are closely interwoven with history. For example, in the
book of Genesis, in the midst of historical narrative, one comes
upon the Joseph epic—the " Epic Incident," as a critic has
called it. " It is an Incident because it is a portion of the
history; it is Epic because the treatment of it touches the
imagination and emotions in the regular way of creative
poetry." [2]

The story of Jephthah is an epic; so is the story of Cain.
One of the particularly interesting Bible epics is the story
of Balaam, for here the narrative bursts into verse several
times. It recounts an incident occuring when the Israelites
were yet in the Wilderness. They had drawn near the region
inhabited by the Moabites, and because of their numbers, the
king of the Moabites feared to attack them. Balaam, although not of their number, worshipped Jahweh, and King
Balak conceived the notion that if Balaam would come and
utter a curse against the Hebrews, by some magic art, the
Moabites might stand a better chance of overcoming them.
" I know that he whom thou blessest is blessed, and he whom
thou cursest is cursed," says Balak, sending messengers to
Balaam with promises of ample reward if he would but come
and curse these enemies. Balaam refused for some time, but
when at length he yielded to Balak, and came to view the band
of Israelites, instead of cursing them, he was inspired to bless
them. Balak supposed that a sight of their numbers overcame him, and led him to a point where only the rear of the
encampment was visible. Still again Balaam broke forth in
verse:

> " Rise up, Balak, and hear;
>   Hearken unto me, thou son of Zippor:
> God is not a man, that he should lie;
>   Neither the son of man, that he should repent:
> Hath he said, and shall he not do it?
>   Or hath he spoken, and shall he not make it good?
> Behold, I have received commandment to bless:
>   And he hath blessed, and I cannot reverse it."

[2]Literary Study of the Bible: Moulton, 229.

Balak is still unwilling to give up, and feels that some way he must compel Balaam to pronounce a curse against his foes, that the spell may work against them, to their confusion in battle.

"At all hazards another attempt must be made. Even Balak has begun to understand that there is some real power restraining Balaam; but if the prophet will accompany him to a third point of view, 'peradventure it will please God' that the enemy shall be cursed from thence.   It happens that from where he is standing his eye just catches the long lines of tents stretching, row after row, with the regularity that distinguished the highly organized Israelites from the tumultuous hordes of desert nomads.   The divine principle of order sinks deep in Balaam's soul, and inspires his song as he turns to face for a third time the king and princes of Moab.

> Balaam the son of Beor saith,
>   And the man whose eye is opened saith:
> He saith, which heareth the words of God,
> Which seeth the vision of the Almighty,
>   Falling down, and having his eyes open:
>
> How goodly are thy tents, O Jacob,
>   Thy tabernacles, O Israel!
> As valleys are they spread forth,
>   As gardens by the river side,
> As lign-aloes which the Lord hath planted,
>   As cedar trees beside the waters.
> Water shall flow from his buckets,
>   And his seed shall be in many waters.
> And his king shall be higher than Agag,
>
> And his kingdom shall be exalted.
>   God bringeth him forth out of Egypt;
> He hath as it were the strength of the wild-ox:
>   Blessed be every one that blesseth thee,
> And cursed be every one that curseth thee." [1]

[1] Literary Study of the Bible: Moulton, 234.

Lyric poetry was originally sung or said to the accompaniment of music—generally to the music of the lyre. Later, when it was no longer accompanied by an instrument, that poetry which was in itself most musical was still called *lyric,* from the word *lyre.*

All translations are unsatisfactory, especially translations of poetry. Goethe's most beautiful verse loses much of its power in English translation. Far truer is this in the case of Hebrew poetry rendered in modern languages. One characteristic has been preserved to us—parallelism, the setting of one thought over against another, balancing phrases or sentences. For example: "A wise son maketh a glad father, but a foolish son is the heaviness of his mother;" "A false balance is an abomination to the Lord: but a just weight is his delight;" "He that gathereth in summer is a wise son: but he that sleepeth in harvest is a son that causeth shame."

The psalms embody the great mass of Hebrew lyrics, although they may be found elsewhere in the Old Testament, as in the songs of Moses, and of Deborah. The Psalms alone contain many variations of the lyric—the ode, song, elegy, pastoral poem, didactic poem. It was once believed that David wrote the great number of the Psalms; it is now known that he wrote very few. Instead of being the production of one man, or of several men, they were written by various writers who lived through eight centuries. Some of the Psalms are perfect gems of poetry; others are perceptibly inferior; all of them have one underlying theme. now subordinate, now predominating: the goodness, power and omnipresence of God.

When the entire contents of the Scriptures were revised and rewritten in their present form of numerically numbered verses, poetry suffered most, and it has recently been the labor of conscientious scholars to restore it to its original form.

Among the one hundred and fifty Psalms that remain to us, are to be found national odes, pilgrim songs, elegies, poems of victory, of repentance, of rejoicing. poems in honor of the new king. of the king's birthday, dedicatory hymns, and so on. It will be possible to consider only a few. Four national hymns are included: the seventy-eighth psalm was the national hymn of Judaea, after the northern kingdom separated from

Rehoboam's realm; the one hundred and thirty-sixth psalm was the hymn of the Wilderness and is very old; the one hundred and sixth was the hymn of Captivity, and the one hundred and fifth, the hymn of the Promised Land.

In the one hundred and fifth psalm, the poet reviews the history of Israel and recalls Jehovah's protection in the past:

O give thanks unto the Lord, call upon his name;
  Make known his doings among the peoples.
Sing unto him, sing praises unto him;
  Talk ye of all his marvellous works.
Glory ye in his holy name:
  Let the heart of them rejoice that seek the Lord.
Seek ye the Lord and his strength;
  Seek his face evermore.
Remember his marvellous works that he hath done;
  His wonders, and the judgments of his mouth;
O ye seed of Abraham his servant,
  Ye children of Jacob, his chosen ones.
He is the Lord our God:
  His judgments are in all the earth.
He hath remembered his covenant for ever,
  The word which he commanded to a thousand generations.

Saying, Unto thee will I give the land of Canaan,
  The lot of your inheritance:
When they were but a few men in number,
  Yea, very few, and sojourners in it;
And they went about from nation to nation,
  From one kingdom to another people.
He suffered no man to do them wrong;
  Yea, he reproved kings for their sakes;
"Touch not mine anointed ones,
  And do my prophets no harm."

He spread a cloud for a covering;
  And fire to give light in the night.
They asked, and he brought quails,
  And satisfied them with the bread of heaven.
He opened the rock, and waters gushed out;
  They ran in dry places like a river.

For he remembered his holy word,
  And Abraham his servant.
And he brought forth his people with joy,
  And his chosen with singing.
And he gave them the lands of the nations;
  And they took the labour of the peoples in possession:
That they might keep his statutes,
  And observe his laws.[1]

The twenty-first psalm was written to celebrate the king's birthday:

  "He asked life of thee, thou gavest it him;
  Even length of days for ever and ever."

The twenty-fourth psalm is much more expressive when given its intended form. "The reader must imagine this sung by a procession of priests and people on some great festival day. Jerusalem is full of pilgrims gathered from all parts of Palestine; a great procession forms in the city; priests lead the way; a band of music composed of lyres, viols, reeds, cymbals, tambourines, drums, trumpets, accompany it. The procession reaches the Temple gates, which are closed; and the following musical colloquy takes place:

Chorus in procession:
  "The earth is the Lord's and the fullness thereof;
  The world, and they that dwell therein.
  For he hath founded it upon the seas,
  And established it upon the floods.

Priest—a solo:
  "Who shall ascend into the hill of the Lord?
  And who shall stand in his holy place?

Another Priest, responding:
  "He that hath clean hands, and a pure heart;
  Who hath not lifted up his soul unto vanity,
  And hath not sworn deceitfully.
  He shall receive a blessing from the Lord,
  And righteousness from the God of his salvation.

[1]Modern Reader's Bible.

Chorus in procession:

"This is the generation of them that seek him,
That seek thy face, O God of Jacob.

Chorus, at Temple gate:

"Lift up your heads, O ye gates;
And be ye lift up, ye everlasting doors:
And the king of glory shall come in.

Response from within:

"Who is this King of glory?

Chorus without:

"The Lord, mighty in battle.
Lift up your heads, O ye gates;
Ye, lift them up, ye everlasting doors:
And the King of glory shall come in."

Then the gates are thrown open, and the procession enters while the priestly doorkeeper repeats the question:

"Who is this King of glory?"

and the procession replies:

"The Lord of hosts,
He is the King of glory."

After David brought the ark of the covenant into Jerusalem and dedicated the city to Jehovah, it became the religious center for all Israel, and several psalms, called "Songs of Ascents," were sung by companies of pilgrims as they marched along to Jerusalem to celebrate the feast days. The one hundred and twenty-second psalm was sung upon reaching the venerated city:

"I was glad when they said unto me,
Let us go into the house of the Lord.
Our feet are standing within thy gates, O Jerusalem;
Jerusalem, that art builded as a city that is compact together:
Whither the tribes go up, even the tribes of the Lord,
For a testimony unto Israel, to give thanks unto the name of
the Lord.
For there are set thrones for judgment,
The thrones of the house of David."

Some lyrics take the form of elegies; such, for example, is the one hundred and thirty-seventh psalm, written after the Hebrews were taken into captivity:

" By the rivers of Babylon
There we sat down, yea, we wept,
    When we remembered Zion.
Upon the willows in the midst thereof
We hanged up our harps.
For there they had led us captives required of us songs,
And they that wasted us required of us mirth:
    'Sing us one of the songs of Zion.'
How shall we sing the Lord's song
In a strange land?"

Some of the songs are didactic, consisting of observations on or concerning life—sentiments which tend to mold opinion, or to teach lessons to the reader. For example, the one hundred and nineteenth:

Blessed are they that are perfect in the way,
    Who walk in the law of the Lord.

Blessed are they that keep his testimonies,
    That seek him with the whole heart.

Wherewithal shall a young man cleanse his ways?
    By taking heed according to thy word.

To the same class belongs the thirty-seventh:

Fret not thyself because of evil-doers,
    Neither be thou envious against them that work unrighteous-
        ness.

For they shall soon be cut down like the grass,
    And wither as the green herb.

I have been young, and now am old;
    Yet have I not seen the righteous forsaken, nor his seed beg-
        ging their bread.

All day long he dealeth graciously, and lendeth;
    And his seed is blessed.

Depart from evil and do good;
And dwell for evermore.
For the Lord loveth judgments,
And forsaketh not his saints."

One more poetical production of the Bible may be considered: The Song of Solomon. The title means that the song pertains to Solomon—not that it was written by him. The poem is pastoral in many of its scenes; it is also dramatic, and has been appropriately called an "idyl." Many interpretations have been offered for it. Most reasonable appears to be this one: "A beautiful Shulamite maiden, surprised by the king and his train on a royal progress in the north, has been brought to the palace at Jerusalem where the king hopes to win her affections, and to induce her to change her rustic home for the honor and enjoyments which a court life could afford. She has, however, already pledged her heart to a young shepherd, and the admiration and blandishments which the king lavishes upon her are powerless to make her forget him. In the end she is permitted to return to her mountain home, where, at the close of the poem, the lovers appear, hand in hand, and express, in warm and glowing words, the superiority of genuine spontaneous affections over that which may be purchased by wealth or rank." [5]

The king's camp is pitched upon the northern hills, and the court is busy providing amusement for his idle hours. He is attracted by the peasant girl and seeks to make her one of his harem. But the flattery of Solomon, the attractions promised by the ladies in his train, are naught in comparison with the man she loves. Taken to Jerusalem, she thinks of her lover by day and dreams of him by night. To Solomon's fulsome flattery she replies:

"My beloved is mine and I am his,
He feedeth his flock among the lilies.
When the day breaks and the shadows flee away
I will get me to the mountain of myrrh
And to the hill of frankincense."

[5]Intro. to Literature of the Old Testament: Driver.

To the women of the train who lend their voices to Solomon's pleas, she returns:

> "I adjure you, O daughters of Jerusalem,
> That ye stir not up, nor awaken love
> Until it please."

One of the most musical songs in this Song of Songs, is sung by the peasant lover—or is imagined by the maiden to be sung by him:

> "Rise up, my love, my fair one, and come away.
> For, lo, the winter is past,
> The rain is over and gone;
> The flowers appear on the earth;
> The time of singing birds is come,
> The voice of the turtle is heard in our land;
> The fig-tree ripeneth her green figs,
> And the vines are in blossom,
> They give forth their fragrance."

At last, it being hopeless to win her affection, she is allowed to return to her peasant lover, and her closing song of love lives on through the ages:

> "Set me as a seal upon thine heart, as a seal upon thine arm:
> For love is strong as death;
> Jealousy is cruel as the grave:
> The flashes thereof are flashes of fire,
> A very flame of the Lord.
> Many waters cannot quench it:
> Neither can the floods drown it:
> If a man would give all the substance of his house for love,
> It would be utterly condemned."

"The Song of Songs is an allegory in the same sense in which marriage is a symbol. The lesson of the Song of Songs is the strength and joy of human love; that is itself a prophetic interpretation of the strength and the joy of God's love for his own, and of their love for him." [a]

[a] Life and Letters of Ancient Hebrews: Abbott.

CHAPTER XVI.

HEBREW DRAMA: THE BOOK OF JOB.

The Book of Job has been variously classified as a didactic poem, an epic, a drama, and a philosophical and religious discourse thrown into verse. As a matter of fact, it partakes of the nature of all these literary types. Genung, the great scholar of this world-masterpiece, calls it an *Epic of the Inner Life*. He thus explains his appellation: "This poem centers in a hero, whose spiritual achievements it makes known to us. I regard this ancient book as the record of a sublime epic action, whose scene is not the tumultuous battle-field, nor the arena of rash adventure, but the solitary soul of a righteous man.

"We know that no other nations have ever approached the Hebrews in their genius for apprehending spiritual truth. If the Hebrews were to give to the world an epic, would it be a story of battle and bloodshed, or of strange adventures beyond the seas? These by no means represent their national character. For the most genuine expression of their life you must look under the surface, in the soul, where worship and aspiration and prophetic faith come face to face with God. And what epos could more truly gather into itself the most sacred ideal of such a nation than this story of Job, the man in whom was wrought the supreme test of what it is to be perfect and upright, who on his ash-heap, a veritable Hebrew Prometheus, continued honest with himself, true to what he saw in the world, loyal to what his soul told him was divine, until the storm was past and his foe shrank baffled away? Is not such a theme worth singing?

"The Epic of the Inner Life,—by this name we may designate the book before us. As such its significance is more than Hebrew; it extends far beyond national bounds to the universal heart of humanity; nay, it is with strange freshness and application to the spiritual maladies of this present century of Christ that the old Arab chief's struggles and victories come to us, as we turn the ancient pages anew."[1]

[1]The Epic of the Inner Life: Genung, 28.

While the Book of Job is rich in religious thought and teaching, we may, nevertheless, study it as a literary masterpiece, quite as we would study other world masterpieces, and with equal candor.

This drama was probably produced during, or shortly after, the united kingdom. Portraying as it does a primitive life in Arabia, it was formerly supposed that it was one of the earliest Hebrew productions. On the contrary, it was probably one of the later writings, and was merely set back into remote times, as Shakespeare placed King Lear in an age distant from his own. Job was an Arabian chief who lived long ago in Uz—a district in Arabia. He was prosperous beyond measure, and was respected by men. Like all old patriarchs, he lived with his children and his flocks around him—his cattle fed on many a hill; his possessions defied estimate. *He had lived a noble and virtuous life, true to the standards of his age.*

Among his people it was everywhere accepted as true that God was a being who rewarded righteousness and punished evil doing. If one were unfortunate, it was believed that his misfortune came as a sign of disfavor; if one prospered, his prosperity was taken as an indication of divine approval.

The prologue represents a scene between God and some restless spirit—called the Adversary, or Satan—in Heaven. Apparently this spirit has found much to criticise among men who were unfaithful to their religious vows. When Job is mentioned as an upright man, the spirit admits it but mockingly says: "Does Job serve God for naught?"—implying that he is righteous simply for personal gain, desiring a continuance of divine favor. To test his fidelity, then, misfortune is sent upon him. His possessions are swept away in a day; his children are taken from him; disease overtakes him. In his wretchedness, his wife turns away and his three intimate friends come to condole with him. Job in the depths of misery, still faithful to God, curses the day when he was born to such a useless, unhappy existence. Eliphaz answers him first:[2]

" Behold, thou hast admonished many,
    And thou hast strengthened feeble hands;

[2] Quotations made from Genung's Translation of the Book of Job.

JAPPA GATE, JERUSALEM.

Thy words have confirmed the faltering,
And bowing knees hast thou made strong;
But now it is come upon thee,—and thou faintest;
It toucheth thee, and thou art confounded.
Is not thy piety thy confidence?
Thy hope—is it not the integrity of thy ways?
Bethink thee now: who that was guiltless hath perished,
And where have the upright been cut off?
As I have seen,—they that plough iniquity,
And that sow wickedness, reap the same.
By the breath of God they perish,
And by the blast of His anger they are consumed.

" Behold, blessed is the man whom God correcteth;
Therefore despise not thou the chastening of the Almighty.
For he it is that woundeth and bindeth up;
He bruiseth, and His hands make whole."

Eliphaz infers that Job's afflictions have come upon him for some misdeed, some secret crime or sin, which confessed and repented, would bring a return of favor. Job is conscious of no misdoing which could have brought upon him any such calamity and suffering, and is already realizing the deficiencies of his previous religious tenets. He replies:

"Doth the wild ass bray over the fresh grass?
Or loweth the ox over his fodder?
Can it be eaten—what is tasteless, unsalted?
Or is there savor in the white of an egg?
My soul refuseth to touch!
They are as loathsome food to me."

As insipid as unsalted food are these beliefs, sufficient heretofore, but now manifestly inadequate, regarding righteousness and prosperity, sin and misfortune. He continued:

" Oh that my request might come,
And that God would grant my longing!
That it would please God to crush me,
That he would loose His hand and cut me off.

II—3

For then it would still be my comfort,—
Yea, I should exult in pain, though He spare me not,—·
That I have not denied the words of the Holy One.
What is my strength, that I should endure?
And what mine end, that I should be patient?
Is my strength the strength of stones?
Is my flesh of brass?
Nay, is not my help within me gone,
And well-being driven away from me?

" Teach me, and I will hold my tongue;
And make me understand wherein I have erred.
How cogent are forthright words!
But your upbraiding—what doth it prove?
Do ye think to censure words,
When they are a despairing man's words to the wind?
Nay, ye would even cast lots for the orphan,
And make traffic over your friends.
But now, be pleased to look upon me,
And surely I will not lie to your face.
Return, I pray; let there be no hardness;
Yea, return;—I am still righteous therein.
Is there perverseness in my tongue?
Cannot my taste discern what is wicked?"

The second friend, Bildad the Shuhite, now speaks, vexed
with Job's insistence that he is still righteous.

" How long wilt thou speak such things?
For the words of thy mouth are a mighty wind.

" Will God pervert the right?
Or will the Almighty pervert justice?
But thou—if thou wilt seek earnestly unto God,
And to the Almighty make supplication,—
So be it that thou art pure and upright,—
Verily then He will awake for thee,
And will restore the habitation of thy righteousness.

" Behold, God will not despise the perfect man,
Nor will he grasp the hand of the wicked."

Job answers him:

" Of a truth I know it is so;
   And yet—how shall a mortal be just with God?
   Should he desire to contend with Him,
   He could not answer Him one of a thousand.
   Wise in heart, and mighty in strength,—
   Who hath defied Him, and remained secure?
   Who removeth mountains, and they know not
   That He hath overturned them in His anger.
   Who doeth great things, past searching out,
   And marvellous things, past numbering.

" Lo, he goeth by me, and I see Him not;
   He passeth along, and I perceive Him not.
   Lo! He snatcheth away, and who will restrain Him?
   Who will say to Him, What doest Thou?

" How much less shall I answer Him,
   Choosing out my words against Him!
   Whom, though I were righteous, I could not answer.

" Perfect were I, yet would He prove me perverse.
   Perfect I *am*,—I value not my soul—I despise my life—
   It is all one—therefore I say,
   Perfect and wicked He consumeth alike."

The third friend who has listened to all the previous argument, takes up the thread of the discussion. His anger has
kindled as Job maintained his claim of uprightness. Zophar
the Naamathite takes up the issue:

" Shall a throng of words go unanswered,
   And a man of lips be counted in the right?
   Shall thy babblings put me to silence,
   That thou mayest mock, with none to shame thee,
   And say, My doctrine is pure,
   And clean am I in Thy sight?
   But oh, that God would indeed speak,
   And open his lips against thee,

And show thee the hidden things of wisdom,—
For there is fold on fold to truth,—
Then know thou, that God abateth to thee, of thine iniquity."

Job has finally lost all patience with their insistence. He
had expected sympathy and has received reproach. He knows
the worn-out argument as well as they, but has lived to see it
refuted. He bursts forth:

" Of a truth, ye are the people,
    And wisdom will die with you!
I also have understanding, as well as you;
I am not inferior to you;
And who knoweth not things like these?
What ye know, that know I also;
I am not inferior to you.

" But I,—to the Almighty would I speak;
I long to make plea unto God.
But ye too,—forgers of lies are ye;
Patchers-up of nothings are ye all.
Would that ye were silent altogether!
And it would be to you for wisdom.
Hear ye now my rebuke,
And listen to the charges of my lips.
Will ye speak *what is wrong*, for God?
And will ye, for Him, utter deceit?
Will ye respect His person?
O will ye be special pleaders for God?
Would it be well, if He should search you out?
Or will ye mock Him, as man mocketh man?
He will surely convict you utterly,
If in secret ye are respecters of persons.
Your wise maxims are proverbs of ashes;
Your bulwarks turn to bulwarks of clay."

From this time forward, Job depends not at all upon his
friends. Their arguments show that *they* do not serve God
for simple love of service. Job appreciates their inability to
cope with the problems that beset his soul. While suffering

greatest anguish, his ideas undergo rapid changes and he comes into clearer light and nobler conceptions. The friends speak once again, but their counsels are unavailing. Having pictured his misery, Job breaks forth in the lines which have lived on through the centuries, and find their finest expression when accompanied by the music of Handel's oratorio, wherein the music sounds forth the confidence of his exclamation:

"Oh that now my words were written!
Oh that they were inscribed in a book!
That, with iron pen, and with lead,
They were graven in the rock, for ever!
    I know that my redeemer liveth;
That he will stand, survivor, over the dust;
And after my skin is gone, they will rend this body,
And I, from my flesh, shall see God;
Whom mine eyes shall behold, a stranger no more!"

After the conclusion of the three older men, Elihu, a young man, addresses himself to Job, picturing the inscrutable power of God, whose plans are past finding out. Then out of the whirlwind, God speaks to Job, and he is led to see that Evil is no more an unfathomable mystery than is Good. The limited vision of man is dwelt upon:

"Where wast thou, when I laid the foundations of the earth?
Declare, if by knowledge thou understandest:
Who set its measurements, so thou knowest;
Or who stretched the line over it?
On what were its piers deep-laid,
Or who placed its corner-stone,—
When the morning-stars sang together,
And all the sons of God shouted for joy?
Who shut up the sea with doors,
And set bars and doors,
And said, ' Thus far shalt thou come, and no farther,
And here the pride of thy waves shall cease '?"

At length Job answered the Lord and said:

"I know that Thou canst do everything;
  Nor is withholden from Thee any design.
'Who is this that hideth counsel without knowledge?'—
  Therefore have I uttered, and understood not,
  Things too wonderful for me, and I knew not.

"I had heard of Thee by hearing of the ear,
  But now mine eye seeth Thee;
  Wherefore I loathe me, and repent,
  In dust and ashes."

In the Epilogue, we are told that the Lord reproved the
friends for not having spoken what was right, as had Job—
that is to say, it was better to question than to contentedly
remain in ignorance of life's greatest truths. And we are
further told that "the Lord blessed the latter end of Job more
than his beginning," and there the story ends.

"To gather the history before us into a sentence:

*There is a service of God which is not work for reward:
it is a heart-loyalty, a hunger after God's presence, which survives loss and chastisement; which in spite of contradictory
seeming cleaves to what is Godlike as the Needle seeks the
pole; and which reaches up out of the darkness and hardness
of this life to the life and love beyond."*

Hebrew Fiction.

Fiction is the work of the imagination; fictitious stories
are imaginative stories. A writer of fiction may weave into
his tale historical happenings, he may describe with accuracy
scenes and given localities; yet if he gives vent to his imaginings, introduces fictitious or unreal characters into his story,
his production is classified as fiction. Ben Hur, Uarda,
Hypasia, are all historical novels. Into each are woven actual
events, each contains descriptions of actual localities; into
each are introduced characters real and fictitious. The circumstances, happenings and details inserted into each narrative
might have been possible during the period in which the
stories are placed, but the writers have given free play to

their imaginations, and have sought to give us pictures of ancient life rather than histories of ancient times.

"The question whether any narrative is history or fiction is not identical with the question whether it is true or false. The literary classification of a narrative depends upon the motive of the author, not upon the accuracy of the narrative.

The question whether any particular narrative in the Old Testament is history or fiction is not to be determined by considering whether the book contains extraordinary events, but by considering the question whether its general spirit and structure are such as to justify the belief that the author thought himself narrating facts as they actually occurred, or whether he consciously gave a free rein to his imagination as he wrote." [3]

When the Puritan reformation swept over Europe, it destroyed works of the imagination as things *untrue*. Paintings, statuary, pictured windows, dramatic plays, fictitious stories—all these were condemned and forbidden. Since this religious reaction, people have slowly learned that our emotions and our imaginations are divinely given, as well as our intellects, and the novel holds an important place in the modern world. For example, a country was divided on the subject of human servitude; the question was agitated for an extended period. Suddenly a novel appeared—fictitious, unreal, no doubt exaggerated, yet so vividly did it picture the condition of those held in bondage that half a nation rose up against the cursed system. Again, the private schools of England had sunk into a pitiable state. Their condition was discussed from time to time with little apparent result. Nicholas Nickleby appeared, portraying these institutions in such a ridiculous light that radical changes were in consequence demanded.

Many novels have no set mission to accomplish, but they portray life and human character, and unconsciously we learn to love the good and despise the evil tendencies they exemplify. "Why then should we think it strange that God should have used the same faculty in the education of the Hebrew race? If today it is one of his instruments for the development of humanity, why should we think it impossible that in olden

[3] Life and Letters of the Ancient Hebrews: Abbott.

time he should have inspired men to use their imaginations for the moral and spiritual culture of the race?"[*]

Folklore is the name given traditions handed down from one generation to another by word of mouth. Some man distinguishes himself among a primitive people; they regard him as a hero; his deeds are told to children as they grow old enough to listen. These children grow up and tell the story to their children. In a comparatively short time there are none living who saw the man or knew personally of his deeds; the tale changes with lapse of time, details are added until the whole resembles slightly the original story; yet it retains the general outlines and some grains of truth. The Greeks had such traditions, or folklore—the Romans, Egyptians, Babylonians and Assyrians had them. In short, all peoples have had their folklore, and the Hebrews had theirs. The book of Genesis contains some of these tales and traditions.

It is generally conceded by biblical students that Genesis was one of the last productions of the Old Testament. Some ancient editor or compiler, arranging the books of Hebrew history, is supposed to have arranged the present book of Genesis from the myths and folklore of his people. In some cases the stories appropriated existed long before the formation of a Hebrew nation—as, for example, the Deluge Story, which was an old Semitic legend. In such instances the compiler simply wrote Jehovah into them. The task he set himself was to prepare a prelude for Hebrew history which should start with the " beginnings," as the word *genesis* literally means. Sometimes the legends he incorporated lay at his hand in two distinct forms and this early editor in several instances inserted both into his book. This explains the repetition and overlapping of certain narratives. The story of the creation illustrates this most plainly. One form of the story is included in the first chapter of the Bible, and the first four verses of the second chapter. This has been called an " epic of creation."

" Its language is not scientific, accurate, technical; it is figurative, poetic, the language of imagination. God broods upon the face of the water like a wind playing upon its surface; he calls, and light comes forth out of the darkness; he gives proper names to both light and darkness, and calls one Day, the other Night; he erects a firmament to divide the waters above from the waters beneath; he again divides the waters below from the land, and gives proper names to both earth and seas; he speaks, and in the heavens above lights appears to illumine the earth. All this is language of poetry and of picture; this is no scientific treatise or cosmogony; it is a poet's sublime epic; a pæan to the Creator of the world. Whether it agrees with the latest conclusions of scientists concerning the order of the processes of evolution by which the world was developed from star-dust is a question as little pertinent to the chapter as would be the question whether geographical exploration indicates any locality for the Purgatory and the Paradise of Dante." [5]

The second story of the creation begins with the fifth verse in the second chapter of the present Genesis. Here again it is a tale of imagination rather than scientific discourse. "How this garden is so fenced in from the outer world that neither they nor their descendants can ever return to it, nor even discover where it is, is left to conjecture, as surely no scientific writer would have left it. The garden disappears absolutely from the face of the earth, and never again is mentioned in the sacred history, or in any other. The man and his wife go out into the wilderness to fight life's battle with thistle-bearing nature; children are born to them; cities are discovered in the wilderness; whence come they?

"It is absolutely certain that if one were to come upon this story in Greek, Latin, or Scandinavian literature, one would not hesitate a moment how to classify it. This, he would say, is a myth of wonderful beauty: What is its significance? What does it mean? The scientific or literary student of the Old Testament sees no reason for refusing to apply the same standards to this story in Hebrew literature which he would apply if he found it in any other." [6]

As we have uniformly found, the prehistoric history of every people is largely preserved in myth and legend, and the Hebrews supply no exception to the general rule. In myth, legend, tradition, folklore, the historian learns to seek for the beginnings of all peoples, and the fact that Genesis has proven

[5]Life and Letters of the Ancient Hebrews: Allott, 60.
[6]Ibid.; 62.

to be a book of Hebrew legends, some of which were common to the Semitic race, does not mean that the value of the literary production is impaired—rather, it helps us to understand these people the better and shows at once for all the futility of attempts to work scientific interpretations into these ancient stories, as well as the wild error of interpreting them literally.

"When neighboring peoples deified nature, worshipping the sun and moon and stars, the birds and beasts, the sacred river Nile, the cattle that browsed upon its shore, the crocodiles that swam in its waters, and the very beetles which crawled along its banks, the Hebrew myth of creation embodied the truth that God is Spirit, and Spirit is creative; that God has made man in his own image; that of created beings man alone is divine; and that nature, which by pagan religions men were taught abjectly to worship, is man's serf whom he is to tame, harness, and make do his bidding. The Hebrew myth of Eden embodies the truth that sin is wilful disobedience of law; that conscience makes cowards of us all; that between sin and the human soul is to be eternal and undying hate; that sin will corrupt the whole human race, but that the human race will destroy sin, or, to relate it in the language of the myth, the serpent shall poison the heel of man, and man shall ·crush the serpent's head.   The tradition of the deluge embodies the truth that destruction of sinners can never cure the world of sin. The Hebrew story of Abraham taught the truth that he who seeks God shall find him, and that to find him no sacrifice of home or friends or child is or can be too great: the epic of Joseph, that he is the Providence of all who put their trust in him—God in Egypt as in the Holy Land, in Pharaoh's prison and Pharaoh's palace, God of gods and Lord of lords."[1]

As we have found didactic poetry in the Old Testament, so we find didactic fiction, *didactic* carrying always with it the sense of *instructive* fiction which bears a moral, teaches a lesson. The story of Ruth belongs to this class. The date of this production is not certain; some think it was written before, some after, the captivity. In any event the Hebrews were always opposed to inter-marriage with foreigners, and after the captivity the feeling was stronger than ever. The heathen—all people except themselves—were intensely hated.

[1] Life and Letters of the Ancient Hebrews: Abbott, 79.

Then the story of Ruth was written by some unknown author, who possessed broad ideas, which he expressed in a delicate way. He wrote this "Idyl of the Common People," and to make the subtle lesson less objectionable, he placed it back in the era of the Judges. The story is briefly this: An Israelite and his wife wandered in the lands of the Moabites, during a time of scarcity in their own land. Their sons grew up there and married Moabite women. In time the sons and the father died, and the three women were left alone. Having no means of support longer, the mother wished to return to her native country, and advised the daughters-in-law to remain in their own country, where they might again be sought in marriage.

One does so; one refuses to leave the old mother, and having maintained her willingness to go with her and espouse her religion, accompanies her back to the old neighborhood. A Hebrew custom required farmers to allow the poor to follow the reapers and pick up whatever they left or dropped in their work. Ruth, the faithful daughter, is directed to the estate of Boaz, a distant relative of Naomi, the mother, and thither she goes to glean. In due time she came under the notice of Boaz, who inquired about the stranger. His servants explained that she had accompanied Naomi out of Moab and had asked permission to gather after the reapers. Boaz spoke kindly to her, and instructed his servants to leave plenty for her to glean. At evening she took what she had collected, beat out the barley and carried it home to Naomi. The wise old Naomi believed that Boaz would take an interest in the maiden, and told her to glean in no other field than his. And the story ends as we might expect: "So Boaz took Ruth, and she became his wife. And she bear a son. And the women said unto Naomi:

"Blessed be the Lord,
    Which hath not left thee this day with a near kinsman,
    And let his name be famous in Israel.
    And he shall be unto thee a restorer of life,
    And a nourisher of thine old age;
    For thy daughter-in-law, which loveth thee,
    Which is better to thee than seven sons,
    Hath borne him."

However deep-seated the prejudice against foreigners, it melted away as one read the simple story—the fidelity of one woman for another yet more unfortunate, and of a different race, and the love of man and woman that reaches beyond all national boundaries to the wider horizon of the universe.

Thirdly, Hebrew fiction falls into historical romance— the book of Esther being a notable example. From its frequent repetition in operetta, as well as story form, it is familiar to all, and space forbids extracts from it.

"One has, it seems to me, but to read this story to feel the life of a romance in it. The contrasted characters—the sensual monarch, the unscrupulous minister, the proud Puritan, the brave woman, brave with true womanly courage—are drawn in few lines, but with marvelous skill. The plot, with its play of character against character, its rapidity of movement, its dramatic incident, its plotting and counter-plotting, shows the highest constructive skill; and the moral inspiration of the story, inciting to hate of the sensuality of Xerxes and the crafty malice of Haman, to admiration for the courage of Mordecai, and a love that is more than admiration for the womanly bearing of the queen, is all the greater because the narrator does not formulate it; and the story is all the more religious in its spirit because it is so wholly free from the phraseology of religion in its language." [8]

Lastly, we may note that Hebrew fiction falls into satirical romance, the book of Jonah being an example. This book is a satire on the narrowness of the Hebrew religion. Just as the Song of Solomon is a song *about* Solomon rather than *by* him, so the book of Jonah contains experiences accredited to Jonah by an unknown of at least a century after the death of the prophet. The whole is the work of an imagination, and the name of Jonah may have been taken by the merest chance.

"It is the anonymous work of some humane and catholic-minded man, so far in advance of his times—in some respect even of ours—that, did even tradition give any clew to his personality, we should gladly subscribe him in the role of the world's greatest teachers. What the author of Ecclesiastes has done in selecting so great a character as Solomon for the spokesman of his wisdom, the author of Jonah has done. He

[8] Life and Letters of the Ancient Hebrews: Abbott, 191.

sets forth contrasting lessons of man's infirmity and God's mercy. as suggested by the personal experiences which he attributes to the great prophet of a former generation." [a]

The substance of the story is this: Jonah is instructed by Jehovah to go eastward and preach the Hebrew faith in Nineveh, a city sunk deep in wickedness and vice. Now the Hebrews hated the heathen—all others besides themselves— and Jonah consequently did not consider the Ninevans worthy of his care. He therefore attempted to escape this duty put upon him by taking passage to the west. Soon a storm arose. He awoke to find the crew imploring their gods in terror for preservation. When he acknowledged himself as one guilty, fleeing from the command of Jehovah, the rest were frightened but hesitated to cast him overboard as he instructed them to do. Thus Jonah was brought face to face with two ideas, hitherto unknown to him: the so-called heathen are as humane as he, and believe as firmly in divine power. For his ultimate rescue a great fish was created—and as several authorities have noted there is no reason whatever for calling this mythical fish a whale. After a time the fish brought him to shore, giving him thus a second chance. Jonah now set out for Nineveh. Reaching the capital of the world-empire, he preached destruction to come upon her citizens because of their iniquity, but as it happened, they repented of their ill-doing and Jehovah spared them. This made Jonah angry. He preferred to see them perish as a just punishment for their evil past. He built him a little hut and in a single night a gourd grew over it, giving grateful shade from the sun's hot rays. In an hour this was stricken and died. Jonah mourned about it, and Jehovah questioned him thus: You are sorry about the gourd, in whose creation you had no part; you would have spared it. May I not then spare a city where dwell thousands upon thousands of poor, blind children of men?

"But he gets no answer. Jonah is left sulky and cross like a petulant child in the hot sun outside the walls of Nineveh, angry because God is merciful. The meaning of the story seems to me to be written in large and luminous characters. 'There is a wideness in God's mercy like the wideness of the sea.' When, from that splendid truth, brought out

[a] The Bible as Literature, ed. Moulton, Whiton, 224.

more clearly in the story of Jonah than in any other book of
the Old Testament, we turn aside to discuss the question
whether a whale has a throat big enough for a man to pass
through, we are abandoning the great lesson which God meant
to teach through our imagination to debate a physiological
fact of absolutely no consequence." [10]

[10]Life and Letters of Ancient Hebrews, 200.

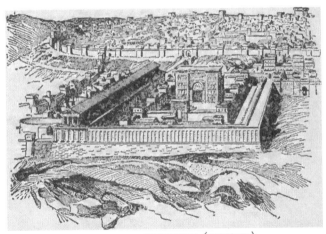

THE TEMPLE AT JERUSALEM (RESTORED).

CHAPTER XVII.

WISDOM LITERATURE.

Literature which among other peoples is called philosophical, has in the realm of Hebrew writing been termed *Wisdom* literature. This difference is to be noted, however: Greek philosophy and modern philosophy which has followed in its wake, seeks to fathom the explanation of things, and to reduce everything to some system; Hebrew *wisdom* taught one how to conduct himself—how to act in the ordinary conditions of life. Three books remaining in the Old Testament—belong to this division: Proverbs, Ecclesiastes, and the book of Job. Two apocryphal books, The Wisdom of Solomon and Ecclesiasticus also contain *Wisdom.*

Israel's teachers, generally speaking, belonged to one of three groups: prophets, priests, and seers or wise men. The prophets brought divinely inspired messages of truth to the people; the priests had charge of the temples, offered sacrifices, and guarded and preserved the ritual: The seers instructed the people in matters of every day life rather than in things eternal.

In the beginning these seers, or wise men, had probably been men conspicuous for their good sense and discretion; as time went on they came to constitute a distinct social class, and became remarkably well versed in human affairs, perplexities, successes and failures. They sat by the city gates and gave counsel to all who sought them out, of whatever class or calling. Their conclusions were based upon wide experience and close observation, and they counselled prudence, industry, moderation, common sense and good policy. Many of their trite sayings have come down to us; others have no doubt been lost. These remaining take the form of proverbs, as for example:

" He that is slothful in his work is brother to him that is a great waster."

" Many will entreat favor of the prince; and every man is a friend to him that giveth gifts."

" He that answereth a matter before he heareth it, it is folly and
shame to him."

" The rich ruleth the poor, and the borrower is servant to the
lender.'

" He that tilleth his land shall have plenty of bread; but he that
followeth after vain persons shall have poverty enough."

Similar in spirit are some of the counsels given Laertes
by his father Polonius:

" Give thy thoughts no tongue
Nor any unproportioned thought its act.

" Give every man thy ear but few thy voice,
Take each man's counsel but reserve thy judgment.

" Neither a borrower nor a lender be:
For loan oft loses both itself and friend."

Neither the advice of Polonius nor the maxims of the
seers are based on the noblest conceptions, but upon expediency, prudence, good policy, as shown by wide observation
and long familiarity with the world.

The *Sayings of the Seers* was the name of a compilation
of these trite sayings taught by the wise men. This book
has disappeared, although it is probable that our book of
Proverbs contains many of its precepts.

Sometimes the *Wisdom* teaching took the form of sonnets:

SONNET ON THE SLUGGARD.

" Go to the ant, thou sluggard:
Consider her ways, and be wise:
Which having no chief,
Overseer,
Or ruler,
Provideth her meat in the summer,
And gathereth her food in the harvest.

CHRISTIAN STREET, JERUSALEM (BAZAAR DISTRICT).

"How long wilt thou sleep, O sluggard?
When wilt thou arise out of thy sleep?
   'Yet a little sleep,
   A little slumber,
   A little folding of the hands to sleep:'
So shall thy poverty come as a robber,
And thy want as an armed man."

Wisdom in Ecclesiasticus takes the form of essays. A collection of disconnected thoughts, bearing merely upon the title, they are not unlike the essays of Bacon and certain other essayists.

FRIENDSHIP.

" Sweet words will multiply a man's friends, and a fair-speaking tongue will multiply courtesies. Let those that are at peace with thee be many; but thy counsellors one of a thousand. If thou wouldst get thee a friend, get him by proving, and be not in haste to trust him. For there is a friend that is for his own occasion, and he will not continue in the day of affliction. And there is a friend that turneth to enmity, and he will discover strife to thy reproach. And there is a friend that is a companion at the table, and he will not continue in the day of thy affliction: and in thy prosperity he will be as thyself, and will be bold over thy servants; if thou shalt be brought low, he will be against thee, and will hide himself from thy face. Separate thyself from thine enemies; and beware of thy friends. A faithful friend is a strong defence; and he that hath found him hath found a treasure. There is nothing that can be taken in exchange for a faithful friend; and his excellency is beyond price. A faithful friend is a medicine of life; and they that fear the Lord shall find him. He that feareth the Lord directeth his friendship aright; for as he is, so is his neighbour also."[1]

In this manner the seers counselled the people regarding the affairs of every day life, exhorting them to be honest, industrious, fair in their dealings with men, moral and up-

[1] Ecclesiasticus VI.

II—4

right—not so much because it was right as because it was
prudent and safest to follow these rules. It was no system of
philosophy that was set forth in the sayings of the seers,
but rather, rules of living that had proven sensible and dis-
creet. All we know of the ancient Hebrews and their social
life leads us to feel that such counsel was needed, and that
such practical guidance worked for good in Israel.

So much has already been said of the book of Job that
no further comment is needed here, reasons for its being
classified with the Wisdom literature being quite apparent.

Ecclesiastes is a book concerning which there has been
much conjecture and wide difference of opinion. The rational,
reasonable explanation seems to be that it portrays the conflicting ideas which so often harass the human mind, these
given utterance without indication of where one begins and the
other ends. Tennyson's Two Voices may be compared with
this biblical book in some particulars.

"The book entitled Ecclesiastes marks the point where
at last observation and analysis are turned upon life and the
external universe as a whole. But this attempt of philosophy
to read the meaning of all things breaks down in failure and
despair: the term ' Wisdom ' disappears from this book, and
in its place we have reiterated the word ' Vanity,' to express
how existence is found ' empty ' of all meaning. This however
does not prevent the book from being full of wisdom in the
other sense of the word; it is a storehouse of miscellaneous
reflections on details of life and conduct."[2]

THE PROPHETS.

We are in the habit of thinking of a prophet as one who
foretells. To the Hebrew the word had a different meaning.
It signified merely *one who speaks for another, one who speaks
forth.*

About one-fourth of the Old Testament is made up of
the writings of the prophets. It is true that some of the
prophets did foretell coming events—sometimes coming events
in Palestine were very apparent to the discerning mind.
Again, happenings foretold did not always occur as prophesied; in other instances they did. It is apparent then that

[2]Intro. to Lit. of the Bible: Moulton, 132.

prophecy was not the only nor yet the most important function of a Hebrew prophet, and we must try to forget our ordinary conception of the word if we are to understand the part taken by this group of Hebrew teachers.

The Old Testament recounts the services and experiences of a number of prophets; sixteen of its books were in all probability written by prophets, yet unquestionably many others of whom we have no record, lived and "*spoke forth*" in Israel. The ones who played the most important *roles,* those who brought messages of greatest force, were remembered, while many others were forgotten. Portions of the Old Testament were written by prophets whose very names remain no longer, as notably the last half of the book of Isaiah, generally accredited to the Great Unknown—a man of wonderful power.

The material for a study of several Hebrew prophets lies open to all, and it would be impossible here to take an individual study of them. How wide a range of subjects were treated by them, and how varied was the character of the forth-speakers of Israel, we may judge from the following lines:

"Amos is a moral reformer, who appears suddenly in the midst of Israel's greatest apparent prosperity, but real corruption and hastening decay, to denounce the nation's profligacy and inhumanity, expose the falsity of hopes built on a traditional theology and a ceremonial religion, and foretell coming disaster and doom; Hosea is a poet, who has learned the deepest truths of human sinfulness and divine love in the school of his own bitter experience. Isaiah is a statesman, strong leader of the people, wise counsellor of kings, whose courage sustains the heart of the people in dire disaster, whose wisdom might have saved the kingdom from destruction had the kings followed his counsels; Micah is the prophet of the poor, the religious socialist of his age, who denounces the greed of the rich and the vices of the capital, and for the nation's redemption looks not to the court or the city but to the country village, and the ranks of the plain people; Zephaniah, living in the superficial and transient reforms of King Josiah, perceives how superficial, and transient they are, and utters the one word of warning against

the hopes which are built upon them; Nahum, with a fine
scorn of imperial greatness inspired by the spirit of cruelty,
foretells the siege and fall of Nineveh, city of blood and of
ceaseless rapine; Habakkum is a skeptic with clinging faith,
whose verse begins with the skeptic's cry, 'O Lord, how long
shall I cry and thou wilt not hear,' and ends with the answer
of faith,   'I will rejoice in the God of my salvation!;
Obadiah is an outraged idealist, whose indignation in the
hour of his nation's apparent ruin cries out against the apathy
of a kindred people gloating over his brother's misfortune;
Jeremiah is the first distinctive individualist among the Hebrew prophets—a Huguenot in an age ruled by the Medici,
a Savonarola in an age of Alexander XI.   strange,
sad, self-contradictory, eloquent, pathetic, despairing, brave, a
Protestant before Protestanism, a Puritan before Puritanism;
Ezekiel is the prophet of the Exile, endeavoring to preserve
the faith of his people by solidifying their religious institutions
and codifying their ecclesiastical laws;   The Great
Unknown is the most catholic of all the prophets—recognizes
even in the pagan Emperor Cyrus the Great a messenger and
servant of Jehovah, foresees the coming of pagan peoples to
share Israel's future glory, is the first of the Hebrew teachers
to see that suffering is not a sign of divine displeasure but a
commission to divine service.   Haggai, Zechariah,
and Malachi are prophets of the restoration: Haggai, a church-
man who urges on the rebuilding of the Temple; Zechariah,
a contemporary of the same school, whose mystic visions are
as untranslatable into prose as those of Percivale in Tennyson's Holy Grail; Malachi, a Puritan prophet who protests
against those corruptions of life and doctrine which always
accompany an ecclesiastical revival.   Joel is a moral
poet of uncertain date who draws from so simple an incident
as a devastating flight of locusts a symbol of the judgment
day of Jehovah; Jonah is a satire written by an unknown
author on the narrowness of Israel and a testimony of the
universality of Jehovah's loving kindnesses and tender mercies;
and Daniel is latest of all the prophets, and his apocalyptic
visions, like those of his antitype in the New Testament, are
still a perplexity to the spiritual and a peril to the literalist."[a]

[a]Life and Letters of Ancient Hebrews, 347, ff.

CHAPTER XVIII.

EXPLORATIONS IN PALESTINE.

In 1865 there was organized in London the English Palestine Exploration Fund, having for its object a scientific and systematic exploration of Palestine. This was the first well organized attempt to make thorough investigations in the Holy Land with the hope of facilitating Bible study. Some little delay was met in collecting sufficient funds, but from 1872-1875, and from 1877-1878, an expedition was kept in the field, under the direction of Conder and Kitchener—later Lord Kitchener. This expedition succeeded in making a geographical survey of the territory west of the Jordan.

" Not only was every place, every little valley, and every hill indicated, but also every road and every spring. All wells and cisterns of any significance were recorded; and all the old structures and graves which were found were measured and sketched. The ground was literally searched foot after foot, and more recent explorers have scarcely succeeded in making any important additions."[1]

In 1878 the German Palestine society was founded, having the scientific exploration of Palestine as its object. Funds provided by its organization maintained Dr. Schumaker and his party of explorers in their work begun in 1884. More recently a Russian society has been formed with the object of effecting new discoveries in the Holy Land.

All efforts to carry on excavations in Palestine are of quite recent date, and no such rich rewards have gratified those in search of buried treasure as have been recovered in Egypt or Babylonia. It is not likely that this country will ever produce finds of like value and detail. However, much that is of interest to the student of Bible history as well as to the archæologist has already appeared.

In addition to complete geographical and topographical maps, of Palestine, without which no systematic work could well be conducted, we have detailed charts of certain small but

[1]Explorations in Bible Lands: Hilprecht, 592.

important localities: the land of the Moabites, east of Jordan, has been thoroughly worked out. The Shephelah has been similarly charted and in this district some considerable digging has been done. Old fortified places—Judah's strongholds on the west, have been discovered, and something has been learned of the earlier inhabitants of the country in this region.

The Jews were not artists, and such tombs as have been unearthed have brought no such ray of light upon their age as has been shed by discovered tombs in the valley of the Nile. Yet to the antiquarian no stone or inscription is unimportant.

The city of Jerusalem has been the coveted arena for explorers, but difficulties occur because the destroyed city—several times laid waste—was later built upon, and modern structures and possessions do not allow of freedom in excavation.

Two or three finds should be mentioned in connection with recent exploration, one being an old mosaic floor which took the form of a map of Syria, Palestine and Egypt. It was probably made about 400 A. D. and has assisted in identifying certain localities previously unknown. Unfortunately the greater part of the floor was destroyed before its discovery, about 49 yards still remaining.

" The difference between plain and highland is strikingly expressed by the artist. The valley of the Jordan, the plain of Sharon, and the wilderness of Mount Sinai are distinguished from the dark mountains of Judaea by being coloured light. A deep green indicates the Dead Sea, while white and light blue fishes sport in the Jordan and Nile. The map accurately shows the location of mountains and hills, of wilderness and forests, of cold and hot springs, of pools and lakes, of palm trees and wells, and represents these in their natural colors. Each city may be recognized by its distinguishing features. The obelisks of Ashkelon; the great street of Gaza which leads to a basilica; the oval place in Lydda: all these are anything but accidental things. To be recognized at the first glance, Kerak is seen enthroned on a high rock. How carefully the artist did his work, even to the minutest detail, is illustrated by the Church of the Sepulchre in Jerusalem.   .   .

" The importance of this new discovery cannot be too highly estimated. By reason of its great mass of details, its exact representation of the form, size and plan of towns and the style and outline of buildings, its references to several hitherto unknown places, its indication of the then current traditions regarding certain sacred places and their location, etc., the map proves to be of inestimable value in the study of Hebrew and Christian archæology and in determining the geography and the historical conditions of the period to which it belongs."[2]

The Tell-el-Amarna letters, so important in the history of Egypt, have thrown light upon the condition of Palestine in 1400 B. C. and the period immediately following, when the Pharaoh was too absorbed with his religious reformation to send help to his outlying provinces.

Recently the American Institute of Archæology has established a school at Jerusalem for the purpose of assisting young scholars to undertake researches on their own account, and there is good reason to think that the next few years will be fruitful in making ancient Palestine better known through the spade of the excavator.

[2] Hilprecht: Explorations in Bible Lands, 618.

THE JEW'S WAILING PLACE OUTSIDE OF JERUSALEM

THE BOOK OF RUTH.

And it came to pass in the days when the judges judged, that there was a famine in the land. And a certain man of Beth-lehem-Judah went to sojourn in the land of Moab, he, and his wife, and his two sons. And the name of the man was Elimelech, and the name of his wife was Naomi, and the name of his two sons Mahlon and Chilion, Ephrathites of Beth-lehem-Judah. And they came into the country of Moab, and continued there. And Elimelech, Naomi's husband died; and she was left and her two sons. And they took wives of the women of Moab; and the name of the one was Orpah, and the name of the other, Ruth. And they dwelt there about ten years. And Mahlon and Chilion both died; and the woman was left of her two children and of her husband.

Then she arose with her daughters-in-law, that she might return from the country of Moab; for she had heard in the country of Moab how that the Lord had visited his people in giving them bread. And she went forth out of the place where she was, and her two daughters-in-law with her; and they went on the way to return unto the land of Judah. And Naomi said unto her two daughters-in-law, Go, return each of you to her mother's house: the Lord deal kindly with you, as ye have dealt with the dead, and with me. The Lord grant you that ye may find rest, each of you in the house of her husband. Then she kissed them; and they lifted up their voice and wept. And they said unto her, Nay, but we will return with thee unto thy people. And Naomi said, Turn again, my daughters; why will ye go with me? Have I yet sons in my womb, that they may be your husbands? Turn again, my daughters, go your way; for I am too old to have a husband. If I should say, I have hope, if I should even have an husband tonight, and should bear sons; would ye therefore tarry till they were grown? would ye therefore stay from having husbands? nay, my daughters; for it grieveth me much for your sakes, for the hand of the Lord is gone forth against me. And they lifted up their voice, and wept again: and Orpah kissed her mother-in-law; but Ruth clave unto her. And she said, Behold, thy sister-in-law is gone back unto her people and unto her god: return thou after thy sister-in-law. And Ruth said,

Entreat me not to leave thee,
  And to return from following after thee:
For whither thou goest, I will go;
  And where thou lodgest, I will lodge;
Thy people shall be my people,
  And thy God my God;
Where thou diest, will I die,
  And there will I be buried:
The Lord do so to me
And more also,
  If aught but death part thee and me.

And when she saw that she was steadily minded to go with her, she left speaking unto her.

So they two went until they came to Beth-lehem. And it came to pass when they were come to Beth-lehem, that all the city was moved about them. And the women said, Is this Naomi? And she said unto them, Call me not Naomi, call me Mara: for the Almighty hath dealt very bitterly with me. I went out full, and the Lord hath brought me home again empty: why call ye me Naomi, seeing the Lord hath testified against me, and the Almighty hath afflicted me? So Naomi returned, and Ruth the Moabitess, her daughter-in-law, with her, which returned out of the country of Moab: and they came to Beth-lehem in the beginning of the barley harvest.

II.

And Naomi had a kinsman of her husband's, a mighty man of wealth, of the family of Elimelech; and his name was Boaz. And Ruth and the Moabitess said unto Naomi, Let me now go to the field, and glean among the ears of corn after him in whose sight I shall find grace. And she said unto her, Go, my daughter. And she went, and came and gleaned in the field after the reapers: and her hap was to light on the portion of the field belonging unto Boaz, who was of the family of Elimelech. And, behold, Boaz came from Beth-lehem, and said unto the reapers, The Lord be with you. And they answered him, The Lord bless thee. Then said Boaz unto his servant that was set over the reapers, Whose damsel is this? And the servant that was set over the reapers answered and

said, It is the Moabitess damsel that came back with Naomi
out of the country of Moab: and she said, Let me glean, I pray
you, and gather after the reapers among the sheaves: so she
came, and hath continued even from the morning until now,
save that she tarried a little in the house. Then said Boaz
unto Ruth, Hearest thou not, my daughter? Go not to glean
in another field, neither pass from hence, but abide here fast
by my maidens. Let thine eyes be on the field that they do
reap, and go thou after them: have I not charged the young
men that they shall not touch thee? and when thou art athirst,
go unto the vessels, and drink of that which the young men
have drawn. Then she fell on her face, and bowed herself
to the ground, and said unto him, Why have I found grace
in thy sight, that thou shouldest take knowledge of me, seeing
I am a stranger? And Boaz answered and said unto her, It
hath fully been shewed me, all that thou hast done unto thy
mother-in-law since the death of thine husband: and how thou
hast left thy father and thy mother, and the land of thy
nativity, and art come unto a people which thou knowest not
heretofore. The Lord recompense thy work, and a full reward be given thee of the Lord, the God of Israel, under whose
wings thou art come to take refuge. Then she said, Let me
find grace in thy sight, my lord, for that thou hast comforted
me, and for that thou hast spoken kindly unto thine handmaid, though I be not as one of thine handmaidens. And at
meal-time Boaz said unto her, Come hither, and eat of the
bread, and dip thy morsel in the vinegar. And she sat beside the reapers; and they reached her parched corn, and she
did eat, and was sufficed, and left thereof. And when she
was risen up to glean, Boaz commanded the young men saying, Let her glean even among the sheaves, and reproach her
not. And also pull some for her from the bundles, and leave
it, and let her glean, and rebuke her not. So she gleaned in
the field until even; and she beat out that she had gleaned, and
it was about an ephah of barley.

And she took it up, and went into the city; and her mother-
in-law saw what she had gleaned; and she brought forth and
gave to her that she had left after she was sufficed. And her
mother-in-law said unto her, Where hast thou gleaned today?
and where wroughtest thou? blessed be he that did take know-

ledge of thee. And she shewed her mother-in-law with whom she had wrought, and said, The man's name with whom I wrought today is Boaz. And Naomi said unto her daughter-in-law, Blessed be he of the Lord, who hath not left off his kindness to the living and to the dead. And Naomi said unto her, The man is nigh of kin unto us, one of our near kinsmen. And Ruth the Moabitess said, Yea, he said unto me, Thou shalt keep fast by my young men, until they have ended all my harvest. And Naomi said unto Ruth her daughter-in-law, It is good, my daughter, that thou go out with his maidens, and that they meet thee not in any other field. So she kept fast by the maidens of Boaz to glean unto the end of barley harvest and of wheat harvest; and she dwelt with her mother-in-law.

And Naomi her mother-in-law said unto her, My daughter, shall I not seek rest for thee, that it may be well with thee? And now is there not Boaz our kinsman, with whose maidens thou wast? Behold, he winnoweth barley tonight in the threshing-floor. Wash thyself therefore, and anoint thee, and put thy raiment upon thee, and get thee down to the threshing-floor: but make not thyself known unto the man, until he shall have done eating and drinking. And it shall be, when he lieth down, that thou shalt mark the place where he shall lie, and thou shalt go in, and uncover his feet, and lay thee down; and he will tell thee what thou shalt do. And she said unto her, All that thou sayest I will do.

And she went down unto the threshing-floor, and did according to all that her mother-in-law bade her. And when Boaz had eaten and drunk, and his heart was merry, he went to lie down at the end of the heap of corn: and she came softly, and uncovered his feet, and laid her down. And it came to pass at midnight, that the man was startled, and turned himself: and, behold, a woman lay at his feet. And he said, Who art thou? And she answered, I am Ruth thine handmaid: spread therefore thy skirt over thy handmaid; for thou art a near kinsman. And he said, Blessed be thou of the Lord, my daughter: that thou hast shewed more kindness in the latter end than at the beginning, inasmuch as thou followedst not young men, whether poor or rich. And now, my daughter, fear not; I will do to thee all that thou sayest: for all the city of my people doth know that thou art a virtuous woman. And now it is true that I am a near kinsman: howbeit there is a kinsman nearer than I. Tarry this night, and it shall be in the morning, that if he will perform unto thee the part of a kinsman, well; let him do the kinsman's part: but if he will not do the part of a kinsman to thee, then will I do the part of a kinsman to thee, as the Lord liveth: lie down until the morning. And she lay at his feet until the morning: and she rose up before one could discern another. For he said, Let it not be known that the woman came to the threshing-floor. And he said, Bring the mantle that is upon thee, and hold it; and she held it: and he measured six measures of barley, and laid it on her: and he went into the city. And when she came to her mother-in-law, she said, Who art thou, my daughter? And she told her all that the man had done to her. And she said, These six measures of barley gave he me; for he said, Go not empty unto thy mother-in-law. Then said she, Sit still, my daughter, until thou know how the matter will fall: for the man will not rest, until he have finished the thing this day.

Now Boaz went up to the gate, and sat him down there: and behold, the near kinsman of whom Boaz spake came by; unto whom he said, Ho, such a one! turn aside, sit down there. And he turned aside, and sat down. And he took ten men of the elders of the city, and said, Sit ye down here. And they sat down. And he said unto the near kinsman, Naomi, that is come again out of the country of Moab, selleth the parcel of land, which was our brother Elimelech's: and I thought to disclose it unto thee, saying, Put it before them that sit here, and before the elders of my people. If thou wilt redeem it, redeem it: but if thou wilt not redeem it, then tell me, that I may know: for there is none to redeem it besides thee; and I am after thee. And he said, I will redeem it. Then said Boaz, What day thou buyest the field of the hand of Naomi, thou must buy it also of Ruth the Moabitess, the wife of the dead, to raise up the name of the dead upon his inheritance. And the near kinsman said, I cannot redeem it for myself, lest I mar mine own inheritance: take thou my right of redemption on thee; for I cannot redeem it.

Now this was the custom in former time in Israel con-

cerning redeeming and concerning exchanging, for to confirm
all things; a man drew off his shoe, and gave it to his neighbour: and this was the manner of attestation in Israel. So
the near kinsman said unto Boaz, Buy it for thyself. And
he drew off his shoe. And Boaz said unto the elders, and
unto all the people, Ye are witnesses this day, that I have
bought all that was Elimelech's, and all that was Chilion's
and Mahlon's, of the hand of Naomi. Moreover Ruth the
Moabitess, the wife of Mahlon, have I purchased to be my
wife, to raise up the name of the dead upon his inheritance,
that the name of the dead be not cut off from among his
brethren, and from the gate of his place: ye are witnesses
this day. And all the people that were in the gate, and the
elders, said, We are witnesses.

> The Lord make the woman that is come into thine house
>   Like Rachel and like Leah,
>   Which two did build the house of Israel:
> And do thou worthily in Ephrathah,
>   And be famous in Bethlehem:
> And let thy house be like the house of Perez,
> Whom Tamar bare unto Judah,
>   Of the seed which the Lord shall give thee of this young
>   woman.

So Boaz took Ruth and she became his wife. And he
went in unto her, and the Lord gave her conception, and she
bare a son. And the women said unto Naomi,

> Blessed be the Lord,
>   Which hath not left thee this day without a near kinsman,
>   And let his name be famous in Israel.
> And he shall be unto thee a restorer of life,
>   And a nourisher of thine old age:
> For thy daughter-in-law, which loveth thee,
> Which is better to thee than seven sons,
>   Hath borne him.

And Naomi took the child, and laid it in her bosom, and
became nurse unto it. And the women her neighbours, gave
it a name, saying, There is a son born to Naomi; and they
called his name Obed: he is the father of Jesse, the father of
David.

Leaders of the people by their counsels,
And by their understanding men of learning for the people;
Wise were their words in their instruction:
Such as sought out musical tunes,
And set forth verses in writing:
Rich men furnished with ability,
Living peaceably in their habitations:
All these were honored in their generations,
And were a glory in their days.
There be of them, that have left a name behind them
To declare their praises.
And some there be, which have no memorial;
Who are perished as though they had not been,
And are become as though they had not been born;
And their children after them.
But these were men of mercy,
Whose righteous deeds have not been forgotten.
With their seed shall remain continually a good inheritance;
Their children are within the covenants.
Their seed standeth fast,
And their children for their sakes.
Their seed shall remain for ever,
And their glory shall not be blotted out.
Their bodies were buried in peace,
And their name liveth to all generations.
Peoples will declare their wisdom,
And the congregation telleth out their praise.

THE PRAISE OF FAMOUS MEN.

(ECCLESIASTICUS XLIV. 1–19.)

LET us now praise famous men,
And our fathers that begat us.
The Lord manifested in them great glory,
Even His mighty power from the beginning.
Such as did bear rule in their kingdoms,
And were men renowned for their power,
Giving counsel by their understanding,
Such as have brought tidings in prophecies:

The Love of the Lord.

A Number Sonnet.

There be nine things that I have thought of,
  And in mine heart counted happy;
And the tenth I will utter with my tongue:
  A man that hath joy of his children;
  A man that liveth and looketh upon the fall of his enemies;
Happy is he that dwelleth with a wife of understanding;
  And he that hath not slipped with his tongue;
  And he that hath not served a man that is unworthy of him;
Happy is he that hath found prudence;
  And he that discourseth in the ears of them that listen;
  How great is he that hath found wisdom!
Yet is there none above him that feareth the Lord.

The Love of the Lord passeth all things:
He that holdeth it, to whom shall he be likened?

—*Ecclesiasticus.*

KING SOLOMON'S BETROTHAL.

The Song of Solomon is a lyrical idyl, celebrating the King's love for a Shulamite damsel. It is divided into five (or seven) parts or scenes. The following is the central division; it opens with the entrance of King Solomon, who afterwards declares the beauty of his beloved, and compares her to a garden. The Shulamite replies briefly, using the same figure.

The Choir.

Who is this that cometh up out of the wilderness
Like pillars of smoke,
Perfumed with myrrh and frankincense,
With all powders of the merchant?
  Behold, it is the litter of Solomon;
  Threescore mighty men are about it,
    Of the mighty men of Israel.
  They all handle the sword, and are expert i war;
  Every man hath his sword upon his thigh,
    Because of fear in the night.
  King Solomon made himself a palanquin
    Of the wood of Lebanon.

He made the pillars thereof of silver,
The bottom thereof of gold,
The seat of it of purple,
The midst thereof being inlaid with love
From the daughters of Jerusalem.
Go forth, O ye daughters of Zion, and behold King Solomon
With the crown wherewith his mother hath crowned him
In the day of his espousals,
And in the day of the gladness of his heart.

SOLOMON.

Behold, thou art fair, my love; behold, thou art fair;
Thine eyes are as doves behind thy veil;
Thy hair is as a flock of goats,
That lie along the side of Mount Gilead.
Thy teeth are like a flock of ewes that are newly shorn,
Which are come up from the washing;
Whereof every one hath twins,
And none is bereaved among them.
Thy lips are like a thread of scarlet,
And thy mouth is comely.
Thy temples are like a piece of a pomegranate
Behind thy veil.
Thy neck is like the tower of David builded for an armory,
Whereon there hang a thousand bucklers,
All the shields of the mighty men.
Thy two breasts are like two fawns that are twins of a roe,
Which feed among the lilies.

THE CHOIR.

Until the day break, and the shadows flee away,
I will get me to the mountain of myrrh,
And to the hill of frankincense.

SOLOMON.

Thou art all fair, my love;
And there is no spot in thee.
Come with me from Lebanon, my bride,
With me from Lebanon:
Look from the top of Amana,
From the top of Senir and Hermon,

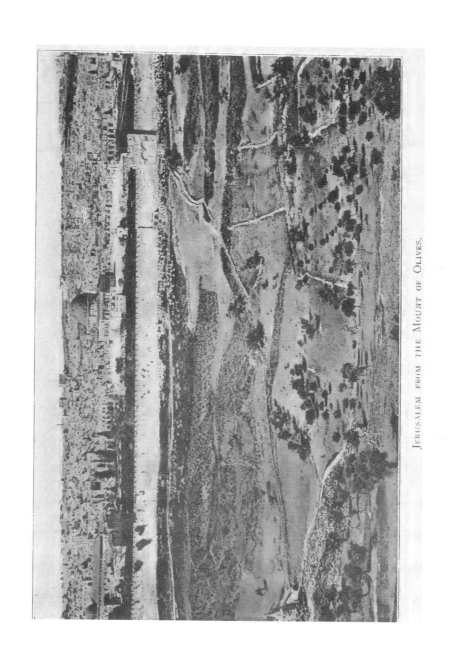

JERUSALEM FROM THE MOUNT OF OLIVES.

From the lions' dens,
From the mountains of the leopards.
Thou hast ravished my heart, my sister, my bride;
Thou hast ravished my heart
With one look from thine eyes,
With one chain of thy neck.
How fair is thy love, my sister, my bride!
How much better is thy love than wine!
And the smell of thine ointments than all manner of spices!
Thy lips, O my bride, drop as the honeycomb:
Honey and milk are under thy tongue;
And the smell of thy garments is like the smell of Lebanon.

A garden shut up is my sister, my bride;
A spring shut up, a fountain sealed.
Thy shoots are an orchard of pomegranates, with precious
fruits;
Henna with spikenard plants, spikenard and saffron,
Calamus and cinnamon, with all trees of frankincense,
Myrrh and aloes, with all the chief spices.
Thou art a fountain of gardens,
A well of living waters,
And flowing streams from Lebanon.

THE SHULAMITE.

Awake, O north wind; and come, thou south;
Blow upon my garden, that the spices thereof may flow out.
Let my beloved come into his garden,
And eat his precious fruits.

SOLOMON.

I am come into my garden, my sister, my bride:
I have gathered my myrrh with my spice;
I have eaten my honeycomb with my honey;
I have drunk my wine with my milk.

THE CHOIR.

Eat, O friends;
Drink, yea, drink abundantly of love.

PALESTINE OF TODAY

For many years travel in Palestine has ceased to be confined to priests, pilgrims and clergymen. It is still true—and will probably always be the case—that the majority of those who visit this renowned land are attracted thither by its historical associations. Palestine is sacred to the adherents of three religions: Judaism, Christianity and Mohammedanism. Yet the followers of these different faiths regard its history from radically different viewpoints, and regard each other with a bitterness ill becoming the disciples of any faith. In addition to the memories and associations that hover over these hills and valleys, however, Palestine fascinates the stranger by its diversity of scenery, its many climates comprised in small area, and its natural beauty.

Accustomed as we are to great magnitudes, it is hard for us to keep in mind the small district which Palestine includes, being altogether not larger than our state of New Jersey. Jerusalem, its most populous city, might be placed four times within the limits of Central Park. From Zion Gate on the south to the Gate of Damascus on the north, the distance is not more than two-thirds of a mile. One can walk from one end of the city to the other in ten minutes; again, from the summit of many a commanding peak throughout the country it is possible to gain a view of its entirety, from the sea on the west to the range beyond Jordan; from Mount Carmel at the north to the desert upon the south.

Taking advantage of the credulence of travelers, natives have ingeniously associated historical events with every possible building, stone, pool and hilltop, to the amusement as well as the consternation of the more discerning. George William Curtis in his letters which were read with such enjoyment several years ago, called attention to the absurd lengths to which the thoughtless acceptance of guides' stories made it possible for this enterprising spirit to go.

"Tons, carloads of boxes, albums, writing desks, paper cutters, crosses, rulers, picture frames, Bible and prayer book covers, tablets and other things are sold and carried off every year by sentimental people, and cherished as souvenirs of the Mount of Olives, when if they had stopped to inquire they would very soon learn that not one of the few trees that remain on Olivet has been trimmed for fifty years.　　　The Garden of Gethsemane is another favorite place for relics, mostly sprigs of cypress and olive, and pressed flowers.　Shiploads of such souvenirs are sent over the world every year. They are sold at church fairs and festivals; they are presented to libraries and museums by pious people, are gratefully received and appreciated, but not one sprig of olive or cypress out of a hundred thousand actually comes from Gethsemane." Guide-books tell one, with no attempt to conceal the humor of the situation, that the location of the house of Simon the Tanner has been recently changed, greatly to the convenience of tourists and pilgrims who may now visit it without loss of time.　The discerning and thinking, by no means in the majority, note sadly the tendency to turn to account unquestioning faith in places sanctified by biblical mention.

"With imagination aflame, multitudes of pilgrims listen and believe.　Have they not come across the lands and the seas to stand in these narrow alleys, to see, to hear, to accept? Would it not be cruel to tell them the plain truth, that the Jerusalem of our Lord is buried far down beneath the mud, the stones, or the dust to which they press their trembling lips?　For some of us it is enough to know that in these depressions and on these stony hills was placed the ancient city where the greatest tragedy of the world was enacted. But for many it is not enough.　So legend steps in.　The mouths of men utter lies, and the minds of men receive them and cherish them."*

There is not lacking plenty to absorb those who do not feel called upon to identify every nook and corner of the land, who care little whether some event occurred by these particular stones, or by others similar in appearance; who find the main outlines of the story enough.　For the general aspect of the region remains unchanged; the same smiling plains reach along the sea as formerly, although this portion was not occupied by the early Hebrews; the same foothills rise with their

* The Holy Land, Hichens, 242.

unending opportunities for concealment in rough border warfare; the mountains, bare and hostile, stand today as they
have for ages, the valley of the Jordan, hot and unhealthful,
cutting them in two divisions; while the desert crouches near,
signifying death, waste, destruction.

Spring and autumn are most enjoyable to the wayfarer.
Summer months are warm and dry, and winter is cold and
wet. Spring mantles the valleys and foothills with beautiful
flowers and fresh verdure, and entices the traveler to wander
through highways and byways familiar although new to the
eye, having been immortalized by the life and ministry of
Christ.

Approaching Palestine by sea, passengers are landed at
Joppa, which bears the distinction of having the worst harbor
in the world. Large vessels cannot come into port because
of shallow water, which necessitates their transfer into small
boats. Because the sea is usually rough, some degree of
determination and fortitude must be summoned by those
unaccustomed to such conditions.

Formerly visitors chose between such mounts as could be
procured or carriages for covering the distance between Joppa
and Jerusalem. Today a railroad accommodates those who
wish either to save time or who prefer travel by train. Except
for the demand created by tourists, this railroad could not pay
for its maintenance, for the natives hold too closely to the
ways of their fathers to make use of conveniences so modern.

Those whose time is limited and others to whom journeying through the country generally would afford no particular
pleasure, find Jerusalem interesting. It is walled today, as
in antiquity. Its present walls, firm and formidable, were
built during the Crusades, but in the main follow the course
of those earlier destroyed. About forty feet high, crowned
by many turrets, they are pierced by several gates. A never-
ending stream of humanity pours through Joppa Gate on the
west. This motley array of people, from many lands and of
many tongues, is faithfully pictured in Ben Hur. For hours
one may watch the strange faces and find entertainment in the
various costumes worn by passersby.

The Gate of Damascus on the north, giving access to the
old Damascus road, is much traveled. Herod's Gate opens

likewise on the north. On the east St. Stephen's Gate, so named because of an erroneous connection with the site of Stephen's martyrdom, is in constant use. This gate is called by the Moslems the Gate of our Lady Mary, because it opens upon the road leading to what is known as Mary's tomb. Golden Gate on the same eastern side has been closed with solid cement work by the Mohammedans, who believe that when God reveals himself on earth, and the reign of Mohammedanism shall end, this gate will be the entrance used, so until that day they intend none to pass through it. Another legend says that it has been foretold that one day a conqueror shall ride through this gate and so extraordinary precaution is thus taken. Zion Gate gives access to the region south of the city

Jerusalem at present includes not only the district bounded by these walls but the immediate vicinity without them, as well. Especially has the population spread out to the north, and many modern buildings such as schools, convents, hospitals and missions have sprung up here. The population of the city is about 60,000, of whom 7,000 are Mohammedans, 13,000 Christians, and the remainder Jews. The Mohammedans are the rulers and hold the rest in contempt; most of them are Arabs and their dignified bearing contrasts strikingly with the unprepossessing Hebrews of the city, few of whom are young, many of whom are dependent upon charity. Ten times as many Jews live in New York as in Jerusalem, and as one writer has aptly remarked, they are ten times more at home there than in their ancient capital. Any notion of an ultimate gathering of Hebrews in the land of their fathers is purely visionary and impractical.

The two sites within Jerusalem of deepest interest to natives and strangers alike are the Church of the Sepulcher and the Dome of the Rock. The first is sacred to Christians; the other, to Mohammedans. Because the Dome of the Rock is built upon the ancient site of Solomon's temple, it has attraction for all. It will be remembered that Solomon's temple was the most splendid edifice in old Jerusalem, and that it was destroyed by the Babylonians when they took the Children of Israel into captivity. Herod rebuilt the temple

and it was his structure that was standing in the time of
Christ. This was in turn obliterated by the Romans in 79.
The very location of the temple area was for long a matter
of dispute but in recent times the Palestine Exploration
workers have settled the question to the satisfaction of
scholars. The top of Mount Moriah in the southwestern part
of Jerusalem was selected by Solomon for his temple. The
hill was formed of rock, bare, rough and originally very
uneven. A series of stairs and terraces led to the top, which
was crowned by the synagogue. The lowest and most spacious
terrace was open alike to Jew and Gentile; it was called the
Court of the Gentiles. Beyond this none but Jews could go
under penalty of death. The second terrace was called the
Court of the Israelites, a portion of it being separated from
the rest and known as the Court of Women. The third terrace
was called the Court of Priests, and upon this stood the temple.
Each terrace was smaller in extent than the one beneath. The
entrance to the temple faced the east and before it stood the
Altar of Burnt Offerings. The temple proper consisted of
three parts: the Portico, Holy Place and Holy of Holies.
This arrangement was undoubtedly borrowed from Egypt.
Today our churches exemplify a similar arrangement: the
nave, choir, and chancel.

After the destruction of Herod's temple, which may have
been even more beautiful than that of his predecessor, the hill
remained in ruins until 130, when Hadrian cleared away the
rubbish and built a temple to Jupiter upon it. In 637 Omar
captured Jerusalem and vowed he would raise a mosque on
the site. Although he began the work, it was finished by his
successors—the beautiful Dome of the Rock.

This is not a mosque in the usual sense of the word,
which signifies a place of worship. Rather, it is a shrine.
Over the rock, which forms the very summit of the hill, a
building has been set. It is made of choicest marble and
porcelain; its shape is octagonal and it is adorned with costly
tiles and mosaics. The huge rough grey-brown stone it
shelters is carefully protected from the polluting touch of
stranger and unbeliever, being regarded as only less sacred
than the shrine in Mecca.

Many legends cluster around this stone. It is said to cover all the waters of the Flood; to be the spot where Abraham prepared to sacrifice Isaac; to be the spot where the Ark of the Covenant rested; that upon it the name of God was divinely written. Upon this rock, it is further expected, the judgment throne of the Almighty will some day rest. So intense is the feeling among the followers of many faiths that it would be unsafe for Christians to visit the Dome of the Rock except under the protection of soldiers provided by the Moslem government. By strange turn of fortune the Jews today are forbidden to go above the first terrace—the boundary they formerly set for those of alien belief. Instead, they come on Friday evenings—the beginning of their Sabbath—and on Saturdays to the lower wall and pour out their grief because of the loss of their temple and the scattering of their people. "Some wail and shriek and tear their garments and their hair. But the old, old men just sit here all day long and nod over their prayer books, and dream of the departed glory of Israel."*

The Church of the Sepulcher, together with all spots held sacred by Christians, is in control of the Mohammedans. And yet, those who are most conversant with existing conditions are obliged to admit that with the present bitterness that divides Greek and Roman Christians and those of various creeds—who, in spite of various differences, take their stand beneath the cross of Christ—any other arrangement would mean unfair treatment of those not in authority. It is difficult for people dwelling in a land where religious differences have almost disappeared from daily thought and conversation, where those of many creeds are content to go, each his own way, to realize the religious feeling and attitude in Jerusalem. Various denominations and Greek and Roman churches, by their inharmony and discord, have caused the Moslems to regard them all with contempt. This condition is particularly manifest during the Easter week, celebrated under such a tension that the Turkish government has had to choose its officers with greatest care to preserve peace and decorum.

* Curtis: Today in Syria and Palestine.

"Perhaps after all it is an evidence of the wisdom of Providence that the central and supreme shrine of the Christian church should be in the possession and under the authority of Islam. The bitterness of the envy and rivalry of the sects is so great that none of them could be trusted to treat the others fairly if a Christian sect were in control, and although their manners are often offensive, the Moslems for a thousand years have always acted impartially and kept the scene of the burial of the Saviour open to all on equal terms."

The Church of the Sepulcher is the name given to a group of more than thirty buildings, all under one roof—chapels, missions, churches, cathedrals and shrines. These are supposed to cover many spots connected with the Passion of Christ and his burial. Even other historic sites quite unrelated—such as the tomb of Adam, the house of Joseph of Arimathea—are also included. The group constitutes a mysterious labyrinth, through which one might easily lose his sense of direction. The interior of many of these chapels is oriental in its dazzling display of barbaric splendor, quite out of keeping with the simplicity of the wonderful life thus commemorated.

The present buildings are not of long standing. Repeatedly has the Church of the Sepulcher been destroyed: by Persian, Turk, Arab, and in 1808 by fire. The present structures have been erected since that time. Shrines stand in memory of the crucifixion, the rolling away of the stone, the meeting of Mary and Christ, the prison where Christ was detained; the place where he was crowned with thorns. Most important is the Chapel of the Sepulcher, over the tomb itself.

Jews are forbidden to enter the Church of the Sepulcher, and they pass quickly by with faces averted, for so tense is religious passion that they would be subject to assault or even in danger of instant death if they were thought to even cast an irreverent glance in this direction.

Easter week finds the city full of pilgrims. Russians have braved the terrors of the steerage to journey thither, in order to worship at this shrine of shrines. Arabs, Syrians, Bedouins, Egyptians, Americans, Englishmen. Greek priests, Catholic priests, Copts and countless others, congregate. Sometimes sacred festivals of the Moslems fall at the same time, increasing the intense excitement. Besides the opportunity of visiting the shrines, praying before them and having treasured articles blessed by contact with them, pilgrims come to witness special ceremonies which occur during the week. The Greeks solemnize the ceremony of the washing of the feet, the Patriarch washing the feet of the twelve bishops; the burial of Christ is enacted; the Easter morning processional takes place; and strangest of all, the miracle of fire. The idea underlying this fast is that on the day before Easter—the Easter of the Greek Church—fire comes down from heaven and with it the patriarch lights a candle which transmits its flame to others until candles everywhere are lighted, being even carried over seas for the purpose of igniting tapers on the shrines of churches remote. Fleet runners are stationed to snatch the brands and set out for the Church of the Nativity and various other places of worship.

Pilgrims gather for days before; the steady line of travelers can be seen ascending the hill and it is impossible not to remember those festivals of ancient time when from all around the Israelites came up to Jerusalem to participate in the ceremonies of the temple. Some of the most beautiful psalms were sung on these occasions. In order to be sure of a place, many spend an entire day in the church, even sleeping in wretched heaps on stones within the court and in every nook and corner of the buildings. All have tapers ready. In course of long hours they grow weary and impatient; thousands of spectators crowd so closely together that they cannot move their arms; the weaker are thrust back by the stronger, and are fortunate to escape injury; armed Moslems are stationed about everywhere to preserve the peace.

Presently upon the appearance of the Patriarch, the vast assembly breaks into a song, ominous, often angry.

> "Christ has redeemed us;
> With His blood has bought us.
> Therefore we are glad,
> But you, O Jews, are sad!"

"I looked down upon what seemed a vast crowd of demented people, who had thrown off every scrap of self-restraint, whose strange passions went naked for all to see, who were full of barbarous violence, savage expectation, and the blood-lust. As I watched them I thought of a pack of hounds leaping up to the fox that the huntsman is about to throw to them. Yet these people, in all the colors of the rainbow, and drawn from all parts of Syria and other lands, wanted only—to light their candles!

"The question that all travelers ask in Jerusalem is: 'Do these crowds believe that what happens inside the Holy Sepulcher is a miracle? Do they believe that, as on the day of Pentecost, fire descends from heaven direct to the Greek patriach who has entered the Chapel of the Angels with the Armenian patriarch? Or do they understand that the ceremony is merely emblematic, that the patriarchs do not pretend that it is anything else?'

"Having watched the people on this extraordinary occasion at close quarters, I am unable to doubt that hundreds, probably thousands, of them do believe they are assisting at a miracle. I cannot otherwise account for their frantic excitement, an excitement such as I have never seen in any other crowd not intent upon violence or slaughter. After the working of the 'miracle,' delirium is the only word that accurately expresses the condition of the multitudes."*

When the fire is first thrust through the wall from the Sepulcher chapel, such slight restraint as has hitherto obtained is lost. The pilgrims fight for a chance to light their candles; they hold the flame to their faces and breasts and exclaim that it cannot harm them. Their garments often become ignited by their own tapers or those of their neighbors. The whole building is filled with heat and smoke and threatens to become a great holocaust. Then in some way that none who have experienced seem rightly to know, the crowds surge out of the Church of the Sepulcher, out of the court, into the streets of Jerusalem, there to sing songs of praise until daybreak.

Much more consistent with the season and its significance to hosts of people is the processional of the glad Easter morn, when those present are moved to compassion rather than bitterness, when the bells swell the praise of song that carries the glad tidings far and near.

* Hichens: The Holy Land.

None visit Jerusalem without passing along the *Via Dolorosa,* spanned by an arch called Ecco Homo today but probably built to commemorate Adrian's triumph in 136. This is supposed to be the road over which Christ bore the cross to Calvary. The stations are marked in the wall, but the spots each designates are not, of course, authentic.

The Garden of Gethsemane is now in the possession of Franciscan monks, who keep it in fine condition and tend it with loving care. The Mount of Olives has been rendered unsightly in modern times by the erection of huge and unattractive buildings. A Russian church crowns the summit. Only two miles beyond the hill—which is outside the city and almost as long—lies Bethany, a squalid village with nothing whatever to commend it. Even the ruins pointed out to strangers as belonging to the time of Christ are comparatively recent in origin.

About six miles south of Jerusalem is the town of Bethlehem, gratifying in its cleanliness and general appearance. The Church of the Nativity is built over the place where the Child is supposed to have been born, and in this instance, reasonable identification has been established. Here the magi came to bring their gifts, and here, too, was enacted the tragedy of the children, when Herod attempted to avert any future danger by the slaughter of the innocents. By many who have never seen the town as well as by those who have traversed its quiet streets, the name of Bethlehem is inseparably associated with the Star in the East, that heralded not alone a birth but the dawn of a new faith of such vitality and power that it has transformed the history of the world.

Greek Mythology

Greek Fables.

Old fables these and fancies old!—
  But not with hasty pride
Let logic cold and reason bold
  Cast these old dreams aside.
Dreams are not false in all their scope—
  Oft from the sleepy lair
Start giant shapes of fear and hope
  That, aptly read, declare
Our deepest nature. God in dreams
  Hath spoken to the wise;
And in a people's mystic themes
  A people's wisdom lies.

J. S. Blackie.

THE STORY OF GREEK MYTHOLOGY.

PREFATORY CHAPTER.

IRST, let us say that it is only the accident of time that makes Greek mythology a subject for study at all. Myths were not invented to be studied, but to be enjoyed. Mythology is in its origin only story-telling, and the object of story-telling is primarily to entertain. The primitive people who first began to give form to these tales of gods and demi-gods and heroes and the invisible semi-human inhabitants of mountain, grove, and stream, told them first of all for their own delight and the delight of their listeners, and the poets who afterwards, in civilized times, lent to the original stories the charm of beautiful language were again actuated by the desire to please themselves and their audience.

It would be a mistake, then, to treat the mythology of the Greeks as a body of scientific knowledge, and to study it with the austere and prosaic purpose of extracting from it mere information. It should be approached rather as a collection of entertaining tales poetically conceived and poetically told. It should be made part of our intellectual equipment, like literature itself, for the enjoyment it gives, and for the sake of its emotional and uplifting appeal.

But it would nevertheless be a great mistake not to study mythology at all, just as it would be a mistake not to study literature at all. Each yields its treasures in full only to those who expend effort in delving after them. We are an immense distance from the time when the tales of Greek mythology came into being, and are unfamiliar with Greek environment. As a matter of fact, there is only one time in its history when a myth is thoroughly understood without comment of any kind, and only one place where the mere telling carries the whole message of the tale—and that is at the very time of its origin, and in the very place. When time has passed, and the story is told to a different people in different surroundings, some of its details are bound to be obscure, and questions must be asked and answered. To appreciate all the content of Greek mythology without study is impossible for various reasons; we are unfamiliar with the geography and physiography of Greece; we are not only far distant from the native land of the myths, but from their time also, and are unable fully to understand the spirit of so ancient a people; we are ignorant of the daily life of the Greeks—their manners, their dress, their laws, their houses, their habit of thought; we know little of the religion they professed; we are unacquainted with the language they spoke as they told the tales; we are more or less unfamiliar with the literature in which they preserved them, and with their art in other forms; and, lastly, we do not possess their exquisite poetic sensibility.

If we are to realize the full enjoyment and profit which mythology has to yield to us, we must not only be familiar with the stories which compose it, but possess something of the knowledge above indicated; and that requires at least a moderate amount of effort.

It requires much less application, however, than might be supposed; there is no reason for regarding the study of mythology as a task. Much of the knowledge necessary to the appreciation of Greek myths may be acquired by nothing more severe than mere careful attention. In fact, one effective way of becoming acquainted with Greek civilization—language, literature, religion, daily life, and all—is to read Greek mythology, which is itself a source contributing much to knowledge of these subjects. Greek mythology may be read for the sake of its illumination of Greek civilization, as well as Greek civilization may be studied through the reading of history and literature for the sake of its illumination of mythology. The acquisition of knowledge for the mere sake of full enjoyment of the myths may become a primary instead of a secondary or contributing purpose.

As a matter of fact, mythology should be studied with both

purposes in mind, though the highest aim should always be the poetic or spiritual appreciation of it, with the uplift that is got only by consistent pursuit and realization of that aim. Just as the careful reading of literature yields, besides the inspiration which is its greatest fruit, a variety of knowledge in itself valuable and interesting, so the attentive reading of the stories of the Greeks may likewise minister to mere intellectual delight as well as to spiritual edification.

With a final admonition not to stop short of this higher delight and profit of the spirit, let us now call attention to the way in which Greek mythology may be made in itself to cultivate our appreciation of Greek civilization in general.

First, mythology helps us to a knowledge of the land of Greece—of its mountains, of its clear skies and islands and brilliant sea, of the charm of its fountains and cool glades, of the mysterious vaporous clefts in its rocks, of secluded recesses in its mountain forests, of foaming torrents and disappearing rivers, of impassable cliffs by the shore, and of the dangers of undrained marshes exhaling miasma. To read Greek mythology is to take a travel trip through Greece.

In the second place, the study of Greek mythology is a traveling backward in time, as well as a traveling abroad in space. It affords glimpses into times when the mind of man was full of simplicity and naiveté—when he did not yet understand the causes of natural phenomena, and took satisfaction and delight in explaining clouds and sun as shepherd and sheep, accounting for earthquakes and volcanoes by the story of gods and giants, seeing in storms the wrath of deities of the deep, and in clear skies, calm seas, and flowing springs the manifestations of ministering spirits. The educated and sophisticated Greeks of historical times, of course, knew better than to believe implicitly and literally such things as these; but the peasant and the shepherd up in the mountain valley knew of the creatures of the invisible world in all ages, and still knows of them; and the people of the cultivated circles of the city never lost their sympathy with the popular attitude of mind, even though their own beliefs became more enlightened. The myths thus throw light on the general spirit of ancient civilization.

Again, we are afforded many an interesting glimpse into

the daily life of the Greeks. The ways of the mythical beings are only reflections of the ways of real people. We see Hephaestus at the forge, Hebe serving as cup-bearer, Heracles cleaning stables, Danae visited by the midnight lover in spite of the care of her father to shut her up, Penelope at her loom, Nausicaä with her girl-servants taking the accumulated linen to the stream and washing it in true southern European fashion on the stones at the beach, and afterward engaging in the ball-game; we are made to sympathize with the loves of Cupid and Psyche, to smile at the jealousy of Venus, to be present at the feast, the wedding, and the sacrifice—and a multitude of other activities. What more illuminating than the passage in the Psyche story which tells of the ancient equivalent of the American recovery of the fugitive slave: "And at the same time Venus handed her brother Mercury a little book containing the name of Psyche, and all the other necessary items of information; having done which, she took her leave and went straight home. And Mercury did not fail to comply with her request; for he went hither and thither on the earth among men, and thus performed the duty of crier laid upon him: 'If anyone can bring back from flight or point out the hiding-place of the runaway daughter of the king, the slave of Venus, Psyche, by name, let him meet Mercury, the crier, behind the Circus goal-posts by the altar of Venus, and he will receive by way of reward for his information seven sweet kisses from Venus herself, and one of them honey-sweet above everything with the delicious touch of her tongue.'"

In the fourth place, the religious ideas and practices of the ancients are again and again exemplified in their mythology. The physical appearance of the gods, their mental and spiritual attributes as conceived by their worshippers, their whereabouts, the offerings made to them, the infinite number of the inhabitants of the unseen world, their kinship and familiarity with mortals—of these and a score of other interesting things in Greek religion, mythology is full.

And yet, a word of caution is advisable here more than anywhere else in the study of mythology. The beginner's ideas are almost invariably confused. Even many who have studied Greek civilization with some thoroughness are guilty of misinterpretation of the connection between mythology and religion, and identify the one with the other.

SEA OF GALILEE.

But mythology is not the equivalent of religion. Not even theology is necessarily identical with religion; and the bond between the mythology of the Greeks and their religion was much looser than that between theology and religion. The truth is, it is only accident that myths tell us anything at all about religion. It should be remembered that mythology is merely story-telling. It affords us information about religion just as it does about other features of Greek life—eating and drinking, and houses, and dress; if it tells us more abundantly about religion, it is only because myths have to do with the supernatural, which, of course, borders on the realm of religion.

Mythology is associated with religion, then, not identical with it. There was no dogmatic, orthodox form of the myths about the gods. No worshipper was under the least obligation to believe in any particular version, or, indeed, to believe at all. He might differ with the priesthood ever so much as to belief in myth. The test of faithfulness lay not in belief but in the proper performance of the traditional rites of worship; so long as the worshipper was careful to transgress no laws whose violation involved offense to deity, and to keep up his prayer and sacrifice in the prescribed manner, he might believe what he chose. If the truth could be known, we should probably find that the priest had little to do with the creation of the myths, but that he only took advantage of them after their invention by people and poet.

Fifthly, through mythology we may gain at least a trifling familiarity with the Greek language. Many of the names of Greek mythology have been made directly into English words —transferred bodily and naturalized—such as Tartarus, the Styx, Chaos, Erebus, Aegis, Hades, Aether. Others have entered the English language as derivatives—as tantalize, herculean, arctic, titanic, panic, gigantic, chronology, halcyon. If the inspiration felt from knowing this little were to lead to the learning of enough Greek to bring Homer or Xenophon in the original within range, the reader of mythology would in this find greatest cause of all to be thankful to the subject.

Further, the study of Greek mythology brings us of necessity into contact with at least some considerable portion of ancient literature in translation, and affords a direct stimulus to the reading of more of it. Homer, Aeschylus, Sophocles, Euripides,

Theocritus, Virgil, Horace, Ovid, Seneca, Apuleius—such are some of the names on the roll of literature based on the tales of mythology.

Again, the study of Greek mythology of necessity brings us likewise into contact with art in other forms than that of literature. Books on mythology are filled with illustrations reproduced from paintings on Greek vases and Pompeian walls, and from Greek sculpture scattered through the museums of the world. Greek art in all its forms was inseparably connected with Greek mythology and religion.

And lastly, familiarity with Greek myths helps us to understand the Greek temperament—their freedom of fancy, their sunny disposition, their exquisite sensitiveness to the moods of nature, their feeling for the art of poetic story-telling.

Here, again, some caution must be observed. Not every Greek was a poet in his interpretation of myth—not more than every Irish peasant is a poet in his conception of the "little people" of Ireland. Myths meant more to some minds than to others. To some, they were merely interesting stories, literal and coarse; to others, they bodied forth the deep things of God. Some men of conscience protested against the instruction of youth in literature that contained the grosser tales about the gods—for example, some parts of Homer himself—because some young people received from these tales only the literal and carnal suggestion; while others defended the myths because they could be spiritually interpreted. The Neo-Platonists, a philosophical-religious school of pagans that arose after the older Greek religion was outworn, and Christianity was rapidly taking possession of the field, reconciled the old religion and the myths inseparable from it with the more advanced moral and religious ideas of their day by investing all the old stories with lofty spiritual significance. The coarse tales of Zeus and Hera, for example, were only allegories of the relation between sky and earth, they said: the revolting story of Cybele and Attis only meant the bond between Mother Earth and her vegetation. Some myths, too, might even be consciously invented, for the purpose of setting forth in attractive form religious or moral teaching. The story of Cupid and Psyche, for example, has been thought, though probably without good reason, to be only an elaborate in-tion to portray the experiences of the human soul (Psyche) amid the trials of life that are begotten by desire in its various forms (Cupid). Elaboration no doubt it was, but on the basis of an old story which had long existed among the common people, and which is known to exist in crude form among many peoples beside the Greeks. And again, myths might be elaborated in literary form by poets whose only desire was to give the rein to their skill. Had Ovid been asked whether he believed the stories he told, or whether he was affected by them morally or spiritually, he probably would have laughed.

Such are the gleanings which await the student of Greek mythology. Nor are they peculiar to the mythology of the Greeks. All mythology—whether Greek, Norse, Egyptian, Hebrew, Indian, or what not—affords ample rewards to those who familiarize themselves with it. Greek mythology, however, is of all the most abundant and rich in its rewards. Let us note why.

First, it is a fuller and richer mythology than any other we possess. Whether fuller and richer in its origin, we cannot say: the presumption is that it was; but, at any rate, it reaches us after transmission through the ages the most abundant and most illuminating mythology in the world.

In the second place, it is much clearer than other mythologies. Its lines are distinct and sure; there is a minimum of the mistiness and obscurity of most mythologies. It is as clear and distinct as the lands and seas of Greece themselves, as Greek sculpture, as Greek literature and Greek thinking.

The result of these two reasons is a third. Greek mythology is so full and so clear that it is a pattern. The Roman gods and heroes are found to be more or less close parallels to the Greek, and the mythologies of Egypt, Assyria, and of the Hebrews and the Germanic races are more easily comprehended after the system of the Greeks is understood—just as all languages and literatures are in a measure acquired through the acquisition of the great basic languages and literatures of Greece and Rome, and just as all sculpture and vases and architecture are much easier of appreciation after a mastery of Greek art in the time of Pericles.

Again, the study of Greek mythology is more profitable than the study of other mythologies because it is inseparably connected with the greatest literature and art and civilization in general of ancient times, and because, more than any other, it is intricately inwoven into modern literature and art and thought. On every hand we meet it—in literature, in such abundance that the intelligent reading of many modern authors is impossible without familiarity with it; in painting and sculpture in the same way; in editorial, lecture, and sermon, and even in ordinary conversation.

To put all my reasons into a word or two, Greek mythology should be studied for the same reason for which all other manifestations of Greek genius should be studied—because it is a part of the civilization which we are still living. The whole basis of modern life is our heritage of Greek civilization through Roman channels. To draw out of the web of the life we are living all the threads contributed by Hellenic genius in architecture, literature, sculpture, painting, religion, philosophy, science, and mythology, would be to ruin it beyond recognition. What the world would have done without Greece, it is idle to speculate; we must, however, recognize what it has done *with it*.

THE GODS OF GREECE.

Ye in the age gone by,
Who ruled the world—a world how lovely then!
   And guided still the steps of happy men
In the light leading-strings of careless joy!
   Ah, flourished then your service of delight!
How different, oh, how different, in the day
When thy sweet face with many a wreath were bright,
   O Venus Amathusia!

   Then the soft veil of dreams
Round Truth poetic, witching fancies wreathed;
   Through all creation overflowed the streams
Of life—and things now senseless, felt and breathed.
   Man gifted nature with divinity
To link and lift her to the breast of Love;
All things betrayed to the initiate eye
   The track of gods above!

   Where lifeless, fixed afar,
A flaming ball to our dull sense is given,
   Phœbus Apollo, in his golden car,
In silent glory swept the fields of heaven!
   Then lived the Dryads in yon forest trees;
Then o'er yon mountain did the Oread roam;
And from the urns of gentle Naiades
   Welled the wave's silver foam.

   Art thou, fair world, no more?
Return, thou virgin-bloom, on Nature's face.
   Ah, only on the Minstrel's magic shore
Can we the footsteps of sweet fable trace!
   The meadows mourn for the old hallowing life;
Vainly we search the earth of gods bereft;
And where the image with such warmth was rife,
   A shade alone is left!

SCHILLER.

CHAPTER I.

WHAT MYTHOLOGY MEANS AND WHY WE STUDY IT.

WERE we to ask the average school girl or boy to tell us why night follows day and why spring succeeds winter, we might receive such an answer as this: The earth is round; every twenty-four hours it makes a complete circuit on an imaginary axis; when we are turned toward the sun we receive its heat and light, and that period is called day, and when our portion of the earth is turned away from the sun, the other half of the earth receives the light, and we have darkness, or night. Furthermore, during one part of the year the number of rays of the sun falling on the earth's surface is greater and we enjoy the luxury of summer; but when its rays fall obliquely and fewer strike its surface, winter holds the earth in its icy grasp. Were we to question further: —What causes rain, and what is snow, why does thunder sometimes roll above our heads and lightning flash around us?—one might reply: The heat of the sun is ever drawing moisture up in the air, and clouds are formed which later send the rain-drops down to a thirsty earth, or freeze in falling, and so come down as snowflakes; while the thunder that accompanies the discharge of electricity, called lightning, seems to be satisfactorily explained by the fact that the electric discharge, in forcing its way through the atmosphere, heats the air and the vapor lying in its path, and the very high temperature causes a violent expansion along the whole length of the flash, the result being a very steep compression wave, or, what is the same thing, a noise.

Such simple facts as these we learn in early years, but we must now attempt to forget them, and to realize, if possible, what these manifestations of nature meant to those who lived long ago, when the world was in its infancy.

Little children do not understand the world around them, they look upon it with wondering eyes.

> " Heaven lies about us in our infancy!
>   Shades of the prison-house begin to close
>   Upon the growing boy,
>   But he beholds the light, and whence it flows,
>   He sees it in his joy;
>   The youth who daily farther from the east
>   Must travel, still is nature's priest,
>   And by the vision splendid
>   Is on his way attended;
>   At length the man perceives it die away,
>   And fade into the light of common day." [1]

In these beautiful lines the poet sets forth the individual experience. The child finds mystery and wonder in everything; as a boy he journeys away from the marvels of childhood, yet the world seems bathed in glowing colors; when a man, a truer comprehension of physical laws is borne in upon him, and the poetry and fresh beauty of the life's morning vanish.

It appears to have been much the same with nations. In the infancy of the world, people looked out upon it with the puzzled eyes of children. Alternating sunlight and darkness, changing seasons, the ebb and flow of the tides and the phases of the moon puzzled them greatly, and there were none to give scientific explanations. In fact it has taken hundreds, even thousands, of years to find out much that is known to-day. In the early years of our race, people did not suppose the earth to be round; they believed it was flat, and it is but a few hundred years since people laughed at Columbus when he attempted to sail around it. To be sure, scholars had believed in the earth's rotundity before 1492, but people generally regarded the idea as absurd. Galileo created vigorous opposition in the early part of the seventeenth century by teaching that the earth and other planets moved around the sun, instead of all moving around the earth as had been previously supposed. Only by recalling such comparatively

[1] Wordsworth: Ode to Immortality.

recent misconceptions as these do we realize how long it has taken to establish some of those truths which today seem most apparent.

People of antiquity, in whose places we are now to imagine ourselves, and with whose eyes we shall attempt to see the early world, saw the sun rise and set, saw the quiet beauty of calm weather, heard the turmoil of the storm, and since there were none to explain such phenomena, gradually they came to devise explanations for themselves. They conceived that beings must exist, more powerful than they, who controlled all these forces, and these creatures they called in time by names which mean gods and goddesses.

"In their total ignorance of causes, they wondered at everything; and their poetry was all divine, because they ascribed to gods the objects of their wonder, and thought that beings like themselves but greater, could alone have caused them. Thus they were like children whom we notice taking into their hands inanimate things, and playing and talking with them as though they were living persons. When thunder terrified them, they attributed their own nature to the phenomenon; and being apt to express their most violent passions by howling and roaring, they conceived heaven as a vast body which gave notice of its anger by lightnings and thunderings. The whole of nature in a like manner, they imagined to be a vast body, capable of feeling and passion."[2]

The kind of divinities called into being by these conceptions, and the stories told of them, were in a large measure determined by the temperament of the people themselves and by the physical conditions of the land wherein they dwelt. The Greeks loved beauty and whatever they touched felt its magic charm. Some of the most exquisite fancies were quickly woven around the gods.

"In this childhood of the world, when the Greek myths came into existence, the sun was called a shepherd, and the clouds were his sheep; or an archer, and the sunbeams were his arrows. It was easier to think of the sea as a husky voiced and turbulent old man, whose true nature none might clearly know because he changed so often and was so secret

[2]Vico.

in his ways, who shook the earth in his anger, and had the white-maned billows of the deep for horses, than to form a theory of the tides. The spring of the year became a beautiful youth, beloved by the whole earth, like Hyacinthus, by the sun, or like Adonis, by the queen of beauty, over whom the fate of death was suspended, and for whose loss annual mourning was made. Such tales the Greeks told themselves in their youth; and it would be wrong to suppose deliberate fiction played any part in their creation. To conceive of the world thus was natural to the whole race; and the tales that sprang up formed the substance of their intellectual activity. They belong to a particular period of human history when it was impossible to think except by pictures, or to record impressions of the world except by stories. That these tales are religious, or partly so, must be explained by the tendency of mankind at an early period of culture to conceive of the powers of nature as persons, and to dignify them with superhuman attributes." [3]

The whole body of legends which these early people developed to account for the origin and progress of the world, with all the lore which came to gather around their divinities, we call mythology. Just as geology may be said to be the science of the earth, sociology the science of society, so the word mythology means the science of myths, and Ruskin defines a myth as a story with a meaning attached to it other than it seems to have at first. The stories, which we call myths and which make up the literature we call mythology, were not the imaginings of poets and dreamers, but they were the explanations devised by grown people, in the childhood age of the world, to account for the mysteries of nature. As ages passed and the real significance of natural changes was better comprehended, stories expanded to meet the expanding ideas, or the stories told in the same way meant more to those who told them. At last, like the mature man, they beheld their beautiful fancies die away and fade into the light of day, but to the Greek they faded only into the light of a glorious day, for beauty ever surrounded and influenced him.

In our age, weary spirits turn gratefully back to the inno-

[4]Symonds: Greek Poets, Vol. I, p. 55.

cent fancies of the infant world, and starving imaginations are fed with the wealth of poetic conceptions born in that far-off time.

> " Unto him who stands afar
>   Nature's marvels greatest are;
>   Who the mountain purple seeks
>   Must not climb the higher peaks."

Recent writers have classified myths in many ways; for example, those which were common to all nations and those which were peculiar to one; those which were devised to explain conditions, and those which were invented purely for amusement. So far as the first class is concerned, no one can be quite sure, and of the latter, the stories may enable each to decide for himself.

And now we come to the second part of our question: Why do we study mythology? One might reasonably urge that while people once believed these tales, in their efforts to understand life—no doubt they did the best they could, but why should we, grown wiser with the flight of centuries, bother about their absurd fancies now? People have asked this question frequently.

One might well reply that without taking into account a people's myths, any complete understanding of its mental activity and daily conduct would be impossible.

" This belief in the gods was connected with every action of human life. The warrior, marching to the field of battle, commended himself to the god who would protect his own. The husbandman plowed his field trusting that the goddess who taught men how to plow and sow, would grant a plenteous harvest. Without the blessing of the gods no seaman could hope for a lucky voyage; the poet's inspiration to song and solemn ode was a divine gift, and so was the skill of the plastic artist. Apart from the favor of the Immortals, the pleasures of social feast and sport could not exist, therefore a prayer and a libation of wine always began the banquet. The study of Mythology brings us into intimate relations with one, and that the most sacred aspect of natural life, and a careful consideration of the religious beliefs of the Greeks and Romans will give us some insight, otherwise unattainable, into their national characteristics." [4]

It is plain, then, that one could get no adequate idea of the life, deeds and writings of these early people without knowing much of the divinities upon whom they so depended. But suppose we were willing to forego the pleasures of classical history and literature. Let us turn to our own English writers. In immortalizing the nautilus,[5] Holmes describes it as found

"In gulfs enchanted, where the *Siren* sings,
　　And coral reefs lie bare,
Where the cold *sea-maids* rise to sun their streaming hair."

And again:

"From thy dead lips a clearer note is born
　　Than ever *Triton* blew on wreathed horn."

In Longfellow's Builders we find this stanza:

"In the elder days of Art
　　Builders wrought with greatest care
Each minute and unseen part,
　　For the *gods* see everywhere."

One of Shakespeare's sonnets runs in this way:

"Thou for whom e'en *Jove* would swear
Juno but an Ethiope were,
And deny himself for *Jove*,
Turning mortal for thy love."

Il Penseroso contains the lines:

"Or bid the soul of *Orpheus* sing
Such notes as, warbled to the string,
Drew iron tears down Pluto's cheek,
And made Hell grant what love did seek."

[4] Petiscus: The Gods of Olympos.
[5] Holmes: The Chambered Nautilus.

And, finally, in Keats' poem run the lines:

"Let then winged Fancy find
    Thee a mistress to thy mind:
    Dulcet-eyed as *Ceres'* daughter,
    Ere the *God of Torment* taught her
    How to frown and how to chide."

Without a knowledge of these ancient myths, then, we find ourselves unable to understand even the writers of our own language, so completely have mythological allusions and ideas become interwoven in all literature.

Should we turn to the realm of art, we would find that some of the rarest productions of the ancient and renaissance artists have had for their subjects these old-time stories. The student of sculpture today can find no study in marble which rivals in perfection the Venus de Milo, while few colorings on canvas surpass those harmonized in Guido Reni's Aurora.

And lastly, we study mythology for the beauty and the aesthetic qualities of the subject itself. These grow upon one as he becomes more and more familiar with it.

The Greeks developed the most highly organized form of polytheism—by which is meant the worship of many gods, —so we shall concern ourselves now with their beliefs for the most part, and subsequently as we follow the story of each nation, we shall note from time to time differences and similarities of other religions with theirs.

With this explanation of the nature and scope of our subject, we come now to the subject itself, waiting only to read thoughtfully these words of Ruskin, who himself approaches this field of thought with a certain reverence and tender patience for the religious beliefs of early peoples.

"To the mean person the myth always meant little; to the noble person, much; and the greater their familiarity with it, the more contemptible it became to one, and the more sacred to the other.   We cannot justly interpret the religion of any people, unless we are prepared to admit that we ourselves, as well as they, are liable to error in matters of faith; and that the convictions of others, however singular, may in some points have been well founded, while our own, however reasonable, may in some particulars be mistaken. You must forgive me, therefore, for not always distinctively calling the creeds of the past 'superstitions.' and the creeds of the present day 'religion,' as well as for assuming that a faith now confessed may sometimes be superficial, and that a faith long forgotten may once have been sincere. It is the task of the Divine to condemn the errors of antiquity, and of the philologist to account for them; I will only pray to you to read with patience and human sympathy the thoughts of men who lived without blame in a darkness they could not dispel, and to remember that whatever charge of folly may justly attach to the saying 'There is no God,' the folly is prouder, deeper, and less pardonable, in saying 'There is no God but for me.' " [6]

[6]Ruskin: Queen of the Air.

THE ACROPOLIS OF ATHENS (RESTORED).

CHAPTER II.

How the Greeks Explained the Origin of the World.

Tradition runs that several hundred years before the Christian era there lived a proud and wealthy man by the name of Homer. The story goes that he was once about to make a voyage to a distant land, but by mistake, boarded a pirate vessel. Before he could make an escape he was seized by the pirates, blinded, and left on a foreign shore by the men who took his possessions and divided them among themselves.

Blind and alone, without friends in a strange country, Homer had to devise some means of getting a living. So he began to tell stories to those who would listen. Of course there were no newspapers in those days, and people gladly welcomed any one who could entertain them with accounts of happenings in other lands. Homer told his stories so well that soon not only the children, but men also, drew near, while he recounted legends which had been handed down from father to son until they were well-nigh forgotten.

Some time later the tales Homer had related were written down, and from these, and from the writings of another poet by the name of Hesiod—who lived some centuries later—we derive much of our knowledge concerning the ideas of the earliest Greeks.

From these poems we find that the Greeks conceived the universe to be a hollow globe. Heaven occupied the upper portion; Hades the lower portion, and between these realms lay the earth, a flat, circular body. Hesiod indicates the distance between these three divisions by explaining that an anvil would fall from Heaven for nine days ere it would reach the earth, and nine days more would pass before it would reach the depths of Hades.

Around the circular-shaped earth flowed the river Oceanus —always tranquil, undisturbed by storm or tempest. Thence came the smaller streams, the rivers of the earth, and waters from Oceanus filled the sea—the Mediterranean—which divided the ancient world into two parts. In the very center of the earth the Greeks located their own country, which they called Hellas; and themselves they called Hellenes. Only in later times did the names Greece and Greeks come into use. In the midst of Hellas was Olympus, the high mountain upon whose lofty heights dwelt the Mighty Ones who ruled heaven and earth, and directed the course of men.

Of their neighbors the early Hellenes had little knowledge. They knew Italy and Sicily vaguely, and were less familiar with more distant lands. As when a stranger sometimes comes into a community, locates apart from others, and never mingles with them, there come to be surmises as to his life and habits, which, if not dispelled by some acquaintance with him and his affairs, come to be generally accepted as facts, so in a more pronounced way a credulous people grew to think of those who lived in regions remote from themselves, of whom they heard only from their more venturesome traders —for daring seamen occasionally skirted along foreign shores, and not infrequently passed strange and unknown ships upon the sea.

The people of Hellas imagined that beyond the high mountains to the north lived a happy tribe who could be reached neither by land or sea; the Greeks called them Hyperboreans, and believed that these fortunate beings were never sick nor did they grow old, but lived always in everlasting peace and joy. When occasionally the piercing winds swept down upon the plains of Hellas, the Hellenes supposed that they came from the caves of the Hyperboreans.

On the east, near the river Oceanus, dwelt the Ethiopians —quite as happy and blissful as the Hyperboreans. To the south, also near the river, lived the Pygmies, and on the west lay the Elysian Fields. Thither mortal friends of the gods were transported without tasting death, to partake of everlasting bliss. We find these plains sometimes spoken of as the " Isles of the Blest."

Between these different peoples and beyond them, the imaginative mind scattered countless mythical creatures mentioned in stories—such as the Sirens, Gorgons, Hesperides, Harpies, and the like. The river Oceanus was never navi-

gated by man, and its further banks were wrapt in perpetual
darkness.

Such was the earth to the early Greek. Now let us see
how it had originally come into being.

In the beginning, all things were in confusion. Earth, air,
and water were mingled together. Chaos ruled over the hopeless mass, which lay in deepest darkness. His wife was Nox
—meaning Darkness or Night; Chaos means Confusion. In
time their son Erebus usurped his father's throne and reigned
in his own right. Later he too was set aside by his children,
Aether, or Light, and Hemera, or Day. By these, the confused mass was for the first time lighted. Conceiving great
possibilities for it, Aether and Hemera determined to evolve
something attractive from the chaotic heap. In time they
created Pontus, the sea, and Gaea, the earth. Nevertheless,
Earth was at first by no means a pleasant place for habitation.
Bare, silent, inanimate, it was but a solid mass. But Eros—
or Love—the son of Aether and Hemera—pierced its bosom
with his darts of love and thus awakened dormant earth.
Aroused from her lethargy she sent up trees to cover the hillsides, grass to make verdant the plains, and flowers to gladden
the whole world. Birds and animals straightway took form,
and the streams were filled with fishes. Responding to the
impulse of life and beauty, Gaea created Uranus, or Heaven.
Not long after, these two asserted themselves, superseding
Aether and Hemera. Their children were the Titans, twelve
powerful sons, whose father, Uranus, feared them greatly.
Lest they disturb his reign, he cast them into a deep pit in the
midst of the Earth. But of them we shall learn more later.

Simpler to understand is this: "In the beginning
the whole world was one mass of stone, and there was no
earth, or sky, or sea. Then Eros, or Love, was the only living
thing; and just as the mother hen warms her eggs till the little
chicks peep out, so the Greeks said Love brooded over the
world until things appeared and the world began to take
shape."

This theory that the Love-spirit was able to transform
opposing elements into a world habitable and attractive for man
is beautiful indeed, and we come upon it again and again.

An endless variety of stories were devised to account for the creation. One told how Chaos once occupied all space. Then, by some unknown means, the lighter portion arose on high and formed the sky while the firm, solid matter took the form of the earth below. Thus Uranus, or Heaven, and Gaea, or Earth, were the first deities of the Greeks. Uranus personified light, heat, purity, while Gaea personified the solid, substantial life-producing earth. These two united in marriage, and this was quite an ingenious conclusion to be reached by people in the childhood age of the world. "Taken in a figurative sense, this union actually does exist. The smiles of heaven produce the flowers of earth, whereas his long-continued frowns exercise so depressing an influence upon his loving partner, that she no longer decks herself in bright and festive robes, but responds with ready sympathy to his melancholy mood." [1]

The first child of this union was Oceanus, the great river which encircled the earth. (In truth, the ocean is formed by the rains of heaven and the streams of earth.) Gaea produced the mountains and the sea, while Erebus and Nox belonged to Chaos. Uranus looked with deep dismay upon the crude Giants and Titans, other children of Gaea, and hurled them into Tartarus, but Gaea became incensed at such treatment, and gave them iron from her veins—and from where else does iron come?—to defend themselves against Uranus.

Mount Olympus, soaring high above the clouds, was the habitation of the gods. On this lofty peak of Hellas the Mighty Ones met in council to plan for the weal or woe of mortals. Far away from this eternal abiding place was Hades, unvisited by the light of day. It was first conceived as a prison house for gods rather than men, while Erebus, the dark country beyond Oceanus, was destined for the final dwelling place of mortals.

Regarding the origin of man, the Greeks never felt sure. The general impression was that people first grew out of trees and stones, or were produced by the rivers or the sea, or better still from the earth. Each spring, when the frosts

[1] Berens: Handbook of Mythology.

II—7

were gone, plants and herbs pushed up into the air from the soil below. So, probably, had it been first with man. Untamed in the beginning, he had lived like the beasts of the field until the gods taught him the arts of civilization.

Thus did the Hellenes try to explain the mystery of creation, which otherwise they could not understand; thus did they think of the realms of Heaven and Hades, and of gods and mortals, and it is not for us to point out the inadequacies of the tale, but to know what were the fancies which had to serve mankind for generations and have since found an abiding place in all literatures.

Having now a world for them to live in, we come back to the Titans. Who they were and what desperate battle they waged will be the subject of another chapter.

CHAPTER III.

The Titans and the Battle of the Giants.

We have seen that Uranus and Gaea had twelve gigantic children. These were so hated by their father and so feared by him that he threw them into a deep cave within the earth, and held them as prisoners. Here also were thrust his other offspring, the one-eyed Cyclops and the hundred-handed monsters. Their mother Gaea, roused by these indignities to her children, incited them to assert their rights, and her son Cronus, sometimes called Saturn, falling upon Uranus with an iron sickle furnished him by his mother, conquered and dethroned him. From the blood-drops of the wounded Uranus sprang giants,—monsters with serpents for legs; the Melian nymphs, and the furies. These last had snakes for hair and girdles of vipers.

Now began the reign of Cronus and the so-called Golden Age. The Titans were set free; they married their sisters and soon had numerous families. The children of the elder brother were the rivers of the earth and three thousand ocean nymphs. Prometheus and Epimetheus were other brothers, but the most important Titan for countless years was Cronus, who ruled during the Golden Age.

"Men were never so happy as they were during Cronus' reign. It was the true Golden Age then. The springtime lasted all the year. The woods and meadows were always full of blossoms, and the music of singing birds was heard every day and every hour. It was summer and autumn, too, at the same time. Apples and figs and oranges always hung ripe from the trees; and there were purple grapes on the vines, and melons and berries of every kind, which the people had but to pick and eat.

"Of course nobody had to do any kind of work in that happy time. There was no such thing as sickness or sorrow or old age. Men and women lived for hundreds and hundreds of years and never became gray or wrinkled or lame, but were always handsome and young. They had no need of houses, for there were no cold days nor storms nor anything to make them afraid.

"Nobody was poor, for everybody had the same precious things—the sunlight, the pure air, the wholesome water of the springs, the grass for a carpet, the blue sky for a roof, the fruits and flowers of the woods and meadows. So, of course, no one was richer than another, and there was no money, nor any locks or bolts; for everybody was everybody's friend, and no man wanted to get more of anything than his neighbors had.

"When these happy people had lived long enough they fell asleep, and their bodies were seen no more. They flitted away through the air, and over the mountains, and across the sea, to a flowery land in the distant west. And some men say that, even to this day, they are wandering happily hither and thither about the earth, causing babies to smile in their cradles, easing the burdens of the toilworn and sick, and blessing mankind everywhere."[1]

Such was life in the Golden Age, the ideal time of which poets have ever since sung. Probably the Greeks loved to think of it as people in all ages have pictured a time when all people should be happy; when all, instead of some fortunate few, should have everything which conduces to true comfort, and when none should have excessive luxuries or increased responsibilities which great wealth is sure to bring.

Cronus had three daughters: Hestia, Demeter, and Hera; and three sons: Poseidon, Pluto, and Zeus. Uranus had foretold that some day Cronus' son would dethrone him, just as he himself had been dethroned by Cronus. Fearing this prophecy, Cronus conceived the unique idea of disposing of his children by swallowing them. Finally Rhea, the mother, sought to save one, her youngest son, Zeus. She wrapped a stone in baby clothing and gave this to Cronus in place of the child. The deception was not discovered, and the little son was sent to the Isle of Crete to be cared for by the nymphs. When he became a man he revealed himself to his father and demanded that his parent produce the children of which he had disposed. All things being possible in mythological times, Cronus first brought forth the stone last swallowed—and this

[1]Baldwin: Old Greek Stories, p. 10.

the Greeks preserved at Delphi—then one by one his children appeared.

And now occurred the mightiest conflict the world had yet seen, when Cronus and his son Zeus contested for supremacy. Some of the Titans sided at once with Zeus, but most of them helped Cronus. Finally wearying of the struggle which lasted ten years, and falling out with his cruel brothers, Prometheus went over to the side of Zeus.

This conflict is known as the Battle of the Giants. The followers of Zeus had their position on Mount Olympus, while the Titans held Mount Othrys. Neither side gained much until Gaea advised Zeus to free the Cyclops and the hundred-handed monsters who all this time had remained in the cave where Uranus had imprisoned them. Grateful for their deliverance, they aided the cause of Zeus by making thunderbolts for him and by causing earthquakes. The earth trembled and took fire, and the waters of the sea boiled. The Titans were driven into the recesses of the mountains, while rocks and hills were hurled after them. The cause of Cronus was lost, and Zeus came into power for all time.

The Greeks placed the site of this conflict in the rockiest portion of Hellas, where deep valleys and steep mountains, sharp rocks and curious earth formations abound. To a credulous people only so great a struggle as this just described, waged by such mighty beings as gods and Titans, could have left such a lasting imprint on the land.

When the Titans were at last defeated, they were thrown into Tartarus, deep within the earth. Over them the Cyclops and the hundred-handed monsters were set to guard. Then Zeus called a council of his victorious family on Mount Olympus, and divided his power among the survivors of the war. Poseidon was given dominion over the sea and all the waters of the earth; Pluto was set to rule over the dark underworld of Hades and over Tartarus; for himself, Zeus retained the earth and heavens. For a long time his throne was insecure, for Gaea stirred up opposition when she beheld the fate of the Titans. This was ultimately overcome, and the authority of Zeus stood forth unquestioned.

Now followed the Silver Age—not so happy as the one

preceding. Zeus divided the year into seasons. It was no longer always spring. On the contrary, it was often hot, and again, it was exceedingly cold. No longer did fruits and other food grow without care, but men had to work for all they had.

"Then men began to grow dissatisfied with their lot. Some wanted to be rich and own all the good things in the world; some wanted to be kings and rule over the others. Some who were strong wanted to make slaves of those who were weak. Some broke down the fruit trees in the woods, lest others should eat of the fruit. Some, for mere sport, hunted the timid animals which had always been their friends. Some even killed these poor creatures and ate their flesh for food. At last, instead of everybody being everybody's friend, everybody was everybody's foe. So, in all the world, instead of peace, there was war; instead of plenty, there was starvation; instead of innocence, there was crime, and instead of happiness, there was misery.

"And that was the way in which Zeus made himself so mighty; and that was the way in which the Golden Age came to an end."[2]

Away from all this turmoil lived Zeus and his wife Hera, together with the other Mighty Ones, on Mount Olympus. In one of his stories Homer speaks of their dwelling place as—

> "Olympus, where they say the ever-firm
> Seat of the gods is, by the wind unshaken,
> Nor ever wet with rain, nor ever showered
> With snow, but cloudless ether o'er it spreads,
> And glittering light encircles it around,
> On which the happy gods aye dwell in bliss."

Here the gods lived, unmindful of the sufferings of mortals, whom, indeed, Zeus wished to wholly exterminate. Prometheus, who had helped Zeus against the Titans in the war of the Giants, now importuned him to spare men, and himself stood forth as their champion. He taught them how to build houses to protect themselves from the storms, for they had only caves for shelter.

To make the condition of mortals worse, Zeus now commanded that woman should be created—for during all these

[2]Baldwin: Old Greek Stories.

years woman had apparently been neither needed nor desired. This new creature was fashioned by the gods, each of whom vied with the rest in bestowing gifts upon her. One gave her beauty, another a gracious and winning manner, a third endowed her with grace, and finally when they had taxed their ingenuity to the utmost, the Graces adorned her with rare ornaments. The name Pandora, meaning 'all-gifted,' was given her and she was sent as a present from the gods to Prometheus by their messenger Hermes. As Pandora was leaving Olympus, a casket was slipped into her hand, while at the same time she was warned not to open it.

Now Prometheus knew well the ways of the gods who dwelt on high, and he straightway refused their proffered gift, attractive as it seemed. His brother Epimetheus, however, ignoring the pleas of Prometheus, gladly accepted the beautiful Pandora. For many days they wandered about, in the forests and through the vales, while the hours passed joyfully. One day, during a brief absence of her lover, Pandora's curiosity concerning the casket overcame her, and yielding to an impulse, she raised the cover ever so slightly, but even so, a myriad of little stinging insects swarmed out. These proved to be the troubles with which the world has ever since been afflicted. One little creature was thrust back as Pandora dropped the lid, and so piteously did she beg to be set free that Pandora, feeling that matters could be made no worse, again lifted the cover, when out flew Hope. The Greeks had many stories of this good fairy who went about always trying to soothe the woe, sorrow and trouble caused by the malicious little sprites which the revengeful gods had tucked into the fatal casket.

> "Fever of the heart and brain,
>   Sorrow, pestilence, and pain,
>   Moans of anguish, maniac laughter,
>   All the evils that hereafter
>   Shall afflict and vex mankind,
>   All into the air have risen
>   From the chambers of their prison;
>   Only Hope remains behind." [1]

[1] The Mask of Pandora: Longfellow.

Prometheus now did a daring deed. Zeus had denied
fire to mortals. This brave Titan stole a spark from the
celestial fire of the gods and concealing it in a reed, brought
it down to men to relieve their misery. This made Zeus so
angry that he ordered Prometheus chained to a rock on Mount
Caucasus, where a vulture came each day and tore away his
vitals, which grew again at night. The mighty god decreed
that Prometheus should be released at once if he would but
submit to him, but this Prometheus scorned to do. It was
prophesied that in the thirteenth generation a son of the mighty
Jove would restore him, and until that time Prometheus chose
to suffer rather than submit. The story of his sufferings, his
transgression and final deliverance, was celebrated by the
Greek poets.

" Do ye also ask
What crime it is for which he tortures me?
That shall be clear before you. When at first
He filled his father's throne, he instantly
Made various gifts of glory to the gods,
And dealt the empire out. Alone of men,
Of miserable men he took no count;
But yearned to sweep their track off from the world,
And plant a newer race there. Not a god
Resisted such desire except myself.
I dared it! I drew mortals back to light,
From meditated ruin deep as hell!
For which wrong I am bent down in these pangs
Dreadful to suffer, mournful to behold,
And I, who pitied man, am thought myself
Unworthy of pity; while I render out
Deep rhythms of anguish 'neath the harping hand
That strikes me thus,—a sight to shame your Zeus!

Beseech you, think not I am silent thus
Through pride or scorn. I only gnaw my heart
With meditation, seeing myself so wronged.
For see—their honors to these new-made gods,
What other gave but I, and dealt them out
With distribution? Ay, but here I am dumb;
For here I should repeat your knowledge to you,

If I spake aught.   List rather to the deeds
I did for mortals; how, being fools before,
I made them wise and true in aim of soul.
And let me tell you,—not as taunting men,
But teaching you the intention of my gifts;—
How, first beholding, they beheld in vain,
And hearing, heard not, but like shapes in dreams,
Mixed all things wildly down the tedious time,
Nor knew to build a house against the sun
With wicketed sides, nor any woodcraft knew,
But lived, like silly ants, beneath the ground
In hollow caves unsunned.   There came to them
No steadfast sign of winter, nor of spring
Flower-perfumed, nor of summer full of fruit,
But blindly and lawlessly they did all things,
Until I taught them how the stars do rise
And set in mystery, and devised for them
Number, the inducer of philosophies,
The synthesis of letters, and, beside,
The artificer of all things, memory,
That sweet muse-mother.   I was first to yoke
The servile beasts in couples, carrying
An heirdom of man's burdens on their backs.
I joined to chariots, steeds, that love the bit
They champ at,—the chief pomp of golden ease.
And none but I originated ships,
The seaman's chariots, wandering on the brine
With linen wings.   And I—oh miserable!—
Who did devise for mortals all these arts,
Have no devise left now to save myself
From the woe I suffer.

           Enough said now of this
For the other helps of man hid underground,
The iron and the brass, silver and gold,
Can any dare affirm he found them out
Before me?   None, I know! unless he choose
To lie in his vaunt.   In one word learn the whole,—
That all arts came to mortals from Prometheus." [a]

[a]Prometheus Bound; Mrs. Browning's trans.

The story of Prometheus has been a favorite theme with poets in all ages. The symbolic meaning of the myth is made sufficiently plain in the following poem by Longfellow:

PROMETHEUS.

Of Prometheus, how undaunted
　On Olympus' shining bastions
His audacious foot he planted,
Myths are told and songs are chanted,
　Full of promptings and suggestions.

Beautiful is the tradition
　Of that flight through heavenly portals,
The old classic superstition
Of the theft and the transmission
　Of the fire of the Immortals!

First the deed of noble daring,
　Born of heavenward aspirations,
Then the fire with mortals sharing,
Then the vulture,—the despairing
　Cry of pain on crags Caucasian.

All is but a symbol painted
　Of the Poet, Prophet, Seer;
Only those are crowned and sainted
Who with grief have been acquainted,
　Making nations nobler, freer.

In their feverish exultations,
　In their triumphs and their yearnings,
In their passionate pulsations,
In their words among the nations,
　The Prometheus fire is burning.

Shall it then, be unavailing,
　All this toil for human culture?
Through the cloud-rack, dark and trailing
Must they see above them sailing
　O'er life's barren crags the vulture!

Ah, Prometheus! heaven-scaling!
  In such hours of exultation
Even the faintest heart, unquailing,
Might behold the vulture sailing
  Round the cloudy crags Caucasian!

Though to all there is not given
  Strength for such sublime endeavor,
Thus to scale the walls of heaven,
And to leaven with fiery leaven
  All the hearts of men forever;

Yet all bards, whose hearts unblighted
  Honor and believe the presage,
Hold aloft their torches lighted,
Gleaming through the realms benighted,
  As they onward bear the message!

                              LONGFELLOW.

People became more and more degenerate. They quarreled among themselves and deceived and ill treated each other until at last Zeus determined to exterminate the race. He called the gods together to agree upon some measure which would accomplish this result. A conflagration was suggested, but others disapproved, since it was urged, the flames might reach even to Mount Olympus and endanger the Mighty Ones. At last it was determined to send a deluge upon the earth. Accordingly Poseidon caused rains to fall in torrents and the waters of the sea to rise. People forgot their contentions and sought safety in the heights. But even here the waters found and overtook them. At last Zeus beheld Prometheus' son Deucalion and his wife Pyrrha seeking shelter in a mountain. He recalled that they alone of all mankind had remained true and noble. So he commanded the waters to recede that they might be spared, all others having perished. He instructed them to cast stones behind them. Those thrown by Deucalion were changed into men; those cast by Pyrrha took the form of women. In this way was the earth re-populated.

This story calls to mind the legend of Noah and the ark, and we shall find that the tradition of a deluge was the inheritance of many peoples.

CHAPTER IV.

ZEUS: RULER OF HEAVEN AND EARTH.

" Leave the rest
To be by me accomplished; and that thou
May be assured, behold, I give the nod;
For this, with me, the Immortals know, portends
The highest certainty: no word of mine
Which once my nod confirms can be revoked,
Or prove untrue, or fail to be fulfilled."
As thus he spake, the son of Saturn gave
The nod with his dark brows. The ambrosial curls
Upon the sovereign One's immortal head
Were shaken, and with them, the mighty mount
Olympus trembled. Then they parted, she
Plunging from the bright Olympus to the deep,
And Jove returning to his palace home;
Where all the gods, uprising from their thrones,
At sight of the Great Father, waited not
For his approach, but met him as he came."

—*The Iliad.*

Zeus, or Jove, as he was called by the Greeks—Jupiter by
the Romans—was the youngest son of Cronus and Rhea. In
the division of the universe which followed the Battle of the
Giants, he retained dominion over heaven and earth. He
married his sister Hera—or Juno—and their dwelling place
was the highest peak of Mount Olympus, while other deities
had dwellings on other points of the same mountain.

We must try to understand that while the Greeks
worshipped and revered their gods, their attitude toward them
was not one of fear, awe, and spiritual adoration. Such was
by no means the case. The Greeks worshipped beauty, grace,
and heroic strength. They had, as Petiscus says, " no aspirations of Heaven—no fear of Hell." The beings whom they
called into existence to account for the natural world around
them, with all its beauty and its variation, while immortal and

unseen, nevertheless were regarded as men and women with passions, preferences, revenges, appetites, and desires similar to those felt by the people themselves. Their gods were their companions—unseen, to be sure, but trusted and depended upon.

As highly imaginative children, placed in new surroundings, see mystery everywhere, so did these Greeks, in the infancy of the world, see signs of divinity around them. Did the leaves rustle in the forest where no breeze was seemingly stirring? Then surely some unseen dryad was there. Did the bees swarm around some mountain cave, and continually hum in a soothing, drowsy fashion? This was then the chosen spot of some goddess, or the abode of some oread. The modern spirit of investigation would have discovered a squirrel among the leaves, and clusters of honeysuckle which allured the bees. But as investigation increases, credulity vanishes, and the age of myth fades away. It is our privilege to wander for awhile in the bay-fringed, island-girt land of Greece, and by means of these old myths to understand the growing consciousness of its early people.

The heavens were Jove's special portion. All the phenomena of the air, thunder, lightning, wind, clouds and snow were ascribed to him—he sending them, it was believed, as signs, warnings, rewards, or punishments.

" As the highest god, and throughout Greece worshipped as such, he was styled the father of gods and men, the ruler and preserver of the world. He was believed to be possessed of every form of power, endowed with wisdom, and in his dominion over the human race partial to justice, and with no limit to his goodness and love. Zeus orders the alternation of day and night, the seasons succeed at his command, the winds obey him; now he gathers, now scatters the clouds, and bids the gentle rain to fertilize the fields and meadows. He watches over the administration of law and justice in the state, lends majesty to kings, and protects them in the exercise of their sovereignty. He observes attentively the general intercourse and dealings of men—everywhere demanding and rewarding uprightness, truth, faithfulness, and kindness; everywhere punishing wrong, falseness and cruelty. As the eternal father of men, he was believed to be kindly at the call of the poorest and most forsaken. The homeless beggar looked to him as a merciful guardian who punished the heartless, and delighted to reward pity and sympathy.'"[1]

It was customary to dedicate some plant or animal to the service of each divinity. Quite naturally it followed that the oak, the grandest of trees, and the eagle, king of birds, were sacred to the service of Jupiter.

In a certain part of Greece there was a forest of magnificent oaks. " It was so thick and dark that the sunbeams scarcely found their way through the leaves to the moss upon the ground. Here the wind made strange, low sounds among the knotted branches, and people soon began to think that this was their great god Zeus speaking to men through the leaves of his favorite tree. So they set this forest apart as sacred to him; and only his servants, who were called priests, were allowed to live in it. People came to this place from all parts of Greece to ask the advice of the god; and the priests would consult with him, and hear his answers in the murmurings of the wind among the branches."[2] This was known as the Oracle of Dodona, and in recent years, leaden tablets have been discovered upon which questions had been asked of Zeus by the believing people. One asked about the welfare of his child; another implored that a business speculation might prove profitable. All valuable adornments had been plundered from the place long since, but these little leaden tablets, having no commercial value, were allowed to lie undisturbed through centuries, and have recently come to light, aiding us to understand the attitude of the early Greeks toward their deities.

However Godlike Zeus may have been in administrating justice, and however awful in hurling his thunderbolts when matters displeased him, he appears to have been quite human in his love affairs, except for his ability, common to all gods and goddesses, to transform himself into any form at pleasure. This ability was most convenient in his case, for his wife Hera has been credited with a distressingly jealous disposition. Since she is the theme of another chapter, we shall not stop here to consider her peculiarities.

Out of Jove's many infatuations immortalized in art was

[1]Murray: Manual of Mythology. [2]Harding: Greek Gods and Heroes.

his passion for Leda. To make love to this mortal maiden he took the guise of a swan. The poet Spencer, ages after, said of swans:

> "Nor Jove himself when he a swan would be
> For love of Leda, whiter did appear."

Zeus courted Danaë through the window of a tower, taking the form of golden rain. Danaë's father had imprisoned her within this tower because it had been prophesied that some day a son of the princess would bring about the father's death. The fact that she was detained in a lofty tower to prevent such a catastrophe could be little hindrance to Jove and seems only to have served as an incentive to his wooing.

The Princess Europa was one day gathering flowers with her companions in the meadows when Zeus saw her and became infatuated with her. To avoid the wrath of Hera, he transformed himself into a bull and came to play with the maiden. So gentle was he that Europa was persuaded to get on his back for a ride, when lo! the bull sprang out to the deep sea, telling her who he was and quieting her fears. Apparently she adjusted herself to such an unusual position without great trouble or alarm. Some writer has suggested that such a legend might have had its beginning in the kidnapping of a princess by a seaman or some neighboring chief, while to comfort the father, his courtiers might have invented the story of Zeus, since it was thought by no means uncommon for gods to appear before mortals in some assumed guise.

To woo Antiope, Zeus took the form of a satyr and he courted Io as a cloud. The story of Io is especially attractive.

"Among Jupiter's other indiscretions was his amour with the nymph Io, a fascinating person of whom Juno conceived a violent and legitimate suspicion. 'Juno,' as Ovid tells us. 'was well acquainted with the intrigues of a husband who had been so often detected.' So Juno decided to visit the earth in search of her missing lord, soliloquizing, 'I am either deceived, or I am injured.' While Jupiter, in the disguise of a cloud, was enjoying the companionship of his fair Io one day, Juno, looking down through the thick atmosphere, was

just in time to see the maiden transformed into a heifer. Juno,
however, had seen so much of metamorphosis in her day, especially in connection with the amorous adventures of her husband, that she decided to set a watch upon the cow. So she
placed her under the observation of the hundred-eyed Argus,
a mythological detective, to whom all these optical advantages
must have been of inestimable benefit. Argus, having so many
eyes, only required to sleep with two at a time, so that really
there was no opportunity for Io to resume her usual shape, or
to receive her Olympian visitor while under his supervision.
Therefore Jupiter sent his trusted Mercury, with the injunction
that he must find a way to make Argus sleep with all his eyes
at once. After some attempts, Mercury related a story so full
of weariness, and sighing, and disappointment, that the hundred eyes of Argus all closed in self-defense. As soon as he
became unconscious, Mercury slew him, and thus restored Io
to freedom. Juno took the eyes of Argus   and immortalized them by setting them in the tail of her peacock."[a]

These various adventures of Zeus have been put on canvas
by artists of the Renaissance or of modern times. Occasionally
they are found, or portions of them at least, on vases of antiquity. It was many years, however, before the Greeks attempted to reproduce the greatest of their gods at all. "The
Greeks usually conceived the Jupiter of war as riding in his
thunder-car, hurling the thunderbolt or lashing his enemies
with a scourge of lightning. He wore a breastplate or shield
of stormcloud like the skin of a gray goat (the *Aegis*), fearful
to behold, and made by the god of fire. His special messenger
was the eagle. It was, however, only with the passage of
generations that the Greeks attempted to represent their greatest of the gods by the works of men's hands. The statue of
Olympian Jove by Phidias was considered the highest achievement of Grecian sculpture. It was of colossal dimensions, and,
like other statues of the period   composed of ivory
and gold. For the parts representing flesh were of ivory laid
on a frame-work of wood, while the drapery and ornaments
were of gold. The height of the figure was forty feet; the
pedestal twelve feet high. The god was represented as seated

[a]Addison: Classical Myths in Art, p. 60.

DEAD SEA.

on his throne. His brows were crowned with a wreath of olive; he held in his right hand a sceptre, and in his left a statue of Victory. The throne was of cedar, adorned with gold and precious stones."[4]

The Greeks thought the face of the statue so wonderful that they said: either the sculptor must have gone up into heaven and seen Zeus upon his throne, or the god must have come down to earth, and shown his face to the artist.

As people in all ages have erected structures to the honor of their deities, the Greeks built temples to their gods. In the most beautiful temple erected to Jupiter this wonderful statue was placed. Since he was worshipped in all Greece, many temples were dedicated to him, and the remains of some of them can still be seen. In these temples were altars. When one wished to invoke the help of one of the gods, he would bring some offering—a dove, a goat, or some other animal, to his temple, and the priest would burn a portion of its flesh upon the altar, since it was supposed that the smell of burning flesh was acceptable to the Mighty Ones.

Festivals were given in honor of the gods. Every four years the Olympian games were held in honor of Zeus. But of how the youths practised for months together for the foot races, the wrestling matches, and other athletic sports, because they thought that to one as mighty as Jove feats of strength and endurance would be pleasing, we shall learn in the story of the Greeks.

Many other myths gathered about the greatest of Greek Gods, but we shall turn now to the stories concerning Hera, his beautiful wife.

Hera: Queen of Heaven.

"The white-armed Juno there enthroned was seen,
Sovereign of heaven and Jove's imperious queen;
Still near his queen her watchful peacock spreads
His thousand eyes, his circling luster sheds;
Where'er she bends the living radiance burns,
And floats majestic as the goddess turns."

[4] Gayley: Classic Myths, p. 63.

II—8

Hera—or Juno, as she was called by the Romans—was the wife of Zeus and the Queen of Heaven. She was tall and very beautiful, being exceedingly proud of her beauty and keenly jealous of the beauty of others. She sat by the side of Zeus in the council-hall of the gods, and shared with him all the honors of his position.

She seems to have been regarded chiefly as the guardian of marriage, watching over its sanctity, and protecting children and mothers.

Hera was cruel to mortal women whom she thought rivaled her in beauty, and meted out to them relentless persecution. "Hera would punish women that she thought were too beautiful, as if they had done something very wrong; she often did this by changing them into animals or birds. There was one woman whom Hera changed into the form of a savage bear, and turned out to wander in the forest because she hated her beautiful face. The poor creature was terribly frightened among the fierce animals of the woods; for although she herself now had the form of a beast, her soul was still human. At last Zeus, who was kinder of heart than Hera, took pity upon her. He lifted her far above the earth, and placed her among the stars of heaven; and so, ever after that, the Greeks called one group of stars the Great Bear."[5]

Even yet Hera's fury pursued the poor creature, and another story relates that the queen of heaven sought out Oceanus, and implored him to see how her rival was exalted when darkness fell upon the earth.

"The god of Ocean was moved, and promised Hera that he would never receive this constellation in his watery domain. Hence it is that the Great Bear continually circles around the pole, and never sinks like other stars, beneath the waves of ocean."

Many myths testify to Hera's revengeful disposition. Notable among them is the story of Echo:

"There was once a wood-nymph named Echo, who deceived Hera, and so made her very angry. Echo was a merry, beautiful girl, whose tongue was always going, and who was never satisfied unless she could have the last word. As a

[5]Harding: Greek Gods and Heroes, p. 19.

punishment for her deception, Hera took away her voice, leaving her only the power to repeat the last word that should be spoken to her. Echo now no longer cared to join her companions in their merry games, and so wandered through the forests all alone. But she longed to talk, and would often hide in the woods, and repeat the words of hunters and others who passed that way.

"At last she learned to take delight in puzzling and mocking the people who listened to her.

"'Who are you?' they would shout at her.

"'You,' would come back her answer.

"'Then, who am I?' they would ask, still more puzzled.

"'I,' Echo would answer in her sweet, teasing manner.

"'One day Echo met in the woods a young man named Narcissus, and loved him. But he was very unkind, and would take no notice of her except to tease her for the loss of her voice. She became very unhappy, and began to waste away from grief, until at last there was nothing left of her but her beautiful mocking voice.

"When the gods found what had happened to the lovely Echo they were very angry. To punish Narcissus for his unkindness, they changed him from a strong young man to a weak, delicate flower, which is now always called by his name."[6]

Another version of the story is this: Echo had known only the satyrs—ugly looking creatures, and, supposing them typical of the entire race of men, she determined to have naught to do with any of them. One day in her rambles she caught sight of Narcissus, and so handsome and godlike did he appear to her that, shy nymph though she was, she could not conceal her admiration. He told her he had vowed to wed any maiden who would enable him to catch sight of his own features. Mirrors were then unknown and he had never viewed himself although often told that he was goodly to look upon.

Echo led him to a crystal stream and bade him gaze upon his countenance. But lo! as he looked into the water he fancied a water sprite looked up to him. He could not be persuaded that it was not his own reflection, but fell passionately in love with it, forgetting lonely Echo. By day he sat ever

[6] Harding: Greek Gods and Heroes.

by the stream, watching his love; when the shades of night
would fall, still by the pale beam of the moon he would keep
vigil to see if the face in the water gazed up to him. At last
he pined and died, and the gods changed him into the flower
that bears his name. It still loves to grow with its head bending over some pool or stream. The blossoms sway so gracefully in the wind, and is so generous with its dainty fragrance
that we are led to think that it has grown less selfish as the
centuries have flown by.

NARCISSUS.

What first inspired a bard of old to sing
Narcissus pining o'er the untainted spring?
In some delicious ramble, he had found
A little space, with boughs all woven round;
And in the midst of all, a clearer pool
Than e'er reflected in its pleasant cool
The blue sky, here and there serenely peeping
Through tendril wreathes fantastically creeping.
And on the bank a lonely flower he spied,
A meek and forlorn flower with nought of pride,
Drooping its beauty o'er the watery clearness
To woo its own sad image into nearness.
Deft to light Zephyrus, it would not move;
But still would seem to droop, to pine, to love.
So while the Poet stood in this sweet spot,
Some fainter gleamings o'er his fancy shot;
Nor was it long ere he had told his tale
Of young Narcissus, and sad Echo's bale.

KEATS.

The Queen of Heaven does not seem to have been a popular subject with artists. Her life had in it too little of the
dramatic. She was greatly loved by the Greeks for her purity
and constancy. The peacock and the cuckoo, as heralds of
the spring, were sacred to her, and in groves set apart in her
honor, whole flocks of peacocks were fed.

Hera is frequently mentioned in the Iliad. These lines
touch upon her appearance and adornments:

"This at length seemed best:
To deck herself in fair array and haste
  to Ida.

She went to her own chamber, which her son
Vulcan had framed, with massive portals made
Fast to the lintels by a secret bolt,
Which none but she could draw. She entered in
And closed the shining doors; and first she took
Ambrosial water, washing every stain
From her fair limbs, and smoothed them with rich oil
Ambrosial, soft, and fragrant, which, when touched
Within Jove's brazen halls, perfumed the air
Of earth and heaven. When thus her shapely form
Had been anointed, and her hands had combed
Her tresses, she arranged the lustrous curls,
Ambrosial, beautiful, that clustering hung
Round her immortal brow. And next she threw
Around her an ambrosial robe, the work
Of Pallas, all its web embroidered o'er
With forms of rare device. She fastened it
Over the breast with clasps of gold, and then
She passed about her waist a zone which bore
Fringes an hundred-fold, and in her ears
She hung three-gemmed ear-rings, from which gleam
She won an added grace. Around her head
The glorious goddess drew a flowing veil,
Just from the loom, and shining like the sun;
And, last, beneath her bright white feet she bound
The shapely sandals. Gloriously arrayed
In all her ornaments, she left her bower.

The son of Saturn spake, and took his wife
Into his arms, while underneath the pair
The sacred Earth threw up her freshest herbs,—
The dewy lotus, and the crocus flower,
And thick and soft the hyacinth. All these
Upbore them from the ground. Upon this couch
They lay, while o'er them a bright golden cloud
Gathered, and shed its drops of glistening dew."

Zeus is sometimes thought of as representing heaven, Hera, earth. From the union of the two results the reproduction of life. This is the idea so beautifully disguised in these lines from Homer.

Argos and Samos both claimed honor as Hera's birthplace, and she was worshipped by special rites in both cities.

Every fifth year the Herae were celebrated. They were races by Greek maidens, and corresponded in a measure to the Olympian games given in honor of Zeus. Previous to these occasions, one woman would be chosen in each of the sixteen cities of Elis, and those so selected would weave a robe for the statue of the goddess. Another festival was celebrated each springtime, at which a wedding was enacted. A figure of the goddess was decked in bridal array and placed on a couch of willow boughs. The willow was sacred to Hera because it was claimed that she had been born beneath the shade of a willow tree.

The most splendid temple erected to her was that at Argos. Within this temple was placed a statue of the goddess, sculptured by Polyclitus, almost rivaling in beauty of perfection the wonderful statue of Zeus done by Phidias.

IRIS.

In early mythology Iris was mentioned as the messenger of Zeus, but as time went on, Mercury became his special herald and Iris was thought of as serving Hera, flitting about on her errands, going swiftly to and fro, executing her plans. Homer tells us that she went like the snow or hail from heaven to the uttermost parts of the universe, carrying out the commands of the gods. Some said that the rainbow was her pathway in the skies; others thought it was the reflection of her many colored robe. Robert Buchanan has written a poem about Iris, so delicately musical that we insert it here because it best expresses the subtle powers of one whose presence was known by the appearance of the rainbow in the sky. Another pretty conception of her is this: "Iris was the granddaughter of Old Ocean. Her sisters were the Dark Clouds; her bridge was the rainbow, which joined heaven to earth. She had golden wings, and her draperies were as many colored as her

bridge, which was made of the most beautiful flower tints ever
seen, and an odor of spring blossoms accompanied her."

IRIS.

'Mid the cloud-enshrouded haze
  Of Olympus I arise,
With the full and rainy gaze
  Of Apollo in mine eyes;
But I shade my dazzled glance
  With my dripping pinions white
Where the sunlight sparkles dance
  In many a tinctured light:
My foot upon the woof
  Of a fleecy cloudlet small,
I glimmer thro' the roof
  Of the paven banquet-hall,
And a soft pink radiance dips
  Through the floating mists divine,
Touching eyes and cheeks and lips
  Of the mild-eyed gods supine,
And the pinky odor rolls
  Round their foreheads while I stain,
With a blush like wine, the bowls
  Of a foam-crusted porcelain:
Till the whole calm peace has caught
  A deep gleam of rosy fire—
When I harken to the thought
  In the eyes of Zeus the Sire.

Then Zeus, arising, stoops
  O'er the ledges of the skies,
Looking downward, thro' the loops
  Of the starry tapestries,
On the evident dark plain
  Speck'd with wood and hill and stream,
On the wrinkled tawny main
  Where the ships, like snow-flakes, gleam;
And with finger, without swerve,
  Swiftly lifted, swiftly whirled,

He draws a magic curve
  O'er the cirrus of the world;
When with waving wings displayed,
  On the sun-god's threshold bright
I upleap, and seem to fade
  In a humid flash of light;
But I plunge thro' vapors dim
  To the dark low-lying land,
And I tremble, float and swim,
  On the strange curve of the Hand:
From my wings that drip, drip, drip,
  With cool rains, shoot jets of fire,
As across green capes I slip
  With the thought of Zeus the Sire.

Thence, with drooping wings bedewed.
  Folded close about my form,
I alight with feet unviewed,
  On the ledges of the storm;
For a moment, cloud-enrolled,
  Mid the murm'rous rain I stand,
And with meteor eyes behold
  Vapory ocean, misty land;
Till the thought of Zeus outsprings
  From my ripe mouth with a sigh,
And unto my lips it clings
  Like a shining butterfly;
When I brighten, gleam, and glow
  And my glittering wings unfurl,
And the melting colors flow
  To my foot of dusky pearl;
And the ocean mile on mile
  Gleams thro' capes and straits and bays,
And the vales and mountains smile,
  And the leaves are wet with rays,—
While I wave the humid Bow
  Of my wings with flash of fire,
And the Tempest, crouched below,
  Knows the thought of Zeus the Sire.

HEBE.

Hebe was the daughter of Zeus and Hera. She symbolized perpetual youth and is represented in art as a young maiden, small, with well rounded contour, brown tresses and sparkling eyes. It was she who passed nectar and ambrosia—the drink and food giving continued youth and immortality—to the gods on Mount Olympus. This function of the daughter of the supreme Zeus carries traces of the old custom observed by early people, whereby the daughter of the household, however noble or high in rank, personally served the guests at her father's table.

One day, however, Hebe slipped while passing nectar in the hall of Jove. For this she was deprived of her office and Ganymede took her place.

Some pleasing pictures have been made of this youthful maiden. In one painting of special grace and beauty she stands simply robed, giving drink to Jupiter's eagle.

After Hercules had performed his many labors, Hera, to atone for her long persecution, gave him her daughter Hebe in marriage, and Jove placed him among the immortal gods.

> " Till the god, the earthly part forsaken,
> From the man in flames asunder taken,
> Drank the heavenly ether's purer breath.
> Joyous in the new unwonted lightness,
> Soared he upwards to celestial brightness,
> Earth's dark heavy burden lost in death.
> High Olympus gives harmonious greeting
> To the hall where reigns his sire adorned;
> Youth's bright goddess, with a blush at meeting,
> Gives the nectar to her lord."

HEBE.

I saw the twinkle of white feet,
   I saw the flash of robes descending;
Before her ran an influence fleet,
   That bowed my heart like barley bending.

As, in bare fields, the searching bees
  Pilot to blooms beyond our finding,
It led me on, by sweet degrees
  Joy's simple honey-cells unbinding.

Those graces were that seemed grim Fates;
  With nearer love the sky leaned o'er me;
The long-sought Secret's golden gates
  On musical hinges swung before me.

I saw the brimmed bowl in her grasp
  Thrilling with godhood; like a lover
I sprang the proffered life to clasp;—
  The beaker fell; the luck was over.

Oh spendthrift haste! await the Gods;
  Their nectar crowns the lips of Patience;
Haste scatters on unthankful sods
  The immortal gift in vain libations.

Coy Hebe flies from those that woo,
  And shuns hands that would seize upon her;
Follows thy life, and she will sue
  To pour for thee the cup of honor.

                              LOWELL.

CHAPTER V.

ATHENA: GODDESS OF WISDOM; QUEEN OF THE AIR.

"Her home was on the radiant shores
    Where snow-white Athens shines;
How beautiful her servitors,
    How stately were her shrines!

And how from farthest east and west,
    And by the unknown sea,
What goddess was so well beloved,
    So much revered as she?"

One day Zeus ordered Vulcan to split open his head with an axe; as he did so, Pallas Athena—or Minerva—goddess of wisdom and of war, sprang out in full armour, chanting a war song. Tempestuous storms occurred at the time on land and sea, announcing her birth to the world. Her curious origin to the Greeks symbolized wisdom springing from the supreme mind.

Best loved of all their deities, Athena had a part or influence in most that concerned the Hellenes. She alone among their divinities committed no foolish or impassioned acts. She avoided intrigues, and remained unmarried, thus symbolizing mind, superior to mortal relationship, having no sex.

As goddess of war she represented skill and military foresight instead of brute force and destructive energy, as exemplified by Mars. She entered war only to protect the oppressed and aid the weak in maintaining their rights. Once entering a struggle, she led through it to a fortunate issue and a prosperous peace.

She was also goddess of peace, of wisdom, of domestic and agricultural arts, and of industries that had prosperity and happiness for their results. She protected state affairs and guarded cities. For this reason her temples were frequently built on the fortification of towns.

When the people of Attica built a citadel for themselves, Poseidon and Athena contended for the honor of naming it. Zeus decreed that the one who should present the city with a gift bestowing greatest benefit upon the people should have the privilege of determining the name. Poseidon struck a rock, and a horse—hitherto unknown—sprang forth. This typified war and suggested the future service of the chariot. Athena struck the earth and an olive tree, symbolic of peace, appeared, ministering to the wants of man with its shade, its fruit, and oil. Her gift was held to be greatest, and she called the city by her own name: Athens. So it has been known ever since. While worshipped throughout Greece, as protector of Athens, the most beautiful temple of the land was there erected in her honor. It was known as the Parthenon.

Athena was sometimes called goddess of the air, and Ruskin has written a beautiful book entitled "The Queen of the Air" in which he considers that particular function of her power. In this book he says: "Athena represents the ambient air, which included all cloud, and rain, and dew, and darkness, and peace, and wrath of heaven. Let me now try to give you, however briefly, some distinct idea of the several agencies of this great goddess.

"First, she is in the air giving life and health to all animals.   Now, of all the people that ever lived, the Greeks knew best what breath meant, both in exercise and in battle, and therefore the queen of the air becomes to them at once the queen of bodily strength in war; not mere brutal muscular strength, that belongs to Ares,—but the strength of young lives passed in pure air and swift exercise.

"When Athena wants to make Penelope bright and beautiful; and to do away with the signs of her waiting and her grief, 'Then Athena thought of another thing; she laid her into deep sleep, and loosed all her limbs, and made her taller, and made her smoother and fatter and whiter than sawn ivory; and breathed ambrosial brightness over her face; and so she left her and went up to heaven.'   You see you may have Athena for lady's maid whenever you choose.

"Again, Athena is the air giving vegetative power to the earth. She is the wind and rain, and yet more the pure air itself, getting at the earth fresh turned by spade or plough, and above all, feeding the fresh leaves.   Thirdly, she is the air giving motion to the sea, and rendering navigation possible.   Fourthly, Athena is the air nourishing artificial light—unconsuming fire.   The torch-race belongs chiefly to her festival, of which the meaning is to show the danger of the perishing of the light even by excess of the air that nourishes it; and so that the race is not to the swift but to the wise.   Lastly, Athena is the air conveying vibration of sound.

"I gather these facts together in brief sum.

"The deep of air that surrounds the earth enters into union with the earth at its surface, and with its waters, so as to be the apparent cause of their ascending into life. First, it warms them, and shades at once, staying the heat of the sun's rays in its own body, but warding their force with its clouds. It warms and cools at once, with traffic of balm and frost: It gives its own strength to the sea; forms and fills every cell of its foam; sustains the precipices, and designs the valleys of the waves; gives the gleam to their moving under the night, and the white fire to their plains under sunrise; lifts their voices along the rocks, bears above them the spray of birds, pencils through them the dimpling of unfooted sands. The air dyes the hills into dark blue, and their glaciers with dying rose; inlays with that, for sapphire, the dome in which it has to set the cloud; feeds the brooks that cease not, and strews with them the dews that cease.   It enters into the separated shapes of the earth it has tempered, commands the ebb and flow of the current of their lives, fills their limbs with its own lightness, measures their existence by its indwelling pulse, molds upon their lips the words by which one soul can be known to another; is to them the hearing of the ear, the beating of the heart; and passing away, leaves them the peace that hears and moves no more. This was the Athena of the greatest people of the days of old."[1]

Ruskin goes into far greater detail regarding this spirit of the air, and in order to fully understand how much Athena meant to the noblest of Greek minds, one must read the entire

[1]Ruskin: Queen of the Air, p. 54, ff.

book, which charms not only in its subject but by the masterly way in which Ruskin always expresses himself.

As goddess of war, Athena came in conflict with Ares and sometimes outwitted him by her cleverness. Such an incident is related in the Iliad. Accounts of her doings in times of peace are quite as absorbing as her attainments in periods of war. Best known probably is her contest with Arachne the spinner.

"There[2] was a young girl in Greece whose name was Arachne. Her face was pale but fair, and her eyes big and blue, and her hair long and like gold. All that she cared to do from morn till noon was to sit in the sun and spin; and all that she cared to do from noon till night was to sit in the shade and weave. And oh, how fine and fair were the things which she wove in her loom. Flax, wool, silk—she worked with them all; and when they came from her hands, the cloth she had made of them was so thin and soft and bright that men came from all parts of the world to see it. And they said that cloth so rare could not be made of flax, or wool, or silk, but that the warp was the rays of sunlight and the woof was of threads of gold.

"Then, as day by day, the girl sat in the sun and spun, or sat in the shade and wove, she said: "In all the world there is no yarn so fine as mine, and in all the world there is no cloth so soft and smooth, nor silk so bright and rare."

"'Who taught you to spin and weave so well?' some one asked.

"'No one taught me,' she said. 'I learned how to do it as I sat in the sun and shade; but no one showed me.'

"'But it may be that Athena, the queen of the air, taught you, and you did not know it.'

"'Athena, the queen of the air? Bah!' said Arachne. 'How could she teach me? Can she spin such skeins of yarn as these? Can she weave goods like mine? I should like to see her try. I can teach her a thing or two.'

"She looked up and saw in the doorway a tall woman wrapped in a long cloak. Her face was fair to see, but stern, oh, so stern! and her blue eyes were so sharp and bright that Arachne could not meet her gaze.

[2]Adapted from Old Greek Stories, by Baldwin.

"'Arachne,' said the woman, 'I am Athena, the queen of the air, and I have heard your boast. Do you still mean to say that I have not taught you how to spin and weave?'

"'No one has taught me,' said Arachne; 'and I thank no one for what I know.' And she stood up proudly by the side of her loom.

"'And do you still think you can spin and weave as well as I?' asked Athena.

"Arachne's cheeks grew pale, but she said: 'Yes, I can weave as well as you.'

"'Then let me tell you what we will do,' said Athena. 'Three days from now we will both weave; you on your looms and I on mine. We will ask all the world to come and see us; and the great Jupiter who sits in the clouds shall be the judge. And if your work is best, then I will weave no more so long as the world shall last; but if my work is best, then you shall never use the loom or spindle or distaff again. Do you agree to this?'

"'I agree,' said Arachne.

"'It is well,' said Athena and she was gone.

"When the time came for the contest in weaving, all the world was there to see it, and the great Jupiter sat among the clouds and looked on.

"Arachne had set up her loom in the shade of a mulberry tree, where butterflies were flitting and grasshoppers chirping all through the livelong day. But Athena had set up her loom in the sky, where the breezes were blowing and the summer sun was shining; for she was the queen of the air.

"Then Arachne took her skeins of finest silk and began to weave. And she wove a web of marvelous beauty, so thin and light that it would float in the air, and yet so strong that it would hold a lion in its meshes; and the threads of warp and woof were of many colors, so beautifully arranged and mingled with one another that all who saw were filled with delight.

"'No wonder that the maiden boasted of her skill,' said the people. And Jupiter himself nodded."

Arachne portrayed many scenes designed to show the weaknesses of the Mighty Ones—Jupiter and his many love affairs, he appearing now as a swan, again as golden grain, and finally as a bull carrying off Europa. This was most daring of the maiden and could not fail to rouse the ire of the gods, even though they admired her skill.

"Then Athena began to weave. And she took of the sunbeams that gilded the mountain top, and of the snowy fleece of the summer clouds, and of the blue ether of the summer sky, and of the bright green of the summer fields, and of the royal purple of the autumn woods,—and what do you suppose she wove?

"The web which she wove in the sky was full of enchanting pictures of flowers and gardens, and of castles and towers, and of mountain heights, and of men and beasts, and of giants and dwarfs, and of the mighty beings who dwell in the clouds with Jupiter. And those who looked upon it were so filled with wonder and delight, that they forgot all about the beautiful web which Arachne had woven."

Athena's web pictured the story of her contest with Neptune when both sought to name the city of Athens, and the details of the circumstance, the horse rising from the rock and the fruitful olive tree were faithfully represented. Spenser touches upon this weaving contest in a poem wherein he says:

"'Among these leaves she made a butterfly,
    With excellent device and wondrous slight,
Fluttering among the olives wantonly,
    That seemed to live, so like it was in sight;

The velvet nap which on his wings doth lie,
    The silken down with which his back is dight,
His broad outstretched horns, his hairy thighs,
    His glorious colors, and his glistening eyes.

Which when Arachne saw, as overlaid
    And mastered with workmanship so rare,
She stood astonished long, nor naught gainsaid;
    And with fast-fixed eyes on her did stare.'

"When Arachne beheld the web of her rival she was overcome with confusion. She turned away her face and wept.

"'Oh, how can I live,' she cried, 'now that I must never again use loom or spindle or distaff?'

"Then when Athena saw that the poor maiden would never have any joy unless she were allowed to spin and weave, she took pity on her and said:

"'I would free you from your bargain if I could, but that is a thing which no one can do. You must hold to your agreement never to touch loom or spindle again. And yet, since you will never be happy unless you can spin and weave, I will give you a new form so that you can carry on your work with neither spindle nor loom.'

"Then she touched Arachne with the tip of the spear which she sometimes carried; and the maiden was changed at once into a nimble spider, which ran into a shady place in the grass and began merrily to spin and weave a beautiful web. I have heard it said that all the spiders which have been in the world since then are her children, but I doubt if this be true. Yet, for aught I know, Arachne still lives and spins and weaves; and the very next spider you see may be Arachne herself."

Certain students of antiquity have found in this famous contest a trace of rivalry which existed between the weavers of Greece and those skillful in this art in Western Asia.

The owl and the olive tree were sacred to Athena. We have seen that the olive tree was her own creation, and the owl can see in darkness—symbolizing thus wisdom that penetrates through ignorance and gloom.

In the Parthenon, beautiful today in its ruins, stood a statue of Athena made of gold and ivory, made by the wonderful artist Phidias. What became of this marble is not known, but it still remained in the fourth century after Christ.

Various festivals were celebrated in honor of the goddess of wisdom. In Greece her festival was called the Panathenaea. Races and contests in athletic sports were participated in and the prizes given the victors were earthen vases of pure olive oil. Some of these jars have come down to us. On one side is frequently painted a picture of the goddess as she called the divine tree into being; on the other side some scene from the sports of the day is pictured.

Every fourth year the entire population joined in a pro-

II—9

cession and escorted women who had previously been chosen
in Athens to weave a robe for Athena, to the Parthenon.   Here
the beautiful robe was draped on the colossal statue—some
forty feet in height.

In Rome Minerva's festival occurred the nineteenth of
March.   A general holiday was declared for five days.   This
was especially observed by the schools—a fact which doubtless
tended to make this particular goddess popular with the youth
of that day.

ATHENA.

CHAPTER VI.

Hymn of Apollo.

The sleepless Hours who watch me as I lie,
   Curtained with star-inwoven tapestries
From the broad moonlight of the sky,
   Fanning the busy dreams from my dim eyes,
Waken me when their mother, the grey Dawn,
Tells them that dreams and that the moon is gone.

Then I arise, and climbing heaven's blue dome,
   I walk over the mountains and the waves,
Leaving my robe upon the ocean's foam ;—
   My footsteps pave the clouds with fire ; the caves
Are filled with my bright presence ; and the air
Leaves the green Earth to my embraces bare.

The sunbeams are my shafts, with which I kill
   Deceit, that loves the night and fears the day ;
All men who do or even imagine ill
   Fly me, and from the glory of my ray
Good minds and open actions take new might,
Until diminished by the reign of Night.

I feed the clouds, the rainbows, and the flowers,
   With the ethereal colours ; the moon's globe,
And the pure stars in their eternal bowers,
   Are cinctured with my power as with a robe ;
Whatever lamps on earth or heaven may shine
Are portions of one power, which is mine.

I stand at noon upon the peak of heaven ;
   Then with unwilling steps I wander down
Into the clouds of the Atlantic even ;
   For grief that I depart they weep and frown.
And what is more delightful than the smile
With which I soothe them from the western isle ?

I am the eye with which the universe
  Beholds itself, and knows itself divine;
All harmony of instrument or verse,
  All prophecy, all medicine, are mine,
All light of art or nature;—to my song
Victory and praise in its own right belong.

—*Shelley.*

Apollo: God of Light.

As Zeus was god of heaven and earth, Athena, the goddess of the air, so was Apollo regarded as the god of light. Most beautiful of all the gods, his father was Zeus himself and his mother Leto, while his sister was Artemis, or Diana, goddess of the chase.

As god of the sun, Apollo brought life-giving rays to the fields and herbs; he was also, and perhaps consequently, god of music—of the natural music of happy waters and singing birds. Again, he was god of prophecy, as light dispels darkness, or the light of knowing drives away the gloom of ignorance.

We must remember that these stories were devised for the most part to explain natural conditions to people of early times. For example, in the myth which shows Apollo as spending six months of the year among the Hyperboreans to the north, then coming in his chariot with the warmth and the spring-tide and the flowers, we see an attempt to explain the position of the sun, now nearer, now farther away from the earth, and the changing seasons.

When quite a boy, Apollo came down to the earth to enjoy the companionship of Hyacinthus. While they were having a game of quoits one day, Zephyrus, god of the south wind, approached. He too was fond of Hyacinthus, and resented Apollo's presence. He blew Apollo's quoit too far aside, and it struck Hyacinthus with such force that it wounded him. Apollo tried in vain to check the flow of blood; Hyacinthus could not be helped, and died immediately. To keep his memory fresh, Apollo changed the blood-drops into flowers which still bear his name—the hyacinths. Each year, as they bloom, the south wind lingers around and caresses them.

Apollo's first love was Daphne, a beautiful river nymph. Seeing her one day, the god would speak with her, but succeeded only in frightening her so that she fled from him. Apollo pursued. In spite of his entreaties she called for her father's help. As she reached the stream, her feet took root in the ground, and a thick bark covered her—for her father, a river deity, had transformed her into a laurel tree. Apollo found himself enclasping a rugged trunk instead of the fair nymph who had so attracted him. When he realized what had happened, he vowed that the laurel should ever be his favorite tree, and that wreaths used to reward victors should be formed from its leaves.

> " I espouse thee for my tree;
>   Be thou the prize of honor and renown;
>   Thou shalt the Roman festivals adorn,
>   But after poets, be by victors worn."

This myth has been interpreted by some to signify the sun trying to overtake the dew, which vanishes at his approach and leaves him embracing only the verdure it has left.

Several of Apollo's acquaintances and friends appear to have found enduring forms as flowers and trees, and this seems natural when we remember that without his life-giving rays of light and warmth, trees and flowers could not exist at all. Clytie was a nymph so beautiful that Apollo, with his usual impulsiveness, fell deeply in love with her and she was happy indeed to be loved by the great Sun-god, and delighted in his companionship. With his habitual inconstancy, however, he straightway discovered a mortal princess whom he was astonished to find he loved even more violently than he had loved the nymph Clytie, so she was soon forgotten. Clytie was at first dismayed by her lover's absence, and then consumed with jealousy as she discovered its cause. She went to the king and told him that his daughter, whom he had commanded to have nothing to do with the fickle gods, was constantly receiving visits from Apollo. In his rage the king ordered the princess to be put to death. To spare her this fate, Apollo changed her into the fragrant myrrh tree and in

high scorn transformed Clytie into a sunflower, which, as
you well know, has no fragrance whatever. But in spite of
all he had done, Clytie still loved Apollo, and it is said that
even today she gazes upon him as he rides across the heavens,
welcoming him as he appears in the east, looking straight to
him at noon, and bending her head to the west as he disappears
at night. This led Moore to exclaim:

> "The heart that has truly loved never forgets
> But as truly loves on to the close—
> As the sun-flower turns to her god when he sets
> The same look that she turned when he rose."

Apollo's special duty was to drive the chariot of day across
the sky. The well-known picture of Aurora has made this
familiar to us. In Comus, Milton speaks of his appearance
at the close of day.

> "Now the gilded car of day
> His golden axle doth allay
> In the steep Atlantic stream
> And the slope-sun his upward beam
> Shoots against the dusky pole,
> Pacing toward the other goal
> Of his chamber in the east."

One day Phaeton, Apollo's son, begged his father to grant
him one request. Apollo gave his oath, which with gods was
irrevocable. Then Phaeton asked that he be allowed to drive
the four horses and the sun chariot across the sky for but one
day. His father urged him to choose anything else, and told
him of the dangers that might thereby result to himself and to
all the world. But this alone would satisfy. Because of his
oath, Apollo had to yield. "The hour had already come when
the Sun usually began his daily journey. The pawing, champing steeds were ready; rosy-fingered Aurora only waited her
master's signal to fling wide the gates of morn; and the
Hours were ready to escort him as usual.

"Apollo, yielding to pressure, quickly anointed his son with a cooling essence to preserve him from the burning sunbeams, gave him the necessary directions for his journey, and repeatedly and anxiously cautioned him to watch his steeds with the utmost care, and to use the whip but sparingly, as they were inclined to be very restive.

"The youth, who had listened impatiently to caution and directions, then sprang into the seat, gathered up the reins, signaled to Aurora to fling the gates wide, and dashed out of the eastern palace with a flourish.

"For an hour or two Phaeton bore in mind his father's principal injunctions, and all went well; but later, elated by his exalted position, he became very reckless, drove faster and faster, and soon lost the way. In finding it again he drove so close to the earth that all the plants shriveled up, the fountains and rivers were dried in their mossy beds, the smoke began to rise from the parched and blackened earth, and even the people of the land over which he was passing were burned black,—a hue retained by their descendants to this day.

"Terrified by what he had done, Phaeton whipped up his steeds and drove so far away that all the vegetation which had survived the intense heat came to an untimely end on account of the sudden cold.

"The cries of mortals rose in chorus, and their clamors became so loud and importunate, that they roused Jupiter from a profound sleep and caused him to look about to discover their origin. One glance of his all-seeing eye sufficed to reveal the damage done the earth, and the youthful charioteer. Jupiter could hardly credit what he saw. In his anger he vowed he would make the rash mortal expiate his presumption by immediate death. He therefore selected the deadliest thunderbolt in his arsenal, aimed it with special care, and hurled it at Phaeton, whose body fell from his lofty seat into the waves of the Eridanus River." [1]

Apollo was so grieved by the death of his son that only the entreaties of the gods persuaded him to resume his place in the chariot of day. Phaeton's sisters grieved for him so long that they were finally changed into larches, overhanging the river, and there they still drop tears of amber in the streams.

[1] Classic Myths, Gayley.

Phaeton's faithful friend Cygnus was transformed into a swan, ever sacred to Apollo.

The ancient Hellenes saw many evil results of this disastrous ride: The Sahara was one of the districts so burned that thereafter nothing would grow within its limits; old river beds left dry had, it was believed, been exhausted on that fatal day, while the sun-spots were places where the infuriated horses had kicked holes in the sun chariot.

The number *seven* was sacred to Apollo, and it was said that in Sicily he had seven herds of cows and seven herds of lambs which he loved to see grazing as he drove by in his chariot. The swan, the laurel, and the lyre were all symbols of him alone.

Temples were erected to Apollo in various parts of Greece, and on the island of Delos, his birthplace. The most splendid of these was at Delphi. Here at an early day it had been believed that an oracle existed. From the fissure of a rock a gaseous vapor issued. This vapor was thought to inspire one to discern the voice of the sun-god. A priestess was maintained here, and to her were put questions by anyone in Greece who chose to consult the oracle. Indeed we read of Asiatic kings sending thence for advice in matters of grave concern. The priestess would inhale the vapor and then, supposedly inspired by Apollo, give replies. Since this temple was constantly the recipient of costly presents made by those who desired to win its favor, it became the richest in all Greece.

Every three years the Pythian games were celebrated at Delphi. In addition to the usual athletic sports, contests in music were held, the prize being a simple laurel wreath.

Even today we cannot fail to feel deep appreciation for the spirit which prompted people of the infant world to worship the life-giving sun, whose glorious orb was ever before them, symbolic of comfort, health, light and joy.

THE SUNFLOWER.

Till the slow daylight pale,
A willing slave, fast bound to one above,
I wait; he seems to speed, and change, and fail;
    I know he will not move.

I lift my golden orb
To his, unsmitten when the roses die,
And in my broad and burning disk absorb
    The splendors of his eye.

His eye is like a clear
Keen flame that searches through me; I must droop
Upon my stalk, I cannot reach his sphere;
    To mine he cannot stoop.

I win not my desire,
And yet I fail not of my guerdon; lo!
A thousand flickering darts and tongues of fire
    Around me spread and glow;

All rayed and crowned, I miss
No queenly state until the summer wane,
The hours flit by; none knoweth of my bliss,
    And none has guessed my pain;

I follow one above,
I track the shadow of his steps, I glow
Most like to him I love
    Of all that shines below.

DORA GREENWELL.

CHAPTER VII.

" That orbed maiden, with white fire laden,
　　Whom mortals call the moon,
Glides glimmering o'er my fleece-like floor,
　　By the midnight breezes strewn;
And wherever the beat of her unseen feet,
　　Which only the angels hear,
May have broken the woof of my tent's thin roof,
　　The stars peep behind her and peer;
And I laugh to see them whirl and flee,
　　Like a swarm of golden bees,
When I widen the rent in my wind-built tent,
　　Till the calm rivers, lakes, and seas,
Like strips of the sky fallen through me on high
　　Are paved with the moon and these."

　　　　　　　　　　　　From The Cloud.
　　　　　　　　　　　　SHELLEY.

ARTEMIS:　GODDESS OF THE CHASE.

Artemis was goddess of the chase, and of the moon. As goddess of the moon she was known as Luna, or Selene; in Hades she was called Hecate, and on earth Artemis by the Greeks—Diana by the Romans.

In infancy she asked her father Zeus that she be allowed to lead always an out-of-door life, on the beautiful mountains of Greece. He granted her wish, and she became the great huntress-goddess. Each evening as her brother Apollo finished his course and sank into the broad Atlantic, the goddess of the moon mounted her car, drawn by snow-white steeds, and was drawn across the sky.

Artemis loved the woods, and, with her company of nymphs, might frequently be seen chasing the deer through the forests, over hill and dale; then she and her attendants would bathe in some clear mountain stream and the woods would resound with their songs and dances.

The story of Niobe is closely associated with Artemis and her twin brother Apollo. The mother of these twins boasted that never had there been such children as her son Apollo and her daughter Artemis. Niobe had seven sons and seven daughters, and she laughed Leto to scorn and forbade her people to worship longer these children of Leto. Thereupon the mother of the twins, one of Jupiter's loves, commanded her children to slay the fourteen offspring of Niobe.

Apollo found the sons hunting in the forest, and with unerring arrows, left them dead within the woods. The mother Niobe was stricken with grief, but still had her daughters left to comfort her, when lo! Artemis began to slay the daughters. The mother, bathed in tears, sought, in vain, to save the last child, and the gods, touched by her grief, turned Niobe into stone just as she stood weeping.

This myth has supplied the subject for a well known marble statue, done again and again by sculptors in all ages. Some see in the myth an allegory: Niobe is winter, and Apollo's arrows, the sunbeams, which kill the winter months. The tears are the rain-drops of springtime.

Orion was a hunter bold who roamed all day through the forest in search of game. One day, he chanced to see the Pleiades, seven nymphs, attendants on Artemis. He at once fell in love with these maidens, it appears, and when they fled from him, he still pursued. In their fear they called upon their goddess to protect them, and sure enough, as Orion drew near, he saw seven white doves ascending to heaven; reaching the skies, they were again transformed, this time into a constellation—the Pleiades. During the Trojan war one of the sisters was so grieved that she withdrew from the sight of man, but the six may yet be seen on a clear night,—pale stars, having never since the fall of Troy regained their former brilliancy. In one of his poems, Tennyson mentions these sisters:

"Many a night I saw the Pleiades, rising thro' the mellow shade,
    Glitter like a swarm of fire-flies tangled in a silver braid."

Both loving the chase, Artemis grew deeply charmed with Orion, but her brother disapproved of him most heartily. Unable to discourage the goddess in giving a mortal her favor, Apollo one day asked Artemis if she thought she could shoot accurately enough to pierce a mere speck, just visible far away in the distance.   Proud of her skill as an archer, never daunting, she pulled an arrow and killed Orion, for it was he.   When she learned what she had innocently done, she was filled with grief, and placed Orion with his dog Sirius as constellations in the sky, where they may yet be seen on any starry night.

Her love for Endymion has been sung by many poets.

" The infrequent absence of Diana from her duties in heaven is said to have awakened suspicion among the deities of Olympus, who doubted whether she actually occupied these intervals with hunting.   It is easy to imagine the satisfaction with which Venus, who so often has been reproached by Diana with her undue fondness of beautiful youths, would welcome news of a corresponding weakness on the part of the cold-hearted and apparently unyielding huntress-queen.   And such satisfaction Venus once enjoyed, if we may trust the later classical and the modern poets, who have identified Diana with Selene, the more ancient goddess of the moon.

" For one calm night Selene looked down upon the beautiful Endymion who fed his flocks on Mount Latmos, and saw him sleeping.   The heart of the goddess was unquestionably warmed by his surpassing beauty.   She went down to him; she kissed him; she watched over him while he slept.   She visited him again and again.   But her secret could not long be hidden from the company of Olympus.   For more and more frequently she was absent from her station in the sky; and towards morning she was paler and more weary with her watching.   When, finally, her love was discovered, Jupiter gave Endymion, who had thus been honored, a choice between death in any manner that was preferable, or perpetual youth united with perpetual sleep.   Endymion chose the latter.   He still sleeps in his Carian cave, and still the mistress of the moon slips from her nocturnal course to visit him.   She takes care, too, that his fortunes shall not suffer by his inactive life; she yields his flocks increase, and guards his sheep and lambs from beasts of prey." [1]

[1] Gayley : Classic Myths.

"On the vaulted arch above
Luna's silver sparks are gleaming;
Latmos shepherd, from thy dreaming,
    Waken to thy tryst of love!
She who chases roe and hart,
Deer, through leafy woodlands straying,
    She has learned a gentler art,
    And she knows a softer mood.
To the shepherd's threshold stealing,
She has found on sweet revealing
Joyful throes of womanhood.
She whose love no god hath won,
Yields within her lover's bower,
'Neath the moon-light's silver shower,
    Smiling to Endymion."

The Diana just described is a totally different being from she who was known as Diana of Ephesus. That deity seems to have been of Asiatic origin, and to have been merely adopted by some of the Greeks who colonized in Asia Minor, in place of the goddess they had known.

Temples were erected to Artemis in many parts of Greece, and a festival called Artemisia was held for her every few years at Delphi.

ENDYMION.

The rising moon has hid the stars;
Her level rays, like golden bars
    Lie on the landscape green,
    With shadows brown between.

And silver white the river gleams,
As if Diana, in her dreams
    Had dropt her silver bow
    Upon the meadow low.

On such a tranquil night as this,
She woke Endymion with a kiss,
    When sleeping in the grove
    He dreamed not of her love.

Like Diana's kiss, unasked, unsought,
Love gives itself, but is not bought;
    Nor voice, nor sound betrays
    Its deep, impassioned gaze.

It comes,—the beautiful, the free,
The crown of all humanity,—
    In silence and alone
    To seek the elected one.

It lifts the boughs, whose shadows deep
Are life's oblivion, the soul's sleep,
    And kisses the closed eyes
    Of him who slumbering lies.

No one is so accursed by fate,
No one so utterly desolate,
    But some heart, though unknown,
    Responds unto his own.

Responds,—as if with unseen wings.
An angel touched its quivering strings:
    And whispers, in its song,
   "Where hast thou stayed so long?"

                LONGFELLOW.

CHAPTER VIII.

ARES: GOD OF WAR.

Ares—or Mars, as the Romans called him, was the son of Hera and Zeus, and was god of war. To give us some conception of his size and strength, one of the Greek poets tells us that he could roar as loud as nine or ten thousand men, and that he covered seven acres of land on one occasion when he fell to earth in a battle.

He cared for nothing but war, and the fiercer the encounter, the better he liked it. The Greeks used to implore his help ofttimes in war, but knowing that he might be fighting at any time against them, they never loved him as they loved their other divinities, and they built few temples to him.

In certain parts of Greece, Ares was worshipped as one who would fight and drive away inclement weather; this however was among a farming people who had little interest in battles.

The Romans, calling him Mars, conceived him as always delighting in the din of war, riding in a chariot in raging fury, or bringing destruction on all force brought against him. He is shown as plunging into battle, caring little which side he helped, indifferent as to whether his faction was in the right —never counting the cost, never planning his campaign in advance, but throwing himself where the fray was thickest, simply for the joy of slaughter. Fear and Terror were said to be his children.

Very few stories have come down to us of the fierce wargod, and he has never been a favorite subject with poets. The reason for this last is plain; poetry catches gleams of beauty, fancy and nobility as these are suggested in life and nature, and setting them forth through its own medium, magnifies and enchances them, until they are visible to eyes, which without such aid, would have known little or nothing of their existence. If the poetry be martial, yet must there be some ennobling strain or motive to dignify the struggle. Such qualities as these were wholly lacking in the god Ares.

Born in tempestuous Thrace, he was first conceived as personifying the fury of the storm, and the transition from this to the province of war was simple. The Greeks were not naturally a warlike people. When in early times they entered upon a campaign, other concerns vied at least with that of battle. The Iliad is composed largely of meetings of the gods, their interposition in the siege of Troy, in council gatherings, and hand-to-hand conflicts between heroes chosen from either side, while general assaults were rare. With the Romans, quite the reverse was true. From the beginning they were primarily a military people, and would have cared little for procedure, even among the deities.

Mars loved a vestal virgin. Her sons were Romulus and Remus. They founded Rome, and their father, Mars, was regarded as the protector of the city. For this reason the god of war was far more important to the Latins than to the Greeks.

In Greece, the Areopagus was named for Ares. The name originated in this way: a son of Poseidon stole a daughter of the war-god, who promptly slew him. Poseidon summoned Ares to appear before a tribunal and answer for the deed. Those concerned met on a hill, called always after Areopagus, or Hill of Ares. The god was soon acquitted, but henceforth those accused of serious crimes were led thither. Their trials took place in the dark, and no rhetorical pleas were permitted. The simple statements of accusing and accused were heard, while the appearance of neither could influence those deciding, since none could be seen.

In Rome the most beautiful temples were dedicated to Mars, and the Campus Martius, an open field where the Roman youth were drilled in military affairs, where armies were reviewed, and where assemblies of the people met from time to time, was named in honor of the war god. In March religious festivals were celebrated in his honor; also on the Ides of October occurred a chariot race at which time it was customary to offer the near horse of the victorious team to the god. The people living in the two oldest portions of the town contended for the head of the slaughtered animal, and the section which obtained it was supposed to receive great blessings.

In arts, Mars is generally shown with helmet, shield, and spear. The horse and the woodpecker were sacred to him.

HEPHAESTUS.

Very different in character was his brother, Hephaestus, or Vulcan, god of fire. Sometimes he has been called the artist, or the smith-god. All other deities were beautiful and fair to see; only Vulcan was deformed by being lame. Some said he had been lame at birth and that his mother was so enraged about it that she cast him out of Olympus; others believed the explanation offered in recent times by Milton:[1]

> "And how he fell
> From Heaven, they fabled, thrown by angry Jove
> Sheer o'er the crystal battlements; from morn
> To noon he fell; from noon to dewy eve,
> A summer's day; and with the setting sun
> Dropped from the zenith like a falling star,
> On Lemnos, the Aegean Isle."

Being a god, and so immortal, such a fall could not kill Vulcan, but it caused him to limp badly.

From his earliest years he fashioned curious and convenient articles of metal, melted by the fire and molded into shape. All the palaces of the gods and their contents were of his making. He had his forges and workshop on Mount Olympus, and in it were not only all kinds of convenient tools, but handmaids to help him, fashioned by the god himself of gold and silver. Of course, only a god could have such perfect assistants.

He made magic shoes that enabled one to walk through the air or water, as well as on the earth; caps that allowed the wearer to pass unseen anywhere; gold and silver dishes for the gods, which would come to the table all by themselves, and go away again.

After his fall from the abode of the gods he would never work again in Olympus, but set up his shop in a volcanic mountain. Here he could usually be found, at work with the cyclops, making shields, spears, and other armour for the

[1]Milton attributes to Lucifer a fall accredited by early Greeks to Vulcan.

II—10

Mighty Ones. He seems to have been on friendly terms, now with Jupiter, now with Juno, but rarely with both at the same time. Being incensed with Juno on one occasion, he manufactured a beautiful and attractive throne, provided with a secret spring to retain whoever sat upon it. This was sent to Olympus as a gift to the queen of heaven. Delighted, she sat down at once upon it. Attempting to rise, she could not free herself, nor could the assembled gods assist her. Mars rushed off to bring Vulcan by force, but the latter brandished a firebrand at him and ordered him away. Finally Bacchus, a jolly sort of god, acted as peacemaker and took Vulcan to the relief of his helpless mother.

It was Vulcan's cunning which created the lovely Pandora, to whose curiosity the world owes so much misery. In the Masque of Pandora the god is made to say:

"Not fashioned out of gold, like Hera's throne,
Nor forged of iron like the thunderbolts
Of Zeus omnipotent, or other works
Wrought by my hands at Lemnos or Olympus,
But molded in soft clay, that unresisting
Yields itself to the touch, this lovely form
Before me stands, perfect in every part."

In appreciation for thunderbolts with which Vulcan supplied him, Jupiter gave the god of fire the lovely Venus in marriage. Venus, however, greatly preferred Mars, and gave Vulcan cause to be very jealous. Finally she left Vulcan's gloomy cave forever, and the god of fire seems to have concerned himself no more with love, but to have applied himself steadily to his work.

Vulcan symbolized fire that burns, wholly different from that of the sun. His fall symbolized the idea of lightning coming from heaven to earth. All results of fire were attributed to him; whenever a mountain smoked the early Greeks fancied that the fire-god was at work within it.

Vulcan was patron of all artisans and blacksmiths; Athens, a city which employed a large number of people in the manufacture of pottery and metal work, and Lemnos, the isle upon which he fell from heaven, were seats of his worship.

A torch race formed a part of the Panathenaic games, held in memory of the early theft of fire by Prometheus. In Sicily a temple was erected to the fire-god where only the pure and good might enter. Two dogs guarded it and being able to divine the wicked from the guileless, they protected the latter and drove the false away.

Vulcan was seldom involved in the constant altercations of the gods, being generally absorbed with his hammer and anvil, creating rare works.

> "Those who labor
> The sweaty forge, who edge the crooked scythe,
> Bend stubborn steel, and harden gleaming armour,
> Acknowledge Vulcan's aid."

HEPHAESTUS.

CHAPTER IX.

APHRODITE: GODDESS OF BEAUTY.

Aphrodite,—or Venus, according to the Romans,—was formed of ocean foam as the spray broke one day over the rocks near Cyprus.   Her hair had caught the glimmer of the setting sun, her eyes were like the clear blue of the summer skies; and her fresh skin gleamed white like the foam from which she sprang.   The nymphs found her, and decking her with ornaments from their coral reefs, led her to the Mighty Ones who dwelt on Mount Olympus.   Here Jupiter, to atone for his severity toward Vulcan, gave him Venus for his wife.

All the gods and goddesses vied with each other in making her gifts, for all loved and adored her.   But none gave such wonderful things as did Vulcan.   He prepared a palace for Aphrodite, as the Greeks always called her, on the isle of Cyprus, where she had first appeared; and in this palace were most wonderful creatures;—handmaids of pure gold who would do her bidding without direction; harps that played themselves; golden birds that sang the sweetest songs.   But Venus cared little for Vulcan and after a time she wearied of him and his artist's skill, and left him altogether.

Now Venus was very lovely; besides being beautiful, she had the power of making everyone love her; animals too, and birds, felt her charm and flocked around her.   Often in pictures doves are shown in her hands or about her.

Again, being born of the sea, she had control over storms and winds, and could give prosperous voyages to sailors.   For these reasons while the Greeks prayed to Zeus and Athena for strength and wisdom, they asked Aphrodite to make those they cared for love them in turn; and seamen invoked her blessing on their long voyages.

This little story shows how great was believed to be the power of this goddess.

" Once a sculptor, named Pygmalion, tried to make a statue that should be more lovely than the loveliest woman.   He chose the finest ivory, and for months and months he worked patiently at his task. As it began to take the form of a beautiful maiden under his skillful chisel, he became so interested in his work that he scarcely took time to eat or sleep. At last the work was finished, and everybody said that the statue was more beautiful than any woman that had ever lived.

"But Pygmalion was not satisfied. All day long he would sit in front of his statue and look at it. He came to love it so that he wished it were a real woman, so that it might talk to him, and love him in turn. He longed for this in secret until finally he grew bold enough to ask the gods for help. Then he went to the temple of Aphrodite, and there before the altar he prayed to the goddess to change his statue into a real woman. As he finished his prayer, he saw the altar-fire flame up three times, and he knew that the goddess had heard him. He hastened home, and there he found that his statue of ivory had indeed been turned into a woman of flesh and blood; and all his life long he blessed the goddess Aphrodite for granting his wish."

Aphrodite gained recognition as goddess of beauty in this way: one day a king of Greece was married to the goddess Thetis—she who closed the western gates when the Sun-god had finished his daily course. All the gods and goddesses were bidden to the wedding—all except one, Discord. She went about making so much trouble that everyone was afraid to invite her. But this slight made her so angry that she set about thinking of some revenge. At last she took a golden apple, wrote something upon it, and being herself invisible, tossed the apple among the assembled guests. Someone picked it up and read: ' For the Most Beautiful!' Now every goddess immediately claimed it as hers, and what a time followed! Discord, who heard it all, grew better pleased as the dispute waxed hotter. Finally all dropped out save Hera, Athena, and Aphrodite, and these appealed to Zeus to settle the question for them. But Zeus was much too clever to get entangled in such difficulties, and after a moment, he replied that mortals were better judges of beauty than were the gods and suggested that they would do well to take the apple to Paris, son of the king of Troy, and ask him to award it. He added that Paris had such excellent judgment that he would be sure to decide the matter justly. So off these fair ones went in search of Paris. They found him leading a pastoral life in spite of his noble blood; contented to dwell away from the turmoil of the world. Appearing suddenly, they explained their errand: he was to bestow the golden apple upon the fairest. Hera promised him wide dominion should it come to her; Athena offered wisdom; and Aphrodite told him she would give him the most beautiful woman in the world for his wife if he awarded the prize to her. Now Paris cared nothing for dominion, little for wisdom, and having a mountain nymph for a wife already, perhaps he cared little about gaining another. But he thought Venus the most beautiful, and to her he gave the apple. Ever afterwards she was conceded to be the goddess of beauty.

The most beautiful woman in all the world—more glorious to behold than any before that time or since, or any who may yet appear, was Helen, wife of King Menelaus of Greece. You may read in Homer's Iliad of the war which ensued when Paris, under guidance of Aphrodite, went to Greece, and while Menelaus was away with his soldiers, took the fair Helen back with him to Troy. The poem tells of the last year during which the Trojans held out bravely against the Greeks, who besieged their walls. Finally when the city fell, it was burned and most of its people destroyed. And all this resulted because Discord was not invited to that wedding and because Aphrodite, jealous of her beauty, was ready to make any concession to have it recognized.

The goddess of beauty had many love affairs both with gods and mortals. Her passion for Adonis is perhaps best known. Adonis was a hunter with whom she fell deeply in love. They had many happy times together, but in spite of all her entreaties, Venus could not persuade Adonis to give up his favorite sport of hunting wild beasts; and so one day it happened as she had feared: while having a contest with a wild boar, Adonis was killed. Venus would not be comforted. Each drop of blood from his wounds she changed into a red rose, and each tear she shed for him sprang up a wall-flower. She begged Jupiter to either bring back her lover or let her go to dwell with him. It was unthinkable that love should leave the earth, so it was finally agreed that six months of the year Adonis should spend in the Elysian Fields, and the remaining six he might return to earth. Each year when he returns, the flowers, trees, and all vegetation assume their gayest colors to welcome him, and it is said that love is more potent at that season—the spring time of the year, than during the months when he is absent.

Venus has always been a favorite subject with artists. She is supposed to embody the most perfect feminine charms. The finest statue left to us of antiquity is the Venus de Milo, now in the Louvre. This was found in 1820 on the island of Melos. The arms are missing and art students frequently try to determine what position the sculptor originally gave them. Other statues of Venus exist, and several modern painters have immortalized her beauty.

April, the month of buds, was sacred to Aphrodite. Then it was that Adonis returned to earth. The dove and rose were symbols of this goddess, while the Graces and the Seasons attended and adorned her. She flitted about in her chariot— a rare sea-shell drawn by snow-white doves,—visiting her various shrines in Greece, where jewels and flowers were offered to her.

CUPID.

Venus' son Cupid has been even a greater favorite with poets and artists than the goddess of beauty herself. Indeed his symbolic character has lived on through the ages.

CUPID AND THE BEE.

Cupid once upon a bed
Of roses laid his weary head;
Luckless urchin not to see
Within the leaves a slumbering bee!
The bee awaked—with anger wild,
The bee awaked and stung the child.
Loud and piteous are his cries;
To Venus quick he runs, he flies:
"Oh, mother, I am wounded through
I die with pain—what shall I do?

Stung by some little angry thing,
Some serpent on a tiny wing,—
A bee it was—for once I know
I heard a peasant call it so."
Thus spoke he, and she the while
Heard him with a soothing smile;
Then said: "My infant, if so much
Thou feel the little wild bee's touch,
How must the heart, ah, Cupid, be,
The hapless heart that's stung by thee?"

In art he is generally shown with wings and a bow and arrow. Anyone pierced by one of his arrows became the victim of love.

"At Venus' entreaty for Cupid, her son,
These arrows by Vulcan were cunningly done.
The first one is Love, as you may behold,
His head, feathers, body, are all of pure gold;
The second is Hate, a foe deadly to love,
And bitter his torments, as many have proved.
The third one is Hope, from whence comfort springs,
His feathers were plucked from out Fortune's wings;
The fourth one is Jealousy—in base minds it doth dwell;
The metal for this last was sent up from Hell."

Although tiny himself, all had to own Cupid's sway.

"For Venus did but boast a son,
The rosy Cupid was that boasted one;
He, uncontrolled thro' heaven extends his sway,
And gods and goddesses by turn obey."

Often he is shown with Venus, she frequently directing his arrows to execute her own designs.

PSYCHE.

Cupid's passion for Psyche has furnished a subject for poets and artists, and many fanciful stories have gathered around these two mythical characters.

Psyche was the youngest daughter of a Greek king; she

was so beautiful that people seeing her often imagined her to be Venus herself. This greatly annoyed the goddess of beauty and she commanded Cupid to pierce the maiden with an arrow so that she might fall in love with the first monster she beheld. In doing so, however, Cupid wounded himself with an arrow's tip, and at once became passionately fond of the princess.

Now it was thought to be a great calamity if a princess did not marry, and while Psyche's older sisters had been wooed and won, she continued to remain fancy free. In distress her parents consulted an oracle and by it they were told to deck their daughter in bridal array and to leave her alone at night-fall on some forsaken mountain, where she would be claimed by one to whom gods and mortals alike yielded submissively. Sorrowing, the parents complied, although they mourned the princess as dead, so sure were they that some harm would thus befall her. Yet the oracle must be obeyed.

> "While Psyche wept upon the rock, forsaken,
>   Alone, despairing, dreading, gradually
>   Still trembling—like the lilies planted high,—
>   Through all her fair white limbs.
>   Her vesture spread,
>   Her very bosom eddying with surprises,
>   He drew her slowly from the mountain-head,
>   And bore her down the valleys with wet eyes,
>   And laid her in the lap of a green dell
>   As soft with grass and flowers as any nest,
>   With trees besides her, and a limpid well.
>   Yet love was not far off from all that rest."[1]

Wakening from a sleep, she discovered a palace in the valley, apparently deserted. Entering timidly, she found a table spread as for a guest. Seating herself beside it, she was served by hands unseen to every dainty. Golden harps played around her and every wish was fulfilled before she was conscious of its being. When darkness fell, the winning voice of Cupid told her that all was hers—that he claimed her as his love, but only through the hours of darkness could he remain

[1] Mrs. Browning.

with her; that if ever she would try to see his face, he would
vanish forever.

Happy and content, she lived in a state of bliss, until her
sisters sought her out and asked what manner of man was this
her lord.   They insisted that he must be some monster biding
a time when he should devour her—some ugly, scaly, serpent-
like creature must he be who feared the light of day and human
eyes.   They urged her to conceal a candle and look upon his
countenance while he slept that she might satisfy herself before
it was too late.   Doubting for the first time, consumed with
fears and misgivings, Psyche resolved to act on their suggestion.   But when she gazed upon the beautiful Cupid, his wings
folded, his golden curls falling about his head, she was so
entranced that she let the burning oil from the candle drop
upon his shoulder.   Awaking, Cupid gave her one reproachful
look and disappeared.   In vain she sought him far and near;
he seemed to have vanished from the world.

Now Venus had learned from a sea-gull of her son's
romance, and she was enraged at the thought of his loving a
mortal.   We might think her own experience in affairs of the
heart should have taught her compassion, but not so, it proved.

When in despair Psyche came at last to the queen of beauty
to gain information regarding the son, Venus told her she must
prove her worth by first performing difficult tasks, otherwise
she could not hope to regain Love.   She required her to sort
into piles a heap of mixed seeds from which her doves were
fed each morning, and insisted that the shades of night must
find the task completed.   Tiny ants performed this otherwise
impossible work for the broken-hearted Psyche.   Then Venus
asked her to fetch a pitcher of water from the fountain of
Forgetfulness, which flowed on the top of a steep precipice,
guarded by a fierce dragon.   Jove's eagle seized her pitcher
and returned it to her overflowing.   Finally, in a rage, Venus
sent her to the realm of Pluto, to ask of Persephone a little
of her beauty.   She was led safely thither, but on regaining
earth, contrary to the caution given her, she peeped into the
jar which contained the beauty of Persephone—which is death
—and fell asleep.   Cupid chanced to find her before it was too
late, and awakening her, he led her straight to Jupiter himself, in whose presence they were united for all time.

The symbolic meaning of the pretty myth is clear: Psyche means soul, which awakens at the approach of love. Let suspicion and distrust creep in and love takes flight. It is only, if ever, regained, when the soul has passed through torrents of anguish which alone bring it again to love's pure heights where doubt and distrust have no part.

THE MARRIAGE OF CUPID AND PSYCHE.

" And Jove's right hand approached the ambrosial bowl
    To Psyche's lips that scarce dared yet to smile:
' Drink, O my daughter, and acquaint thy soul
    With deathless uses and be glad the while!
No more shall Cupid leave thy lovely side:
    Thy marriage-joy begins for never-ending.'
While yet he spake, the nuptial feast supplied,
    The bridegroom on the festive couch was bending
O'er Psyche on his bosom. Jove and other deities
    Alike ranged round. The rural cowboy came
And poured Jove's nectar out with shining eyes,
    While Bacchus for the others did as much,
And Vulcan spread the meal, and the Hours
    Made all things purple with a sprinkle of flowers—
Of roses chiefly, not to say the touch
    Of their sweet fingers; and the graces glided
Their balm around; and the muses through the air
    Struck out clear voices which were still divined
By that divinest song Apollo there
    Intoned to his lute; while Aphrodite fair
Did float her beauty along the tune and play
    The notes right with her feet. And thus the day
Through every perfect mood of joy was carried.
    The muses sang their chorus; Satyrus
Did blow his pipes; Pan touched his reed: and thus
    At last were Cupid and his Psyche married."

                      MRS. BROWNING.

CHAPTER X.

HERMES.

Much must he toil who serves the Immortal Gods,
And I, who am their herald, most of all.
No rest have I, nor respite.   I no sooner
Unclasp the winged sandals from my feet,
Than I again must clasp them, and depart
Upon some foolish errand.   Forth I launch
On the sustaining air, nor fear to fall
Like Icarus, nor swerve aside like him
Who drove amiss Hyperion's fiery steeds.
I sink, I fly!   The yielding element
Folds itself around me like an arm,
And holds me as a mother holds her child.

My errand done, I fly, I float, I soar
Into the air, returning to Olympus.
O joy of motion!   O delight to cleave
The infinite realms of space, the liquid ether,
Through the warm sunshine and the cooling cloud,
Myself as light as sunbeam, as a cloud!
With one touch of my swift and winged feet,
I spurn the solid earth, and leave it rocking
As rocks the bough from which a bird takes wing.

LONGFELLOW.

HERMES: MESSENGER OF THE GODS.

You will remember the Pleiades who were placed in the
sky by Artemis.   The eldest of these, Maia, was one of
Jupiter's numerous loves.   Her son, born in a mountain cave,
was certainly the most remarkable baby that ever lived, or yet
again is likely to live in the future.   When but a few hours
old he stole out of his cradle, wandered away and drove off
some cattle belonging to Apollo, concealing them in a cave.

> " The babe was born at the first peep of day;
> He began playing on the lyre at noon,
> And the same evening did he steal away
> Apollo's herds."

Then finding a tortoise shell, from it he made a lyre. The story of that first day's escapades has been told in this way:

" Running out of doors to play in the sunshine, he saw a spotted tortoise shell lying in the grass. He laughed with pleasure at sight of the pretty thing, and carried it into the cave. Then he bored holes in the edge of the shell, fastened hollow reeds inside, and with a piece of leather and strings made a lyre of it. This was the first lyre that ever was made, and most wonderful music lay hidden in it.

" That night, when his mother was asleep, Hermes—or Mercury—crept slyly out of his cradle and went into the moonlight; he ran to the pasture where Apollo's white cattle were sleeping, and stole fifty of the finest heifers. Then he threw his baby shoes into the ocean, and bound great limbs of tamarisk to his feet, so that no one would be able to tell who had been walking in the soft sand. After this, he drove the cattle hither and thither in great glee for awhile, and then took them down to the mountain and shut them into a cave—but one would think from the tracks left in the sand that the cattle had been driven up, instead of down the mountain.

" A peasant, who was hoeing in his vineyard by the light of the full moon, saw this wonderful baby pass by, driving the cattle, and could hardly believe his own eyes. No one else saw Mercury; and just at sunrise, the little mischief went home, to his mother's cave, and in a twinkling was in his cradle with his tortoise shell lyre held tightly in his arms, looking as if he had been sleeping there all night.

" Apollo soon missed his cattle. It happened that the man who had been hoeing his grape vines by moonlight was still working in the same field. When Apollo asked him whether he had seen any one driving cattle over that road, the man described the baby he had seen, and told him how he had driven the cattle backward and forward, and up and down.

' By daylight, the road looked as though the wind had

been playing havoc with the young evergreens. Their twigs were scattered here and there, and great branches seemed to have been broken off and blown about in the sand. There were no tracks of any living thing, except the tracks of the cattle, which led in all directions. This was very confusing, but Apollo, knowing that no baby except his own baby brother could drive cattle, went straight to Maia's cave.

"There lay Mercury in his cradle, fast asleep. When Apollo accused him of stealing his white cattle, he sat up and rubbed his eyes and said innocently that he did not know what cattle were; he had just heard the word for the first time. But Apollo was angry and insisted that the baby should go with him to Jupiter to have the dispute settled.

"When the two brothers came before Jupiter's throne, Mercury kept on saying that he had never seen any cattle and did not know what they were; but as he said so, he gave Jupiter such a roguish wink that he made the god laugh heartily. Then he suddenly caught up his lyre, and began to play. The music was so beautiful that all the gods in Olympus held their breath to listen. Even Jupiter's fierce eagle nodded his head to the measures. When Mercury stopped playing, Apollo declared that such music was well worth the fifty cattle, and agreed to say no more about the theft. This so pleased Mercury that he gave Apollo the lyre.

"Then Apollo, in turn for the gift of the wonderful lyre, gave Mercury a golden wand, called the caduceus, which had power over sleep and dreams, and wealth and happiness. Besides, he made him herdsman of the wonderful white cattle. So the quarrel was made up and the two brothers became the best of friends." [1]

Few stories seem to have gathered around this particular god, and yet he appears to have been concerned, as a messenger at least, with most plans of the Immortal Ones.

He was supposed to travel more rapidly than lightning, executing the commands of Zeus. The Greeks thought their dreams came down to them from the mightiest of all gods, and fancied that Hermes brought them from him while they slept.

[1]Hyde: Favorite Greek Myths.

Since he himself was such a traveller, it naturally followed that he was regarded as the friend of travellers. Posts of wood with the head of Hermes carved upon them, called Hermae, were erected along the roads to direct the way. Stones were piled around these posts, and passersby were asked to add a stone to each pile, the object being to clear the road of stones, and so facilitate commerce.

Hermes was the patron of all roguery and gambling. The Romans conceived of him chiefly as a god of commerce. In those days most commercial dealings depended largely on envoys, and considerable travelling back and forth was necessary to carry on trade. Hermes was supposed to enable these men of commerce to outwit others in their business dealings. Having begun his own career by thieving, it was concluded that he ought to be an authority on the subject.

Perhaps in consequence of this, he was looked upon as the god of " persuasive speech," and suave eloquence, and the tongues of animals were offered to him in this capacity. In all matters of dexterity he excelled. So it followed that in schools where boys were trained, his statue was always seen.

The Greeks, and Romans too, expected to find in their gods qualities that they themselves possessed, and Mercury embodied many qualities with which they were only too familiar in their every day life.

Hermes is thought to have symbolized the wind,—the clouds, Apollo's sheep; hence the wind, but a few hours old, was able to drive the clouds from the sky. The whistling, singing, sighing wind suggested the music of the lyre.

It was his trusted messenger Mercury, you will remember, that Zeus sent to the relief of Io, when to shield her from the queen of heaven, he had transformed her into a cow, and the jealous goddess had set Argus to watch over her. The hundred eyes of Argus calls to mind the sky sprinkled o'er with stars, and Mercury, by scattering clouds across the heavens, could close the watchful eyes, or stars, from earthly view.

The splendor of the starry night has always strongly appealed to people of all ages.

In recent years, someone with the imagination of a poet, has exclaimed that God made the violets and forgetmenots from fragments of the blue sky, and that the stars are the tiny places from which the blue was taken, allowing the glory of heaven to shine through. And, you see, the fancy is just as poetical, ethereal, and filmy as the explanation given by people in the infancy of the world.

The rapid speed of the wind which suggested travel, while its sudden changes, apparently having no particular cause, brought in an element of chance. Of course it was the wind, favorable or the reverse, which largely controlled commerce in a day when much of the travel was by means of water.

Thus you see these fancies were not vague, indefinite dreamings, but each had its own significance when fully understood, and to the Greek these tales seemed very simple and plain. So we come to realize what Ruskin meant when he defined a myth as a "story with a meaning attached to it other than it seems to have at first."

HERMES.

THE FINDING OF THE LYRE.

There lay upon the ocean's shore
What once a tortoise served to cover.
A year or more, with rush and roar,
The surf had rolled it over,
Had played with it, and flung it by,
As wind and weather might decide it,
Then tossed it high where sand-drifts dry
Cheap burial might provide it.

It rested there to bleach or tan,
The rains had soaked, the suns had burned it;
With many a ban the fisherman
Had stumbled o'er and spurned it;
And there the fisher-girl would stay,
Conjecturing with her brother
How in their play the poor estray
Might serve some use or other.

So there it lay, through wet and dry,
As empty as the last new sonnet,
Till by and by came Mercury,
And, having mused upon it,
" Why, here," cried he, " the thing of things
In shape, material, and dimension!
Give it but strings, and lo, it sings,
A wonderful invention!"

So said, so done; the chords he strained,
And, as his fingers o'er them hovered,
The shell disdained a soul had gained,
The lyre had been discovered.
O empty world that round us lies,
Dead shell, of soul and thought forsaken,
Brought we but eyes like Mercury's
In thee what songs should waken!

—Lowell.

II—11

CHAPTER XI.

LESSER DIVINITIES: HESTIA.

Hestia was the goddess of the domestic hearth. To the Romans she was known by the name of Vesta, and by both Greeks and Romans she was greatly venerated.

The hearth was of greater importance in early times than it later became. Meals were prepared upon it, to be sure, but upon it stood the ancestral gods; there the father of the family offered sacrifices upon all special occasions, such as births, deaths, and on the eve of unusual undertakings.

Daughter of Cronus and sister of Zeus, Hestia never married, although Poseidon and Apollo were among the many suitors for her hand. In the council of the gods she was given a prominent seat and at the feast of the Mighty Ones choice morsels of food were reserved for her.

In Greece, since every home was her dwelling, no special temples were erected to Hestia, but one of note was early erected to her honor in Rome. It was round in shape, and on the altar in the center of the temple burned the fire which was never allowed to go out. Six vestal virgins were chosen to guard it. They were selected from the noblest families of Rome, and were sent to live in the temple when but six years of age. For thirty years they served—first learning the duties from older virgins, then performing these duties and finally they taught novices to serve as they had done. After thirty years had passed, they were at liberty to leave the temple and follow whatsoever lives they chose. In the Story of Rome we shall meet these vestal virgins again.

Hestia personified the fire which ministers to the wants of mankind—the spark of fire within each breast, extinguished only with life itself, and the fire upon the hearth—that most treasured spot within the home—where food and warmth were supplied and where sacrifices were offered to the gods.

In the midst of each Greek city was a public hall where the fathers of the community met together and considered the general welfare; here too, was a table around which they

were fed, and in the midst of the hall the fire of Hestia was
ever burning.   Whenever a family removed to another town
or country, a portion of this sacred fire was taken along with
their most cherished treasures.   In those days fires could only
be started anew at great trouble, and the fires of Vesta in the
temples were rekindled only from the sun's rays.

Not many stories seem to have gathered around this goddess; in the older Greek poems she is not mentioned, which
fact goes to show that she was a later conception than others
of the great divinities.

THE MUSES.

Begin we from the Muses, O my song!
Whose mansion is the mountain vast and holy
Of Helicon; where aye with delicate feet
Fast by Jove's altar and purpureal fount
They tread the measured round; their tender limbs
Laved in Parnassian waters, or the stream
Of blest Olmius, or pure Hippocrene,
On the high top of Helicon they wont
To lead the hazy measures, breathing grace,
Enkindling love, and glance their quivering feet.
Thence break they forth tumultuous, and enwrapped
Wide with dim air, through silence of the night
Shape their ethereal way, and send abroad
A voice, in stilly darkness beautiful.
Jove Aegis—armed they praise, in choral hymns
Of adoration; and of Argos named
Majestic Juno, gliding on her way
With golden-sandaled feet: and her whose eyes
Glitter with azure light, Minervan born
From Jove; Apollo, sire of prophecy,
And Dian, joyous in the sounding shaft;
Earth-shaker Neptune, earth-enclasping god;
And Themis, lovely with her tremulous lids;
And Hebe, who with fillet golden binds

Her brow; and fair Dione, and the Morn,
And the great Sun, and the resplendent Moon;
Latona and Iapetus and him
Of mazy counsel, Saturn; and the Earth,
And the vast Ocean, and the sable Night,
And all the holy race of deities
Existing ever.

The Muses were nine in number, and Apollo was their leader. It is said that a number of springs rippled down the east side of Mount Olympus in an early day. These clear mountain streams leaped from rock to rock, over grass and stones, and their sparkles in the sunlight and the singing of the waters led people to suppose that some spirit of song presided over the locality. Apparently the Muses were evolved to carry out this theory.

Their father was Zeus and Memory was their mother. Calliope, the beautiful voiced, was muse of epic poetry. Clio —she who praises—was muse of history. She was usually shown carrying a scroll. Euterpe—the charmer—was muse of lyric poetry and of harmony. Thalia—the joy of life— presided over comedy. Terpsichore—joyful in the dance— carried a lyre and was muse of the dance. Urania—the heavenly one—held a globe of the heavens, and was muse of astronomy. Erato—the beloved—was muse of love and love-songs. Polyhymnia—rich in hymns—was muse of divine song. She was always closely veiled. Melpomene—the singer— bore a tragic mask, indicating that she was muse of tragedy.

Mount Helicon became the later home of the muses. At feasts and special gatherings of the gods, they, with Apollo, provided music for the feasts and banquets.

Because of their close connection with poetry and song, the Muses have frequently been invoked by poets of all time when about to undertake some prodigious task.

Of the other divinities who lived above the clouds we shall consider simply the Fates, since the remainder played but obscure parts.

THE FATES.

The ancients saw children come into the world, and spend lives wrapped more or less in obscurity and uncertainty. They observed that now young persons were cut off just as they reached years of understanding and activity, while others lived on when life no longer attracted them. To explain the mystery of birth, life, and death, they conceived that there must be three inexorable sisters in whose hands rested the destiny of all beings. One sister, Clotho, youngest of the three, spun the thread of life; Lachesis twisted it to make it strong, and the most relentless of the three, Atropos, held the shears and snapped it short when it pleased her to do so.

The Fates were dreaded because it was thought they could not be moved by prayers; indeed, gods as well as mortals, were powerless to cause them to alter their plans. They are spoken of as " Daughters of the Night "; and no matter how many people came into the world. for each there was a separate thread held by these sisters of destiny.

The Greeks and Romans offered flowers and money to the Fates, and believed implicitly in them.

Artists have conceived the Fates differently. The picture of the sisters, long accredited to Michael Angelo, is now thought to have been the work of another. It is interesting to compare this with the conceptions of modern artists.

> " In their dark House of Cloud
>   The three weird sisters toil till time be sped:
> One unwinds life; one ever weaves the shroud;
>   One waits to cut the thread."

CHAPTER XII.

Earth Deities: Demeter, Goddess of Harvest; Persephone.

Demeter represented the crust of the earth, while Gaea, mentioned in an earlier chapter, embodied the whole terrestrial globe, with its internal molten fire and its subterranean divisions.

Demeter, or Ceres, as she was called by the Romans, taught men how to reap and sow; she watched over the growing corn and ripening fruits, and brought them to a plenteous harvest. In the beginning men had not known how to make the earth yield; they pastured their flocks in some fertile valley and when this was exhausted, they roamed on in search of fresh pastures and food for themselves. Ceres taught men how they might abandon a roving life and have a fixed habitation. Of all divinities she was kindest to mortals and loved them as her children.

Now Demeter had a daughter, Persephone, whom she dearly loved. Persephone aided her in her duties as goddess of the fields. One day while plucking flowers for her friends, the ocean nymphs, she became separated from her companions. Pluto, passing by, was struck with her surpassing beauty, and immediately desired her for his queen. Several times before this Pluto had sought a queen for his dark realm, but none could be induced to live in his cheerless world, where the sun's rays never penetrated, and bright flowers never grew. So on this occasion he wasted no time entreating Persephone to accompany him, but seized her where she stood picking the lovely blossoms, and, whipping up his coal-black steeds, rushed away to his underworld. Persephone's cries of alarm were soon lost to mortal ears beneath the caves of earth.

When night fell, and her daughter did not return, Demeter grew dismayed. She lighted a torch from a flaming mountain and for nine days and nights did not cease to search for the missing Persephone. In vain she sought her—no traces could she find. At last a fountain nymph told Ceres what had happened—how Pluto had stolen her daughter and hurried her away to his land of shades.

Ceres refused to be comforted. For months the fields were neglected. The trees no longer blossomed, nor bore fruit. The corn did not grow and a famine threatened the land. Mortals cried aloud to Zeus to help them; they petitioned him to compel Pluto to give back Ceres' daughter, that she might come once more to give heed to their needs, and watch over their fields.

At this expression of sympathy Ceres began to take an interest in life again. She came forth from her cave and added her prayers to those of mortals. None had ever returned from Hades and it was questioned whether or not such a thing were possible. Jove inquired of the Fates, and they replied that Persephone might be restored if she had not yet tasted food in Hades.

Now when Pluto first brought Persephone to his world, she had vowed she would eat nothing whatever there—that she had no desire to live longer, and so she spent her time mourning for her mother and for the bright world she had left. Shortly before Zeus questioned the Fates, however, Pluto had persuaded her to eat a few pomegranate seeds. For each seed she had eaten, it was decreed she must spend one month with Pluto in the realm of Hades, but this left her yet six months to pass with her mother. Mercury was sent to bring her, and when she appeared, the earth covered herself with brightest colors, the singing of birds was once more heard, and all life took on hope and happiness anew. When the six months were passed, Persephone returned to Hades, and earth laid aside her gay apparel and mourned until she came once more with the coming year.

Of all mythological stories this is the most beautifully symbolic. Persephone is vegetation—the life of trees and plants, and all that springs from the earth. In the fall she descends to the sunless regions under the earth—to the roots of trees and plants.

The restless, melancholy autumn represents the mother searching for her child, with no thought or care for the leaves and flowers which die, so neglected. Before winter is wholly gone, there come days which seem to bring with them a breath of spring—a hope of life renewed. This calls to mind Demeter coming forth from her cave and taking fresh measures for the recovery of her child. And last, spring comes, with its yearly glory and mystery. Persephone returns and the story of the resurrection is once more symbolized.

PERSEPHONE.

She stepped upon Sicilian grass,
　　　Demeter's daughter fresh and fair,
A child of light, a radiant lass,
　　　And gamesome as the morning air.
The daffodils were fair to see,
They nodded lightly on the lea,
Persephone—Persephone!
Lo! one she marked of rarer growth
　　　Than orchis or anemone;
For it the maiden left them both,
　　　And parted from her company.
Drawn nigh she deemed it fairer still,
And stooped to gather by the rill
The daffodil, the daffodil.

What ailed the meadow that it shook?
　　　What ailed the air of Sicily?
She wondered by the brattling brook,
　　　And trembled by the trembling lea.
"The coal-black horses rise—they rise:
O mother, mother!" low she cries—
Persephone—Persephone!

"O light, light, light!" she cried, "farewell;
O shade of shades, where I must dwell,
　　　Demeter, mother, far from thee!
Ah, fated doom that I fulfill!
Ah, fateful flower beside the rill!
The daffodil, the daffodil!"

What ails her that she comes not home?
  Demeter seeks her far and wide,
And gloomy-browed doth ceaseless roam
  From many a morn till eventide.
" My life, immortal though it be,
Is nought," she cries, for want of thee,
Persephone, Persephone!

" Meadows of Enna, let the rain
  No longer drop to feed your rills,
Nor dew refresh the fields again,
  With all their nodding daffodils!
Fade, fade and droop, O' lilied lea,
Where thou, dear heart, wert reft from me—
Persephone—Persephone ! "

She reigns upon her dusky throne,
  'Mid shades of heroes dread to see;
Among the dead she breathes alone,
  Persephone—Persephone!
Or seated on the Elysian hill
She dreams of earthly daylight still,
And murmurs of the daffodil.

A voice in Hades sounded clear,
  The shadows mourn and flit below;
It cries—" Thou Lord of Hades, hear,
  And let Demeter's daughter go.
The tender corn upon the lea
Droops in her goddess gloom when she
Cries for her lost Persephone.

" From land to land she raging flies,
  The green fruit falleth in her wake.
The harvest fields beneath her eyes
  To earth the grain unripened shake.
Arise, and set the maiden free;
Why should the world such sorrow dree
By reason of Persephone ? "

He takes the cleft pomegranate seeds:
    "Love, eat with me this parting day!"
Then bids them fetch the coal-black steeds—
    "Demeter's daughter, wouldst away?"
The gates of Hades set her free;
"She will return full soon," said he—
"My wife, my wife, Persephone."

Low laughs the dark king on his throne—
    "I gave her of pomegranate seeds."
Demeter's daughter stands alone
    Upon the fair Eleusian meads.
Her mother meets her. "Hail," saith she;
"And doth our daylight dazzle thee,
My love, my child Persephone?

"What moved thee, daughter, to forsake
    Thy fellow-maids that fatal morn,
And give thy dark lord the power to take
    Thee living to his realm forlorn?"
Her lips reply without her will,
As one addressed who slumbereth still—
"The daffodil, the daffodil!"

Her eyelids droop with light oppressed,
    And sunny wafts that round her stir,
Her cheek upon her mother's breast—
    Demeter's kisses comfort her.
Calm Queen of Hades, art thou she
Who stepped so lightly on the lea—
Persephone, Persephone?

Demeter sighs, but sure 'tis well
    The wife should love her destiny:
They part, and yet, as legends tell,
    She mourns her lost Persephone;
While chant the maids of Enna still—
"O fateful flower beside the rill—
    The daffodil, the daffodil!"
                  JEAN INGELOW.

BACCHUS.

The praise of Bacchus then the sweet musician sung,
Of Bacchus ever fair and ever young.
The jolly god in triumph comes;
Sound the trumpets, beat the drums;
Flushed with a purple grace
He shows his honest face:
Now give the hautboys breath; he comes, he comes,
Bacchus, ever fair and young,
Drinking joys did first ordain;
Bacchus' blessings are a treasure,
Drinking is the soldier's pleasure;
Rich the treasure,
Sweet the pleasure,
Sweet is pleasure after pain.

DRYDEN.

DIONYSUS, GOD OF WINE.

Of all mortal maidens loved by Zeus, for none did he more tenderly care than for the fair Semele. Hera, discovering the love between the two, appeared to Semele as her nurse and persuaded her to ask Jove to visit her in all his glory instead of in his usual disguise. Having exacted a promise from her lover that he would grant any wish she might ask, Zeus was bound by his oath, and sorrowfully complied with Semele's wishes, although of course, no mortal could gaze upon such splendor and live, and at his first appearance as lord of heaven, she fell dead before his glance.

Her son, Dionysus, was cared for by the nymphs. He was early recognized as god of wine. As a boy he was entrusted to a tutor, Silenus, a reveling, half-tipsy fellow, half-man, half-goat. When sober he would teach his pupil many things, and together they roamed through distant lands, showing people how to grow the grape vine, and to make wine from its delicious fruit.

On one occasion Silenus became separated from Dionysus —or Bacchus, as the Romans called him. He wandered about until he came to the palace of King Midas. This king seems to have been possessed of some leisure, and hardly endowed with kingly habits, for he at once offered to escort Silenus back to his god.

When they finally found Bacchus, he was so rejoiced to see Silenus again that he offered to grant any wish the king might choose to make. Now Midas had hoarded gold all his life, and naturally he thought first of that. He asked Bacchus to make everything he touched turn to gold. The god replied that this was a very foolish wish, but the king would not alter it. Accordingly it was fulfilled.

At first it seemed very gratifying to pick up a stone and have it immediately transformed into precious gold. Midas was rapturous to find that he had really acquired the Golden Touch. When, however, he sat down to eat and grapes became hard balls in his mouth, when water changed into liquid gold, and wheaten cakes into blocks of the same metal, the disadvantages of the situation grew gradually upon him. In a golden bed with his head resting upon a golden pillow, he came rapidly to the conclusion that every effort must now be made to get free from this power he had so recently coveted. Early morning found him once more before the god Bacchus, this time a humble suppliant. He begged that the Golden Touch be taken from him; whereupon the god smiled and bade him bathe in the river Pactolus. Having done so, King Midas was released from his gift which had caused him such anxiety. The river, it is said, still flows over sand made golden by the touch of king's feet.

On another occasion, Bacchus wandered away from his friends. Feeling tired, he dropped down upon the shore for a nap. Some pirates passing, saw the youth upon the sands and quickly carried him while he slept to their ship. Awakening, Bacchus found himself some distance from home. The sea-rovers laughed heartily when he insisted that they take him back. Shortly, to their own consternation, they beheld grape vines growing out of the waves and twining around their ship which rapidly became a floating arbor. Deprived of reason the pirates leaped over the side of the vessel and were changed by Bacchus into dolphins.

DRINKING SONG.

Come, old friend! sit down and listen!
  From the pitcher placed between us,
How the waters laugh and glisten
  In the head of old Silenus!

Old Silenus, bloated, drunken,
  Led by his inebriate Satyrs;
On his breast his head is sunken,
  Vacantly he leers and chatters.

Fauns with youthful Bacchus follow;
  Ivy crowns that brow supernal
As the forehead of Apollo,
  And possessing youth eternal.

Round about him, fair Bacchantes,
  Bearing cymbals, flutes and thyrses,
Wild from Naxian groves, of Zante's
  Vineyards, sing delirious verses.

Thus he won, through all the nations,
  Bloodless victories, and the farmer
Bore, as trophies and oblations,
  Vines for banners, ploughs for armour.

Judged by no o'er zealous rigor,
  Much this mystic throng expresses:
Bacchus was the type of vigor,
  And Silenus of excesses.

LONGFELLOW.

To tell the story of Bacchus' love we must diverge from the
incidents of his life to relate the doings of a mortal, Theseus
by name. Son of an Athenian king, he came to the relief of
Athens under peculiar circumstances. The king of Crete,
King Minos, had exacted cruel tribute from the city of Athens.
Every nine years he required seven sons and seven daughters
of the noblest families to appease a monster that infested his
borders. Theseus came forward and offered to kill the monster. Sailing away with seven daughters and six other noble
princes, he came at last to the palace of King Minos. The

king's daughter saw and loved him. Unable to persuade her father to save him, she resolved to do so herself. Appearing to him in the night, she urged Theseus to attack the monster at once while he slept, and provided him with a sword for the deed. Since the monster lived in a labyrinth—a mystery of many caves and windings so bewildering that once in them one could never hope to reach the open air again—Ariadne gave him a ball of twine, the end of which she retained. By winding it up he might reach the opening of the cave, should he live indeed after his conflict with the horrible monster.

Theseus did all that Ariadne advised. He was successful in making way with the dreaded one and, emerging from the cave, he found the brave princess waiting with his Athenian companions. They took their way to the ship which had brought them thither. In gratitude for all she had done, Theseus made many vows to the fair Ariadne, and entreated her to accompany him home, there to become his bride. To this plan the princess gave her consent. Embarking speedily, they stopped only on the island of Naxos. Landing for a brief rest and to explore the place, Ariadne fell asleep, where-upon the inconstant Theseus gathered together his companions and set sail. Waking, the princess saw their sails far over the sea.

> " The daughter of a king, how should I know
>   That there were tinsels wearing face of gold,
>   And worthless glass which in the sunlight's hold
>   Could shameless answer back my diamond's glow
>   With cheat of kindred fire? The current slow
> And deep and strong and stainless, which has rolled
> Through royal veins for ages, what had told
> To them that hasty heat and lie could show
>   As quick and warm and red as theirs? Go free!
>   The sun is breaking on the sea's blue shield
> Its golden lances: by their gleams I see
> Thy ship's white sails. Go free if scorn can yield
> Thee freedom! Then alone, my love and I,—
> We both are royal: we know how to die." [1]

[1] Helen Hunt Jackson.

But the lovely Ariadne did not die. By some chance Bacchus and his merry crew now descended on the island. The god of wine heard her story and loved her. After a time they were married, and their marriage festival was splendid indeed. Bacchus gave his bride a crown set with seven diamonds, which she afterwards wore. But their happiness was short-lived. In a few months his loved one sickened and died. Bacchus threw her crown up in the sky and there the diamonds were changed to stars, and even yet the constellation of Ariadne's crown shines bright above.

Theseus has been interpreted to symbolize the sun; the monster which he slew, darkness. The sun was assisted by Ariadne or the Dawn, which he was soon compelled to desert. Bacchus probably had his origin in some noble prince who first taught the people how to make good use of their land—to cultivate fruits, as they thought Ceres had first taught them to cultivate grains. Bacchus is the god of the nature that men produce, and in art he is always shown with the leaves and fruit of his favorite vine.

Some of the Dionysian festivals early fell into boisterous occasions, those participating often indulging too heartily in wine and questionable pastimes. However, the great festivals held in Athens, and elsewhere in Greece, in honor of this god, gave rise in time to plays, and the history of the Greek drama may be traced back to the early celebrations of the god of wine.

> " And as I sat, over the light blue hills
> There came a noise of revellers : the rills
> Into the wide stream came of purple hue—
>   'Twas Bacchus and his crew!
> The earnest trumpet spake, and silver thrills
> From kissing cymbals made a merry din—
>   'Twas Bacchus and his kin!
> Like to a moving vintage, down they came,
> Crowned with green leaves, and faces all on flame ·
> All madly dancing, through the pleasant valley,
>   To scare thee, Melancholy!

" Within his car, aloft, young Bacchus stood,
  Trifling his ivy-dart, in dancing mood,
        With sidelong laughing;
  And little rills of crimson wine imbrued
  His plump white arms, and shoulders, enough white
        For Venus' pearly bite;
  And near him rode Silenus on his ass,
  Pelted with flowers, as he on did pass
        Tipsily quaffing.

" Whence came ye, merry Damsels! whence came ye!
  So many, and so many, and such glee?
  Why have ye left your bowers desolate,
        Your lutes and gentler fate?—
' We follow Bacchus! Bacchus on the wing,
        A conquering!
  We dance before him through kingdoms wide:—
  Come hither, lady fair, and joined be
  To our wild minstrelsy!"

" Whence came ye, jolly satyrs! whence came ye!
  So many, and so many, and such glee?
  Why have ye left your forest haunts, why left
        Your nuts in oak-tree cleft?—
' For wine, for wine we left our kernel tree;
  For wine we left our heath, and yellow brooms,
        And cold mushrooms;
  For wine we follow Bacchus through the earth;
  Great God of breathless cups and chirping mirth!
  Come hither, lady fair, and joined be
  To our mad minstrelsy !'"

                                    KEATS

CHAPTER XIII.

GREAT GOD PAN.

Sing his praises that doth keep
  Our flocks from harm
Pan, the father of our sheep;
  And arm in arm
Tread we softly in a round,
Whilst the hollow neighboring ground
Fills the music with her sound.

Pan, oh, great god Pan, to thee
  Thus do we sing!
Thou that keep'st us chaste and free
  As the young spring;
Even be thy honor spoke,
From that place the morn is broke,
To that place day doth unyoke!

FLETCHER.

PAN, GOD OF NATURE.

While Bacchus was the god of that nature which men produce and cultivate, Pan was god of nature as found in its wild, native state. He was god of shepherds and their flocks; god of hunting and of fishing; god of the beautiful natural world, open to the skies above, extending in mountains, valleys and forests beneath; god of rustic rural life.

It was believed that Hermes was Pan's father; his mother, a wood-nymph. In any event, Pan was always the amusement as well as the pet of the Mighty Ones. For his feet were like those of a goat; with a face and body human, he had horns and pointed ears.

Pan once fell in love with a nymph named Syrinx, but she, shy creature, thought him insupportably ugly and ran away. When Pan pursued—and it seems to have been impossible to dismiss a god—the terrified nymph called to the gods to protect her, and she was transformed into a number of reeds. As the wind sighed through them it suggested music to the god of nature, so, sorrowing for his lost love, he cut seven pieces from the reeds and made a sort of flute which he called a syrinx. Upon this simple instrument he poured out his passion to the lost nymph.

You will remember Midas—he of the Golden Touch. He was especially fond of the music which Pan made on his flute, and one day told him that he played as well as Apollo himself. Some mischief-making sprite repeated this to Apollo at her earliest opportunity, and Apollo challenged Pan to a contest. The god of a nearby mountain acted as judge; Midas made up the audience; and Apollo with his golden harp, and Pan with his reed flute, began to play. Soon the mountain-god told Pan that it would be better for him to drop out of the contest and listen to the harp, thereby learning to appreciate how far its liquid notes surpassed any efforts he could make. The god of nature had taken the whole thing in a jesting manner and quickly complied, but King Midas cried that it was unjust, that Pan's music was as acceptable as Apollo's. In his scorn Apollo changed the king's ears into those of an ass—the better to hear with, perhaps. Anyway, King Midas was greatly concerned. He summoned a barber to make him a wig, threatening him with death should he reveal the secret of his ears. Somehow this bit of information seems to have preyed continually on the barber, and at last he went to the river bank, dug a deep hole, and whispered into it the secret—King Midas had ears like an ass. This done, he went his way relieved. But he had whispered it to the roots of growing reeds and when they grew tall, and the wind blew through them, they would say: "King Midas has ears like an ass!" Of course everybody heard them, and then all the world knew the secret.

Pan symbolized natural life, free from restraint—Arcadian. He was the natural person, care-free, impulsive, giving play to each emotion, expressing his joy of life by gamboling, and dancing, always to natural music.

So people have always loved to think of Pan. Even now, when the first spring days come, simple souls who care little for the wisdom of the world, think they sometimes catch glimpses of the god among the trees, and they are sure they hear him.

The Greeks believed that each wood, rill, dale, mountain, and tree had its special deity who watched over it. The woods were filled with nymphs, shy maidens, immortal like the gods. Echo, we have seen, was one of them, and she hovers yet in many forests. Call in the woods, and she will answer. Each tree had its dryad, which was born with it and died with it. For this reason, wanton destruction of trees was severely punished.

OREADS.

The Oreads were tall, slender maidens, young huntresses who attended on Diana, and presided over the mountains. The Satyrs were youths, having, like Pan, a form half-goat, half-man. Pan was their leader, and they danced to his music. Silenus, Bacchus' tutor, was of their band.

Ruskin has well said that our attitude toward the new-born day depends upon what that day is likely to bring us. To the Greeks it brought joy. Each dawn meant a fresh opportunity to enjoy life and to feel divinity around them. The hearth was guarded by a goddess whose purity insured safety to all who drew near it. The air they breathed was sanctified by a goddess; across the sky moved daily the great sun god, and when he had gone to rest, his sister followed him in her snow-white chariot. Any of the deities might be at any time in their midst. The spring from which they found water to quench their thirst was presided over by a water nymph who would hear all they might say.

With such bright fancies, it is little wonder that these people developed the most perfect language the world has heard, that they gained great physical perfection and every grace, while their art stands yet unsurpassed, and their poems still awaken admiration and inspire responsive hearts.

After the old gods were swept away by the truer conceptions and teachings of Christianity, in the reaction which followed, all that antiquity had valued was tossed aside, and in blind misunderstanding, much that was useful and ennobling was cast away with much that was no longer worthy. In the

centuries that followed, poets cried that Pan was dead. Only
in comparatively recent times have noble, fearless minds shown
that beauty and truth are but different aspects of the same
principle, that the spirit of the brotherhood of man reaches
back and includes these far away people, recognizing their
efforts to reach upward and to fathom the mysteries of life;
and finally, it has been shown that Pan is not dead—or that
those things he symbolized still live, and are today drawing
men from the artificial to the natural, from the city to the
woods, from leading strings of custom to the freedom of simplicity.

The Living Pan.

Who weeps the death of Pan? Pan is not dead,
But loves the shepherds still; still leads the fauns
    In merry dances o'er the grassy lawns,
To his own pipes; as erst in Greece he led
The sylvan games, what time the god pursued
The beauteous Dryope. The Naiads still
    Haunt the green marge of every mountain rill;
The Dryads sport in every leafy wood;
Pan cannot die till Nature's self decease!
    Full oft the reverent worshipper descries
    His ruddy face and mischief-glancing eyes
Beneath the branches of old forest-trees
    That tower remote from steps of worldly men,
    Or hears his laugh far echoing down the glen!
                            Saxe.

CHAPTER XIV.

The monarch Neptune kept no idle watch;
Soon he descended from those rugged steeps,
And trod the earth with rapid strides; the hills
And forests quaked beneath the immortal feet
Of Neptune as he walked.   Three strides he took,
And at the fourth reached Æger, where he stopped,
And where his sumptuous palace-halls were built,
Deep down in ocean, golden, glittering, proof
Against decay of time.   These when he reached,
He yoked his swift and brazen-footed steeds,
With manes of flowing mail, and took his scourge,
Wrought of fine gold, and climbed the chariot-seat,
And rode upon the waves.   The whales came forth
From their deep haunts, and frolicked round his way:
They knew their king.   The waves rejoicing smoothed
A path, and rapidly the coursers flew;
Nor was the brazen axle wet below.

Deep in the sea there is a spacious cave,
Between the rugged Imbrus and the isle
Of Tenedos.   There Neptune, he who shakes
The shores, held back his steeds, took off their yokes,
Gave them ambrosial food, and binding next
Their feet with golden fetters which no power
Might break, or loosen, so that they might wait
Their lord's return, he sought the Grecian host.

—*Iliad.*

Water Deities: Poseidon, God of Ocean.

When Zeus divided the power of the universe, after the
Battle of the Giants, he gave his brother Poseidon, or Neptune,
dominion over the sea, and made him ruler of all sea-creatures.

While Poseidon had a palace on Mount Olympus, he generally lived in his wonderful home beneath the ocean.   Very
wide and spacious was this dwelling, covered on the outer side

with gold, kept shining and bright by the constant wash of the
waves. Beautiful columns divided the apartments and the
draperies were of sea-weeds, bearing softest of pink blossoms.
Coral grottoes and caves were to be found here and there;
pearls, born of the sea, might be seen in profusion; fountains
sent up their sprays in unexpected places; brooks and springs
abounded, while fish of every sort, sea-plants of all descriptions, mermaids and all sea creatures, added their charms to
this wonderful palace. The whole dwelling, with its broad
courts, was lighted by the glow-worms of the sea.

Still, with all his dominions, Poseidon was not contented.
He saw the wider estate of his brother Zeus, and envied him.
He longed especially for territory on land. We have seen
how he contended with Athena for the city of Athens, and he
was deeply chagrined when she was chosen as its guardian.

On one occasion he united with Hera and Apollo in a con-
spiracy against the mighty Jove, the three plotting to seize his
power for themselves. Fortunately for the great father,
someone betrayed the plot to him and put him on his guard.
He banished Apollo from Olympus for nine years, and commanded Poseidon to build the walls of Troy as punishment
for his treachery.

One day the great sea-god saw one of the nereids, Amphitrite, and loved her. She was so shy however, that he despaired of ever winning her for himself, so he besought a dolphin to intercede for him. The dolphin returned with her
consent to become Queen of the Sea, and Poseidon was so
delighted that he placed him in the skies, where he still shines
as a constellation.

Most noted of Amphitrite's children was Triton, a youth
half-man, half-fish. He acted as Poseidon's herald, and often
preceded him, blowing a conch-shell as a horn. All the numberless Tritons of the sea were said to be his offspring, and so
took their name from him.

Like most of the ancient deities, Neptune had various love
affairs. He was very fond of Ceres, but far from returning
his devotion, she wearied of his attention. When seeking
her lost daughter, Neptune persisted in accompanying her,
until she took the guise of a mare in self-protection. But

Neptune accordingly assumed the form of a horse and trotted along by her side. Arion, a winged horse, was the result of this union. This fabled horse was said to have frequently won races at the Olympian games.

Neptune also loved Theophane, but fearing lest some of her other suitors might steal a march on him, he changed her into a sheep, himself taking the form of a ram. Their offspring was the ram of the Golden Fleece, celebrated in hero-lore.

This ram saved the lives of two noble children by carrying them out of danger on his back, and then died of exhaustion. Thereupon his wool was changed to gold. His fleece was hung high in a tree, in the Garden of Mars, where it was guarded by a monster, to say nothing of a wicked king who did everything in his power to frustrate the effort of any ambitious youth who tried to secure it.

Jason was the son of a king who had been wrongfully deposed. Seeking to recover the crown which was rightfully his, he was bidden to win first the Golden Fleece, whereupon the usurping monarch agreed to renounce the throne—thinking, of course, that he had named an impossible exploit.

Jason, nothing daunted, instructed Argus, the great ship-builder, to build the Argo, the first great vessel to plow distant seas. Manning it with fifty brave youths, called Argonauts, they journeyed together to Colchis, where hung the Golden Fleece, carefully guarded. Here dwelt Medea, daughter of the king who ruled over the Garden of Mars, as well as the surrounding country. Medea, who possessed magic power, happened to be won over by Jason's charms, and promised to aid him in his efforts. With her assistance, difficulties melted away, and Jason won the Golden Fleece, as well as the throne which he sought.

This story, only remotely connected with the great god of ocean, well illustrates what Ruskin had in mind when he said that following Greek myths was like tracing the variously colored threads of a tapestry. Now they are interwoven, and twine side by side; now they diverge until in tracing one you lose sight of the other, when suddenly they cross and together weave a new and previously unseen pattern. Patience and time are often required to seek them out, but the reward is ample.

To the early people, personifying everything about them, the sea constantly encroaching upon the land, suggested a deity dissatisfied with his own possessions, and eager to grasp the dominions of another. The great billows, rolling deep and breaking into white foam, suggested angry horses, impatient of control. The sudden squalls, succeeded by calm sea and wave, brought to mind a person of changeful mood. And with these qualities they came to endow Poseidon.

As time went on, and commerce by water grew in importance, it was necessary indeed to propitiate the god of the seas, and the festivals celebrated in honor of Poseidon came to be second only to those held in honor of Zeus himself. The distant seas were unknown and the primitive mind imagined them to be filled with all kinds of malicious water creatures, themselves subservient to the great sea god.

In art, the god of ocean is always shown with his trident; often in his chariot—an ocean shell drawn by champing steeds. One favorite painting shows the wedding of Neptune and Amphitrite, fifty nereids celebrating the occasion by a mazy dance.

The Sirens.

The ships of the early Greeks and Romans were frequently wrecked off their rugged coasts. Frail crafts would either be blown against the rocks in severe storms, or coming unexpectedly upon treacherous and unseen islands of the sea, they would go down with their helpless crews.

As time went on, it was believed that there were malicious creatures, having forms half-woman, half-fish, who inhabited these rocks, and by enchanting music, lured sailors on to their destruction. Very enticing, it was thought, were their songs, leading seamen to leap overboard in their desire to join the creatures, only to find a watery grave. Sometimes, it was believed, the sailors would be induced to row up to the rocks to partake of refreshment offered them. But the food given had power to make them forget the past, and put them to sleep forever. For those who waited their return, the result was the same—they never reached home again.

It was said that if any mortal should pass these sirens unmoved, their charm would be destroyed. Ulysses, on his homeward course, on drawing near the enchanted rocks, had his sailors fill their ears with wax in order that they might pass unharmed. Danger-loving as he himself was, he had his men bind him securely to the mast, cautioning them not to release him until well past the dreaded sirens. As with others, his strength of will gave way before the seductive music and he begged his men to let him go, but they left him bound until danger was past. Thus was he saved again for his home-coming.

Orpheus, however, without wax or chains, sailed by these maidens by simply producing music of his own more beautiful than theirs. Whereupon the sirens, in deep chagrin, leaped into the waves and were changed to rocks. Their memory lived on in the minds of the Greeks, and centuries after, the tradition of sea creatures working ill for seamen drifted into other lands. Today one journeying up the Rhine may see the rock, the Lorelei, where it was thought a maiden sang, luring sailors on to ruin.

Song of the Sirens.

Long have you buffeted the winds,
  And urged the weary oar;
Now you reach our little isle,
Furl your sail, and rest awhile,
  On the happy shore.

What is here that you should fear
  What is there so deadly here?
A quiet island in the sea,
Grass-fringed, and shadowed deep with palms,
  Winds that winnow summer balms,
Flowers in each vale, and fruit on every tree.

We weave slow dances in the shade,
  With lifted arms and floating hair;
Or, when the golden moon is come,
List the wild-bee's drowsy hum,
  Or watch the insects in the air,
  Or kiss each other on the lips,
And so softly swoon away in sleep's divine eclipse.

What is there to fear in this?
　　Where's the danger of a kiss?
But if dangerous it be,
　　It is to maids like us—not men like thee!

STODDARD.

You will remember the princess Danaë, whom Zeus wooed in the tower as golden rain. Her father had thus confined her because it had been foretold that some day his grandson would be the cause of his death. By thus retaining his only daughter in this lofty tower, he fancied that he had placed her beyond the reach of suitors, and so evaded the fates. But we have seen that Zeus found the maiden and won her for his wife, just as though she had been accessible, instead of imprisoned in a guarded turret.

Now when a little baby with golden curls was born in this turret, Danaë concealed him until he was four years old, but then, one day, the king passed by and heard his childish prattle. Discovering the babe, he ordered both mother and child to be put in a strong chest and set afloat on the waves. So afraid was he of losing his kingdom that he could plan a watery grave for his own daughter. The mother and babe did not drown however. A kind fisherman found them and cared for them until the boy Perseus grew to be a man.

The king of the island, where this good fisherman brought Danaë and her boy, was an evil-minded man, and most of his subjects were like him. They wished to harm the fair Danaë and her son just because they were nobler than these evil-minded subjects and their king. So one day the king sent for Perseus and told him that he had promised his bride the head of Medusa for her wedding present, and that he had been chosen to obtain it.

THE GORGONS.

Medusa was one of the Gorgons—dreadful sea-creatures, with long, snakey locks, bodies covered with scales as hard as iron, and eyes so fierce and wild that whoever gazed upon their faces was instantly turned to stone. So you can easily see that no ordinary bride would covet such a gift, and the evil-minded king had simply devised this method of getting rid of Perseus that he might be free to wreak his vengeance on the mother.

Perseus was a hero, and in early mythological times, that meant that his father had been a god, even though his mother was mortal. Naturally then, he was much braver than ordinary men. So Perseus was not at all dismayed when the king gave him this mission, but promised that the bride should have the head of the Medusa, ignoring the king's sneers.

However when he set out to accomplish his task, he began to meditate. Where were the gorgons, anyway? What reason had he to expect he might escape the stony fate that had befell others who had gazed upon the awful face of the Medusa? While thus debating with himself, and feeling for the first time dismayed by his task, Mercury appeared before him. Learning of his difficulty, Mercury offered to assist him. You may be sure that Perseus gladly welcomed any help in such a moment, and listened eagerly to the advice Mercury gave. First, he was told, they must seek out the Graeae—or the Grey Sisters, who lived in the land of mist, and who served the gorgons. They alone could inform him where he might find the nymphs who supplied the winged sandals and other enchanted accoutrements he would need.

Now the Grey Sisters were simple old women, having but one eye, one tooth, and one wig among them. These they passed around from one to the other, and so took turns in seeing, eating, and probably in looking well. Anyway, Perseus' only hope lay in snatching their one eye as they shifted it from one to another, and in retaining it until he had gained the necessary information.

This plan, characteristic of Mercury, since it was crafty, worked out well. Much as they hated to disclose a secret, they hated total darkness worse; but some say that never after that catastrophe did the Grey Sisters appear to mortal eyes again.

Equipped with a cap that made him invisible, winged sandals that gave him the speed of the wind, a sword that would cut iron as easily as thread, and the shield of Athena, that shone like the finest mirror, Perseus was conducted by Mercury and Athena to the western sea, where abode the dreaded gorgons.

Cautioned repeatedly only to look at the image reflected in
the shield, Perseus was told to drop down upon Medusa as she
and her sister-gorgons lay asleep. The snakes covering her
head like hair were for the most part quiet, and with one
master stroke, Perseus severed the head, thrust it in a magic
purse before the snakes could bite him, and rose up again
before the other gorgons, wakened by the noise, could avenge
the death of their sister. They struck around in all directions,
and the snakes sprang out with their deadly stings, but
Perseus was invisible, and so they could not harm him.

ATLAS.

As he journeyed homeward, he came upon Atlas, who had
been doomed to support the world upon his shoulder since the
battle of the Giants, when he had taken part against Zeus.
Atlas now begged Perseus to show him the head of Medusa.

"But," objected Perseus, "to behold the face would turn
you into stone. None can look upon its gaze and live!"

"But," returned Atlas, "that is what I have long been
wishing. As stone I would be insensible to the burden I now
bear."

So Perseus showed him the face of the slain gorgon, and
accordingly in the place where but now had stood Atlas,
Perseus beheld the mountain range that now bears his name,
with its snowy summits and rugged peaks.

Reaching home, Perseus found that the king had ill-treated
his noble mother. No one had expected the son to return
again, and now when the king and his courtiers beheld him,
they cried: "Show us the Medusa's head! Show us the
Medusa's head! Show us the head of the gorgon!"

Although he and his mother had suffered much at their
hands, the hero hesitated to display the fatal head and
accordingly he cautioned them.

"Show us the head or we will have yours!" cried the evil-
minded people, and so Perseus drew forth the head of Medusa
from the magic purse. Of course all the people were immediately turned to stone, and henceforth Perseus and his mother
had no more to fear from them.

Some have seen in the story an allegory of sunlight and
darkness. Perseus, born of Dawn, meets the Grey Sisters,

or the early mist, slays Medusa, or the terror of darkness, as
the sun's rays dispel night.

MEDUSA.

A face in whose voluptuous bloom there lies
  Olympian faultlessness of mold and hue;
Lips that a god were worthy alone to woo;
Round chin, and nostrils curved in the old Greek wise.
But there is no clear pallor of arctic skies,
  Fathom on crystal fathom of livid blue,
  So bleakly cold that one might liken it to
The pitiless icy splendors of her eyes!
Her bound hair, colored lovelier than the sweet
Rich halcyon yellow of tall harvest wheat,
  Over chaste brows a glimmering tumult sheds;
But through the abundance of its warm soft gold,
Coils of lean horror peer from many a fold,
  With sharp tongues flickering in flat clammy heads!

EDWARD FAWCETT.

CHAPTER XV.

To the Winds.

Ye viewless minstrels of the sky!
I marvel not in times gone by
    That ye were deified:
For, even in this later day,
To me oft has your power, or play,
    Unearthly thoughts supplied.

Awful your power! when by your might
You heave the wild waves, crested white,
    Like mountains in your wrath;
Ploughing between them valleys deep,
Which, to the seaman roused from sleep,
    Yawn like Death's opening path!

Graceful your play! when round the bower
Where beauty culls spring's loveliest flower,
    To wreathe her dark locks there,
Your gentlest whispers lightly breathe
The leaves between, flit round the wreath,
    And stir her silken hair.

Still, thoughts like these are but of earth,
And you can give far loftier birth:—
    Ye come! we know not whence!
Ye go! can mortals trace your flight?
All imperceptible to sight,
    Though audible to sense.

The Sun,—his rise and set we know;
The Sea,—we mark its ebb and flow;
    The Moon—her wax and wane;
The Stars,—man knows their courses well;
The comet's vagrant paths can tell;—
    But you his search disdain.   BARTON.

DEITIES OF THE WIND: AEOLUS.

There is, of course, no special reason for classifying the wind gods with the water deities; neither would they be classified wholly with the divinities of earth; the truth is that while the winds affected the land materially, they were of still more consequence to the seafaring people. For that reason we consider them here.

Aeolus was a mighty god who lived on an island, far removed from other lands, and indeed his island differed from any other which has existed then or since, because it floated around at the will of its ruler.

Now the god of wind loved Eos, or Aurora, goddess of the Dawn,—she who flung open the gates of day for the great Sun-god when he began his daily journey through the heavens. She had two swift steeds of her own, Brightness and Lustre, and is often represented in art, riding after them.

The wind-god loved Aurora as we have seen. But unfortunately she had a mortal husband, and his career was so remarkable that we shall interrupt the tale of the wind-gods long enough to find out what it was.

" If you have ever seen the sun rise, you have seen the wings of Aurora.

" Aurora is the dawn; and as she opens her wings, you see all their colors—first pale grey; then a delicate amber, which deepens into saffron; then the tint of a pink-rose, which grows fuller and fuller till it becomes crimson and purple, which turns to gold when the chariot of the Sun appears. It is she who throws open the gates of the sky for Phoebus Apollo to start upon his daily journey, just as it is Thetis who shuts them, and brings the twilight when his journey is done.

" Aurora is always glad and beautiful and young; always full of hope, because she closes her splendid wings and goes to sleep before the troubles of the day begin; and her only work is to feed the flowers with dew. But once upon a time she fell in love with a mortal named Tithonus; and she promised to grant him whatever boon he most desired.

" I suppose almost everybody has tried to think of what he would wish for if a goddess or fairy gave him such a chance. Tithonus thought hard for a minute, and then said :—

" 'Great and beautiful goddess, my wish is that I may never die, so that I may see you every morning forever.' Now of course it was against all the laws of Hades that a mortal should never die—unless, of course, he was allowed to taste the Ambrosia, the food of the gods, which was very seldom allowed. How Aurora managed it I cannot tell. But she kept her word somehow, and Tithonus got leave to live forever.

" And so long as he was young and strong, and could get up early in the morning to look at the color of Aurora's wings, that was all very well. It did just as well as if he were to die, in the end, like other men. But it happened at last that, while Aurora remained as young as ever, Tithonus began to get old. The promise of endless life did not prevent him from growing bald, and toothless, and liable to catch cold if he went out into the keen morning air. By the time that he was a hundred years old, he became tired of getting up to see the sun rise day after day. At two hundred he felt like a bundle of aches and pains, and he liked a doze in the sun better than a thousand Auroras. At three hundred he became tired of living, and wanted to be able to creep into some quiet corner of Hades, drink a cup of Lethe, and go to sleep and think of nothing. But he could not; for though racked with pain and weary of life, he could not die!

" He could only shrink and shrivel till, after many hundreds of years, he was less than two inches long. His skin turned dry and brown. His voice became cracked, and thin, and shrill. He lost his senses, and kept on chirping the same thing over and over again. He never stirred from the warmth of the chimney corner, night or day. His legs grew as thin as threads of cotton, and he dwindled into a dry, wooden-like insect—in short, a Cricket.

" And such he remains today. But Aurora is as young and as beautiful and as fresh as ever, and has entirely forgotten him. While he spends his life in trying to be merry and in chirping: 'Oh, how I want to die!' " [1]

Tithonus and Aurora were the parents of Memnon, who fell before the siege of Troy. His mother has never ceased

---

[1] Francillon: Gods and Heroes.

POSEIDON.

weeping for him, her favorite son, and the dew is said to be composed of her tear-drops.

As wife of the wind-god Aeolus, she became the mother of six sons and six daughters, gods and goddesses of all the varieties of wind.

On his floating island Aeolus had a strong tower, and within this tower he kept his boisterous sons imprisoned, only letting one out at a time to take a little exercise. These sons were most of them rough and unruly. The oldest was Boreas, god of the north wind. He brought the piercing cold and the snow. The Greeks thought that he lived in the caves of the Hyperboreans, lying as they did to the north. The wind sent by Boreas was health-giving, and it filled the sails of the mariners and sent them rejoicing on their way.

Boreas once fell in love with the maiden Orithyia. Now how to woo was beyond the wildest imagination of the north wind. He could not even blow gently, and giving vent to lover-like sighs defied his bravest efforts. At last in despair, he seized the maiden and carried her off to his caves. Their children were two of the heroes who accompanied Jason on his quest for the Golden Fleece.

Corus was the northwest wind. He brought the winter storms and clouds of snow came before him. Eurus was the east wind. He was an impetuous youth, who brought warm rains. He was supposed to hold an inverted vase of water in his hand, ready to pour it out at any moment.

Aquilo, god of the west wind, was an old man with grey hair. Rain and sudden showers were in his wake. Zephyrus was the mildest of all the brothers. He, the south wind, brought the spring. Chloris, or Flora, goddess of flowers, and one of Aeolus' daughters, was his wife.

Aura, goddess of the morning wind, was another daughter, but of the remaining four we know little.

Ulysses, returning from the Trojan war, had many adventures and mishaps, recounted in the Odyssey. He happened upon this floating island ruled by Aeolus. The god of winds received him cordially, and for one month he and his weary men rested and enjoyed his bounty. Then the god, to accord him still greater favor at parting, tied all the winds into a great leather bag, fastening it at the top with a silver rope,

and gave it to Ulysses. The west wind was needed to waft
him and his crew over the seas with full spread sails, and bring
them soon to the homeland, while all the reverse winds, which
might otherwise have delayed the journey, were given into
Ulysses' keeping, and on his home arrival he was to set them
free.

Now Ulysses' men were not so wise as he. They looked
at the bag with envious eyes, supposing it contained rich gold
and precious stones. Probably Ulysses thought they would
not believe the story should he tell them that all the adverse
winds which otherwise they would have encountered were
therein held prisoners, so he simply watched through the days
and nights, that no harm might befall the precious bag. At
last they came in sight of the beloved Greek harbor. Two or
three hours would bring them into port. Ulysses was worn
out by long vigils, and now, feeling all danger past, he fell
asleep. Immediately his men seized the leather bag and un-
tied the silver rope. Instead of finding rich booty as they
had hoped, they scarce knew what had happened. The north
wind, and the east wind, the south breeze and all the other
winds took that vessel, whirled it around, sent it first in one
direction, then in another, until altogether, they brought it
back to the floating island.

The god of the winds was greatly offended. No more
would he help those who apparently had incurred the displeasure of the mighty gods, so he left them to reach home
as best they might. Seldom did the west wind blow now,
and most of the long distance had to be covered with weary
rowing. Probably the mariners had time to weigh well their
hasty action before they again came in sight of the Greek
shores they had left so long before.

When the Persians attempted to invade Greece, reverse
winds frustrated their plans. In gratitude, the Athenians built
a temple to the wind-gods; it was six-sided, and on each side
a flying figure of one of the winds was carved. These may
still be seen today.

HARPIES.

In connection with the winds we may consider the Harpies
—curious, spiteful creatures. who were thought to have faces

like women, and to be otherwise like birds. Three in number, they were the deadly enemies of the sons of Boreas. These harpies were thought to snatch and devour food set before those they hated. They were identified with the whirlwind, and with those little eddying gusts which blow the sand in spiral coils just before a storm. Spiteful, malicious beings, they were always being driven off by the sons of Boreas. The next time the wind whirls the sand before you, catching your clothing and tangling your hair, blowing in quick little spiral gusts, you can see for yourself something of the nature and disposition of the harpies.

We may note one more story of the winds. Halcyone was one of the daughters of Aeolus. She married a mortal king —Ceyx, and very happily they ruled in Thessaly for many years. At length the king was obliged to undertake a long voyage. His wife pleaded to go with him, but he feared the dangers of the deep for her. Promising a speedy return, he finally left her. She daily offered prayers for the king's safety, but it seems that early in the journey the sea-god raised a fearful storm to work out some other plan, and this king perished with all on board.

Hera, realizing that Halcyone would never be happy without her husband, sent her a dream telling her of the mishap and guiding her to the place where the king lay. Then the queen of heaven changed them both into king-fishers, and left them again united.

Each year these birds built their nests on the waves, and while Halcyone brooded over it, no wind or storms disturbed the sea, but all was serene, peaceful, brooding and quiet. From this it came to be said that the halcyon days had come when such peaceful weather reigned.

Some think that the story of Aeolus arose because an astronomer lived in any early day on a volcanic mountain. By watching the smoke he was able to foretell storms when yet far off. So the credulous people grew to think that he caused these storms and governed the winds.

Aurora was considered mother of the winds because they are generally born at break of day.

CHAPTER XVI.

DIVINITIES OF HADES: PLUTO, GOD OF THE DEAD.

> " 'Tis Pluto who is deaf to prayer
> And ne'er relents, and he, of all the gods,
> Most hateful is to men."

When Zeus, retaining heaven for his portion, gave Poseidon dominion over the seas, Pluto was made ruler of Hades, and god of all treasure concealed within the earth.

We have already come to know something of this grim god in connection with Persephone, daughter of Demeter. Now let us see to what sort of country he took his fair bride.

Hades was dark and gloomy. The light of the sun never penetrated its obscure recesses. The usual entrance to this dreaded region was near a volcanic mountain. Sulphur and other gaseous vapors here abounded, and suggested a passage to Hades in a credulous age. All dark and grewsome caves were thought to lead ultimately to the land of the dead.

The entrance of the wide gate was guarded by Cerberus, the three-headed dog, who was agreeable to those who entered, but showed his teeth to any one who tried to escape. His tail was a serpent with a fiery tongue, and altogether you can imagine he was quite a formidable enemy.

> " A mighty dog with three colossal necks,
>   And heads in grand proportion; vast as fear,
>   With jaws that bark the thunder out that breaks
>   In most innocuous dread for ghosts anear,
>   Who are safe in death from sorrow: he reclines
>   Across the threshold of Queen Persephone's
>   Dark-sweeping halls, and there, for Pluto's spouse,
>   Doth guard the entrance of the empty house."

A deep cave led from the gateway. Somber trees and bushes grew around. Lifeless groves, gloomy ravines, and bare hills made up the region surrounding Pluto's palace. The palace itself was made of gold and lighted with flashing diamonds. A thousand rooms were enclosed in its broad dimensions, and an army of servants ministered to the wants of Hades' king. Having all the riches concealed within the earth at his command, his palace was naturally very splendid, but when Persephone was taken thence that bright summer day, she thought one sunbeam worth all the sparkling diamonds, and one bunch of violets more to be desired than gardens of jeweled flowers.

In the midst of the palace Pluto sat upon a throne of sulphur, which he shared with his queen. He wore a crown of ebony and in his hand he bore a huge key, which gave him somewhat the appearance of a stern jailer who would make flight impossible for any of his charges.

THE GARDEN OF PERSEPHONE.

Here life has death for neighbor,
    And far from eye or ear
Wan waves and wet winds labor,
    Weak ships and spirits steer;
They drift adrift, and whither
They wot not who make thither;
But no such winds blow hither,
    And no such things grow here.

No growth of moor or coppice,
    No heather flower or vine,
But bloomless buds of poppies,
    Green grapes of Proserpine,
Pale beds of blowing rushes
Where no leaf blooms or blushes
Save this whereout she crushes
    For dead men deadly wine.

Pale, beyond porch and portal,
    Crowned with calm leaves, she stands
Who gathers all things mortal
    With cold immortal hands;
Her languid lips are sweeter
Than love's, who fears to greet her,
To men that mix and meet her
    From many times and lands.

> She waits for each and other,
>   She waits for all men born,
> Forgets the earth her mother,
>   The life of fruits and corn;
> And spring and seed and swallow
> Take wing for her and follow
> Where summer song rings hollow,
>   And flowers are put to scorn.
>
> SWINBURNE.

All kinds of attractive dishes were served on his table, but whoever once partook of them might never hope to see the light of earth again.

When Psyche was sent on an errand by Aphrodite to seek out Persephone, she was instructed by a kindly spirit, to take with her a crust for her own refreshment and to decline any food offered in that realm—for it would be the food of death.

> " Then Psyche entered in to Proserpine
>   In the dark house, and straightway did decline
>   With meek denial the luxurious seat,
>   The liberal board for welcome strangers spread,
>   But sate down lowly at the dark queen's feet,
>   And told her tale, and brake her oaten bread."

When a soul was brought to Hades, he must first be rowed over a river, deep and black as night—Acheron, river of woe, whose rapid current defied the bravest swimmer. Charon, a grim boatman, meanly clad, ferried shades across, provided they had a fee for him. To meet this need, relatives put a coin in the mouth of their dead. Lacking a fee, one must wait a hundred years, whereupon the boatman begrudgingly ferried the unfortunate shade over for nothing.

Approaching the throne where Pluto and his queen, robed in black, were seated, shades were questioned first by three judges—Aeacus, Minos, and Rhadamanthus,—kings who had ruled so justly in their earthly kingdoms that they were chosen as judges of Hades. They ascertained by close questioning what the past life of the shade had been, and the decree was announced by Pluto. The guiltless were allowed to pass at once to the Elysian Fields, while all others were doomed to Tartarus, there to meet their fate, were it labor or punishment, or both.

The Elysian Fields were in the west, across the river Lethe, stream of forgetfulness. One drink of its waters eliminated all the sorrow of a life time, and prepared one for the everlasting joy of the Blessed Isles. Here one lived as he had lived on earth, knowing neither grief, sorrow, misery or pain. He never grew old, and in the pleasant fields and quiet groves led a blissful existence. It must be said, however, that the shades were not always contented. Aeneas visited his father there, and Anchises said he would rather be a laborer on earth than to share the joys of the Isle of the Blessed.

Light was supplied to Hades by a sun which shone on no other land; stars twinkled above, but they never looked down on other lands. Everything was apparently provided to make the place attractice. Pluto had once loved a nymph. When she died he changed her into a silver poplar, whole groves of which abounded here. The sacred Styx flowed through this portion of Pluto's realm. An oath sworn by this river was binding even upon the gods.

Sometimes mortal friends of the gods were transplanted to the Elysian Fields without tasting death at all. Here they lived in perpetual spring.

Very different was existence in Tartarus. Thither were dispatched all who had sinned, all who had injured others, all who had lived regardless of their fellow men. No deceit could keep their misdeeds secret. Tartarus was as far below Hades as earth is below heaven. The Cocytus, one of its rivers, was filled by the tears of those doomed to spend eternity within this region.

The Phlegethus was the river which surrounded the dismal place, and it was a stream of liquid fire. Gates of adamant guarded the only entrance, and a fifty-headed hydra watched all who entered. Care, hunger, toil, grief, disease, fear, and remorse crouched around, while the terrible furies goaded on the workers.

Certain special punishments were meted out to those whose

crimes had been flagrant. Tantalus had once been a proud
and wealthy king.   He had even been admitted to the feasts
of the gods, but carried away by these honors, he had stolen
their nectar and ambrosia, had been presumptuous to Zeus,
and had murdered his own son.   For these crimes he was
doomed to stand in a lake whose water reached to his very
chin, but when, consumed with thirst, he tried to drink, the
water always receded.   Delicious grapes hung over his head,
but when he sought to eat them, they rose high above his
reach.   From this story has arisen our word *tantalize.*

TANTALUS.

I at the banquet of the gods have sate
  Above the clouds that shroud these earthly plains,
Their nectar quaffed, and their ambrosia ate,
  And felt Olympian ichor in my veins.

Apollo, like a glory in a gloom,
  Jove's thunderous brow, and Juno's face serene,
Chaste Dian's grace,—the auroral blush and bloom
  That Venus owns,—these mortal eyes have seen.

Mad with desire I strove the charm to seize
  That should again renew to sense and soul
On earth below those heavenly ecstasies—
  And I their nectar and ambrosia stole.

But who against the Gods shall e'er prevail?
  The bliss of heaven on earth we may not own,
Stale tastes the nectar here, the ambrosia stale,
  The ethereal flavor lost, the aroma flown.

And so the gods condemn me here to stand
  Thirsting within the stream that from me flees,—
Hungering 'mid fruits ambrosial that my hand
  Forever vainly reaches out to seize.

O Poets, in whatever realm or clime,
  Pity me—Tantalus—for you must feel
How nature lures us on with dreams sublime,
  And hints the secrets she will ne'er reveal.

STORY.

Sisyphus too, had been a king, most wicked and greatly feared by his people. He was told that his task would be to roll a heavy stone up hill and down on the opposite side. He fancied that this would be an easy undertaking, but someway, each time he got the stone almost to the top of the hill, off it would go, back to the place from which he had started it, and no effort of his could quite make the peak, although each time he thought he was about to succeed.

Some maidens who had killed their husbands were set to fill a bottomless cask which never filled, notwithstanding all their efforts.

Pluto signified death to the Greeks. Naturally therefore, they did not love him. The mere mention of his name would make them shudder and feel chilly on the warmest summer day. They built few temples to him, and only a few statues of the god have been found.

Sacrifices were offered to him at night by priests robed in black. The offerings were invariably black-colored animals —perhaps because the steeds which drew his golden chariot were black, but more probably because everything connected with him was dismal. The cypress, emblem of mourning, was sacred to him.

Persephone, who was gay and loving on earth, grew to share the disposition of her husband when she returned to Hades. Confirming all his decrees, she herself issued others quite as relentless. But instead of his stern expression, her brow was always wrapped in sadness, as though her heart denied the sentences of her lips and the sights that her eyes beheld.

We see, then, that no life was so desirable to the Greek as the one he lived on earth; that while he believed in a continued existence, he would certainly have preferred oblivion to the fate awaiting him unless his life were pure.

THE ISLES OF THE BLEST.

" There was no heavy heat, no cold,
  The dwellers there wax never old,
    Nor wither with the waning time,
  But each man keeps that age he had
    When first he won the fairy clime.
  The night falls never from on high,
    Nor ever burns the heat of noon;
  But such soft light eternally
    Shines, as in silver dawns of June
  Before the sun hath climbed the sky!
  All these their mirth and pleasure made
    Within the plain Elysian,
  The fairest meadow that may be,
  With all green fragrant trees for shade,
    And every scented wind to fan,
    And sweetest flowers to strew the lea;
  The soft winds are their servants fleet
    To fetch them every fruit at will
    And water from the river chill;
  And every bird that singeth sweet,
    Throstle, and merle, and nightingale,
    Brings blossoms from the dewy vale,—
  Lily, and rose, and asphodel,—
    With these doth each guest twine his crown
    And wreathe his cup, and lay him down
  Beside some friend he loveth well."

                        LANG.

CHAPTER XVII.

ORPHEUS, THE WONDERFUL MUSICIAN.

Apollo was, as you know, the leader of the Muses. Now Calliope was the sweetest singer among the nine gifted singers, and the great sun-god became deeply in love with her. She consented to marry him, and their little son was Orpheus. Of course, having the god of music for his father, and the sweet-voiced Calliope for his mother, he himself was a wonderful musician. Apollo gave him a harp, almost as splendid as his own.

As a youth, Orpheus used to play the sweetest strains on his lyre. Even the wild animals would gather around to hear him, and under the spell of his music they would become harmless and affectionate. The birds thought that some new feathered singer had come into their groves, and the fishes paused in their streams to listen; the bees forgot to gather honey from the blossoms, the butterflies stopped fanning through the air; trees and mountains even left their places to hear the harmony Orpheus produced.

Shakespeare sang this song of the wonderful musician:

> "Orpheus with his lute made trees,
> And mountain-tops, that freeze,
> Bow themselves when he did sing:
>
> To his music plants and flowers
> Ever sprung; as sun and showers
> There had made a lasting spring.
>
> Everything that heard him play,
> Even the billows of the sea,
> Hung their heads and then lay by."

So you can well imagine that Orpheus was a remarkable musician, for even our most skillful artists of today experience no such results as these.

Orpheus joined Jason in the expedition for the Golden Fleece. When the Argo was ready to be launched, and the fifty heroes were eager to spring to the oars, their united strength could not start the boat. A large number of workmen and some spectators aided them, but still the vessel stood unyielding. At last the deity aiding Jason whispered to him that the heroes must take their places at the oars, that all the rest must release their hold and that Orpheus must play. This being done, at the first chord from Orpheus' lute, the boat moved, and as he continued to play, it slipped easily from its moorings and glided into the water.

We have seen how Orpheus, producing more alluring music than the sirens, fulfilled a prophecy, and these were changed into rocks.

Now Orpheus had apparently cared for nothing but his music, but one day he beheld a water-nymph, Eurydice, daughter of the sea-god Nereus. He loved her passionately and she soon learned to love him. Their wedding was duly celebrated, but shortly after, the fair Eurydice stepped on a snake concealed in the grass and died directly from its sting.

Orpheus was disconsolate. He wandered around with his lute, playing the most heart-rending strains. At length in his anguish, he wandered to Zeus and besought him to allow him to see his wife, if but for a moment. The mighty god gave his consent, but assured the sorrowing man that it was a most dangerous undertaking. No danger was great enough to deter the musician, and he straightway started for the gloomy realm of Hades. Reaching the gate, Cerberus came to meet him. The dog was cross to mortals, knowing only shades and his master Pluto, but nevertheless, the music Orpheus produced rendered the animal harmless as a young dove or lamb.

Never had the cheerless region heard such dulcet sounds; for a few moments all the grief and sorrows of the comfortless place were forgotten; punishments were suspended, and all listened in wonder to the soft strains.

> " E'en Tantalus ceased from trying to sip
>   The cup that flies from his arid lip;

> Ixion, too, the magic could feel,
> And, for a moment, blocked his wheel;
> Poor Sisyphus, doomed to tumble and toss
> The notable stone that gathers no moss,
> Let go his burden, and turned to hear
> The charming sounds that ravished his ear;
> And even the Furies,—these terrible shrews
> Whom no one before could ever amuse,—
> Each felt for a moment her nature desert her."

Penetrating to the very throne of the dark king and queen, Orpheus poured out his sorrow for the lost Eurydice in such profusion that even the relentless Pluto was moved to help him. Persephone told him that he might regain his wife if he could retrace his steps to earth without once looking back to see if the loved one was following. Promising gladly, all went well until he felt the salt breath of the ocean once again on his brow. Forgetting the gates of Hades were yet unpassed, Orpheus glanced round to see if his wife were there. Instantly she retreated and like a pale phantom glided out of his sight.

Further efforts to recover her he felt to be useless. Well nigh bereft of reason, he led a hermit's life, filling the caves which sheltered him with strange and appealing music. All his passion, his lost love, and his hopelessness were in the strains he played. Birds, beasts, and ocean nymphs tried to soothe his woe, but in vain.

It has been said that followers of Bacchus, angry because he would not play gay music for their festival, finally killed Orpheus and tossed him into the river, while the name Eurydice was last on his lips.

The gods placed his harp in the skies as a constellation, where it shines today on all the trees, stones, and mountains that once listened in raptures to the harmony it gave forth.

NIGHT: THE CAVE OF SLEEP.

In one of the many caves beneath the earth, Thanatos—Mors or Death,—and his twin brother Hypnos—Somnus, or Sleep,—took up their abode.

This cave was far removed from all disturbing cares and sounds; no cock heralded the appearance of the dawn, no breezes swayed tree or branch or vine; conversation of mortals was unknown, while the light of the sun never penetrated the gloom. Twilight reigned forever. Sounds there were in this deep cave, but they were those sounds which lull to sleep, and make deep repose still deeper,—the languid music of waters, the drowsy hum of insects.

> " And more to lull him in his slumber soft,
>   A trickling stream from high rock tumbling down,
>   And ever-drizzling rain upon the loft,
>   Mixt with a murmuring wind, much like the sound
>   Of swarming bees, did cast him in a swoon."

Nox, or Night, mother of these sons, was herself tall and beautiful. She was robed in black, and wore a long veil. Her chariot was black, as were also her noiseless steeds, while the stars were her attendants.

> " I heard the trailing garments of the Night
>   Sweep through her marble halls!
> I saw her sable skirts all fringed with light
>   From the celestial walls."

Before this cave Nox had planted a world of poppies, and at night she went about, unseen, placing drops of their distilled juices on the eye-lids of weary mortals.

Now Sleep was a kindly spirit, gentle and loved by mortals, but Death was grim and cruel, and was feared by all mankind.

Sleep was represented as bearing poppies—emblems of drowsiness—while Death held an inverted torch, indicating that the flame of life had been extinguished.

In one chamber of the cave stood the ebony couch of sleep, its coverlet sprinkled over with bright stars, while black plumes hung over all. In another chamber lay Death, hideous to look upon; for his eyes were hollow, and he was wrapped in a white shroud. In one hand he held an hour-glass; in the other, a sickle.

> " There is a Reaper, whose name is Death,
>   And with his sickle keen
> He reaps the bearded grain at a breath,
>   And the flowers that grow between."

As time went on, people came to think of Death as merely an interlude between life on earth and in the Elysian Fields, and then Death was conceived as a beautiful youth, but still ghastly and deathlike.

Somnus, or Sleep, had three sons: Morpheus, god of dreams, who could imitate persons perfectly in dreams; Icelos, who could take the form of birds, beasts and serpents; and Phantasos, who represented woods, meadows, rivers—in short, nature.

MORPHEUS.

" He, making speedy way through yielding air,
    And through the world of waters wide and deep,
    To Morpheus' house doth hastily repair,
    Amid the bowels of the earth full steep,
    And low, where dawning day doth never peep,
    His dwelling is; there Tethys his wet bed
    Doth ever wash, and Cynthia still doth steep
    In silver dew his ever-drooping head,
While sad Night over him her mantle black doth spread.

Whose double gates he findeth locked fast;
    The one was framed of burnished ivory,
    The other all with silver over-cast;
    And wakeful dogs before them far do lie,
    Watching to banish Care, their enemy
    Who oft is wont to trouble gentle sleep.
    By them the sprite doth pass in quietly,
    And unto Morpheus comes, whom drowned deep
In drowsy fit he finds; of nothing he takes heed.

The messenger approaching to him spake;
But his waste words returned to him in vain:
So sound he slept, that naught might him awake.
Then rudely him he thrust, and pushed with pain,
Whereat he gan to stretch: but he again
Shook him so hard, that forced him to speak.
As one then in a dream, whose dryer brain
Is tossed with troubled sights, and fancies weak,
He mumbled soft, but would not all his silence break.

The sprite then gan more boldly him to wake,
And threatened unto him the dreaded name
Of Hecate: whereat he gan to quake,
And, lifting up his stupid head, with blame
Half angry asked him, for what he came.
"Hither," quoth he, "me Archimago sent,
He that the stubborn sprites can wisely tame,
He bids thee to him send for his intent
A fit false dream, that can delude the sleepers sent."

The god obeyed; and calling forth straightway
A diverse dream out of his prison dark,
Delivered it to him, and down did lay
His heavy head, devoid of careful care;
Whose senses all were straight benumbed and stiff.
He, back returning by the ivory door,
Remounted up as light as cheerful lark;
And on his little wings the dreams he bore
In haste unto his lord, where he him left before.

SPENSER.

The dwelling of Morpheus had two gates. One was made of ivory; dreams passing out of this gate were false and misleading. The other gate was made of horn; dreams issuing thence were true and never failing.

Merely a child in size, furnished with wings for rapid movement, Morpheus was surrounded by all sorts of dreams—happy, pleasing fancies; ugly phantoms; restless, irritating dreams; soothing, restful visions. Sometimes Morpheus was conceived as ever bending over his father, Somnus, carrying out the latter's wishes.

When King Ceyx was obliged to depart on a long sea-voyage, leaving his anxious wife at home, Hera, you will recall, sent a dream to her, acquainting her with the shipwreck.

"The gods could do wonderful things. At a word from Juno, Iris set her beautiful rainbow bridge in the sky, while her sisters, the dark Clouds, gathered together behind it. She came swiftly down the bridge to the earth, then flew toward the cave of Somnus, the god of sleep and dreams. She flew low over the great fields of scarlet poppies—the flowers that bring sleep—and heard the trickling water of the river Lethe, which had its source within the cave of Somnus. Soon she reached the dark, cool silent cave, and there lay Somnus, sleeping very soundly on a great bed heaped high with black feathers. Around the god were dreams of every kind—good dreams and bad ones, beautiful and ugly, true and false. As Iris entered, her coming lighted up the darkness and the wonderful colors of her garments were reflected to the farthest recesses of the cave. She roused Somnus and delivered Juno's message—that night Somnus sent a dream to Halcyone."[1]

This story in one form or another, may be found in all mythologies, and allusions to it occur in many poems.

> "Tired Nature's sweet restorer, balmy sleep!
> He like the world, his ready visit pays
> Where fortune smiles; the wicked he forsakes;
> Swift on his downy pinion flies from woe
> And lights on lips unsullied with a tear.
>
> Night, sable goddess! from her ebon throne,
> In rayless majesty, now stretches forth
> Her leaden scepter o'er a sleeping world,
> Silence, how dead! and darkness how profound!"[2]

---

[1]Hyde: Favorite Greek Myths.
[2]Young: Night Thoughts.

CHAPTER XVIII.

HECATE.

First Witch: "Why, how now, Hecate! you look angerly.

Hecate: "Have I not reason, beldams as you are,
      Saucy and overbold? How did you dare
      To trade and traffic with Macbeth
      In riddles and affairs of death;
      And I, the mistress of your charms,
      The close contriver of all harms,
      Was never called to bear my part,
      Or show the glory of our art?
      And, which is worse, all you have done
      Hath been but for a wayward son,
      Spiteful and wrathful; who, as others do,
      Loves for his own ends, not for you.
      But make amends now: get you gone,
      And at the pit of Acheron
      Meet me i' the morning. Thither he
      Will come to know his destiny.
      Your vessels and your spells provide,
      Your charms and everything beside.
      I am for the air; the night I'll spend
      Unto a dismal and a fatal end:
      Great business must be wrought ere noon.
      Upon the corner of the moon
      There hangs a vaporous drop profound.
      I'll catch it ere it come to ground;
      And that distill'd by magic heights
      Shall raise such artificial sprites
      As by the strength of their illusion
      Shall draw him on to his confusion.
      Hark, I am call'd; my little spirit, see,
      Sits in a foggy cloud, and stays for me."

MACBETH.

HECATE: GODDESS OF THE BLACK ARTS.

Another being connected with the cheerless realm of Pluto
was Hecate. Confounded in some way with the moon, she
came to be regarded as mistress of all magical and mysterious
incantations.

The early Greeks did not understand why on some nights
the moon was only partly seen. Again it shone full in its silver
glory, and sometimes was not visible at all. They fancied
that when not in the heavens, it was doubtless detained in
Hades. Artemis rode across the sky with the moon as her
chariot, but she was goddess of the chase, and during the day
was known to be hunting deer·over hill and dale; Hecate was
devised therefore, it may be, to fill out the tale, and account for
the moon's frequent changes.

She was pictured as a miserable woman whose sole delight
was found in being miserable, and the more wretched she could
make herself, the deeper satisfaction she seemed to find in life.
She was imagined to have a head like a dog, with a crown of
serpents coiled around her locks.

When Ceres lost her daughter, she wandered at length to
the cave of Hecate, questioning her, as she questioned everyone,
whether or not she had seen anything of the child. Hecate replied that nine days earlier she had heard her cries, and thought
it most probable that she had been devoured by some wild
monster. The answer was characteristic of Hecate; she looked
ever on the darkest side of life. She advised Ceres that she
would best take up her abode within her cave and together they
would be the two most wretched women in the world. Attractive as this must have appeared, Ceres preferred to continue her
search, persuading Hecate to join her. Of course the unhappy
woman was loath to leave her cave where everything was so
conducive to misery, but she thought Ceres' grief might en-
shroud her in sufficient gloom, and taking her torch, which in
the bright day cast a lurid light, they started out together.

Hecate hated the sun as much as Pluto possibly could, and
presently she was glad to leave Ceres to seek Persephone all
by herself, while she hurried back to her gloomy cavern.

The Greeks believed that Hecate was seldom seen by mortals, since she wandered around in the deep night. She was

supposed to haunt cross-roads, and places where dire deeds had been committed. Her approach was known by the continued barking of dogs.

Places she was likely to visit were marked by posts having the head of a dog carved on them. She was thought capable of working good as well as ill when so disposed, and naturally people desired to propitiate her favor.

Hecate spent much of her time gathering herbs and plants which possessed magical properties. With these she worked her spells and carried out her designs.

Witchery and magic never had the hold on the Greeks that it came to have on many people during the middle ages. The Greeks had sunny dispositions in the main, and were not haunted by gloomy fears. They believed in the beautiful and were more absorbed with trying to attain it than in seeking to escape the evils of uncanny creatures. After the old gods were cast aside, witchery and sorcery became stronger forces.

Many of the superstitions still afloat in the world can be traced to the time when there was believed to be a charm in odd numbers, and when ghosts and haunted places were firmly believed in.

We shall consider only one more character of Hades, namely, Nemesis, goddess of equity.

NEMESIS.

In these days we have come to recognize a law of compensation in the world. It has often been noted that if one person had great wealth, he frequently had little happiness; if another seemed especially gifted, he might not be blessed with the best health; if a third appeared to have all that life could offer, those who made life alone desirable for him were sometimes taken from him. These might be cited as examples of the compensating law.

Instead of thinking of the matter thus, the early Greeks thought there was a goddess whose function it was to maintain a balance in the affairs of men. She rewarded merit which had not won recognition; she punished pride, arrogance, and presumption. For example, it was Nemesis who avenged the insult Niobe gave to Latona by taking away her children, while

Apollo and Diana were simply the agencies through which she worked.

The Greeks believed that a true balance was necessary in a well ordered civilization—a compensating force. They regarded it as wholly fitting that one who had some particular thing should be deprived of something else, which would serve to keep the balance true.

Nemesis was thought of as tall and queenly, with a diadem upon her brow, and preserving a quiet, thoughtful demeanor.

DEMETER.

CHAPTER XIX.

HERCULES: THE NATIONAL HERO OF EARLY GREECE.

Hercules was the son of Zeus and a mortal princess. He was, then, a hero, instead of a god. So brave did he prove, and so strong did he become, that his triumphs quite eclipsed the undertakings of other early heroes of Hellas. For this reason Hercules became the great and favorite hero of Greek story.

Hera hated him from his birth, and tried hard to think of some means by which he might be destroyed as a child. Finally when he was eight months old, she sent two serpents to sting him in his cradle. You see these divinities could be very revengeful when they were displeased. But the hero-baby wakened, clutched one serpent in either hand and strangled them to death. Hera saw that she could not destroy the child, so she determined to annoy him in as many ways as possible and so make his life as unbearable as she could.

When a boy, Hercules had the best teachers in the land. He was taught to stand in the chariot, to shoot well, to wrestle, and to fight with lance and shield. By this kind of training he became perfectly developed physically, and possessed great endurance. The accomplishments of his time were not forgotten, and his music teacher was a brother of Orpheus. Being reproved by this teacher one day for some trivial mistake, Hercules in anger struck the man with his lute. Now it was impossible for this strong youth to strike anything lightly, and the musician fell dead, to the great horror of his pupil. For this deed, the boy was filled with remorse. It seemed best to send him into the mountains for a time, to learn from the herders what they could teach.

Here in a vision one night the youth saw two roads stretching out before him: one was smooth and pleasant, and led into a city lying far down into a valley; the other road followed over hills and rocks and ended at last in the clouds themselves. Two women stood by, each urging him to take the road by which she stood. One was called by a name which we might interpret Pleasure: she pointed to her broad road, smooth and even, and asked Hercules to see into what shady streets it finally led. In this city, she assured him, was to be found all enjoyment and all pleasure, and thither, should he choose her road, she would guide his steps.

The other woman was called by a name which we may translate Duty: she said her road was rough and stony, that it often led over hills and steep mountains, and reached wholly away from personal desire and ease. She said the joys of the city to which Pleasure led were but empty, shallow, fleeting joys which would not satisfy, while her road, though thorny, came finally to the land of the gods, and to immortality. Hercules answered that he would follow her.

Now at his birth, Hera had exacted an oath from Zeus whereby Hercules was bound to serve his cousin, Eurystheus, king of Argos, for a given term of years. This man was a person of no strength, either of mind, body or character.

The mighty Jove discovered Hera's scheme when it was too late to alter it—for he had been induced to swear by the river Styx. The queen of heaven began to urge this king to exact the service due him, thinking thus to humiliate the young man who was even now conceded to be the most wonderful man in all the world. Hercules at first promptly refused to serve any one. Then Hera sent a fit of madness on him. Lucid at last, he consulted an oracle, and was told that since it had been decreed by the gods that he should serve a certain number of years, peace would never come to him save by yielding to this decree, in fulfillment of duty. Finally he conquered his pride and spirit sufficiently to comply.

Presenting himself at the court of Argos, Eurystheus saw at a glance the wide difference between his cousin and himself. Hercules was taller than any other man in Greece, and his muscles had been so developed that they were strong as iron bands; he towered above the king not only physically but in his courage and mental attainments, so Eurystheus wished for nothing so much as to get him away, out of his kingdom.

Being asked what he would have his cousin do, Eurystheus tried to think of something desperately hard, in performance of which the young giant might be overcome. Suddenly he bethought him of a lion which had been working havoc in a wide district of his land. It had devoured many people already and he thought it likely that it would add Hercules to its long list of victims, so in a loud voice he commanded Hercules to bring him this lion's skin!

That you may understand how brave the king really was, no sooner was Hercules departed on his errand than Eurytheus had three hundred subjects at work, constructing a huge brass tower. One opening alone it should have, and that near the top. And for what, think you, did he erect this tower? That he might withdraw into it upon Hercules' return—if indeed he should return—for he feared the young giant's strength.

Since he was obliged to serve, Hercules was glad that his task was worthy of his strength and pride, at least, and quite fearless, he journeyed to the neighborhood of the terrible Nemean lion. He found that it had consumed whole herds of cattle and flocks of sheep, while any who tried to stay its ravages were crushed by its mighty jaws. It was said to have a skin which no arrow, however keen, could penetrate, so Hercules was obliged to find some other method of attacking it. He pulled up a forest tree as he journeyed, bringing it up, roots and all, with one jerk of his powerful arm. He trimmed it down and it became his favorite club, usually seen in pictures of him.

Finding the lion's lair, he closed all entrances save one, and walking boldly into that, he seized the lion by the throat and strangled it to death, as he had strangled the serpents when a baby. Taking its skin, he returned to Argos. Arriving suddenly in the city, the king had no knowledge of his coming, and hence no opportunity to climb into his tower. The first thing he knew there was a great commotion in the streets, and there came Hercules, walking right up to the palace with the skin of the Nemean lion thrown over his shoulder. The skin frightened the king almost as much as the lion could have done. He commanded Hercules never to bring his trophies within the city walls henceforth, but to display them outside the fortifications. He could not get the hero off again too soon, so he gave him a task he supposed impossible, commanding him to slay the Lernean Hydra!

Now killing the lion was mere pastime compared with slaying this hydra, for it was a monster serpent, having many heads—some say seven, some nine, and some again say fifty; but it does not matter very much, for the trouble was that as rapidly as one of its numerous heads was cut off, two more grew in its place. However, Hercules regarded all things as possible and first he made himself a robe of the lion's skin. A skin which was proof against arrows would certainly protect him from the hydra's fangs. Having cut off one or two of the serpent's heads and seen others immediately grow in their places, Hercules had to devise some other method of dealing with the matter. He believed that if the wounds were instantly seared with a red hot iron, the new heads could not grow. This proved true, and in this way he finally slew the hydra. This was a very great triumph for the mere breath of the creature made a large tract of land uninhabitable. It poisoned the water all around so that the cattle died in vast numbers, and the people who could not get away, perished.

This time the king had knowledge of the hero's approach. He probably had maintained sentinels on every road leading into his capital since Hercules' last departure, for certainly he would not care for many such frights as the skin of the Nemean lion and Hercules together had given him. So from the brazen tower he heard of the victory of the hydra, and it is to be feared that he did not rejoice as greatly as he should have done. However, from the tower he commanded Hercules to bring him the Arcadian Stag *alive!* How he ever dared to risk anything being brought to him alive, I cannot fathom, but it is likely that he thought Hercules would spend the rest of his life pursuing this fleet deer, which scarcely touched the earth with its hoofs when it sped through the air. Only a few had ever claimed to see it, and most people thought it a hunter's story; but those who had seen, said it had hoofs of brass and antlers of pure gold. To have brought this stag in any condition would have been a stupendous task, but to bring it *alive!* Yet Hercules had no choice.

After watching for many days, Hercules at last caught sight of the fabled stag, and it was a sight to reward a long vigil. It was a noble animal, and its antlers gleamed about its head like a halo of the sun. Knowing that he might never get sight of it again, Hercules started after, and what a chase it led him! For one long year, scarce stopping for food or sleep, he followed it over hill and dale, across rivers and over mountains. At last he drove it into a snowdrift far to the north, and so captured it, wearied and exhausted.

This is another version of the story:

"The Arcadian stag was sacred to Diana; and no wonder, for besides being so swift that no horse or hound could follow it, it had brazen feet and horns of pure gold.

" Of course this labor was not so dangerous as the others had been, but apparently more utterly impossible.

" Impossible as it was, however, Hercules had to try. Had he been ordered to bring the stag to Argos dead, he might perhaps hope to catch it with an arrow; but his orders were to bring it alive. So, having started it from its lair, he followed it with his utmost speed and skill. At first he tried to run it down; but the stag was not only the swifter, but had as much endurance as he. Then he tried to drive it to bay, but it always managed to escape out of the seemingly most helpless corners. He tried to catch it asleep; but his slightest and most distant movement startled it, and off it raced again. All the arts of the deer-stalker he put in practice, but all in vain. And thus he hunted the stag of Arcadia, scarce resting day or night for a whole year. It looked as if he were to spend the rest of his life in pursuing what was not to be caught by mortal man; and the worst of it was that, while there was some real use in destroying wild beasts and monsters, lion and hydra, his present labor, even if accomplished, would be of no use at all.

" Still it had to be attempted; and I suppose you have guessed that he succeeded, and that it was in some wonderful way. Well—he did succeed at last, but it was not in a wonderful way at all. It was just by not giving in. One of the two had to give in, and it was not Hercules. One day he managed to drive the stag into a trap and to seize it by the horns.

" As he was returning to Argos, dragging the stag, he met a tall and beautiful woman, dressed for the chase, and carrying a bow and quiver. As soon as her eyes fell upon the struggling stag she frowned terribly.

"'What mortal are you,' she asked, 'who have dared lay hands on my own stag sacred to me, who am Diana? Loose it, and let it go.'

"Hercules sighed. 'I would gladly do so, great goddess, but it is not in my power.'

"'Not in your power to open your hand?' she asked, in angry surprise. 'We will soon see that,' and she seized her stag by the other horn to pull it away.

"'I am sorry to oppose a goddess; but I have got to bring this stag to Argos, and neither gods nor men shall prevent me, so long as I am alive,' answered Hercules.

"'I am Diana,' she said again, 'and I command you to let the stag go.'

"'And I,' said he, 'am only Hercules, the servant of Eurystheus, and therefore I cannot let it go.'

"'Then I wish,' said Diana, 'that any of the gods had so faithful a servant as has Eurystheus! So you are Hercules?' her frown changing to a smile; 'then I give you the stag, for the sake of the oracle of my brother Apollo. I am only a goddess; you are a man who has conquered himself, and whom therefore even the gods must obey.'

"So saying, she vanished. And the stag no longer struggled for freedom, but followed Hercules to Argos as gently and lovingly as a tame fawn."[1]

"Eurystheus began to realize that no matter what sort of a task he planned for Hercules, some means would be found for accomplishing it. While the deer had been fleet of foot, yet it was not a dangerous animal to encounter. Now the king commanded that Hercules bring him the Erymanthian boar alive! The ferocious beast lived in a cave in the Erymanthian mountain, down whose side flowed a river bearing the same name. It ravaged all the valley below, and no one lived on the rugged peak.

"Hercules was fast growing out of sorts with life. Why should he, a man of prodigious strength, steadfast of purpose and having lofty ambitions, why should he be ensnaring wild beasts for the entertainment and gratification of a foolish, cowardly king? He decided to visit his old friend and teacher,

[1] Francillon: Gods and Heroes.

Chiron, a centaur, and this gives us an opportunity to find out what the centaurs were like. They had heads, arms and shoulders like men, and legs and bodies like a horse. The Greeks were very proud of the horse which Neptune had called into being for them, and they thought the centaurs acceptable companions anywhere. The famous teacher Chiron was most noted of their race, for he kept a school attended by most of the old Greek heroes.

"This learned schoolmaster was one of the people, or quadrupeds, called Centaurs. He lived in a cavern, and had the body and legs of a white horse, with the head and shoulders of a man. His name was Chiron; and, in spite of his odd appearance, he was a very excellent teacher, and had several scholars who afterwards did him credit by making a great figure in the world. The famous Hercules was one of them, and so was Achilles, and Philoctetes, and Aesculapius, who acquired immense repute as a doctor. The good Chiron taught his pupils how to play upon a harp, and how to cure diseases, and how to use the sword and shield, together with various other branches of education, in which the lads of those days used to be instructed, instead of writing and arithmetic.

"I have sometimes suspected that Chiron was really not very different from other people, but that, being a kind-hearted and merry old fellow, he was in the habit of making believe that he was a horse, and scrambling about the school-room on all fours, letting the little boys ride on his back. And so, when his scholars had grown up, and grown old, and were trotting their grandchildren on their knees, they told them about the sports of their school days; and these young folks took the idea that their grandfathers had been taught their letters by a Centaur, half man and half horse. Little children, not quite understanding what is said to them, often get absurd notions into their heads, you know.

"Be that as it may, it has always been told for a fact, and always will be told, as long as the world lasts, that Chiron, with the head of a schoolmaster, had the legs and body of a horse."[2]

Hercules determined to visit Chiron and get what comfort he could from him.

---

[2] Hawthorne: Tanglewood Tales.

A barrel of wine, common property of all the Centaurs who lived on the mountains, was in Chiron's cavern, and to this Hercules helped himself. The other Centaurs smelled the wine far off, and rushed into the cave. In their rage they did not stop to know who the giant was, but made for him, right and left. Hercules struck out in all directions, and soon centaurs of various sizes lay stretched upon the ground. Sad to tell, in the scramble, Chiron scratched himself with one of Hercules' poisonous arrows and shortly died of the wound. Thus ended the race of Centaurs, and heroes, too, apparently. None seemed to have appeared when there was no longer a suitable school for them to attend.

Saddened by the loss of his old friend, Hercules set out for the wild boar. When the snows of winter came, it was held a prisoner in its cave. It was then that Hercules captured it and returned to the king.

Perhaps the severe storms of winter had interfered with the king's watchmen. Anyway, you can imagine Eurystheus' feelings when the hero approached him dragging behind him the most dangerous boar in all the land! He whisked into his brass tower quicker than lightning, but Hercules pretended not to have seen him, and cried: " Why, that brass tower will be the very place to keep this wild boar!" and thereupon threw him in after Eurystheus. It is remarkable that the poor man did not lose his reason. But the boar was so frightened that it crouched down beside him, and did him no harm, although we may be sure the king did not trust long to its friendship.

Eurystheus was now so angry that he racked his brains to conjure up the most disagreeable task conceivable for Hercules, At last he had it. He commanded him to clean the Augean stables.

King Augeus ruled in Elis. He was a son of Apollo, and he had so many cattle that no one had ever been able to count them. At night they flocked into his stables from all directions, as the fleecy clouds gather before the wind. Some of his bulls were as white as snow, and one was said to gleam far off like a star. These stables had never been cleaned, and this was the task the king devised for Hercules.

Without delay the hero went to work to change the course

of a nearby river. Damming up its old channel, he directed its current to flow through the stables, and in this way, cleanse them. The river emptied at last near Sicily, and the fertility of that island is said to be due to the barn litter washed down from the Augean stables.

Eurystheus in despair, set him next to drive away the Stymphalian birds. These mighty birds had talons of iron and feathers like arrows. Flying above, they could send their flesh-piercing feathers down to the injury of all below. Frequently they would swoop down in a neighborhood and carry little children away to their nests, later to be cruelly devoured. They lived around a pool in the Stymphalian valley. Protected by a huge shield, Hercules rang a bell incessantly, making such an unearthly din that most of the frightened birds, finding their feathers no avail, flew off to the isle of Mars, while the rest were easily shot.

His seventh task was to capture the Cretan bull. Years before, Minos II., grandson of him who judged the dead in Hades, aspired to be king of Crete. Upon being crowned, he hastened to the shore to make an offering to Jupiter. He called upon the sea to produce an offering worthy of the god and Neptune caused a snow-white bull to appear. Struck by its beauty, Minos determined to keep it for himself and substitute something else in its place. This so incensed Neptune that he drove the bull mad and sent it raging around the island.

You may remember the monster that Theseus killed, by the aid of Ariadne. It was an offspring of the mad Cretan bull.

Hercules went to meet it with simply his club—the old forest tree uprooted. Even this he cast aside as it came bellowing toward him. As he took it fearlessly by the horns, it recognized him as its master, and followed him like a gentle lamb.

His eighth task was to capture the horses of Diomedes. Diomedes was the cruel king of Thrace. He was said to be the son of Mars, who, you will remember, was born in that wild, tempestuous country. He had two horses which were very fierce in battle, and people believed the reason they were so wild was that they were fed on human beings who chanced to be shipwrecked on the Thracian shore. Since its coast was very rocky, many were cast upon its inhospitable banks.

Hercules overcame the guards of the horses, and led them easily to the shore—although ordinarily they had to be held by iron chains, and only the king could drive them. Diomedes and his subjects became aware of an invading stranger and rushed to the coast. Hercules overcame them in turn, and brought the steeds to Eurystheus, who doubtless was persuaded to peep out at them from the secure brass tower.

Eight labors had now been accomplished, and they had taken eight long years. We cannot wonder that Hercules despaired of ever earning his release, while we are forced to admit that Eurystheus exercised originality and ingenuity in keeping him so constantly occupied.

The story of the ninth labor has been recounted in the following way:

"Soon after the capture of the horses of Diomedes, Hercules was sent to the country of the Amazons to get Queen Hippolyte's girdle.

"The Amazons were a race of women who delighted in warfare and hunting. They lived at some distance from Greece, on the Caucasian Mountains, and on the borders of the Black Sea. Their Queen, Hippolyte, had a very famous girdle, which was a gift to her from Mars, the war-god. It was said to be some magic power of this girdle which made the onslaught of the Amazons so like a rushing, irresistible storm. The Greeks, in their wars, had more than once found themselves opposed to the Amazons, and knew them as a formidable enemy.

"The daughter of Eurystheus, who was a princess, thought that Hercules could not do a better service for the Greeks than to secure this girdle of Queen Hippolyte. So Eurystheus sent him for it.

"Hercules, therefore, crossed the Black Sea, and went to the country of the Amazons. He anchored his ship in the harbor, not far from the queen's palace, and Queen Hippolyte and some of her women went on board, to see who had come among them. The queen, who was brave herself, and admired courage in others, welcomed the famous Hercules and gave him the girdle. But one of the Amazons, seeing the queen on board the ship, raised a cry that a stranger was carrying off their queen by force.   The Amazons then armed themselves and flew toward the ship in all directions.   In spite of this, Hercules escaped with the girdle—although not without fighting,—and was soon crossing the Black Sea on his way home.

"Reaching the court, he presented the famous girdle, which was set with precious stones and heavy with gold, to the daughter of the king.   And so ended his ninth labor."[3]

[3]Hyde: Favorite Greek Myths.

CERBERUS.

CHAPTER XX.

THE REMAINING LABORS.

Hercules had now relieved Greece and all nearby countries of dangerous creatures, and the king began to feel anxious lest difficult tasks would fail him. You can imagine, then, how he welcomed a stranger to his court who told stirring tales of a mighty giant who lived in Gades. Now Gades was the old name for Cadiz, which is, as you all know, in Spain. Consequently it was considered quite the end of the earth. "Go to Gades," cried Eurystheus to Hercules. "Bring me the cattle of Geryon."

Geryon was a giant possessed of three bodies, three heads, six arms, six limbs, and a pair of wings; so you see he was rather well prepared for a hand-to-hand conflict.

Hercules borrowed the golden boat in which Apollo rode each night from west to east, that he might be ready for the next day's journey. This boat was most convenient of its kind, for it expanded or contracted to suit the burden it bore.

Coming to the end of the sea, Hercules made the opening now known as the Straits of Gibraltar, to enable ships to pass into the ocean. Then he sought for the cattle he had been sent to find.

First a two-headed dog attacked him; this he promptly killed with his club; then a herdsman appeared, uglier than the dog. Finally Geryon himself spied a stranger and made for him with all his bodies, heads, arms, and legs; but for him Hercules had brought one of his poisonous arrows, and giant though he was, he was shortly translated to some division of Pluto's realm.

A greater problem now confronted the mighty hero—that of transporting his herds, numbering far into the thousands, to the king of Argos. At last he succeeded in accomplishing this too, but if you will look at your map and trace a line from Cadiz to Greece, then think what it would mean to drive, not five thousand but five cattle thence, you will realize what a wonderful man was Hercules.

The Golden Apples of the Hesperides.

His eleventh labor was perhaps most interesting of all: to secure some of the golden apples from the garden of Hesperides.

It seems that when Hera was married, on the very day of her wedding, she was given a tree which yielded golden apples. Now it is often the case that when things are rare and difficult to obtain, they acquire a fabulous value. For instance, we have heard of people sending long distances to procure the seeds of dandelions, and growing the blossoms with great care in their gardens, and yet many of us have tried diligently to free our lawns from the same bits of yellow. The truth in this instance is that in one locality the flower is so rare that it awakens admiration, and in the other, so common that it is discarded as a weed. To return to the apples. Hera did not wish every god and many mortals growing golden apples, for then her gift, so marvellous even in the day of wonders, would lose its interest and become ordinary. So the tree with its golden fruit was placed on an island in the western sea, where the sun's last rays might be reflected in all its branches. The three daughters of Atlas, called the Hesperides, were set to watch over the lovely tree, and to aid them, a hundred-headed dragon was placed in the garden, to protect it from invading foes. Few knew of the garden, although it was extolled in song and story, and ambitious youths often planned to set out to find it, and to secure an apple or two for their sweethearts, but most of them became absorbed in matters nearer home, and tradition ran that the rest furnished a welcome meal for the hundred-headed dragon. However that may be, when Eurystheus commanded Hercules to bring him some of the golden apples, he knew no more where they were than you would know today, were you to receive the same commission, but he supposed it would be possible to ascertain. So according to his habit when he was given a task, he at once got about it, and as he journeyed away, he often asked people this question: " Where are the apples of the Hesperides? "

Some said they were in the north, others said in the west, and some simply shook their heads and hurried along, for they did not like the size of the club Hercules carried.

To be safe, he took a north-westerly course, and continued until he came upon some lovely nymphs, making garlands of flowers. To them he put this question. Now the nymphs thought Hercules much too promising a man to become the meal of any dragon, quite regardless of how many heads he boasted, so they told him of all the dangers he would encounter should he continue in his purpose. In every way they thought to discourage him in this wild adventure. Hercules listened to them, then smiled and did what for him was a rare thing: he sat down and told these sea-nymphs of all the terrors he had met, and how, since a babe in the cradle, his life had been made up largely of conflicts and difficult problems. He told of the terrible lion, whose skin he still wore; of the hydra, into whose blood he had dipped his fatal arrows; of the fleet stag which had led him such a chase, over much of Europe indeed before it was finally captured. Then he described the boar and explained how the snows of winter had aided him in trapping it at last—and we shall hope he told about dropping it down upon the cowardly king in the brazen tank. When he mentioned having cleaned some stables, one of the sea-nymphs tossed her pretty head and said that most country swains could match him in that, but when he quietly went on to tell of the mighty river he had turned out of its course in order to cleanse them, she doubtless changed her mind. The birds with arrow-tipped feathers, the Cretan bull, and the fiery steeds that had yielded submissively to a strong fearless hand,— these were described in turn. But when he related the difficulties of procuring the girdle of the Amazon queen, the nymphs could not understand why any princess wanted it, unless like Venus' girdle it would make all love her when she wore it.

Hercules' last adventure with the five thousand cattle taken from the giant Geryon was fresh in mind. You see it had not been like taking something away from a rightful owner, for this terrible giant stole all the cattle he could lay hands upon, and since he had three pairs of hands, that amounted to thousands in course of a few years. He killed all the rightful owners, so really Hercules had done the world a good turn by making way with him. Much did he tell the maidens of the western land where the dreaded Geryon had lived.

While he told them these stories, the nymphs decked him with their bright garlands, and feasted him on delicious grapes. They thought him very brave and noble, and perhaps we too are glad that the mighty Hercules had not dwelt among monsters so long that he could be wholly impervious to the lively nymphs with their soft, winning ways. There is something very human and appealing in this great child of nature here, telling of his exploits, without pride or boasting, showing how his victories already won had prepared him for this, his greatest undertaking so far. He appeals to us far more in this light than when overcoming the fiercest monster.

When they were convinced that nothing would move him from his purpose, they told him to follow the river until he came to the sea, and there he would be likely to find the Old Man of the Sea—Nereus—asleep. If he would only hold him fast enough so he could not make an escape, he could tell him where to find the garden of the Hesperides.

Accordingly Hercules took leave of the sea-nymphs, with expressions of gratification for their kindness, and sought the Old Man of the Sea. Sure enough, he beheld a funny old man asleep; his hair was a deep blue, and his beard was snowy white. Does not that suggest a foaming billow? Hercules seized his arms firmly and asked "Where are the apples of the Hesperides?" Now the old man of the sea had an unpleasant habit of changing his form when any one bothered him with questions, because in the first place he wished to sleep undisturbed, and in the second place, he did not wish to reveal his secrets, for then, you see, they would no longer be secrets. So Hercules immediately found himself clutching a screaming sea-gull; nevertheless, he clutched the tighter; then Nereus became a roaring sea-horse, then a serpent, and finally a reef of sea-moss, but Hercules held him close. Seeing that nothing would frighten him away, Nereus took his own form again, and asked him in disgust what in the world he was bothering him for, and why, by the blue sea's sparkling waters, he clutched his arm as though he were standing by the yawning mouth of Hades? Then for the first time, Hercules had an opportunity to explain his errand, and Nereus told him how to reach Atlas, who alone could get the apples for him.

Journeying thither, Hercules came upon Prometheus, still bound to the rock, where we left him in an earlier chapter. It was easy for Hercules to release him, just as had been foretold, and Prometheus, in gratitude, assisted him with what information he could give.

To reach Atlas, Hercules had to pass through the land of the Pygmies, who lived, as you will remember, to the south of Greece. These Pygmies were tiny people, something like Gulliver's Lilliputians. They had serious trouble in protecting themselves from the large sized people who often came into their country and annoyed them, and again, from great numbers of cranes which swooped down upon their fields of grain —quite destroying them. So at last they had engaged a giant, Antaeus by name, whose duty it was to protect them from any invading thing. One glimpse of Hercules brought cries for Antaeus from all sides. We know that Hercules wished only to pass through their land in order that he might find Atlas, but the Pygmies did not know, nor did they stop to find out. They roused Antaeus who flew at Hercules with terrible fury. Now this giant differed from other giants, in that every time he was thrown to the earth he gained new strength, so that being thrown down five times, he would be just five times stronger than he was in the beginning. It was quite a problem to deal with a giant possessing such a nature. It was said that he was a child of Gaea, or earth, and that she strengthened him each time he was thrown against her. Hercules, perceiving the difficulty, held him high in the air and in that way overcame him.

Without further adventure, the lofty form of Atlas dawned at last upon his vision. There he stood, his feet on the earth, his head in the clouds, supporting the skies upon his shoulder. Hercules shouted to him his errand. Atlas shouted back that if Hercules could support the heavens a little while, he, the only one who could enter the gardens of the Hesperides without making a dinner for the hundred-headed dragon, would get the apples for our hero. For once Hercules hesitated. Did he dare attempt to hold the universe in place while Atlas went on his errand? Atlas called him up on the highest mountain, and, climbing to its loftiest peak, Hercules managed to take the burden. But a few stars were shaken out of place, and the clouds were driven about somewhat, although there was no wind stirring.

Atlas planted his huge feet in the ocean, whose water came only to his waist, and a few strides brought him to the tree where hung the tempting apples. The Hesperides were dancing around it, singing one of their songs. They knew Atlas, since he was their father, yet occupied with holding the heavens in place, they had little opportunity to see him. The dragon, which at the first sound of footsteps, had thrust its hundred heads out in every direction, seeing only Atlas, withdrew at once. He plucked three of the apples from the treasured tree and strode away.

Now Hercules was wellnigh spent. The burden of the skies bore down upon him with a weight he had never known. You can imagine how he welcomed Atlas when his tall head once more appeared. But Atlas had found liberty too sweet; he told Hercules that he was tired of holding up the heavens anyway and that he would just step over and give the apples to Eurystheus himself, while for the next few hundred years Hercules might serve his turn holding the world in place.

Inwardly Hercules trembled so that all the stars and most of the planets, day though it was, appeared to see what was the matter. Outwardly, however, he was calm and willing. He asked Atlas to wait a moment, if he would, and let him make a cushion of his lion's skin, so that his shoulders would not feel the burden quite so much. Accommodating him, Atlas slipped into place for the minute, while Hercules, snatching up the apples thrown on the ground, rushed away as fast as ever he could. How Atlas stormed at him! He ordered him to come back, and scolded him furiously. Long years after, when thunder rumbled in the distant mountains, people said it was Atlas storming after Hercules.

The Song of the Hesperides.

" We sing of the old, we sing of the new,—
Our joys are many, our sorrows are few;
    Singing, dancing,
    All hearts entrancing,
We wait to welcome the good and the true.

The daylight is waning, the evening is here,
The sun will soon set, the stars will appear.
    Singing, dancing,
    All hearts entrancing,
We wait for the dawn of a glad new year.

The tree shall wither, the apples shall fall,
Sorrow shall come, and death shall call,
    Alarming, grieving.
    All hearts deceiving,—
But hope shall abide to comfort us all.

Soon the tale shall be told, the song shall be sung,
The bow shall be broken, the harp unstrung,
    Alarming, grieving,
    All hearts deceiving,
Till every joy to the winds shall be flung.

But a new tree shall spring from the roots of the old,
And many a blossom its leaves shall unfold,
    Cheering, gladdening,
    With joy maddening,—
For its boughs shall be laden with apples of gold."

As for Eurystheus, when he beheld the golden apples, he
simply gasped: " Bring me the dog Cerberus, from Hades,"
adding softly to himself: " None ever returns from Hades,
for that means death."

It had been foretold that when Hercules had successfully
performed twelve labors, he would be released from his service
to the king, and would be once more free to follow his own
course of life. When he received his last commission, therefore, he was determined to move heaven or hell to accomplish

it. He set out at once for Hades. At the gate Cerberus came bounding to meet him, but Hercules gave him such a blow with his club that it required all three heads for some minutes at work to tell what had happened. On Hercules strode to the very throne of Pluto himself. There he stated his errand —to take Cerberus to earth!

Pluto was so dumbfounded that he granted the request before he realized what he had said, and without waiting for him to recover, Hercules seized the dog by its serpent tail, and strode on with it to earth.

Dragging that monster into Eurystheus' court, the king ashy white and trembling in every limb, ordered him out of his sight forever. We may be sure that this was a welcome command.

From this time forth, Hercules was at the call of many nations, aiding them to rid their lands of monsters, and they seem to have gotten them pretty generally destroyed. Ages after, we find some monsters mentioned in northern lands, but whether they were the last of the race that once infested Greece, or whether they always belonged to the northland, is one of the many unanswered questions.

Finally Hercules was taken up to Mount Olympus, where Juno, to atone for her actions, gave him Hebe for his wife.

> " Deep degraded to a coward's slave,
> Endless contests bore Alcides brave,
> Through the thorny path of suffering led;
> Slew the Hydra, crushed the lion's might,
> Threw himself, to bring his friend to light,
> Living, in the skiff that bears the dead.
> All the torments, every toil of earth
> Juno's hatred on him could impose,
> Well he bore them, from his fated birth
> To life's grandly mournful close."

Some have seen in the labors of Hercules, sun-myths, where light overcomes darkness, night and gloom. They probably have several origins, for instance, the boar on the mountain might easily have been the river flowing down its side, when swollen by winter snows and spring rains. The hydra was possibly a marshy exhalation, giving birth to fevers and disease, which vanished when the land was cleared up and drained. In accounting for these stories, we must remember that they grew up in an age when people wrapped everything in mystery, and were very credulous. Then again, they worshipped heroic strength, as all nations seem to have done at some stage of their development. Samson was the giant of the Hebrews; Beowulf of the Saxons, and their victories were not entirely different from those of Hercules.

·And are these *all* the stories of Greek Mythology? By no means. It would be impossible to compass them all, and the same tales are told again and again, with infinite variety. Poets have retold them, and have changed each into many a key. Sometimes a mere reference to one of these old-time stories brightens up a dreary page, wearisome indeed without it.

It is wonderful to think how these fanciful beliefs came into being. It is even quite as wonderful to realize how much they have meant to humanity in later years, making life more pleasurable to all who know them.

We may think of mythology as a mighty stream, giving freely of its refreshing waters to all who are athirst; we may think of it as an inexhaustible treasure-box, whose rare gems never lose their luster with the lapse of time, but by their beauty and scintillating rays rest eyes wearied with sad and sordid sights. These myths belong to the starry circlet of tales which never grow old, and they carry a message to the responsive of all ages. Each finds among them what he alone seeks, and the sun, moon and stars, each hill and vale—the very air we breathe, grow to have fresh significance when seen reflected in the mirror of Greek Mythology.

I know it all is true.   For I have seen
The light upon the Aegean's purple waves,
And I have heard the silence of the caves
Where wreathed sarcophagi in darkness lean;
And I have smelt the breath that from the green
Slopes of Hymettus all my sense enslaves.
And in Dodona's whispering forest naves
Felt the dim Presences that hold demesne.

And now I know 'tis more than an old song
Wrought by a poet of his sweet desire—
For Pan still wanders the slow stream along,
Bacchantes dance round every midnight fire;
And from the hills where purple shadows throng
Steals the low music of a vanished lyre.

ARTHUR DAVIDSON FISKE.

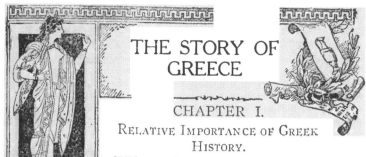

THE STORY OF GREECE

CHAPTER I.

RELATIVE IMPORTANCE OF GREEK HISTORY.

WE turn from the earliest group of nations to trace the development of classical civilization as evolved on Greek and, later, on Roman soil. Europe, rather than Asia and Africa, henceforth demands attention, and of all European peoples to emerge from barbarism, earliest were the Greeks.

There are many reasons why the history of the ancient Greeks has lively interest for us today. In the first place the Greeks, like ourselves, belonged to the Aryan race—the great white race which has peopled Europe and America, and whose civilization dominates the foremost nations of the present time. Aside from a bond of racial kinship, we sympathize deeply with the attitude of the early Greek, who wondered at everything around him, and set himself to the task of discovering causes and effects, differences and relationships, after the manner of the scientific inquirer today.

Again, the early Greeks possessed a quick appreciation of beauty and a rare sense of proportion—qualities stimulated by the nature of the land wherein they dwelt. Because they were thus gifted, the people as a whole attained more nearly to perfection in whatever they attempted than have other nations. The most perfect language so far evolved is the Greek language; the noblest literature, the Greek literature. The finest specimens of sculpture are those which remain to us of Greek execution; the greatest philosophers the world has yet produced have been Greek philosophers. In the domain of civil life the Greeks strove for equality, and they tried many experiments in government which we may still study with profit.

" They had faults in abundance, and a great part of their history is the history of discord and violence. But in the midst of these evils we shall meet with instances of the most striking goodness; and while the vices of the Greeks belonged to other ancient nations, their good points raised them in many respects above all the rest of mankind. No other race ever

did so many different things as well as the Greeks. They were
the first people who thought of finding out the truth and the reason in everything. Busy men in our own day take pleasure in
what remains of Greek poetry and history, and artists know
that they can never make anything more beautiful than what
is left of Greek sculpture. Men will always be interested in
ancient Greece, not only because the Greeks were so bright and
so clever themselves, but because so many things which we value
most in our own life, such as the desire for knowledge, the
power of speaking eloquently, and the arts of music and painting, have come down to us from the Greeks." [1]

Since the civilization we possess has been inherited largely
from the Greeks, and our debt to them is greater than to any
other people, it is natural that we should wish to know by what
successive steps these children of the Aryan race, these first
scientific inquirers after truth, came into an understanding of
the world around them; how they organized themselves into
little states, and attained to a superior degree of civilization.
We can only hope to consider the general development of their
race, establishing certain landmarks which shall serve to guide
all our subsequent study of this ancient people. The importance of our subject, however, cannot be too often called to
mind, for without some understanding of Greek history it is
not possible to comprehend modern civilization. Among the
Greeks modern civilization had its beginnings.

While the influence of oriental progress swept westward,
we shall find that whatever ideas came to Greece from Egypt or
western Asia underwent such changes that they soon ceased
to resemble their earlier forms—remodeled as they were by
Greek thought and temperament.

The Greeks were no mere imitators, like the Phœnicians.
They were susceptible to ideas on every hand, but they invariably improved upon legacies left them, and in turn bequeathed
a nobler gift than they had themselves received.

" For you must know that of all the peoples that have
ever lived the Greeks were the greatest. the keenest-witted, the
most intelligent, the most artistic. There was nothing they did
not seem to know, or if they did not know it they divined it.

[1]History of Greece: Fyffe, 5.

They had the noblest and most perfect language ever invented by any nation; and not only that: they had the most to say, and said it better, than any other race of men that ever lived. Others took lumps of stone and modelled and chipped and hammered them into rude likenesses of human figures and faces; the Greeks took the snowy marble and made it live, filled it with heavenly grace, charged every limb with mysterious force, and did everything but make the marble talk. Others built great pyramids and labyrinths and systems of artificial irrigation, or filled their land with mummies and sphinxes; the Greeks with the wand of enchantment made their glorious shrines and dwelling-places for their gods, their porticoes and market-places, their theatres and colonnades, rise all over their cities and filled them with a varied throng of folk eager to inquire, to learn, to study political life, to buy and sell, to teach and to worship. Finally the Greeks gave the world the most perfect poems and dramas, and the most eloquent discourses that we can ever hope to have." [2]

THE PHYSICAL GEOGRAPHY OF GREECE.

The early people whom we call *Greeks* never called themselves by that name. They believed that they were descended from an illustrious ancestor Hellen, and taking his name, they called themselves *Hellenes* and their country *Hellas*. By the time authentic history begins they were established not only in the little country we know as Greece, but upon the islands of the Aegean Sea, along the western coast of Asia Minor and the shores of Italy. Wherever Hellenes lived, there was Hellas, and although continental Greece may be regarded as their especial home, they set no limits to their territory.

It is quite impossible to understand aright the temperament of the ancient Greeks or to comprehend their history without some knowledge of the physical conditions of the land wherein their race developed. The far-reaching effects of topography upon a people is universally conceded, and nowhere can we find more immediate and more apparent results of such influence than in ancient Greece. Let us consider then, somewhat in detail, the various land areas that constituted Hellas.

[2] Story of Greece: Story of the Nation Series.

European Greece occupies the peninsula constituting the south-eastern extremity of Europe, and is said to be one of the newest land formations of that continent. Nearest to Asia, intercourse with the East was possible from earliest times.

Although smaller than Portugal or the state of Ohio, Greece nevertheless possesses a remarkable length of coast-line. A glance at the map will show how deeply the shores are indented with harbors and gulfs, bays and estuaries. The water has encroached so far upon the land that the country has been happily likened to a leaf-skeleton, retaining at last but the ribs of its former structure.

After the long stretch of coast-line, one is struck by the appearance of the mountains, which rise everywhere with little system or order. Nor are these mountains forested and wild —rather, they rise white and bare, with definite contour and scanty soil. Aristocratic mountains they have been called, because of their stern aloofness and abrupt, unverdured peaks.

Greece is sometimes compared with Scotland, analogies existing in the size of the countries and their irregularity of coast. Both are fringed with islands, both possess a poor and rocky soil, and both are mountainous. Greece possesses comparatively few plains, nine-tenths of its surface being mountainous. One can never get more than ten miles away from the hills nor forty miles distant from the sea.

Few rivers of importance flow through the land and none are suited to navigation. In the rainy months many of the streams become rushing torrents, while in summer their dry channels often serve as routes for travel.

Many varieties of climate are found within this limited area, much depending upon the latitude and the proximity to the sea. The damp, thick atmosphere of Boeotia, the cold of mountain heights, cool breezes of the low hills, warmth of the sunny plains—all exist with many gradations, yet altogether, the habitable portions of the country are usually blessed with clear skies and a mild temperature. This condition leads to much out-of-door life, and we shall find that the ancient Greeks developed into a strong and healthy people.

Greece possesses singular beauty: a soft haze enveils the rocky peaks, and catching the sun's last rays, reflects shimmer-

ing tints and colors.   The beauty of their land had much to
do with fostering a deep overpowering love of beauty in the
hearts of the people.   They developed beautiful bodies, artists
strove to reproduce beautiful human figures in marble—the
Greeks worshipped beauty.   It is not possible to conceive of
such a passion for the beautiful in a people who dwell always
under grey skies, where a cold, forbidding climate leads to
a sheltered life.

"In its physical characteristics Greece was a land of singular contrasts.   A remarkable singularity of conditions between
the eastern and western shores of the Aegean was matched
by a remarkable difference of conditions between the eastern
and western coasts of Greece itself, and still more between its
southern and northern provinces.   The Aegean was a highway between two halves of one country—a sea exceptionally
suitable for commerce.   The air is clear.   Islands—that is,
landmarks, are frequent.   Bays and safe anchorages are in-
numerable.   During a great part of the summer there are
regular winds which blow daily from the north.   On the other
hand, while the eastern side of Greece is rich in fertile lowlands
and has a deeply indented though accessible coast-line, the
western side consists of little else than rocky ridges skirting
a savage shore with few harbors.   But the contrast between
south and north is more striking yet.   There is not on the
entire surface of the globe, it has been said, any other region
in which the different zones of climate and flora meet one
another in so rapid a succession.   The semi-tropical products
of the Cyclades and the Peloponnesus have vanished in Boeotia.
The olives of Attica are not seen in Thessaly.   Even the myrtle
disappears in the northern shores of the Aegean." [3]

Having noted these general characteristics of Greece, let
us consider more at length some of the constituent districts
which made up Hellas.

Northern Greece is composed of the state of Thessaly upon
the east and Epirus on the west.   Nature has done much for
Thessaly; on three sides mountain ranges enclose a fruitful
plain, early famous for its horses and its fertile fields.   Rich
in cities, Thessaly became known for its self-indulgent citizens.

[3]Rise of the Macedonian Empire: Curtius, 2.

The very fertility of the soil led to the demoralization of the people. Little labor brought rich reward, and having few obstacles to overcome in gaining a livelihood, the Thessalians turned to discord among themselves. Through much of their history, anarchy was rife. Epirus was not inhabited by pure Greeks and its mountainous districts were little known in early times. The oracle of Dodona attracted visitors, but Epirus was at no period one of the leading Grecian states.

Central Greece is for the most part a mountainous country, stony and devoid of forests. Along the eastern coast deep gulfs and bays abound. Small forested plains are shut in by mountains which here extend in an easterly and westerly direction—as opposed to the northerly and southerly trend of the ranges in northern Greece. Crystal brooks hurry down the mountain-sides, and the bare rocky peaks glimmer bright in the clear atmosphere.

Of the several political states into which central Greece is divided we shall at present note but two: Boeotia and Attica. Quite a part of Boeotia is marshy. Lake Copais, largest of Grecian lakes, is here. Enclosed by mountains on three sides and infested with fogs that rise constantly from the moist earth, the air is thick and uncomfortable. In the long ago days of Hesiod he characterized it as " bad in winter, oppressive in summer, and never good." Yet this state grew to be one of the densely populated portions of Hellas and the fate of the whole nation was frequently decided within its borders. Thebes considered herself as head of the Boeotian cities.

Attica was a rocky, barren land. Greatest of her cities was Athens, situated in a plain, well nigh surrounded by mountains.

The Peloponnesus, or the peninsula of Pelops, has been called the citadel of Hellas. It consists of a high ridge of hills, some of which reach out to the very sea, forming rocky promontories. Well-watered plains nestle between the hills, and in the center of the peninsula is Arcadia—land of pastoral life, beloved of poets in all ages. Arcadia has been likened to Switzerland, her people to the peasants of the Alps. Both have possessed a sense of freedom inborn, and both have been eager for gain. Pan and his pipers originated on the eastern slopes

ATHENA.

of Arcadia, where brooks sparkle along and the air is fresh and cool. Southeastward reaches Laconia, land of heroes. Rough and mountainous, this region is watered by the Eurotas, purest of Grecian rivers. On its banks stood Sparta—her citizens her only walls.

East of Arcadia lay Argolis, with Argos the capital city. Here too was Mycenae, in Homeric times the home of Agamemnon. Here also was Nemea, where games were held in honor of Poseidon. Argolis, however, never took first rank among the states of Greece.

West of Arcadia is Elis—holy land, thrice blessed of the gods. Several rivers flow down from Arcadian heights across its borders. Here were celebrated the Olympian games. Elis was a land of peace; wars were not allowed to desecrate its soil. Armies marching through its precincts laid down their weapons upon entering its borders, receiving them only when they left them. On the banks of the Alpheus stood the grove sacred to the Mighty Ones. Altars and shrines, beautiful statues and temples made splendid its entire area. Here was the temple of Jove wherein was placed the masterpiece of Phidias. Pausanias relates that he counted twenty-three statues of Zeus alone, while Pliny estimates the whole number of statues in the grove as approximately three thousand. When we remember that only the finest works of art were admitted to the grove sacred to the gods, we can understand the deep pride of the Greek, returning from the celebration of the Olympiad, and viewing scornfully the achievements of other races in comparison with his own. Achaea reaches away to the north. This land was noted for the wisdom of its men. It was a maritime country; once occupied by Ionians, later came the Achaeans, giving the land its name.

Central and southern Greece were connected by an isthmus, sometimes not more than four miles broad. In view of the Corinthian Gulf it is easy to understand why geographical unity in Greece was effected by water instead of land.

From this knowledge of physical Greece we may draw certain inferences: (1) This was not a country to be governed easily from one central point. Rather, it was destined to develop small city-states—(states growing up around a leading town)—each state jealous of its own freedom but willing

to encroach upon the liberties of its neighbors.   (2) This was
not a country suited to the development of one industry at the
expense of all others.   Instead, the fertile plains drew the
farmer to till the soil, while the ever present coast enticed to
the sea.   The mere geographical position of a state determined
in advance whether its citizens were to dwell apart, as for
example, the Aetolians, so far remote from routes of travel
that they were always two or three hundred years behind their
neighbors in the matter of progress; or whether, like the inhabitants of Attica, the citizens were to keep closely in touch
with outside influences.   (3) The few plains of Greece could
not produce sustenance sufficient for a large population, and
intercourse with other countries early became a necessity.
(4) With a varied economic life was to come a keen intellectual
development, well-nigh impossible in a land where one particular industry absorbs general attention.   (5) People of two
temperaments were to grow out of this peninsula of Europe:
the mountaineer, who loved his home and wished not to leave
it; the restless sea-farer, whose home was anywhere.   One was
to become the bulwark of the homeland; the other was to
scatter settlements south, east and west, and to build up a
mighty commerce.

Other effects of topography upon the Greeks will be noted
from time to time; we shall now glance over the remaining
lands early settled by Hellenes.

Insular Greece included the numerous Greek islands.
Islands dot the sea from the eastern coast of Greece to the
shores of Asia Minor.   This entire region is doubtless a sub-
merged land area and has the appearance of a sunken mountain
range, the islands being the peaks which still hold their heads
above the water.   Euboea is separated from the mainland by
a narrow channel only ten feet deep in one locality.

Crete was the largest of all Greek islands.   Until the period
of Roman submission it contained thirty republics, each in
reality a country town, maintaining its own freedom and independence.   Several of the smaller islands—Melos and Thera
for example—built up an extensive sea-trade in early days.
These countless islands—stepping stones, they have been called
—played an important role in the maritime interests of Greece,
for while the open ocean was full of imaginary dangers, the

sailor was lured along from one island to another, until the sea became his home.

The coast of Asia Minor was early settled by Hellenes, and the first Greek civilization developed there. Asia Minor is an elevated plateau with a slightly depressed center. Its coast-line is extensive, and is deeply indented with bays and natural harbors. Along this shore Greek settlements were made and because of their proximity to the east, the Ionian tribes of this district attained earliest a superior degree of culture.

The islands and peninsulas on the west of Italy offered safe havens for the mariner, and here the Greeks migrated in the eighth century before Christ. The peninsula farthest west received the name of *Magna Graecia* because of its large Greek population. It is important to notice that Greece faces the east, Italy the west, and that the two countries lie with their backs to each other. This fact proved a telling factor in their development.

In view of these wide spreading colonies it has been said that " ancient Greece was the Grecian Sea with all its coasts from Asia Minor to Sicily and from Cyrene to Thrace."

The importance of the position of the country should be constantly emphasized. " Greece was the point of communication between the old and new world. All the art, all ideas, all movements, which passed from the east to the west must necessarily pass through her. She had it in her power to modify and recast whatever was transmitted from one to the other." [4]

[4]Tozer : Geog. of Greece.

CHAPTER II.

A GREAT DISCOVERY.

Until recent years the Iliad and the Odyssey were the chief
sources for earliest Greek history. They portrayed a stage of
development which preceded that of organized Greece and
which, aside from the two poems, appeared to be unrecorded.
Out of the obscurity of ages two masterpieces shone forth and
then again came darkness. The society these depicted became
known as Homeric society. It was long supposed that the
period which gave them birth must always remain a subject
for doubt and conjecture. During the last thirty years, however, wonderful remains have been laid bare by the spade of the
excavator, and it has been conclusively shown that instead of
portraying a new, undeveloped condition of life, these poems
reflect a culture in its decadent stage—perhaps, in the last glow
whose brightness signaled an approaching end.

The discovery of this early civilization in Greece has been
largely due to the energy and perseverance of one man, and
he, strange to say, a man of affairs rather than a student,—a
merchant rather than an archæologist. Since the world of
today owes so great a debt to Dr. Schliemann, we may well
stop to consider his part in this remarkable recovery before
entering upon a discussion of the remains he brought to light.

Dr. Henrich Schliemann was born in 1822 in a little German village. His father, a Lutheran clergyman, was a good
student and fond of the classics. He often related stories of
the Greek gods and heroes to his children. When but a little
lad Henrich was shown a fanciful picture of the burning of
Troy. He already knew of Helen and the Trojan War, but
the strong walls in the picture held his attention and he asked
his father if they had really been so massive. When told they
were, according to the poem, the boy insisted that they could
not have been totally destroyed by fire—that some portion of
them must still remain in ruins. He concludes the incident in his

autobiography by saying that his father and he agreed he should some day go to search for the ruined walls of Troy.

Misfortune came upon his family and while a mere lad Henrich was taken from school and put to work in a grocery shop. Here for five years he worked early and late, finding small opportunity for the studies to which he had been attracted. The monotony of this life was unexpectedly terminated when he injured himself by attempting to lift a cask too heavy for him. Being at once discharged as no longer useful, and having no one to whom he might turn for help, Henrich walked one hundred and thirty miles to Hamburg, where he obtained a place as cabin bóy on an outgoing vessel. The ship was wrecked before it had been long at sea, and Henrich was among those saved. Taken to Amsterdam, he found work as an office boy with a firm in that city. His wages were small but his time was not fully occupied, and he eagerly seized the chance to continue his education. Half of his earnings were spent for books. Having become well acquainted with his own literature, he attempted foreign languages. Not being able to pay a teacher, he taught himself. He would take a French copy of some story known well in German, read it aloud and commit pages to memory. In this way he gradually mastered one language after another. After learning two or three, others were acquired more easily.

After a time Henrich secured a position as clerk with a mercantile house having interests in Russia. Here his services were appreciated and his salary soon raised; whereupon Schliemann set himself to the mastery of the Russian language, believing that by so doing he would become more useful to his employers. Sent by them to Russia as their agent, he was able to undertake business in his own behalf, importing tea and indigo. At the age of forty he found himself possessed of a fair fortune and free at last to devote himself to studies he had long wished to pursue. He commenced the study of Greek and soon was able to use the language as readily as his own. Retiring from business, he travelled in the east, spending much time in Greece—land of his beloved Homer. He married a Greek lady of learning and their children were named Andromache and Agamemnon.

The child-dream of finding the city immortalized by Homer

remained and finally, overcoming many oppositions to his plan, Schliemann began to dig on the supposed site of Troy. Ridicule hailed him on all sides. The Iliad, scholars said, was a moral poem and had no geographical locality. As well try to find the Inferno of Dante's poem, or the scene of Milton's epic—as well seek the pot of gold at the rainbow's end.

Indifferent to such comments, Schliemann sunk a shaft through a hill called Hissarlik—a Turkish word meaning *citadel*. Soon the workmen came upon ruined huts and other evidences of earlier habitation. Striking through nine successive settlements, they came at last to the foundation rock whereon the first village had been built. Most extensive appeared to be the ruins of the second city, which also gave evidence of having been burned. In exultant enthusiasm Schliemann gave out the premature announcement that he had recovered the city of Priam.

One has but to look back through the files of the leading magazines to find specimens of the sarcastic retorts which greeted this statement. One critic journeyed to see the ruins and then gave to the public his opinion that had Schliemann contended these rude structures once sheltered Trojan pigs, he should not have wondered greatly, but the royal Priam? Never!

Such idle talk naturally had little effect upon the man who was bringing to light the buried secrets of centuries. Having recovered considerable treasure, together with many specimens of pottery and weapons, Schliemann transferred his operations from Asia Minor to Mycenae. Here the unearthing of royal tombs containing the embalmed bodies of princes accompanied with great profusion of gold and jewels, caused him to believe he had found the tomb of Agamemnon, and he sent the following telegram to the King of Greece:

NOVEMBER 28, 1876.

"*To the King of Greece*:

"I have the greatest pleasure in announcing to your majesty that I have discovered the tombs which tradition, according to Pausanias, pointed out as the graves of Agamemnon, Cassandra, Eurymedon, and their companions, all murdered at a banquet by Clytæmnestra and her lover Aegisthus. I have found im-

mense treasure in these graves, sufficient by themselves alone to
fill a great museum, which will be the most wonderful in the
world, and for centuries will bring thousands of strangers to
Greece."

Such discoveries silenced the flow of ridicule. Students
would not at once be persuaded that they belonged to Homeric
days, but beyond question they were valuable contributions to
Greek history and caused no little excitement in the student
world.

As a matter of fact, it was proven later that the city Schliemann, supposed to be Troy of the Iliad, was of far earlier date,
and the sixth settlement, through which he had passed with
little notice, was probably the scene of Homer's poem. Again,
the tombs unearthed in Mycenae belonged to an age prior to
that of Agamemnon, and were probably contemporaneous with
the second city of Troy.

Subsequently Schliemann made his home in Athens, where
he built a palatial residence, reviving the most perfected Grecian style of architecture. One who visited this home wrote
of it thus: " All visitors to Athens know the marble mansion
on the street of the University, with its beautiful frescoes on
the front, and its sculptured gods and heroes guarding the
battlements; with its garden full of oranges and climbing roses
on either side and in the rear. Even in its exterior it is a
splendid palace, with its front looking across the city upon the
Acropolis. But enter once and the charm of the house becomes commanding. The ground floor is a great museum,
full of the rude, prehistoric things of Troy. Adjacent are the
working rooms where one finds antiquity piled pell-mell, waiting for classification. Hence a wide marble stairway leads up
to the second floor, with its ball room, drawing room, music
room, dining rooms—while verses of Homer are inscribed on
every possible panel. In the mosaic floors the chief specimens
of the Trojan vases and urns are represented. Friezes with
classical landscapes and pictures from the Greek epic are found
with appropriate Homeric quotations."

Greek was the language of this household, except as other
languages were spoken for the accommodation of guests. The
butler, porter, and all the household servants were given Greek
names, whatever their original names had been. Dr. Schlie-

mann loved to surround himself with an air of ancient Greece His entire crew of workmen had special names given them by him—such as Aeneas, Priam, Telamon and the like.

Schliemann had unbounded faith in himself, yet it was this inordinate self-confidence which led him, in the face of ridicule, to succeed in a gigantic undertaking. Seeking at random to give reality to a dream, he incidentally brought to light a wonderful civilization. He always realized fully his tremendous contribution to history and spoke of it in no slight terms. Yet as some of his commentators have said, " one can but regret that he anticipated their praises."

The bulk of the finds at Troy were presented to the German government and are today in the Ethnological Museum at Berlin, while those found in Greece remain in the home of Schliemann—called by him the Hall of Troy. This has become a museum and is open to all who desire to see the remains of Mycenaean civilization.

The government of Greece is carrying on the work begun by Schliemann, and other valuable contributions are being added each year.

We are compelled to admire the spirit of this man who could hold unfalteringly to the dream of his youth, resolutely denying himself comfort in order to pursue an education which would fit him for its realization. To his memory the contents of the Great Treasure and of the Princes' Tombs remains a lasting monument.

MYCENAEAN LIFE AND CULTURE.

Remains of a civilization corresponding to that unearthed at Troy have since been found in various parts of Greece, in Asia Minor and on the islands of the Aegean Sea. This is known today as Mycenaean civilization—from the town in Greece where first discovered—although the name Aegean would be equally as good and more comprehensive. We shall first give attention to some of the discoveries made in Troy and Mycenae, and shall then consider the culture as a whole.

The prehistoric ages of Greece are now known as Mycenaean ages, and it appears that in these remote times, settlements were clustered around commanding heights. A fortified acropolis, or citadel, was erected on a hill, and guarded by massive walls. These were called Cyclopean by the Greeks

who believed that only the fabled giants—the one-eyed Cyclops
—could have built them.

The hill was crowned by the palace of the chief, or king,
who dwelt secure, like some feudal lord of the Middle Ages.
Around the fortress reached away the lands of the tribe, who
in time of danger flocked within the shelter of the fenced city.
Such settlements were sprinkled over the whole country, and
as a rule each chief was served by a comparatively small number of followers. As in all ages when war is ever imminent
and plundering bands infest the land, hills and elevated rocks
were chosen as fortresses, not only because they were the more
easily defended, but because they served also as outlooks over
a more or less extensive area of grain fields.

While the less substantial portions of Mycenaean settlements have perished, the walls remain in a ruined condition in
various parts of Greece, and invariably they are found to have
been built on hill-tops—as those at Troy, Mycenae and Athens.

Of all thus far unearthed, the first settlement at Troy appears to be the oldest. The village was built on a rock about
115 feet above the sea, and perhaps 150 feet broad. In this
strata Schliemann found axes, knives and saws—always of
stone; vases of crude pottery lacking handles, and having
instead small holes through which strings were tied to hang
them by.

The second village, built on top of the earlier settlement,
was from ten to twenty-five feet higher than the first, and its
walls enclosed an area 320 feet in breadth. Most interesting
in this stratum is the citadel with its one remaining wall, and
the outlines of a ruined palace. Stone and copper utensils
were found, and the pottery still appears to have been made
by hand. The third, fourth and fifth settlements were probably made entirely by poor people, for little has been discovered
in their huts, built of quarry-stone or clay. It is plain that
for several generations the hill was occupied by practically
one continuous village and the remains of these three settlements are so intermingled in their ruins that it is difficult to
separate them. Bronze was known, but copper continued to
be commonly used for weapons and utensils.

In Greece—especially at Athens, Delphi and Sparta—in

Crete and other islands of the Aegean, traces of a civilization similar to that shown in these first four settlements of Troy have been found. It corresponds to what is generally known as the Copper Age among primitive people, and in Greece is called *Pre-Mycenaean*, since it preceded that higher culture which in its flower we call *Mycenaean*. To summarize the progress made up to this point: "The knowledge of copper working has progressed; bronze has made its first appearance. Pottery has progressed and vague attempts to imitate animals and people are found among the vases. Ruins of town walls and gates show the knowledge of building to be in advance of pottery. The dead are buried—not burned."

An ax-head of white jade, found in the ruins of one of the earliest settlements, proves conclusively that at least indirect intercourse was established at this early time with the far east, for white jade was found alone in China. Amber from the Baltic, tin from Spain, possibly from Britain, and ivory from northern Africa, all go to show how wide was the intercourse among peoples of this remote age. It is difficult to assign dates to these stages of progress. Some think that the first settlement at Troy was contemporaneous with predynastic ages in Egypt, and hence reaches back 5000 years before Christ—3000 B. C. is by others considered a safe date for the dawn of Pre-Mycenaean civilization, 1500 B. C. as its close, or the beginning of Mycenaean culture. Such dates, in the nature of the case, can be but approximate.

The sixth settlement at Troy has greatest interest for us, since this is now thought to have been the Troy of Homeric song. At least we may say that it exemplifies such a culture as the Homeric poems portray. While stone implements were yet known, copper had largely superseded stone; bronze was used for knives and weapons, and while iron was known, it was still rare and used only for ornaments and exchange. The area enclosed by the city walls had expanded. Temples, as well as the palace of the king, adorned the citadel.

It is often difficult to determine to which period articles found in the various settlements properly belong. Schliemann connected the Great Treasure with the second city, but judg-

¹Earliest Civilization of Greece: Hall.

ing from the workmanship of ornaments and the artistic skill evinced, it has been more fittingly associated with the sixth— or Homeric Troy. The Great Treasure was the name applied by Schliemann to a chest of jewelry and other valuable articles discovered by him in May, 1873, buried deep in a ruined wall of Troy. The chest contained women's ornaments, such as two beautiful diadems—worn over the forehead and hanging down over the ears; bracelets, ear-rings, and a necklace; six flat bars of silver, thought to have been used for purposes of exchange; silver vases with cap-covers; cups of gold, silver and electrum. It was surmised that the chest had been hidden for immediate safety in the wall, and was unknown to those who later occupied the site. We can imagine Schliemann's excitement on the morning when a gleam of gold in the ruined wall rewarded his long search for buried articles. Great care had to be exercised to protect these articles from workmen, and as it was, several ornaments of gold were stolen and traces of them discovered only after they had been melted down and fashioned into modern jewelry.

This was one of the greatest finds at Troy, and from a study of the articles, evidently secreted by some member of the royal family, much light has been thrown on the age which produced them.

The remaining settlements crowning the site of the ancient city belong to the Graeco-Roman period and so have no particular interest here. Abundant records of this late age exist.

Crossing from Asia Minor to Greece, the remains at Tiryns give evidence of great antiquity. Tiryns was the ancient seaport of Argolis, and owed its importance to its sea-trade. The walls defending the citadel were of prodigious strength, the stones being held in place by their own weight. They were rough, unhewn stones, weighing from three to fifteen tons. This ruined wall was reckoned by the ancients as one of the wonders of the world. The Greeks called them Cyclopean walls, believing that they had been built by the Cyclops, or giants of mythological fame—the only creatures powerful enough, they thought, to fit the huge stones into place.

At Tiryns were found also the ruins of a great palace, containing many apartments. Marked similarity was found between it and a palace described by Homer in the Odyssey.

Fragments of an alabaster frieze especially recalled the Homeric palace.

Of somewhat later date was the settlement at Mycenae, which city had soon risen to first place and long held Tiryns in vassalage. Private houses as well as a royal palace were here unearthed. The wall, built of smaller stones than those of Tiryns, was built in a similar fashion. From the wall stretched a roadway to a tower within, and guarding one end of this approach stood the lion-gate, so-called because two lions keep watch over the gateway. Between them was once a tablet bearing, no doubt, an inscription of the king. This, with the heads of the two lions, long since disappeared.

The most remarkable recoveries at Mycenae were the royal tombs, which we have already seen were believed by Schliemann to enclose the remains of Agamemnon and his companions, but were proven later to belong to a much earlier age.

"The incomparable splendor with which these dead were buried has never been equalled elsewhere. They were dressed in robes of state, were lain in their tombs with golden diadems upon their foreheads, wearing their richest jewels and most sumptuous raiment. On their heads were crowns, belts and baldrics of gold around their breasts, while their faces, by a custom which seems to have been borrowed from the East, were covered by a golden mask which reproduced the features of the deceased. Their garments were ornamented with thin plates of gold, 700 of which were found in a single tomb; and their richly inlaid swords, whose sheaths are curiously adorned with bosses of gold, lay within reach. The women were no less splendidly attired; they also wore diadems upon their heads, necklaces around their throats, rings on their fingers, as well as broaches, ear-rings, and bracelets of admirable workmanship. Lastly by the side of each of the corpses were placed vessels, often of gold and silver, which contained the provisions needful for sustenance of the dead in the lower world. Certainly there were no insignificant personages buried here,—they were sovereigns interred in state, and in this respect at least, Dr. Schliemann's hopes were not deceived." [2]

---

[2]Excursions in Greece: Diehl, 18.

Estimating the contents of these tombs merely at the value of the gold they contained, their value was above 5,000 pounds, while their worth to students has been inestimable. There is a remarkable concurrence between the traditions regarding the wealth of Mycenae as reflected in the Iliad, and the revelations of these tombs. They give proof of the existence, long before the Doric invasion, of a great and thriving empire; we are also enabled to judge of the conditions under which primitive Greek art was born.

Mycenaean civilization flourished from approximately 1500 B. C. to 1000 B. C.—these dates being accepted, like those of the age preceding, as reasonable conjectures. This is the Bronze age of the Aegean basin, reaching from the coast of Asia Minor, across the islands of the sea, and far into Greece. Who the people were who developed such a high degree of culture is not known. They are generally called Pelasgians. The Dorian invasion swept away the remains of their civilization, replacing it by that of a ruder race. The Phœnician traders ceased to come this way during the unsettled years which followed, and the new race was left to destroy much, to absorb much, and eventually to evolve a greater culture than that which it had overcome.

More definite knowledge concerning men of the Mycenaean age may be forthcoming in future years. At present we can only say that between the fifteenth and tenth millennium before Christ, a people having attained a high degree of culture occupied the Aegean basin—an area which their ancestors had occupied before them in a more primitive stage of development. At what time they emerged from Asia cannot be estimated, but they were able to maintain a close relationship with the Orient. They built large and convenient houses, amassed wealth and attained to a superior excellence in art. While the effects of Egyptian and Asiatic contact are very apparent in their decorative efforts, yet a certain originality and inventive skill which came later to characterize Greeks of a later day were from the beginning evident.

The Post-Mycenaean, or better, the Homeric period, followed as the Mycenæan age gradually declined, and we shall consider it in connection with the two great poems which belong to it.

CYCLOPEAN WALLS.

Ye cliffs of masonry, enormous piles,
Which no rude censure of familiar time
Nor record of our puny race defiles,
In dateless mystery ye stand sublime,
Memorials of an age of which we see
Only the types in things that once were ye.

Whether ye rest upon some bosky knoll,
Your feet by ancient myrtles beautified,
Or seem, like fabled dragons, to unroll
Your swarthy grandeurs down a bleak hillside,
Still on your savage features is a spell
That makes ye half divine, ineffable.

With joy, upon your height I stand alone,
As on a precipice, or lie within
Your shadow wide, or leap from stone to stone,
Pointing my steps with careful discipline,
And think of those grand limbs whose nerve could bear
These masses to their places in mid-air;

Of Anakim, and Titans, and of days
Saturnian, when the spirit of man was knit
So close to Nature, that his best essays
At Art were but in all to follow it,
In all,—dimension, dignity, degree;
And thus these mighty things were made to be.

LORD HOUGHTON.

CHAPTER III.

THE HOMERIC POEMS.

The Iliad and Odyssey are quite unlike in style and character, and although tradition ascribes to both a common authorship, such was probably not the case.

In the story of Greek Mythology we have learned of the strife among the fair ones of Mount Olympus for the possession of the Golden Apple marked: *For the Most Beautiful*—how Hera, Aphrodite and Athena took their cause before Paris, who awarded the apple to Aphrodite, thereafter known as Goddess of Beauty; how by her aid he abducted Helen, wife of Menelaus and most beautiful of mortal women. Priam, king of Troy and father of Paris, received his son and the stolen Helen at his court, and so laid the country open to the revengeful attack of King Menelaus and his Greek allies.

Owing to the nature of primitive warfare and to the strength of the Trojan walls, the siege of the city continued year after year with little apparent result. Finally in the ninth year an estrangement occurred between the Greek leaders Agamemnon, king of Mycenae, and Achilles, bravest of Greek heroes. This incident, the Wrath of Achilles, with the causes leading up to it, its results and the final reconciliation, supplied the general theme of the Iliad. Incidentally however, much pertaining to the life of the times and the manners and customs of the people, was woven into the epic. On this account, the poem furnishes us valuable material for a study of primitive civilization in Greece.

The Greeks themselves believed the Iliad and the Odyssey to have been composed by Homer, a blind poet, who went about from place to place, singing his verses to the accompaniment of a lyre. During the last hundred years scholars have been trying to arrive at a more satisfactory conclusion, for it seemed improbable that from a seemingly impenetrable darkness should suddenly shine forth two masterpieces of literature, the work of a genius unparalleled in human history. Wide differences of opinion have resulted from critical study of the two poems. Some hold the Iliad to be a collection of early ballads, having a similar origin, strung together like pearls on a silken strand. A few still hold to the first idea of a Homer who produced the Iliad in as full a sense as Shakespeare produced *Hamlet,* or Tennyson *In Memoriam.* Without attempting to set forth all the conflicting ideas upon the Homeric question we shall note simply the most probable explanation, as accepted by the leading Homeric scholars.

After the Trojan war and before the Dorian invasion, there probably lived some bard—either in Central Greece, or more probably, in Asia Minor—who composed the Iliad in its general form. That is to say, he may have outlined the story largely as we have it today, bringing it into much smaller compass. This may have occurred as early as the eleventh century before Christ, although the date is much disputed. Writing was not commonly known in Greece until two or three hundred years later, and the epic passed from father to son, by word of mouth, for many generations. There was no " authorized " version of the epic; each one who related it added to the original story, modified and changed it as seemed best to him. Thus it is probable that minstrels in different parts of the country were contemporaneously singing the story of Achilles' Wrath in a variety of ways.

During times of national rejoicing over military successes, national epics are likely to take on a new significance, and it may be that some blind bard who lived two hundred years after the composition of the original Iliad, possibly bearing the name Homer, gave a new importance to the tale by bringing it forward in a more elaborated form. At last, probably in the time of Pisistratus, the epic was edited and given a final shape, and this version is the one known to us today.

The Iliad reflects the age when Mycenaean culture was being supplanted by a ruder condition of life, yet had not been wholly extinguished. No reference is made to the radical change produced in Greece by the Dorian migration, and it is scarcely to be believed that so momentous an event would have passed unnoticed had it yet occurred. While the poem sings of war, it shows a growing sentiment against its barbarism. War and carnage are no longer carried on for the mere pleasure of slaughter. The advantage of trade was drawing on the primitive Greek mind, and this checked the earlier and wilder joy of warring.

The style of the poem is spirited, full of energy and fire—wholly in contrast with that of the Odyssey.

The Odyssey is a poem of peace. It was composed in an even vein, breathing of calm and deliberation. Ulysses, the hero, has set out for his home in Ithaca after the fall of Troy, and his adventures during ten long years are related. Having incurred the displeasure of Neptune, adverse fate attends his way. Sirens entice his sailors to dangerous rocks: Circe, the enchantress, brings his men under her magic spell. Monsters of the deep and giants of the mountains do their best to injure him, and he despairs of ever seeing his native shores. Such experiences, together with domestic scenes from his home in Ithaca, where his faithful wife Penelope awaits his return, while suitors clamor for her hand, make up the tale.

The Odyssey was probably composed about eight centuries before the Christian era, and it is believed that its present form more closely conforms to the original than does the Iliad. Both poems are invaluable for the light they throw upon the decaying Mycenaean culture and the new civilization just dawning.

No other literature offers such a varied picture of life during the transition stage of a primitive people. Who wrote the poems will never be determined, for their origin is wholly lost. Realizing this, it is nevertheless necessary to keep in mind the attitude of the Greek toward them. He believed that they were both the creation of the divine Homer. No murmur of doubt is found among Greek writers. The two epics were read for many years at the celebration of the Olympiads, and the memory of him who was supposed to have sung them first was fondly cherished.

HOMERIC LIFE.

We are now to consider certain aspects of Homeric Life as set forth in the Iliad and Odyssey. Instead of entering

II—17

upon a discussion of minute details, the fundamental institutions, manners and customs, presumably common to the primitive Greeks as a whole, will be noted, while citations from the epics themselves will frequently be made.

The form of government maintained by a people constitutes one criterion for judging the degree of progress to which it has attained. The Iliad represents the Greeks as still divided into many tribes, each under leadership of a chief, or petty king. In war, he commands the force of fighting men; in times of peace his acknowledged military skill insures him continued honor and distinction; at all times with the elders of the tribe he settles disputes among tribesmen and upholds the accepted ideas of justice. Ulysses states the attitude of the tribe towards their king in this fashion:

> " We, the Greeks,
> Cannot be all supreme in power.   The rule
> Of the many is not well.   One must be chief
> In war, and one the king, to whom the son
> Of Saturn gives the sceptre, making him
> The lawgiver, that he may rule the rest."
>
> —*Iliad,* II., 252.

The council was made up of the heroes, or nobles, who deliberated with the king on all matters involving the welfare of the tribe.   In the council meeting each had a voice, and no king would act in direct opposition to the will of his nobles.

> "Atrides Agamemnon, glorious king!
> What I shall say begins and ends with thee,
> For thou dost rule o'er many nations.   Jove
> Hath given to thee the sceptre, and the power
> To make their laws, that thou mayst seek their good.
> Thou, therefore, of all men, shouldst speak and hear
> In council, and shouldst follow willingly
> Another's judgment when it best promotes
> The general weal; for all depends on thee."— *Iliad,* IX., 115.

The Assembly was made up of all freemen.   This body merely voted or rejected plans presented to it by the council.

The functions of the council and the assembly are sufficiently brought out in that passage where Agamemnon presents his plan of continuing the siege of Troy:

> " Agamemnon bade
> The shrill-voiced heralds call the long-haired Greeks
> Together; they proclaimed his will, and straight
> The warriors came in throngs.   But first he bade
> A *council* of large-minded *elders* meet
> On Pylian Nestor's royal bark, and there
> Laid his well-pondered thought before him.
>
> He spake, and left the council, and the rest,
> All sceptred kings, arose, prepared to obey
> The shepherd of the people.   All the Greeks
> Meanwhile came thronging to the appointed place.
> As, swarming forth from cells within the rock,
> Coming and coming still, the tribe of bees
> Fly in a cluster o'er the flowers of spring,
> And some are darting out to right and left,
> So from the ships and tents a multitude
> Along the spacious beach, in mighty throngs,
> Moved toward the *assembly*.
> And when the crowd was seated and had paused
> From clamor, Agamemnon rose.
>
> He spake, and in the bosoms of the crowd
> Stirred every heart; even those who heard him not
> Were moved; the assembly wavered to and fro
> Like the long billows of the Icarian Sea,
> Roused by the East wind and the South, that rush
> Forth from the cloudy seat of Father Jove;
> Or like the harvest-field, when west winds stoop
> Suddenly from above, and toss the wheat.
> So was the assembly swayed."—*Iliad*, II., 65, 110, 177.

In times of war, troops were led forth by clans, or brotherhoods.   Nestor gives one reason for the perpetuation of this custom:

> " Marshal the Greeks by tribes and brotherhoods,
>   That tribe may stand by tribe, and brotherhoods

Succor each other; if thou thus command
And they obey, thou shalt discern which chief
Or soldier is faint-hearted, which is brave,
For each will fight his best, and thou shalt know
Whether through favor of the gods to Troy,
Or our own cowardice and shameful lack
Of skill in war, the town is not o'erthrown."—*Iliad*, II., 445.

The Iliad pictures camp rather than civil life, and so the manner of attack, kind of armour and weapons used are described at length. It was customary for a battle to open with a duel between two champions chosen by either side. This repeatedly happened during the siege of Troy. As a champion was worsted or slain, his countrymen made a charge upon the enemy, rescuing his body if such a thing were possible.

" Then first Antilochus, advancing, struck
The Trojan champion Echepolus down,
Son of Thalysius, fighting in the van.
He smote him on the helmet's cone, where streamed
The horse-hair plume. The brazen javelin stood
Fixed in his forehead, piercing through the bone,
And darkness gathered o'er his eyes. He fell
As falls a tower before some stubborn siege.
Then Elephenor, son of Chalcodon,
Prince of the brave Abrantes, by the foot
Seized the slain chieftain, dragging him beyond
The reach of darts, to strip him of his arms;
Yet dropped him soon, for brave Agenor saw,
And, as he stooped to drag the body, hurled
His brazen spear and pierced the uncovered side
Seen underneath the shield. At once his limbs
Relaxed their hold, and straight the spirit fled.
Then furious was the struggle of the Greeks
And Trojans o'er the slain; they sprang like wolves
Upon each other and man slaughtered man."
                                    —*Iliad,* IV., 576.

The simplest armour for a Homeric hero consisted of a helmet, shield, sword and lances. The earliest shield protected the entire body, but it was unwieldy and impeded motion. With the short shield came the breastplate and greaves, or leathern gaiters.

Shields were made of several thicknesses of oxhides, bordered with a rim of bronze. They hung suspended by a strap over the left shoulder, the handle being grasped inside by the left hand, while the right was free to wield the sword. The shield of Ajax was fashioned after the manner of his time:

> " Ajax, drawing near, upheld
> A buckler like a rampart, bright with brass,
> And strong with ox-hides seven. The cunning hand
> In leather-work, had wrought it at his home
> In Hyla. He for Ajax framed the shield
> With hides of pampered bullocks in seven folds,
> And an eighth fold of brass,—the outside fold."
>
> —*Iliad*, VII., 285.

The Greeks took great pride in the workmanship and adornment of their shields. Most wonderful was the shield of Achilles, made for him by Vulcan before his famous encounter with Hector. Only a god could have fashioned so splendid a piece of armour in so brief a time.

> " And first he forged the huge and massive shield,
> Divinely wrought in every part,—its edge
> Clasped with a triple border, white and bright.
> A silver belt hung from it, and its folds
> Were five ; a crowd of figures on its disk
> Were fashioned by the artist's passing skill,
> For here he placed the earth and heaven, and here
> The great deep and the never-resting sun
> And the full moon, and here he set the stars
> That shine in the round heaven,—the Pleiades,
> The Hyades, Orion in his strength,
> And the Bear near him, called by some the Wain,
> That, wheeling, keeps Orion still in sight,
> Yet bathes not in the waters of the sea.
> There placed he two fair cities full of men.
> In one were marriages and feasts ; they led
> The brides with flaming torches from their bowers,

Along the streets, with many a nuptial song.
There the young dancers whirled, and flutes and lyres
Gave forth their sounds, and women at the doors
Stood and admired.　Meanwhile a multitude
Was in the forum, where a strife went on,—
Two men contending for a fine, the price
Of one who had been slain.　Before the crowd
One claimed that he had paid the fine, and one
Denied that aught had been received, and both
Called for the sentence which should end the strife.

Around the other city sat two hosts
In shining armor, bent to lay it waste,
Unless the dwellers would divide their wealth,—
All that their pleasant homes contained,—and yield
The assailants half.　As yet the citizens
Had not complied, but secretly had planned
An ambush.

There too he sculptured a broad fallow field
Of soft rich mould, thrice ploughed, and over which
Walked many a ploughman, guiding to and fro
His steers, and when on their return they reached
The border of the field the master came
To meet them, placing in the hands of each
A goblet of rich wine.　Then turned they back
Along the furrows, diligent to reach their distant ends.

There too, the artist placed a field which lay
Deep in ripe wheat.　With sickles in their hands
The laborers reached it.　Here the handfuls fell
Upon the ground; there binders tied them fast
With bands, and made them sheaves.　Three binders went
Close to the reapers, and behind them boys,
Bringing the gathered handfuls in their arms,
Ministered to the binders.　Staff in hand,
The master stood among them by the side
Of the ranged sheaves and silently rejoiced.
Meanwhile the servants underneath an oak
Prepared a feast apart ; they sacrificed

A fatling ox and dressed it, while the maids
Were kneading for the reapers the white meal.
A vineyard also on the shield he graved,
Beautiful, all of gold, and heavily
Laden with grapes. Black were the clusters all;
The vines were stayed on rows of silver stakes.
He drew a blue trench round it, and a hedge
Of tin. One only path there was by which
The vintagers could go to gather grapes.
Young maids and striplings of a tender age
Bore the sweet fruit in baskets. Midst them all,
A youth from his shrill harp drew pleasant sounds,
And sang with soft voice to the murmuring strings.
They danced around him, beating with quick feet
The ground, and sang and shouted joyously.

There also did the illustrious Vulcan grave
A fair, broad pasture, in a pleasant glade,
Full of white sheep, and stalls, and cottages,
And many a shepherd's fold with sheltering roof.
And there illustrious Vulcan also wrought
A dance,—a maze like that which Daedalus,
In the broad realm of Gnossus once contrived
For fair-haired Ariadne. Blooming youths
And lovely virgins, tripping to light airs,
Held fast each other's wrists. The maidens wore
Fine linen robes; the youths had tunics on
Lustrous as oil, and woven daintily.
The maids wore wreaths of flowers; the young men swords
Of gold in silver belts. They bounded now
In a swift circle,—as a potter whirls
With both his hands a wheel to try its speed,
Sitting before it,—then again they crossed
Each other, darting to their former place.
A multitude around that joyous dance
Gathered, and were amused, while from the crowd
Two tumblers raised their song, and flung themselves
About among the band that trod the dance.
Last on the border of that glorious shield

He graved in all its strength the ocean-stream.
And when that huge and massive shield was done,
He forged a corselet brighter than the blaze
Of fire; he forged a solid helm to fit
The hero's temples, shapely and enchased
With rare designs, and with a crest of gold.
And last he forged him greaves of ductile tin.
When the great artist Vulcan saw his task
Complete, he lifted all that armour up
And laid it at the feet of her who bore
Achilles. Like a falcon in her flight,
Down plunging from Olympus capped with snow,
She bore the shining armor Vulcan gave."
—*Iliad,* XVIII., 600.

The donning of the armour is minutely described several
times in the Iliad, the equipment of Patroclus being typical:

" Patroclus then in glittering brass
Arrayed himself; and first around his thighs
He put the beautiful greaves, and fastened them
With silver clasps; around his chest he bound
The breastplate of the swift Æacides,
With star-like points, and richly chased; he hung
The sword with silver studs and blade of brass
Upon his shoulders, and with it the shield
Solid and vast; upon his gallant head
He placed the glorious helm with horse-hair plume,
That grandly waved on high.   Two massive spears
He took, that fitted well his grasp."—*Iliad,* XVI., 170.

When an army in all its array marched to battle, the sun's
rays caught the gleam of polished metal, and the sight was
formidable indeed to the opposing force.

" As when a forest on the mountain-top
Is in a blaze with the devouring flame
And shines afar, so, while the warriors marched,
The brightness of their burnished weapons flashed
On every side and upward to the sky."— *Iliad,* II., 561.

When a battle was ended and the enemy put to flight, the plunder was always divided among the Greeks. A certain portion was set aside for the king; the rest was apportioned among the warriors.

> " To Thebe, Eetion's sacred town,
> We marched, and plundered it, and hither brought
> The booty which was fairly shared among
> The sons of Greece."—*Iliad*, I., 460.

The dead were burned, and since both Greeks and Trojans laid great stress upon the care of the dead, truces were often declared for the accommodation of both armies. Nestor addresses Agamemnon thus:

> "Give thou, then, command,
> That all the Greeks tomorrow pause for war,
> And come together at the early dawn,
> And bring the dead in chariots drawn by mules
> And oxen, and consume them near our fleet
> With fire, that we, when we return from war,
> May carry to our native land the bones,
> And give them to the children of the slain."
> —*Iliad*, VII., 420.

Considerable light is thrown upon private life of the Greek. Agriculture was still the leading occupation—indeed, in times of peace all Greeks were farmers, and their wealth consisted in herds and flocks. Money was not in circulation. Any commodity might serve as a medium of exchange, and oxen were taken as the standard in values. Three thousand horses were reckoned as great riches. Lack of cattle in Homeric times was equivalent to barbarism. Possessing them, one could barter for what he wished.

> "Her, in her early bloom
> Laertes purchased for a hundred beeves,
> And in his palace honored equally
> With his chaste wife."—(Od. I., 530.)

In the Odyssey there is preserved to us a description of a
kingly palace, singularly like the one unearthed at Tiryns:

"Ulysses toward
The gorgeous palace of Alcinous turned
His steps, yet stopped and pondered ere he crossed
The threshold.   For on every side beneath
The lofty roof of that magnanimous king
A glory shone as of the sun or moon.
There from the threshold, on each side, were walls
Of brass that led towards the inner rooms,
With blue steel cornices.   The doors within
The massive building were of gold, and posts
Of silver on the brazen threshold stood,
And silver was the lintel, and above
Its architrave was gold; and on each side
Stood gold and silver mastiffs, the rare work
Of Vulcan's practised skill; placed there to guard
The house of great Alcinous, and endowed
With deathless life, that knows no touch of age.
Along the walls within, on either side,
And from the threshold to the inner rooms,
Were firmly planted thrones on which were laid
Delicate mantles, woven by the hands
Of women.   The Phaeacian princes here
Were seated; here they ate and drank, and held
Perpetual banquet.   Slender forms of boys
In gold upon the shapely altars stood,
With blazing torches in their hands to light
At eve the palace guests; while fifty maids
Waited within the halls, where some in querns
Ground small the golden grain; some wove the web
Or twirled the spindle, sitting, with a quick
Light motion, like the aspen's glancing leaves.
The well-wrought tissues glistened as with oil.
Without the palace-court, and near the gate,
A spacious garden of four acres lay.
A hedge enclosed it round, and lofty trees
Flourished in generous growth within,—the pear
And the pomegranate, and the apple-tree

With its fair fruitage, and the luscious fig
And olive always green.
At the garden's furthest bound
Were beds of many plants that all the year
Bore flowers.   (Od. VII., 100.)

Wide hospitality was dispensed within the palace.   No
stranger was turned away.   The banquet prepared for Ulysses
when he came a stranger to the home of Alcinous is paralleled
by many other feasts.

" But you, ye sceptered princes, come at once
To my fair palace, that we there may pay
The honors due our guest; let none refuse.
Call also the divine Demodocus,
The bard, on whom a deity bestowed
In ample measure the sweet gift of song,
Delightful when the spirit prompts the lay.

                              They went with speed
To their wise monarch in his spacious halls.
There portico and court and hall were thronged
With people, young and old in multitude;
And there Alcinous sacrificed twelve sheep,
Eight white-toothed swine, and two splay-footed beeves.
And these they flayed, and duly dressed, and made
A noble banquet ready.

And when their thirst and hunger were allayed,
The muse inspired the bard to sing the praise
Of heroes; 'twas a song whose fame had reached
To the high heaven, a story of the strife
Between Ulysses and Achilles, son
Of Peleus, wrangling at a solemn feast
Made for the gods."   (Od. VIII., 50.)

Visitors were welcome indeed in those remote times when
news traveled slowly, and opportunity to hear of distant lands

was limited to such occasions as brought travellers thither from foreign shores. Feasts were prepared for them and speeches made, while harpers beguiled the hours which followed the banquet.

> "A sacred bard
> Amidst them touched the harp and sang to them
> While, as the song began, two dancers sprang
> Into the midst and trod the measure there."—(Od. IV., 25.)

During the Homeric age women occupied themselves in managing the household, superintending the slaves, weaving linen and stuffs for all garments worn by the family, and draperies which adorned the home.

> "She drew near
> To Helen, in the palace, weaving there
> An ample web, a shining double-robe,
> Whereon were many conflicts fairly wrought,
> Endured by the horse-taming sons of Troy
> And brazen-mailed Achaians for her sake
> Upon the field of Mars."   —*Iliad*, III., 160.

Ulysses was told to make himself known to the queen at the royal palace:

> " Go quickly through the palace till thou find
> My mother where she sits beside the hearth,
> Leaning against a column in its blaze,
> And twisting threads, a marvel to behold,
> Of bright sea-purple, while her maidens sit
> Behind her."   —(Od. VI., 385.)

One might continue indefinitely to draw pictures of life and customs from the Iliad and Odyssey, but to reproduce them all would be little short of reprinting the poems. They are accessible to all today and afford delightful reading.

The people believed implicitly in the power of the gods and goddesses. These took part in the mighty struggle before the walls of Troy, some aiding, some injuring the assailants.

They were believed to move unseen among the armies, driving weapons aside, or making blows effectual. To win their favor, sacrifices were offered at their shrines, and libations of wine were unfailingly poured out to them at every feast. Chryses, the aged priest, prays thus to Apollo:

> "Hear me, thou bearer of the silver bow,
>   Who guardest Chrysa, and the holy isle
>   Of Cilla, and art lord in Tenedos,
>   O Smintheus! if I ever helped to deck
>   Thy glorious temple, if I ever burned
>   Upon thy altar the fat thighs of goats
>   And bullocks, grant my prayer, and let thy shafts
>   Avenge upon the Greeks the tears I shed."—*Iliad,* I., 50.

and again:

> "They burned to Phoebus chosen hecatombs
>   Of bulls and goats beside the barren main,
>   From which the savor rose in smoke to heaven."—*Iliad,* I., 398.

With the passing of Mycenæan life, culture and civilization, we find an age of darkness, dispelled ere long by the new life of the vigorous race of Hellenes; and there begins Greek history, properly so-called.

LION GATE, MYCENAE.

CHAPTER IV.

SOURCES OF GREEK HISTORY.

We have just learned that the material for a knowledge of prehistoric ages in Greece is to be found in the field of archæology, and in the Homeric poems. Another poem survives from remote times: *Works and Days,* by Hesiod. This was composed perhaps two centuries after the Homeric poems, and while these sing of court life and the nobility, *Works and Days* treats of humble concerns and people. The various duties of the farmer and the sailor are enumerated, and the poet explains what days are lucky for the performance of each. Although written later than the Homeric epics, the civilization portrayed is not very different from that of Homeric times. The Greeks have become a nation, and a more settled condition prevails. Love of gain is growing, but no radical changes appear. Lacking wholly any particular literary spirit or artistic quality, the poem has lively interest for the student of early Greece.

For historical periods in Hellas there are several important sources from which modern historians have drawn material for the reconstruction of Greek development. A treatise on the Athenian Constitution by Aristotle is one of these. Since this particular writing is discussed later, we shall merely note here that Aristotle briefly reviewed the history of Athens from earliest times with the special purpose of tracing constitutional development in the city. Several points have been cleared up by the recovery of this manuscript, and we are now able to understand Athenian government to an extent previously impossible.

Herodotus was the first Greek historian. Born in Halicarnassus in 484 B. C., or thereabouts, he spent many years in traveling over the ancient world, writing his histories which, for the most part, remain to us. Most important for Greek history is his account of the Persian War, written in nine books, named after the muses. This division of the history, however, was probably the work of another. Herodotus expressly states his reason for writing his history: "That human events may not become obliterated by time, and that the great and wonderful deeds performed by Greeks and barbarians may not lose their glory." Whatever Herodotus himself observed or gained through personal investigation has proven in light of modern research to be generally true, but he was obliged to take much on hearsay, and he was too ready to incorporate mere guides' tales into his writings to give them great value for the student.

Thucydides wrote a history of the Peloponnesian War. As a scholarly work, this far exceeds the writings of Herodotus. It is written in a calm, dispassionate style, and while the sympathies of the writer are naturally with his native country, he is fair to all. The value of the work is enhanced by the fact that Thucydides incorporated into it many orations delivered during the early part of the war. While these were probably in no case set down as rendered, we get the spirit of the times from sentiments that Thucydides puts into the mouths of Greek statesmen.

Xenophon's writings are also of first value. He was an Athenian, born about 431 B. C., and distinguished himself by leading the Retreat of Ten Thousand, after the death of Cyrus the Younger. The story of the Greek expedition and its retreat is told in the Anabasis—the "march up,"— the *retreat* comprising six of the seven books.

The Hellenica, another writing of Xenophon, continued the story of the Peloponnesian War from the point where Thucydides left it to the fall of Athens. The style of the book is not equal to that of Thucydides, but we are quite dependent upon it for the years intervening between 411-362 B. C.

Polybius lived during the transition period between Alexandrian and Roman Greece. He wrote a history of the world from the beginning of the Second Punic War to the fall of Corinth, 221-146 B. C. Much of this work has been lost. Of the original forty books, the first five, long extracts from the next thirteen, and only fragments of the rest remain.

Plutarch's Lives of Illustrious Men form a valuable source. He lived in Bœotia about 50 A. D. He was educated in Athens and travelled extensively. The author of several treatises, he is generally known by his Lives,—forty-six parallel lives of Greeks and Romans having survived. The life of a Greek is followed by the life of some Roman and then a comparison drawn between the two. "For his lives of Greeks he drew from the writings of historians, poets, philosophers, orators and geographers, some one hundred and thirty-one having been counted, while, doubtless, many more have been utilized. Much, or the most, of this material has been lost, and the historian goes to the lives of the Greeks by Plutarch to find traces of these lost records. Unfortunately, Plutarch was not a critical historian, and although his narrative is made of material gathered from other writers, he does not feel impelled at all to name his source, and in borrowing does not always select the most valuable material." [1]

Strabo was born about 63 B. C. and wrote a valuable *Geography*. He travelled extensively, and his work is especially useful for the light it throws on Greek colonies. Not only was the geographical knowledge of the time therein accumulated, but much information regarding the resources of a country—its products and minerals, the people and their manner of life, was also incorporated. The work originally comprised seventeen books and has been almost wholly preserved.

Some two centuries later, Pausanias wrote his Description of Greece. This was the first guide book of Greece, and is historically valuable for the descriptions of buildings, monuments, statues and other evidences of human greatness to be seen in his day but now for the most part wholly obliterated or fallen into ruin. Besides monuments remaining in his own time, Pausanias consulted earlier works and described still more ancient ones.

In addition to these distinctively historical writings, the literature of Greece contains much that is helpful for the historical student. For example, the odes of Pindar were written to commemorate victories at the national games. Traditions connected with the house of the victor, or better, connected with the origin of the festivals themselves, are sometimes incorporated into these odes.

[1] Source Book of Greek History: Fling. 345.

The Greek plays are important; the tragedies are based upon some tradition or event in Greek development; the comedies satirized Athenian life and institutions. Æschylus was the first great tragic poet. He is believed to have written over seventy plays, seven alone having been preserved to us. *The Persians* was rendered in Athens eight years after the victory of Salamis.

Sophocles was the greatest tragic poet of Greece. He is said to have composed one hundred and twenty-three plays. Only seven survive. Euripides wrote many plays, and Aristophanes was greatest of Greek comedy writers. His comedies were so severe in their criticism of prominent men that finally personalities were barred from comedies altogether and institutions and existing customs became the butts of the comedy poets.

Orations of various Greek statesmen are repositories of historical material, notably the orations of Demosthenes. These were delivered upon matters which vitally concerned the Athenians, especially upon the encroachments of Philip of Macedon into Greece. These last are known as the Philippics and well express the sentiments of the discerning who understood Philip's ambitious plans for empire from the beginning of his movement for expansion.

Odes, folk-songs, early sonnets and fragments of verse remaining to us have some value for students of social history. However, these would be too numerous and possessed of too questionable assistance to be mentioned in a list of Greek sources. Strictly speaking, the historical writings of the ancient Greeks, philosophical discourses as they turned on Greek affairs and government, the tragedies for Greek mythology and tradition, and the odes commemorating public celebrations—these, together with the orations of Greek statesmen, supply the sources for all modern histories of Greece

EARLY MIGRATIONS.

The origin of the Hellenes is lost. During those centuries when the later Greek states were forming, people were occupied with matters of immediate concern, and no records were kept. Indeed, the art of writing was not commonly known

II—18

until some time later. When peace and settled conditions gave opportunity for reflection, all traces of the beginnings of the Hellenes were gone. Imagination, however, came to the aid of the Greek, and legends and traditions took the place of historic facts.

There had been a time, so the legend ran, when gods came down to earth in the guise of men. They took mortal wives, and the sons of these unions were heroes, possessing less power than gods, on one hand; excelling the strength and skill of mortals on the other. These heroes undertook great exploits; they freed the land of dangerous monsters and braved the terrors of the deep to seek out distant realms. From these superhuman beings sprang the leading families of Greece, receiving as part of their inheritance the transmitted courage and genius of their ancestors.

This simple conception expanded into a mass of legends, each augmented and amplified by minute details as time went on. These hero myths have value for us today, not as explaining Greek origins, but because they set forth Greek ideals and ideas.

The modern historical student cannot accept the fanciful stories of the Hellenes regarding their beginnings. It would be a long story to tell by what language tests and other methods of scientific inquiry certain general hypotheses have been established regarding their origin, and we shall confine ourselves simply to the conclusions which are now considered as at least highly probable.

The nucleus from which the later Greek tribes sprang probably came at a remote time from regions beyond the Black Sea, and gradually took up an abode in the northwestern part of the Balkan peninsula; 3000 B. C. is sometimes assumed as the date of this early removal, but no definite time can be assigned to it. We know that primitive people did not make long and rapid removals; when they migrated they took with them their flocks and herds, and this necessitated slow progress.

After a lapse of centuries, probably a movement of the tribes was once more started. A pastoral people, possessing flocks and herds, require wide grazing lands. Again, in a wild and barbarous age, one tribe resents the near approach of an alien people, for difficulties of common pasturage are likely to occur and lead to open war. Thus we shall find that lack of pasturage and the pressure of alien tribes were two motives which prompted early migrations. It frequently happened that one tribe setting out upon the march gave the signal for a general commotion.

Pressed by the Illyrians it may be, the Aryan people who had settled in the northwestern part of the Balkan peninsula moved south, while about the same time the Trojans probably journeyed into Asia Minor. The Hellenes pushed into Epirus, Acarnania and Ætolia. After a while, part of these newcomers crossed the Corinthian Gulf and settled Elis, Achæa, Messenia and the highlands of Arcadia. Contemporaneously, the Ionians, bound to them by language ties at least, settled in Attica and Argolis.

It must be remembered that these incoming tribes came not as conquerors, subduing all before them; rather, they crept in quietly, occupied unclaimed lands at first and finally appropriated the fertile valleys for themselves. The civilization of the country had long been Mycenæan, and was not changed at once. On the contrary, the invaders gave their language to the country and in turn absorbed in a measure the culture they found around them. In various districts of Greece life and language developed differently and for generations changes took place so gradually that they were unnoticed.

It has been suggested that the myth of the Battle of the Giants grew out of the overthrow of Mycenæan gods. "There are clear enough memories of conflict and conciliation between the gods of the invaders and the older deities of the land. The legend of the war of the gods and the giants can hardly be anything else than a mythical embodiment of the conflict of religions; the giants, or earth-born beings, represent the older gods whom the gods of Greece overthrew. And we can hardly be wrong in regarding Cronus, whom Zeus dethroned, as one of these older gods. But Zeus, who dethroned him, became his son; that was the conciliation." [2]

With the decline of Mycenæan power, intercourse with

[2] Hist. of Greece: Bury, 53.

lands across the Ægean became infrequent. The story of the
Argonauts may have grown out of attempts on the part of
the Hellenes to cross the sea. In such legends, numberless
journeys are summed up into one, and the various experiences, real and imaginary, recounted by returning seamen, are
attributed to one hero. When the Ægean became well known,
the objective port was set along the Black Sea, for terrors no
longer credited in nearby waters might yet be attributed to a
remote sea.

After the Trojan war, or after the period to which the
original Homeric poems belong—the tenth or eleventh centuries before Christ—an invasion of a somewhat different character occurred. This is known as the Dorian invasion. The
Dorians presumably belonged to the race which had earlier
migrated to the northern part of the Balkan peninsula. Before
900 B. C. they spread over lands around Parnassus. Doris
was one of their famous settlements in this locality, and it continued Dorian throughout Greek history. The great mass of
Dorians, however, sought more fertile lands and pushed southward into Peloponnesus, some travelling by boat, some over-
land. Three different conquests can be distinguished—the conquests of Laconia, of Argolis, and of Corinth.

The inhabitants of these districts, who would not submit
to new overlords, sought refuge in Attica, whose barren soil
and isolated position protected her from disturbance. Many
of the fugitives crossed the Ægean sea and made settlements
in Asia Minor.

A general commotion accompanied the advent of the Dorians, and some generations passed before readjustment was
completed. Arcadia and Attica were little influenced by these
changes, and this fact remained in the Greek mind long after.
Thus arose the tradition that "the Arcadians had lived in
their country before the moon was born and the people of
Attica were children of the earth"—which was one way of
saying that invaders and unsettled conditions had affected these
regions scarcely at all.

With the readjustment that followed the Dorian invasion
comes the dawn of Greek states.

CHAPTER V.

SPARTA.

Land of the lordly mien and iron frame!
Where wealth was held dishonor, luxury's smile
Worse than a demon's soul-destroying wile!
Where every youth that hailed the Day-God's beam,
Wielded the sword, and dreamt the patriot's dream;
Where childhood lisped of war with eager soul,
And woman's hand waved on to glory's goal,
Ay, she sent forth her son in battle's face,
Feared not his death, but only his disgrace;
Dropped on his home-borne corpse no woman's tear,
So he had died in valor's red career;
Wept only for the son who lost his shield,
And, choosing life to honor, fled the field.

NICHOLAS MICHELL.

EARLY SPARTA.

Little is definitely known concerning the beginnings of the Greek states. When written records began many changes had already taken place within them. We are led to believe that each state was at first a mere settlement around some easily fortified height, the inhabitants of the immediately surrounding district being governed by those in the village, and in times of danger taking refuge within the fortifications. Government was vested in a chief, or petty king, a council of elders,—advising and aiding the king,—and an assembly made up of all freemen. The assembly heard plans presented by the council and merely accepted or rejected them.

Were we in a position to follow the progress of the many Grecian states from their earliest formation to historic times, we should have little to pay us for our trouble—for the history of one but repeated that of another in some modified form, and few advanced along lines which from the beginning insured future greatness.

Sparta was the first Greek state to exert a wide influence. While this Dorian settlement was largely devoid of the fullness and richness of later Greek life, yet from its beginnings Sparta built for the future, and the very austerity of her customs raised her ultimately to power.

When the Dorians entered the Peloponnesus, they took the rich Eurotas valley region for themselves, forcing the earlier occupants of the land farther away. Five smaller villages seem to have been settled by them. These united as time went on and became known as Sparta.

Two co-equal kings were retained by the Spartans and it may be that the union of the two strongest settlements resulted only on condition that the kings of each be retained. Lycurgus was the traditional lawgiver of Sparta. Just as in the case of Moses, he having given the children of Israel some early laws and consequently been acknowledged as a lawgiver, for centuries later, whenever new laws were promulgated, to give them force they were attributed to him—so, probably in the case of the Spartans; they later attributed laws to their first statesman, Lycurgus, which in reality came into being long after his death. We have, however, two objects in the study of Greek history: to find out what was historically true, and to ascertain what the Greeks themselves thought was true regarding facts in their own development.

Eight hundred B. C. is a date assigned for the age of Lycurgus, whose character is so shadowy that he has often been declared a myth. Since it is impossible to determine which of Sparta's laws were formulated by him, we shall simply consider her system of government as a whole, remembering that its general character was always believed by the Spartans to have been the result of the far-sighted statesmanship of Lycurgus.

Besides her two kings, whose offices were hereditary, Sparta had a senate of twenty-eight old men. These were chosen from the leading families of Sparta in the following manner: a few men would be stationed where they could not see those in the assembly, yet could hear. Men who were deemed fitted for place in the council, or senate, would be brought before the popular assembly, one at a time. He who was greeted by the loudest cheers from the assembly in the judgment of the listeners, was declared elected. Only men above sixty years of age were eligible, but when elected they served for life. The two kings met with them and had equal vote with them. The body of thirty thus accounted for, was called the *Gerousia*.

The Apella, or popular assembly, was made up of all freemen of Sparta above thirty years of age. They met monthly, in the full of the moon, in the open air; they remained standing while the plans of the Gerousia were made known to them; there was no deliberation upon these, but they shouted for or against their adoption.

When the invading Dorians conquered the Eurotas valley, they pushed the earlier possessors of the soil out on less arable lands. These people probably belonged to one of the many tribes known later by the general name of Hellenes. The Spartans called them Periœci—dwellers apart, provincials,—and allowed them to have their own local government under Spartan supervision. The Periœci fought with the Spartans in time of war, and retained quite a degree of freedom.

The country people of more remote districts, together with captives taken in war, on the other hand, became serfs or helots. Belonging to the state of Sparta, they were put out to service among the Spartans and Periœci. They tilled the soil, and were allowed to retain for themselves whatever they produced in excess of the yearly amount of produce required by the overlords. Since these helots had recently been freemen, they were very bitter toward their conquerors, and remained a constant menace to the state.

Citizens of Sparta were alone called Spartans. To maintain his full citizenship, a Spartan was required to conform to these general requirements: he must submit to the military discipline of Sparta; he must take his meals at the Syssetia, or public mess, to the support of which he must contribute monthly; he must acknowledge the right of the state to supervise the training of his sons; he must not engage in trade or business.

It was once the custom to see confusion and disorder in Sparta, until Lycurgus, an inspired statesman, came into view, formulating a code of laws by whose observance the state grew to great power. Extended study among ancient peoples has shown that such is not the course of nations. While men of strong personality leave their stamp upon their age, and frequently exert an influence which lives on after they are gone, nevertheless a man, however gifted, does not make an epoch; he merely directs forces already at work. So here, it is probable that Lycurgus codified long existing customs of the Dorians, and any laws which were in advance of these were only enforced when their practical value had been demonstrated.

The Dorians were a warlike people. They were cruel and relentless, like most primitive peoples, but they did not outgrow these traits as many others, because of their continued military character. They were a sturdy race of mountaineers, desiring above all to perpetuate their fighting strength. To this end it is probable that they had always abandoned weak or deformed offspring. Hence the law which required a father to present his new-born babe before a committee for inspection, allowing it to be raised only if well and strong. The law in this case was plainly no innovation but a custom crystallized. Again, in the matter of training the youth. It was desirable that soldiers be brave, able to endure severe marches, scanty food, and hard fare. Because parents might be indulgent with their own children it was provided that when seven years of age the boys should be taken from home and put under the care of those responsible to the state. Their training was vigorous in the extreme, but in the end they were able to endure great hardships. Little time was spent with those things which are today considered necessary to education; rather, the boys took exercise, foraged for their food, grew accustomed to getting about in the dark and in all respects prepared for their life-long careers as soldiers. It is at once apparent that one who engages in trade or industry comes to look at the world from a personal standpoint; interest in his own hope of gain grows rapidly to modify his interest in the welfare of his country. The Spartans knew this well, and so all forms of trade were forbidden among them. To discourage the accumulation of wealth, iron money was established for internal commerce. A wagon and oxen would be required to

NIOBE.

move a few hundred dollars' worth of this inconvenient coin, and no one could easily secrete it. All forms of self-indulgence and luxury were scorned. Long afterwards the poor dwellings and unpretentious temples excited comment among the Greeks. Thucydides once spoke of Sparta in this way: "Suppose the city of Sparta to be deserted and nothing left but the temples and the ground plan, distant ages would be very unwilling to believe that the power of the Laconians was at all equal to their fame. And yet they own two-thirds of the Peloponnesus, and are acknowledged leaders of the whole, as well as of numerous allies in the rest of Hellas. But their city is not regularly built, and has no splendid temples or other edifices; it rather resembles a straggling village like the ancient towns of Hellas, and would therefore make a poor show." [1]

The states in other parts of Greece gradually outgrew their kings, and passed through various experiments in governments, becoming oligarchies, democracies, often falling under the rule of Tyrants. Such was not the case in Sparta. Retaining their traditional kings, they gradually limited the kingly power. The kings had formerly exercised supreme command in time of war, and directed foreign affairs. Later a board of five men, called ephors, or overseers, was instituted. They served only a year, but owing to the curious manner of election—by acclamation rather than by vote,—the same men were often able to keep the office in their own hands. The ephors were in reality the important officials in the state. They convened the Apella and Gerousia, and presided over both. They negotiated with foreign ambassadors, gave directions to the generals, and interfered in the name of the state in affairs of other cities. They criticised and punished at their discretion all citizens and officials of the realm. In time of war the king still commanded the troops but one or more ephors accompanied him to battle and later made a report of any action which met with disapproval.

The Apella tried at times to gain more authority. For example, when measures were brought before this body for adoption, conditions would be inserted, or omissions of certain

[1] Thucydides: Bk. 1.

clauses would be made which entirely changed the nature of the measure. To prevent initiative power being taken by the Apella, a provision was brought forward providing that the senate, with the kings, should have power to reverse any crooked decisions of the people.

Such changes were slight when compared to the constantly varying conditions in other parts of Greece, and the fixed and conservative trend of affairs in Sparta called forth frequent comment. One writer says: "The Spartans became as self-satisfied as the Chinese and more arrogant and exclusive." Thucydides regarded this conservatism as the secret of Spartan success: "For although Laconia, after the conquest of the country by the Dorians, who now inhabit it, remained long unsettled, and indeed longer than any country which we know, nevertheless she obtained good laws at an earlier period than any other, and has never been subject to tyrants. She has preserved the same form of government for more than four hundred years, reckoning to the end of the Peloponnesian war. It was the excellence of her constitution which has given her power, and thus enabled her to regulate the affairs of other states."

Having established herself securely at home, it was inevitable that Sparta should turn to conquest. The Messenians occupied the western portion of southern Peloponnesus, and possessing fertile and alluring land, the envy of the Spartans was aroused, especially as they felt an increasing need of more territory. Wars with Messenia lasted for many years, for her people proved as sturdy soldiers as the Spartans. In the end they were reduced to submission, many of their number being taken as helots and their lands divided among Spartan subjects. As a result of these wars Sparta extended her rule to the western sea. Other Peloponnesian states became allies and the Peloponnesian League was established, whereby the ally states agreed to furnish Sparta a certain number of fighting men in time of war, and to acknowledge her leadership.

Such in the main was the course of affairs in Sparta before 500 B. C.

CHAPTER VI.

ATHENS.

O land of Solon, Plato, and of men
Whose glorious like earth ne'er shall see again!
Thou art not dead,—thy every plain and hill
Sends forth a voice, and teems with spirits still!
What though no more they teach, with valor burn?
Thy sage and warrior breathe from out the urn,
And each lone wreck that moss and ivies bind
Points to bright days, and speaks of godlike mind.
But rock-crowned Athens calls our thoughts away.
There sits she, lovely, in her calm decay,
The eye of Greece, Fame's daughter sad and lone,
The queen of Wisdom on her mouldering throne.

Athens! thou birthplace of the great, the free!
Though bowed thy power, and dimmed thy name may be,
Though old Renown's once dazzling sun hath set,
Fair beams the star of Memory o'er thee yet.
City! where sang the bard, and taught the sage,
Thy shrines may fall, thou ne'er wilt know old age;
Fresh shall thy image glow in every heart,
And but with Time's last hour thy fame depart.
                                        NICHOLAS MICHELL.

We have seen that the acropolis of Athens was one of the heights occupied in the Mycenæan age, and portions of its Cyclopean walls, built at a remote period, remain to the present day. As this civilization died away, and rude Hellenes replaced an earlier people, the commanding rock was in turn appropriated by them.

Attica contains approximately 1,000 square miles, and like all Greek states was at one time the dwelling place for several tribes, each under the rule of its own chieftain or king. Few valleys, scanty soil, and a generally rugged character saved the country from invasion when the Dorians spread into Greece, and while we find Attica united at a comparatively early time under leadership of Athens, the union was brought about by assimilation rather than conquest. This was fortunate for Athens, as it left no strongly drawn lines between social classes, as, for example, existed in Laconia between conquerors and conquered.

"Certainly Attica, of which the soil was poor and thin, enjoyed a long freedom from civil strife, and therefore retained its original inhabitants. Attica through immigration increased in population more than any other region. For the leading men of Hellas, when driven out of their own country by war and revolution, sought an asylum at Athens, and from the very earliest times, being admitted to rights of citizenship. so greatly increased the number of the inhabitants that Attica became incapable of containing them, and was at last obliged to send out colonies to Ionia." [1]

Theseus was one of the mythical kings of Attica, and according to Thucydides, it was he who effected the union of the state.

"In the days of Cecrops and the first kings, down to the reign of Theseus, Attica was divided into communes, having their own town halls and magistrates. Except in the case of alarm the whole people did not assemble in council under the king, but administered their own affairs, and advised together in their several townships. But when Theseus came to the throne he, being a powerful as well as a wise ruler, among other improvements in the administration of the country, dissolved the councils and separate governments, and united all the inhabitants of Attica in the present city, establishing one council and town hall. They continued to live on their own land, but he compelled them to resort to Athens as their metropolis; and henceforward they were all inscribed in the role of her citizens. A great city thus arose, which was handed down by Theseus to his descendants, and from his day to this the Athenians have regularly celebrated the national festival of the Synœcia, or 'union of the communes,' in honor of the goddess Athena." [2]

[1] Thucydides: I, 2. [2] Ibid, II, 15.

The processes of unification in Laconia and Attica were thus wholly unlike. The unification of Laconia might be compared in some respects to that brought about in England when the Normans invaded the land and held its various elements in control by military force; the unity of Attica was accomplished more as a modern city expands, gradually absorbing within itself all outlying boroughs and villages,—its citizens coming to feel greater pride in belonging to the united whole than they knew when members of only a part.

Tradition has it that Codrus was the last Athenian king, the people feeling that none was worthy to succeed him. However that may have been, when authentic history begins in Attica, the king had lost many of his earlier royal prerogatives and an oligarchy was already established.

Until recently little was understood concerning government in Athens before the time of Solon. It was known that Aristotle, four centuries before Christ, had written about the constitutions of one hundred fifty-eight Greek states, but these treatises were lost and were known only from excerpts made by later Greek and Roman writers. However, in 1891, among some papyri found in an Egyptian tomb and stored some time in the British Museum, a copy of Aristotle's Constitution of Athens was discovered. This was immediately translated and given to the world, much to the gratification of Greek history students.

This valuable manuscript consisted of four rolls of papyrus, 18 feet 8 inches long and 11 inches wide. It had at one time been used by the bailiff of an Egyptian farm for his reports. Certain years of Vespasian's reign are mentioned, 78 and 79 A. D. being probably those referred to. Apparently when these reports were no longer valued, Aristotle's Constitution was copied on the reverse sides—not by one but by four different writers. The first and last portions of the treatise are lacking, and many words in the text are badly blurred. Nevertheless it has been possible to read the manuscript, and in spite of the fact that no author's name and no title attaches to the papyrus, it is unquestionably a copy of that writing known to ancient scholars as Aristotle's Constitution of Athens. Quotations from the original treatise were made by early writers, and these have been found for the most part in this recently discovered copy, which had lain undisturbed for hundreds of years in an Egyptian tomb, found its way at last to the British Museum, where it is treasured today among other priceless heritages of antiquity.

Some facts of Athenian history long established have thus been verified; other inferences and suppositions have in turn proved erroneous. It appears that before the time of Codrus, either certain kings had shown themselves to be poor military leaders, or else it was not thought best that they expose themselves to the dangers of war. Consequently a Field-Marshal, or Polemarch, was chosen as commander of the army. Next, a Regent, or Archon, was added, and these two officers shared the responsibility of government with the king. All three were elected for life by a council known as the Areopagus.

In the story of Greek Mythology we found that Ares was once brought by Poseidon to answer to a charge of murder, the hearing before the gods taking place on an Athenian hill known thereafter as Areopagus, or "hill of Ares." From earliest times in Athens the Council of the Areopagus met on this traditional hill, and here at night those accused of dire deeds were summoned to answer charges brought against them.

Besides electing the three Archons, and hearing criminal cases, the Areopagus had other functions; it was composed of nobles and exercised general supervision over affairs of government. In 752 B. C., tenure of office for the archons was lessened from life to a period of ten years. In 682 B. C. it was reduced to one year, and six new magistrates, called Thesmothetæ—or recorders of court decisions—were added. These nine officers, sometimes called nine archons, were elected by the Areopagus, and henceforth the council itself was composed of ex-archons. Once becoming a member of the Council of Areopagus, one held his seat for life.

While the king had considered the welfare of all his subjects, the nobles ruled for themselves alone; hence the lower classes fell into miserable condition. Society was made up of nobles, free farmers, artisans, and a rapidly increasing class which was compelled to till the land for the nobles, receiving but one-sixth of the crops raised for themselves. Poor seasons forced free farmers into this class. When they were compelled to borrow money, they could only pledge themselves and their families as security for the debt. In this way land fell more and more into the hands of the nobles, and the unfortunate poor sank deeper into poverty and servitude.

It was under such conditions as these that Cylon, a noble of power and prominence, thought the opportunity favorable for him to seize control of the government. This had been successfully done by tyrants in Corinth and other Grecian states. Accordingly, he raised a following and made an unexpected raid on the Acropolis; but while the common people would have welcomed any change, since their lot could scarcely be worse, the nobles were very jealous of one another, and they put down this demonstration, killing Cylon and his followers.

Thus far there had been no code of laws in Athens. In days when there were neither laws nor a written constitution, decisions rendered upon cases in court took the place of these, and were themselves used as a precedent for future decisions. On this account it was important that all renderings should be preserved for reference. This was the duty of the Thesmothetæ—"writers of dooms." Nevertheless, only these court recorders, as we would call them, were familiar with the decisions, and since nobles held the position, the masses remained ignorant of laws by which they were tried and sentenced. About the year 621 B. C., therefore, the people clamored for a publication of the laws of Athens, that all might know what they were. This demand was reasonable, and Draco, an archon, was directed to prepare them for the public.

Until the copy of Aristotle's Athenian Constitution came to light, it had been supposed that Draco merely codified old laws found in court decisions, and originating in tribal customs. In this manuscript, however, he is credited with having given Athens her first Constitution. It would appear that Draco allowed all men who had means sufficient to equip themselves in time of war for infantry service, to constitute the popular assembly, which body henceforth elected the nine archons, choosing them only from the nobility. Furthermore, he created a Council of 400; its members were required to have certain property qualifications, since they possessed legislative powers. The Council of the Areopagus was left as guardian of the laws and chief power in the state.

Penalties for crime were made severe by Draco, who has become famous for his cruel and relentless character. However, he made distinction between intentional and unintentional murder, and tried to take punishment out of private hands and so abolish the blood feud, still common in his day.

Neither the publication of the laws nor the new constitution accomplished much in relieving the misery of the time, for Aristotle says: "After this there was contention for a long time between the upper classes and the populace. Not only was the constitution oligarchial in every respect, but the poorer classes, men, women and children, were in absolute slavery to the rich. They were called Hectemori (those who receive a sixth portion) because they cultivated the lands of the rich for a sixth part of the produce. The whole country was in the hands of a few persons, and if the tenants failed to pay their rent they were liable to be haled into slavery and their children with them. Their persons were mortgaged to their creditors. But the hardest and bitterest part of the condition of the masses was that they had no share in the offices now existing under the constitution. At the same time they were discontented with every other feature of their lot; for, to speak generally, they had no part nor share in anything."

When the state seemed on the very verge of ruin, Solon was brought into public view. "Now seeing that such was the organization of the constitution and that the many were in slavery to the few, the people rose against the upper class. The strife was keen and for a long time the two parties were face to face with one another, till at last, by common consent, they appointed Solon to be mediator and archon."[3]

A noble by birth, Solon had been forced into commercial life to earn a livelihood. He had journeyed in different parts of the ancient world and had seen points of advantage in various governments. In 594 B. C. he was elected archon for the following year. Instead of promising to protect each man's property intact, as had been customary, he immediately issued

[3] Aristotle: Constitution, Kenyon's trans.

a proclamation that all existing debts were thereupon can-
celled, that all persons held in servitude for debt should be
set free, and those who had been sold into other countries
should be ransomed. He, moreover, forbade loans being further made on security of the debtor's person or family. These
were radical reforms and were only justifiable because of the
alarming situation. They gave freedom to many slaves and
rescued a large number of people from hopeless poverty. The
occasion was celebrated by a public feast, and was held in
memory as the "release of burdens."

Solon next turned to financial matters. In place of the
old currency he caused new coins to be made, placing Athens
on equal footing with the leading commercial states of Greece
and Asia Minor. At the close of the year it was plain that
he did not intend to use his position for personal ends, and
being trusted by all classes, was again elected archon, with
legislative as well as executive authority. He was urged to
give Athens a new constitution.

Thus far the government of Athens had been the exclusive
right of the nobles. To break away from old class distinctions,
Solon made ownership of land the basis of citizenship. He
divided the entire population into four classes: the first class
included all those whose yearly incomes from their lands were
equal in value to 500 measures of grain, or more; the second,
those whose income ranged from 300-500 measures; the third,
from 150-300 measures; the fourth and last, those whose
incomes fell below the value of 150 measures of grain. From
the first class alone were archons to be chosen; lesser magistrates were chosen from the first three classes. Members of
the fourth class could not hold office, but on the other hand,
they were not compelled to share the expense of maintaining
the government.

The Council of 400, or the Boulê, was retained. As before,
it was composed of 100 members from each of the four tribes
of Attica. This body considered all measures which were to
be brought before the assembly. No matter could be presented before the ecclesia without previous deliberation upon it
in the boulê.

The ecclesia, or the assembly of the people, was composed

of all citizens of whatever class, above twenty years of age.
Solon gave the popular assembly new functions. Not only
could they accept or reject plans put before them by the
boulê, but they had the right of investigating the doings of
any magistrate upon the expiration of his term of office. Such
hearings were made before a body of jurymen, drawn annually
from the community at large. Here, too, appeals might be
made by any citizen who thought himself unfairly treated by
the archons. Finally the Council of Areopagus was retained
in name, although its duties were somewhat modified. All
cases of murder, arson, treason and other serious crime were
brought before it. Its decisions were irrevocable, and it
retained the highest respect of all citizens throughout its administration. Laws passed by the boulê and agreed upon by the
ecclesia were here rejected if they were found contrary to the
common good.

Such in the main were the constitutional reforms of Solon.
Certain other laws and measures provided by him might be
noted—some of them to be understood only when considered
in the light of his times. One of these provided that a man
in time of civil strife must take one side or the other, or lose
his right of citizenship. Another allowed foreigners to
renounce their native allegiance and become metics at Athens.
This was enacted to accommodate merchants who might desire
to make permanent homes in the Attic city. Still another
made idleness an offense. It was thought that the welfare of
the state demanded the activity of all its citizens.

These far-sighted reforms gave Solon place with the world's
statesmen. The events immediately following seemed to show
that his efforts in favor of a democracy had been in vain.
However, looking at the matter in the light of later history,
we can see that Solon laid the foundation for Athenian democracy and greatness. Making property instead of birth the
basis of citizenship, he enabled all industrious and capable men
to avail themselves of its privileges. Because of his unselfish
efforts and simple justice, Solon was always revered in Athens
as one who loved the people.

" I gave to the mass of the people such rank as befitted their need,
I took not away their honor, and I granted naught to their greed;
But those who were rich in power, who in wealth were glorious
      and great,
I bethought me that naught should befall them unworthy their
      splendor and state;
And I stood with my shield outstretched, and both were safe in
      its sight,
And I would not that either should triumph when the triumph
      was not with right." ⁴

    ⁴Aristotle: Constitution, Kenyon's trans.

A GREEK THEATER, ATHENS.

CHAPTER VII.

FROM THE AGE OF SOLON TO THE PERSIAN WARS.

After the adoption of Solon's constitution, peace reigned for a few years; but the rich were discontented because they could no longer control affairs as they had done before, and the poor, having been somewhat relieved by legal enactment, desired that they be further benefited and aided to become better off without hard labor. So presently the city split up into factions again. There were three political parties, each of which strived to gain the upper hand in the community; the party of the Shoremen, or traders, under leadership of Megacles; this faction stood for a moderate government. Second, the party of the Plain-men, or wealthy owners of valley lands, for the most part nobles. Their leader was Lycurgus and they wished to get control out of the hands of the people and bring it once more under their own management. In other words, they wanted to abolish the democracy and re-establish the old oligarchy. Third, the party of Hill men, or the poor shepherds and farmers, joined by the masses of whatever calling. Their leader was Pisistratus, strangely enough, a noble, who claimed to care not at all for his own social class, but desired only to help the people. We shall see that his attitude was not so entirely disinterested as it first appeared. Feeling between these parties and their leaders ran high, and the spirit of unrest was abroad in Athens.

One day Pisistratus drove into the market place covered with wounds which he had inflicted upon himself, but which he claimed to have received at the hands of the Plain-men because he espoused the cause of the people. He told the gathering crowd that he was no longer safe in Athens, and they at once declared that they would call a meeting of the ecclesia and give him a body guard, which was promptly done. Solon tried in vain to be heard and warned the people against the young noble, but to no purpose. Having soon increased the original guard of fifty, which had been voted him, Pisistratus was soon able to seize the acropolis and establish himself as tyrant of Athens, in 561 B. C.

By the word *tyrant* we at present mean a selfish and unprincipled ruler. To the Greeks the word at first merely signified one who gained control of the government in an irregular and unconstitutional manner, whether he used the power so gained for good or ill. However, so many of their tyrants proved to be unprincipled men that the term grew to have its present significance.

In spite of this high-handed way of seizing the government, Pisistratus ruled wisely. He helped the poor and did not oppress the rich. Nevertheless, the other parties united to drive him out of the city, but with characteristic fickleness he was shortly allowed to return. Expelled again, he gathered a force and a third time established himself as tyrant. He did not violate the constitution Solon had given, but he saw to it that members of his own family always appeared on the board of archons. He imposed a tax of one-twentieth on all produce of the land, but the revenue thus derived was spent to improve the roads, beautify the city, and for other internal purposes. He gathered literary men around him, and tradition says that the Homeric poems were now given their present form. This, however, is a matter of dispute.

In his treatise on the constitution, Aristotle says of him: "His administration was more like a constitutional government than the rule of a tyrant. Not only was he in every respect humane and mild and ready to forgive those who offended, but, in addition, he advanced money to the poorer people to help them in their labors, so that they might make their living by agriculture. In this he had two objects: first, that they might not spend their time in the city but might be scattered over the face of the country, and secondly, that, being moderately well off and occupied with their own business, they might have neither the wish nor the time to attend to public affairs. In matters in general he burdened the people as little as possible with his government, but always cultivated peace and kept them in quietness. Hence the tyranny of Pisistratus was often spoken of proverbially as "the age of gold," since later the government became much harsher, owing

to the excesses of his sons. The quality which gave most satisfaction of all was his popular and kindly disposition. The
majority alike of the upper class and of the people were in
his favor; the former he won by social intercourse with them,
the latter by the assistance which he gave to their private
purses, and his nature fitted him to win the hearts of both." [1]

When Pisistratus died in 527 B. C., his sons Hippias and
Hipparchus succeeded him as joint rulers. They are often
spoken of as the Pisistratidæ, the Greek terminal *idæ* meaning
'sons of.' For a time they ruled as acceptably as their father.
Then, as a result of a private quarrel, Hipparchus was killed.
Hippias, not knowing how far-reaching was the plot against
him, was embittered by the death of his brother and began to
oppress the people and to lessen their privileges. Finally a
popular uprising occurred and Hippias was banished from
Greece. Thus in 511 B. C. the republic was restored and
democracy triumphed again in Athens.

After the overthrow of tyranny, Clisthenes became the
leader of the popular party, while Isagoras was leader of the
nobles. Feeling need of additional strength, Isagoras called
upon the Spartan king for aid. It was repeatedly demonstrated in Greek history that while the Greek could be loyal
to his personal interests, or to the interests of his party—which
generally furthered his personal interests—few hesitated to
expose their country to dangers from outside powers when
these might give temporary assistance to some cherished
project. Sparta was the most powerful state in all Greece at
this time, and her interference in Athenian matters was most
of all to be avoided, yet Isagoras did not scruple to invoke her
aid in his cause. The Spartans enabled the aristocratic party
to win, but when an attempt was made to impose upon the
Athenians a Spartan-like constitution, a popular uprising drove
out the Spartan king, the Laconian army and Isagoras, killing
many of his supporters.

The people were left in control, and some important constitutional changes were soon inaugurated by Clisthenes, their
leader. He saw that strongly drawn party lines were ruinous
to a pure democracy. To cut loose from them—for the fac-

[1] Aristotle: Athenian Constitution.

tions of Shoreman, Plain-men and Hill-men—he divided all Attica into ten districts, or, as we might call them, counties. These were named from ten national heroes whose statues were placed in the market place. These districts were again divided into their various villages, burroughs, etc., called by the term *deme*. All the people of Attica were then divided into ten tribes, but the tribe had no geographical significance. Had such been the case, one district would have been composed of merchants, another of farmers, and so on. Instead, a tribe might be made up of demes in two or three counties. All met in Athens for important matters, so no inconvenience attached to this scheme. All men dwelling in a deme were enrolled in its records as Athenian citizens, and freed slaves and foreigners who desired to become citizens were given full rights. Henceforth, as a result, each felt a pride in being a citizen of Athens, and factional feeling gave way to patriotism for country.

The Council was increased from 400 to 500 members, fifty being chosen from each of the ten tribes. The year was divided into ten periods and fifty council members managed affairs of state for each period. A new chairman was elected each morning and for twenty-four hours was entrusted with keys to the acropolis, treasury, and seal of state. The following morning, upon the election of the succeeding chairman, these were turned over to him.

The old assembly, or ecclesia, was continued and a new feature introduced into it. Clisthenes thought that strong rival party-leaders were detrimental to the welfare of Athens. Therefore he evolved the plan of banishing one until the crisis was passed. Each year if the ecclesia so desired they might vote the name of one citizen whom they wished to banish. The name was written on bits of pottery, called ostraka, and dropped like a ballot into a box. If one man received 6,000 votes or more, he was compelled to go away for ten years, at the expiration of which time he might return to enjoy full rights of citizenship.

The ecclesia decided on peace or war, heard reports of magistrates at the close of the year, passed new laws and repealed old ones, determined questions of revenues and taxation and elected the archons.

While influences had been long working in furtherance of popular government, in spite of backsets during the age of tyranny, pure democracy was first realized in Athens under the leadership of Clisthenes. All citizens were then able to share in the affairs of state, and magistrates were no longer limited to those of wealth and noble birth. From this time forward Athens advanced rapidly, and instead of being one of the backward states, soon took her place with the leading states of Greece.

We have thus far considered but two of the Grecian states: Sparta and Athens. Sparta developed an aristocratic government and went no further. She became the leading power in the Peloponnesus, bringing much of southern Greece under her direct influence and making alliances with nearly all the remaining states. Athens developed a democracy, and by this time was not even first state in central Greece. Other states came rapidly forward, some possessing great commercial strength, others striving for wide political influence. Nearly all passed from the rule of kings to oligarchies, then to republics and tyrannies. Some experienced all these changes in a comparatively brief time.

It is neither possible nor desirable that we enter upon a discussion of all Greek states, nor even study those few which at one time or another took first rank. It is very necessary, on the other hand, that we understand what in general was the usual course of a Greek state, and further, that we note what influences were tending to union and disruption in the country as a whole.

By a *state* the Greeks did not understand what the word signifies to us. Their state centered around some city and included only those surrounding settlements whose people might easily assemble in the city for religious and political duties. If we imagine all Greece as corresponding to one of our states, and all Greek states as corresponding to our counties, each independent of the rest, we will get a truer conception of the real situation than by comparing the country to some country known to us today. The Greeks never understood nor developed representative government. In the United States, for example, it would not be conceivable that all men should repair to the capital and participate in making the laws; yet this was just what every Greek citizen desired to do. Hence it was only possible to develop states of limited size, wherein general assemblies would be practicable. We do indeed find certain states gaining supremacy over others, but no successful effort was made to interfere with local affairs. Unions were made for outside considerations—for protection against a common foe, or against a state which was becoming too strong for common safety.

As has been pointed out, Greece was divided up into many inaccessible parts, and the topography of the land tended to divide rather than unite the people. It was easier to trade with foreign countries than with certain peoples within Greece itself. During much of the year land communication between neighboring states was frequently impossible. To these strongly marked topographical divisions we must add the character of the Greek,—jealous of increasing influence on the part of others, and guarding with stubborn determination his own freedom. It is plain, then, that there were powerful forces tending to hold states apart.

On the other hand, certain influences tended to produce a degree of union among the Hellenes. They came originally from the same stock, spoke a common language, and shared a common religion. It is true that various fusions of blood made the people of one district somewhat unlike those of another; it is true that their language grew richer and more perfect in an active, intellectual locality than in mountainous districts peopled only by herdsmen; and finally we find wide differences in the cults of various states. In spite of all this, the Athenian, for instance, felt a kinship with citizens of Hellas which he could not feel for any other people; with all modifications of speech, the inhabitants of Thessaly could converse with the Spartan; and above all varying religious customs, all Greeks regarded Mt. Olympus as the dwelling place of deities they held in common.

Racial relationship and bond of language are easily understood. Somewhat more complicated were the religious leagues, which lived on after their first objects had been accomplished or superseded. The religious significance of these leagues belongs to later consideration. Here we are concerned with their political functions. The Amphictyonic League may be cited as typical and most important. It had two centers: the temple of Demeter in Anthela, in the land of the Malians, near the Pass of Thermopylæ; the second, the temple of Apollo at Delphi. Twelve peoples composed this league. Among them were the Malians, Dorians, Ionians, Thessalians, Boetians and Phocians. The league dated from a time when the Dorians had not yet brought the Peloponnesus under their sway, and was a union of northern and central Greece. Each of the twelve peoples had equal vote and sent two delegates to the bi-yearly meetings, held spring and fall. Not only were sacrifices offered to the deities of the temples, but regulations were made to govern the states thus leagued together in time of war. They agreed that they would not cut a city off from its supply of water, and that they would not ruthlessly destroy any Amphictyonic town. Their most sacred duty was to protect the shrine of Apollo at Delphi from disturbances or interference of neighboring tribes. Four different so-called sacred wars were declared on occasions when free access to the oracle had been denied pilgrims. The authority of the league was vague; fidelity to religious custom made it effective; yet political importance was closely allied to the religious aims, and as states grew stronger, the political aspect gained prominence.

Finally the Greeks found a powerful bond of union in their national games, most famous of which were those celebrated at Olympus every four years, after the summer solstice. Athletic contests were open to free-born Greeks from all states; the foot-races had originally been of first interest, but soon contests in jumping, wrestling, casting javelins and disc throwing were added. Later, chariot races were allowed, but these led to display of wealth rather than agility and healthy competition, and were scarcely in accord with the original spirit of the Olympiads.

While these celebrations lasted, a sacred truce was declared throughout the land. Besides athletic sports, men of learning gathered to read their poems and literary productions, for the entertainment and edification of visitors. Herodotus

read portions of his histories before audiences gathered in
honor of the great Zeus.   Here the Homeric poems were
recited and new poets strived for laurels.   In the grove adjacent the finest art of Greece was brought to the honor of
Olympic deities.   Temples were erected and beautifully
adorned.   The visitor to Elis returned home with renewed
pride in his countrymen and his race.   It was natural that a
feeling of kinship should have been strengthened as a result of
such gatherings, and the Olympian games continued for generations and worked for unity in the land.

GREEK VASE.

CHAPTER VIII.

STRUGGLE WITH PERSIA.

When the Dorians pressed into the Peloponnesus and sub-jected earlier occupants of the land, some of the sturdy Hel-lenes refused to recognize their authority and wandered away to seek other homes.   They migrated to Athens in many cases, and thence to Asia Minor, where they appropriated cities already existing, or founded settlements of their own.   These early colonists were followed by others for many generations. Gradually the Greeks became a commercial people, rivaled only by the Phœnicians as carriers for the ancient world.   Their settlements reached all countries where commodities of civili-zation were demanded and their outposts were fixed on the outskirts of the ancient world.   Before 600 B. C. they had planted colonies in Italy, Africa, among the islands of the Ægean, along the shores of western Asia, and in the region of the Black Sea.   So far as political organization was concerned, colonies were generally not controlled by states from whence they came.   Some established oligarchies, others democracies, and many passed through the same changes of government which we have seen in continental Greece.   Like the home states, these colonies were divided among themselves, jealous of one another, and unable to remain in close or lasting unions.

Leaving the Greeks for a moment, it will be remembered that the great empires of Babylonia and Assyria were followed by the Persian Empire, which was quickly brought into being by Cyrus the Great.   Having overcome the Medes, he fell heir to whatever remained of the old Assyrian state, and Babylon he won for himself.   In time Persian territory reached from the river Halus on the northwest, while across this stream lay the fair kingdom of Lydia.

Lydia had been a state of minor importance, but under the kingship of Crœsus she had expanded into activity.   Finding his land shut off from the great sea-ports held by the Ionic Greeks, Crœsus undertook a campaign against the shore cities and in 560 B. C. succeeded in bringing them under tribute to Lydia. Crœsus was himself imbued with the Greek spirit, and having gained commercial advantages for his country, he did not attempt to interfere with the internal affairs of these conquered cities, requiring only tribute. Consequently, peace came again, and the yoke of Lydia was light.

When the armies of Cyrus penetrated to Lydian borders, Crœsus did not wait for attack, but instead carried the war into Persian territory. In the struggle which followed, Lydia fell to the share of the great conqueror. Naturally her tribute cities came also under Persian control. It was soon found, however, that submission to Lydia and to Persia were two different things. In addition to tribute exacted, soldiers and ships were required of the Ionic cities in times of war. Moreover, when Darius ascended the Persian throne, he instituted radical changes. For purposes of administration the entire Persian empire was divided into satraps or provinces with a Persian provincial governor over each. The first province included these Ionic cities along the shore, and the seat of administration was in Sardis.

For fifty years the Greeks in Asia Minor chafed under foreign rule. The Greek spirit, naturally free and unrestrained, was restless under oppression of any sort. At length, in 512 B. C., Darius led a military expedition into the Black Sea region, destroying the partially Greek town of Gelonus— an outpost for Hellenic traffic in furs, obtained still farther north.

In the struggle which now opened between Greek and Persian, economic features must be taken into account. Darius possessed remarkable executive and administrative ability. The Phœnicians—Asiatics—who had earlier controlled sea commerce, were now replaced, or at least closely rivaled, by the Greeks, who were Europeans. In other words, the planting of Greek colonies in Asia had been largely undertaken for advantage in trade, and amounted to an encroachment of Europe in Asia for benefits of commerce. To some extent the course now followed by Persia was reactionary—an attempt to recover the valuable sea-ports and bring back trade into Asiatic channels. These economic motives have been often wholly ignored.

Having been forced to provide soldiers for a campaign in the Black Sea region, this resulting disastrously for their own interests, the Ionic cities waited but a chance to revolt. An opportunity came in 501 B. C. A conference of delegates from the different cities met at Miletus, and Aristagoras was sent into Greece to secure aid for the Ionians in the struggle with Persia, now imminent. He went first to Sparta, as recognized head of Greece. The Spartans refused to take part in a war against a king so remote from themselves. In Athens he was received more cordially. The Athenians were closely allied to the Milesians in kinship and commercial affairs. Twenty ships were promised and Eretria offered five more.

The Persian provincial governor had seen trouble ahead and called for troops. When the twenty-five ships arrived at Ephesus, the Greek soldier marched to Sardis, burning the city. They were met, however, by the Persian cavalry and worsted, hastened back to their ships and set out immediately for home. Thus it is plain that they rendered little assistance to their Ionic neighbors. But the burning of Sardis and the evident willingness they evinced to take part against Persia were not to be forgotten.

It was not possible for the Ionic cities to follow any protracted plan of concerted action. Soon all but Miletus surrendered. This largest of Ionic towns underwent a siege and when at last the assault was carried, the town was destroyed and her citizens taken in captivity to Susa, the Persian capital. Only then was Darius free to avenge the action of Athens and Eretria. Furthermore, he undoubtedly realized that the Greeks in Asia Minor would never become faithful subjects while their kinsmen across the Ægean remained free.

In 492 B. C. a fleet was sent to attack the offending cities, but it was practically destroyed by storm off the tempestuous coast of Thrace, and never reached its destination. Then water and earth, Persian symbols of submission, were demanded by Persian legates, who visited the Grecian states. Many of the weaker states gave these at once; in Sparta, however, and in Athens, the officials were tossed into wells and invited to help themselves to these elements.

In 490 B. C. a second fleet was sent out from Samos with

instructions to sail directly across the sea, take Athens and
Eretria and bring back their inhabitants to Susa. Eretria was
betrayed into the hands of the Persians by one of her own
citizens. The town was laid waste and the population deported
to a neighboring island to await the return of the invaders.
Then the fleet entered the bay of Marathon. A broad plain
stretches along the shore and here the army encamped.

Nine thousand Athenian soldiers had been sent to intercept
them, and Platæa in turn, for friendly protection of Athens,
supplied 1,000 more. Sparta had been invoked for aid, but
delayed sending troops until a festival had passed. When at
last dispatched, they arrived too late.

Miltiades commanded the Greek forces and won the battle
of Marathon against great odds. Six thousand four hundred
Persians fell, while the Greeks lost but 192 men. It was a
glorious victory, and was so regarded even by jealous Sparta.

There were those within the city of Athens who for
money would betray her to the Persians, as had been done in
Eretria. A signal flashed from the direction of the acropolis
to the enemy was observed by the Athenian army. Knowing
that the town would be helpless in their absence, the army
hastened homeward, leaving a small detachment to take the
plunder and bury the dead. By a forced march the Athenians
reached the city before the fleet. When the Persians saw
again the soldiers who had just defeated them, they did not
attempt a landing, but set out for Asia with the Eretrian
captives.

The battle of Marathon had a tremendous effect upon the
Greeks. It showed that they could stand against the soldiers
of the Great King. It was accounted a splendid triumph, and
Miltiades was hero of the day. Athens rose at once to first
rank among Greek states.

On the other hand, the effect upon the Persians was slight.
A few thousand slain in battle was a trifling matter to Darius.
His motley armies were levied upon many tribute lands, and
while the survivors of this battle would hesitate to encounter
an army which had defeated them, news traveled slowly in
those days, and a sturdy resistance did not become generally
known at once. Persian provinces were wide and more sol-

diers could be levied as they were needed. The pride of the Persian king was touched, however, and he immediately gave orders for a third expedition to be fitted out. Elaborate preparations were undertaken and years passed before the campaign was put into the field. Meanwhile, Darius died, enjoining his son Xerxes to blot out the stain upon Persian arms sustained at Marathon, and to humble the stubborn Athenians.

Aristides and Themistocles were rival leaders in Athens during the ten years of truce intervening. Themistocles saw that the Persian struggle was but ebbing for a brief rest. The hope of Athens must be in her navy and so he labored unceasingly to strengthen and increase her fleet. Aristides, called "the Just," differed with Themistocles in many of his projects. At last the rivalry between the leaders became so great that Aristides was ostracised in order that the factional feeling might abate and concerted action be taken.

In 480 B. C. a congress of Greek states convened at Corinth to take measures for common safety against Persia,—for a third attack was now expected. Some of the lesser states favored Persia—money of the Great King having been used plentifully among them; others were prevented by natural jealousies from aiding Athens. Sparta joined, however, in face of impending danger, and several other states did likewise.

The same year Xerxes left Sardis with a great army and well equipped navy. Herodotus relates that his was the largest army ever mustered on the field, and were we to accept his figures, it exceeded any since brought into action. But as we have seen, Herodotus did not find it necessary to verify his statistics, and the more numerous the foe, the greater glory for Greece in overcoming it. While it is impossible to ascertain the actual numbers brought into Europe, we should understand the great difference in the relative resources of the two countries.

Xerxes ruled over a wide area and levied troops from his whole dominion. Some were Persians, others Scythians, Phœnicians, and so on. His was a motley army, made up largely of men who did not want to fight, and who had been forced against their wills to leave home and make war upon a people in whom they felt no interest, in behalf of a country they hated. Xerxes, their king and leader, was not himself a brave man and could not inspire bravery in his generals. On the other hand, while some of the Greek states, notably Sparta, maintained well disciplined troops, many of the soldiers who took part in the last war with Persia were untrained. But they were fighting for their country in face of an invading host. If defeated, it would mean loss of home, freedom and nationality—to whatever extent they possessed it. Under these conditions the enormous regiments of Persia counted for less than a much smaller number of Greeks.

Xerxes was borne along with his army in a litter or chariot, according to the condition of the roads. For some distance no resistance was offered the invaders. The mountaineers of the north and the sparse population of certain districts submitted at once to the Great King as he passed along. Opposition came first at the Pass of Thermopylæ, where Leonidas commanded a band of Spartans. Through mountains which barred the way, a narrow pass led between the sea and a lofty range. For two days the mighty army of the Persian king was checked, because the Spartans were in a position to hold the pass. Finally a traitor—seldom lacking in Greece—showed a Persian general a defile over the mountain. Picked troops were dispatched thither and soon the Spartans were surrounded, all hope of retreat being lost. This mattered little to a Spartan who held death preferable to ignoble defeat. Fighting bravely, Leonidas and his three hundred Spartans fell before overwhelming numbers, but the loyalty of this little band has been extolled ever since. On a rock by this pass an inscription was raised which might be translated in this fashion:

> Go tell the Spartans, he who passeth by,
> That here, obedient to her will, we lie."

The resistance at the Pass of Thermopylæ was not decisive, but it showed the Persians with what sort of mettle they had to fight.

On Those That Died at Thermopylae.

Of those who at Thermopylae were slain
    Glorious the doom and beautiful the lot!
Their tomb an altar : men from tears refrain
    To honor them, and praise, but mourn them not.
Such sepulchre nor drear decay
Nor all-destroying time shall waste : this right have they!
Within their grave the home-bred glory
    Of Greece was laid : this witness gives
Leonidas the Spartan, in whose story
    A wreath of famous virtue ever lives.

Trans. John Sterling, from Simonides.

As the Persian army advanced, consternation ruled in Athens. Some favored defending the acropolis and taking refuge on its height; however, Themistocles persuaded the people that their hope lay in their fleet. Most of the women and children were transported to an island for safety, and the fleet anchored off Salamis. Ships of various Greek states composed this navy, with Themistocles in general command, but when the city of Athens was taken many thought the fleet ought to move south, where each ship could hasten home to its own people in case of attack. The Persian fleet had drawn near, and Themistocles knew that the time to strike was in the bay of Salamis. When he was persuaded that the Greek fleet would divide if held there longer, he sent a secret message to the Persian naval commander that the Greek fleet was about to move out of the bay. Thinking advantage on their side, the Persians shut off chance of escape. Consequently the allied Greeks were forced to offer battle.

From his throne on the shore Xerxes watched the engagement. His fleet was much greater than that commanded by Themistocles. Nevertheless, the ships were so crowded in the bay that they could not handle themselves advantageously and trireme after trireme manned by Persians went down. The defeat of the Persian fleet was decisive, and well-nigh destroyed the hope of Xerxes. When next day the Greeks prepared to continue the fight, they found that the Persians had set out for home under cover of the night. The army was left to winter in Greece under command of Mardonius, but the Great King returned to Sardis with his surviving ships.

The victory of Salamis was long celebrated by the Greeks, and we today are thrilled as we read of it. While in case of defeat at this critical moment the Greeks would probably have won out in the long run, yet success just then saved them from the bitter experience of pillaged country and scattered forces.

The following spring, earth and water were once more demanded from the Greek states, but their recent triumph had so elated them that few were friendly to the Persian legates. The battle of Platæa during the summer of 479 B. C. ended the war in Greece and caused the evacuation of the Persian army. During the next three years, moreover, the Greeks in Asia Minor and in the Ægean islands gained freedom from Persian rule.

It is important for us to remember the significance of this war. This was not a case of countries seeking aggrandizement, although that was one motive, doubtless, of the eastern monarch. Rather, it amounted to a struggle between two civilizations, and settled for all time that the freedom of the west should not go out and be replaced by the despotism of the east; that the higher conceptions of western progress should dominate in Europe as against the less noble elements of orientalism. The Greeks fought for more than their own safety at Marathon, Salamis and Thermopylæ, and for that reason we rejoice two thousand years later for their glorious victories.

(From Aeschylus' great play called *The Persians*.)

The Persians.

(Messenger returns to Xerxes' court to announce the disaster of Salamis to Atossa, mother of the Great King).

Messenger:
" Woe to the towns through Asia's peopled realms!
Woe to the land of Persia, once the port
Of boundless wealth, how is thy glorious state
Vanished at once, and all thy spreading honours

Fallen, lost!   Ah me! unhappy is his task
That bears unhappy tidings : but constraint
Compels me to relate this tale of woe.
Persians, the whole barbaric host is fallen.

Chorus:

O horror, horror!   What a baneful train
Of recent ills!   Ah Persians, as he speaks
Of ruin, let your tears stream to the earth.

Atossa:

This is the height of ill, ah me! and shame
To Persia, grief and lamentation lend.
But tell me this, afresh renew thy tale,
What was the number of the Grecian fleet
That in fierce conflict their bold barques should dare
Rush to encounter with the Persian hosts.

Messenger:

Know then, in numbers the barbaric fleet
Was far superior: in ten squadrons, each
Of thirty ships, Greece ploughed the deep; of these
One held a distant station.   Xerxes led
A thousand ships; their number well I know;
Two hundred more, seven that swept the seas
With speediest sail: this was their full amount.
And in the engagement seemed we not secure
Of victory?   But unequal fortune sunk
Our scale in fight, discomfiting our host.

The morn, all beauteous to behold,
Drawn by white steeds bounds o'er the enlightened earth;
At once from every Greek with glad acclaim
Burst forth the song of war, whose lofty notes
The echo of the island rocks returned,
Spreading dismay through Persia's hosts thus fallen
From their high hopes; no flight this solemn strain
Portended, but deliberate valor bent
On daring battle; whilst the trumpet's sound
Kindled the flames of war.   But when their oars
The paeans ended, with impetuous force
Dashed the resounding surges, instant all

Rushed on in view; in orderly array
The squadron on the right first led, behind
Rode their whole fleet; and now distinct we heard
From every part this voice of exhortation:
" Advance, ye sons of Greece, from thraldom save
Your country, save your wives, your children save,
The temples of your gods, the sacred tomb
Where rest your honoured ancestors; this day
The common cause of all demands your valor."
Meantime from Persia's hosts the deepening shout
Answered their shout; no time for cold delay;
But ship 'gainst ship its brazen beak impelled.
First to the charge a Grecian galley rushed;
Ill the Phœnician bore the rough attack,
Its sculptured prow all shattered. Each advanced
Daring an opposite. The deep array
Of Persia at the first sustained th' encounter;
But their thronged numbers, in the narrow seas
Confined, want room for action; and deprived
Of mutual aid, beaks clash with beaks, and each
Breaks all the other's oars; and skill disposed
The Grecian navy circled there around
With fierce assault; and rushing from its height
Th' inverted vessel sinks; the sea no more
Wears its accustomed aspect, with foul wreck
And blood disfigured; floating carcasses
Roll on the rocky shores; the poor remains
Of the barbaric armament to flight
Ply every oar inglorious; onward rush
The Greeks amidst the ruins of the fleet,
As through a shoal of fish caught in a net,
Spreading destruction; the wide ocean o'er
Wailings are heard, and loud laments, till night
With darkness on her brow brought grateful truce.
Should I recount each circumstance of woe,
Ten times on my unfinished tale the sun
Would set; for be assured that not one day
Could close the ruin of so vast a host."

—Aeschylus. Potter's trans.

CHAPTER IX.

THE ATHENIAN EMPIRE.

The Greeks did not deem it prudent to abandon the cities of Asia Minor to their own course after the victories of Salamis, Plataea, and Mycale, for although a severe blow had been dealt the Persian army, and her fleet was much reduced, yet the resources of the great empire were not materially affected, and vigilance alone could save the Greeks from recurring attacks. For this reason the Greek navy, composed of ships supplied by the various allied states, cruised among the Aegean islands, aiding such as had been brought under Persian rule to regain independence; reducing Persian garrisons in the west, and otherwise crippling the Great King.

Because of differences arising, Sparta at length withdrew from the fleet. She uniformly exhibited a selfish policy, and now demurred at guarding the Ionic cities, claiming that those peoples in Greece who had favored the Persian king ought to be deported and their lands given Hellenes in Asiatic towns, where protection would not be required. This ingenious scheme suited none save the Spartans, who now withdrew and for some years contented themselves by maintaining pre-eminence in the Peloponnesus. To the Athenians, therefore, fell the responsibility of conducting the aggressive defense against Persia.

To produce more concerted action, in 478 B. C. the Confederacy of Delos was organized. This league had for its object the maintenance of at least one hundred ships—a permanent fleet—to patrol the Aegean waters and make Persian encroachment impossible. It was not incumbent on any island-state to join this league, although safety prompted to such action; but having once entered into the confederacy, no state would be allowed to withdraw. Each ally pledged herself to contribute ships, men, or money, according to her strength. With no express privileges, leadership fell naturally to Athens. Meetings of delegates from all states in the league were held on the island of Delos, long sacred to Apollo. Here also was kept the treasury of the confederacy.

Meantime the Athenians had returned to find their city in ashes. Even before they rebuilt their dwellings and temples, Themistocles urged the building of walls around the city, so that Athens could be defended in case of future attack. The entire population, including the women and children, set to work to erect these walls, and all kinds of material were used in their construction. Sparta remonstrated when she heard that Athens was fortifying herself in this way, fearing her rival would thus become unduly strong. Themistocles realized that this would be an inopportune time for war, so he cleverly managed to evade the ambassadors until the walls were well under way. Then he replied to the Spartans that the walls were indeed in construction, and that thereafter when Sparta desired to negotiate with Athens she must recognize her citizens as "men who knew quite well what was best for their own and for the common good."

Having been indirectly involved with the Spartan general Pausanias, in secret dealings with Persia, Themistocles was exiled. It is not easy to believe that he had any notion of giving advantage to the old enemy of his people, but he apparently had known of Pausanias' treasonable letters to the Persian court, and had not made them public. Probably the treatment he received from his fellow-citizens embittered him. A charge of treason being brought against him, he took refuge at the court of Persia and afterwards died there.

Much has been said concerning Themistocles' later conduct. Since it is impossible at this time to get full light on the subject, we can only dwell upon his earlier service to his country. Themistocles was unquestionably one of Athens' most clear-sighted statesmen. To his excellent judgment the victory of Salamis was due; the brief supremacy of Athens was largely due to the policy he outlined; the maintenance of a strong fleet, the securing of sea-port advantages for Athens by connecting the city with the harbor, four miles away, and the fortification of the city by strong walls.

After the ostracism of Themistocles, Cimon, son of Miltiades, became commander of the navy. Having won great victories in the eastern Aegean, he returned to Athens and became leader of the conservative party. This was the faction which always stood for oligarchial government, or, failing this, for limiting the powers of the people so far as possible.

Sparta had been planning to humble her northern rival, but in 464 B. C. her city was destroyed by an earthquake. While the people were still dazed by their misfortune, the helots, brutalized and embittered by long servitude, rose in revolt. They were joined by some of the Perioeci, and Sparta's plight was for some time alarming. In her distress, she appealed to Athens for help. Her usual hostile attitude made the popular party averse to sending aid, but Cimon held that refusing aid to a city that had helped in common cause against Persia would be an action unworthy of Athens. This argument led the Athenians to dispatch soldiers to support Sparta, and help her to put down her incited slaves. But no sooner had they arrived than the Spartans, jealous to an extreme, conceived a notion that while Athens was ostensibly helping them, she was attempting to get a foothold in southern Greece, and as this was not to be thought of, her army was dismissed with scant ceremony. This insult so enraged the Athenians that they ostracised Cimon, whose advice had brought them into such a humiliating situation.

Here it would be best to explain one peculiarity of democratic government in Greece, which if not understood is often perplexing. In the United States it is usual for a member of either legislative house to bring forward a measure, which if it gains support, regularly becomes a law. This plan is followed likewise in our states, and in our municipalities a measure becomes a city ordinance if sanctioned by the council and the mayor. If in course of time such laws or ordinances prove to be unsuccessful or undesirable, they are revoked, but no blame necessarily attaches to the one who originally proposed them. Quite the reverse was true in Greece. It was there thought that he who voted for a measure took no such responsibility as the man who brought it before the people for consideration. In fact, a citizen who advocated a measure was held responsible for its outcome. This seemed to the Greek to be the plainest common sense, for how could the average voter understand the full significance of a given policy as well as he who planned it? Holn states this attitude very clearly: "The Athenians rightly held that a citizen who moves the adoption of a resolution affecting the welfare of many individuals must be prepared to take a greater responsibility than the man who merely gives an affirmative vote." This explains why men who had advocated unsuccessful measures were treated with such ill favor, and in a case like this, ostracised from their country.

The alliance made with Sparta before the invasion of Xerxes was abruptly broken off and a new one made with Argolis, Sparta's enemy.

About this time a change is discernible in the character of the Confederacy of Delos. Because of its vigilant fleet, Persian ships were no longer seen in Aegean waters, and one by one the island-states began to begrudge money contributed to the further support of the navy. Most of them had grown to make a money payment instead of furnishing ships, and so the fleet practically belonged to Athens. However, when Naxos tried to withdraw from the league, the fleet was sent promptly to coerce her. Her walls were razed to the ground and she became a dependency of the Confederacy, or of Athens, as head of this confederacy. Similar treatment was meted out to other seceding allies, and in time Athens assumed a sort of over-lordship towards the lesser states of the Confederacy, while the treasury was removed from Delos to the acropolis. And so the Athenian empire had its beginning.

PERICLES.

In 461 B. C. Pericles became leader of Athenian affairs. Supported by the popular or democratic party, he brought in a new policy. He wished above all things to see Athens an empire, preserving her strength on the seas, to be sure, but making equally effective her power on land. Two constitutional changes at once inaugurated indicated the bent of his ambition. One was lessening of the powers possessed by the Areopogus. Its duties were greatly curtailed; indeed, the hearing of homicide cases and the care of the sacred olives were the chief functions left this ancient body, while its earlier duties were apportioned among the council, the assembly, and

the law-courts. Again, those engaged in the service of the
state, especially jurors, were now paid. Reasons for these
measures are apparent.   The Areopogus was composed of
ex-archons and they were almost invariably wealthy, conservative men.   If all officials were to continue to be accountable
to this body at the close of their terms, the people—the masses
—could not successfully carry out their policy of reform.
Again, citizens had hitherto given service to the state without
compensation.   The result was that only men with a fixed
income could hold certain offices, or, if others were called to
serve, they could give but limited time to matters for which
they received no returns.   Now, while remuneration was
small, it enabled one to live frugally; hence more men were
ready to fill public positions.

Regarding foreign affairs, Pericles favored peace.   In
459 B. C. a Libyan king who had incited Egypt to revolt
against Persian rule, called upon the Athenian fleet for aid.
This was sent, but the expedition ended disastrously, 250 ships
being lost.   Soon after this a treaty of peace was made with
Artaxerxes, king of Persia.   It is doubtful whether we should
apply the term "treaty" to the concessions made by Persia,
but she did not recognize Greece as a power equal with herself. Great uncertainty attaches to the matter, and some have
even doubted the existence of a written agreement at all.   It
appears that by the so-called Peace of Callias, the Persian king
agreed to send no more warships into the Aegean sea, and
Athens promised to keep her fleet out of Persian waters.   The
Greeks in Asia Minor were to be independent, and Athens was
not to attack Persian allies.   Thus terminated a struggle which
had lasted over forty years

It is not strange that members of the Confederacy of Delos
held the mission of the league accomplished with these nego-
tiations of peace, and that they desired to assume their earlier
freedom.   Two parties existed in each state—the oligarchal,
and the democratic.   Everywhere the oligarchal party chafed
under Athenian leadership; the democratic faction sympathized
on the whole with Pericles' policy.   The great Athenian leader
believed that only by the perpetuation of the league could
safety be assured, and, moreover, he realized that this was the

only way to accomplish his hopes for a Greek commonwealth. So while meetings of delegates no longer convened at Delos, annual payment for the maintenance of the fleet was regularly required.

In connection with this we must note Pericles' home policy. He wished to beautify Athens. Opportunity offered to replace the temples destroyed by the Persian by more perfect architectural structures. Phidias, the greatest sculptor of antiquity, was engaged to superintend the adornment of the acropolis. Most of the marble structures which made Athens famous in antiquity and which have made her attractive in ruins, were erected at this time. This was naturally an undertaking suited to gain favor among her citizens, but when the treasury of Delos was drawn upon, the allies murmured bitterly. Some of the Athenians themselves—notably Thucydides—protested that money collected for defense should be preserved for that alone. Pericles replied that Athens had undertaken to protect the members of the Delian Confederacy from attack, and so long as they were not attacked, she was keeping her part of the bargain, and they should keep theirs. He probably did not fail to see how entirely conditions had changed, but he dreamed of establishing a great Greek empire, with Athens at its head— first in government, commerce, literature, and art, and he believed that the perpetuation of the Confederacy, with Athens as leader, was his sole means of giving reality to this hope. Something may be said to justify Pericles' action regarding the treasury of the allies; Athens had borne the brunt of the Persian war and the later defense largely herself; it had been a comparatively simple matter for the members of the league to make an annual payment, since this tax was much less than under other conditions they would have been compelled to expend for defense; while construction of ships and equipment had fallen almost entirely to the care of the Athenians. So long as they kept the seas free from foreign vessels and allowed commerce to push on unhindered, Pericles maintained that the allies ought to continue their ship tax and never mind how the money was expended, since they realized that for which they were paying. This logic was hardly likely to satisfy other than Athenians, however.

The attempt to make Athens supreme on land caused constant strife among those states which looked to Sparta for protection and among the discontented Delian Confederates. From 461 B. C., when Pericles assumed leadership, until 445 B. C., war waged most of the time in some quarter. The struggle with Corinth was especially serious. At last the Spartan king invaded central Greece, yet returned home without striking a blow. This gave rise to the rumor that he had been bought off by the Athenian leader. This report was later strengthened when Pericles refused to account for a sum of money that had passed through his hands, saying merely that it had been used for a necessary purpose. Since neither Athens nor Sparta felt ready for the struggle which both knew must come sooner or later for the supremacy of Greece, a thirty years' truce was declared in 445 B. C.

The years of peace which followed were remarkable for great achievements in literature and art. Since Athens excelled in the arts of peace rather than war, we must regard this period as most splendid in her history.

PERICLES.

CHAPTER X.

GREAT ATHENIAN STATESMEN: ARISTIDES; THEMISTOCLES.

The careers of Aristides and Themistocles were so interlinked during the greater part of their lives that it is convenient to consider them together.

In character and temperament these two men differed widely. Aristides was a few years the elder. He was a quiet, thoughtful man, of gentle habits. . Before all else he held the welfare of Athens, and for himself appears to have been devoid of purely personal ambitions. Strict obedience to law he regarded as the first duty of a citizen. No modern jurist views illegal proceedings with greater alarm than he did. It was probably his high sense of honesty and conformity to law that early won for him the complete confidence of the people. "Nor has any man ever possessed a deeper and more lively comprehension of the mission of Athens—the union of free mental progress with the discipline of the law."

Themistocles exemplified the direct opposite of these qualities. His father was an Attic citizen, while his mother was probably of Thracian birth. Since marriages with foreigners were not given legal sanction in ancient Greece, Themistocles while a boy was made aware of his sullied birth, being debarred from certain athletic contests open only to youths of pure Greek parentage. With a stormy temper, he possessed rare ability, clearness of reason, good judgment, and quick intelligence. He, too, was ambitious for Athens, but he was not lacking in aspirations for personal preferment. While Aristides held to the safe, conservative policy, Themistocles, with magnificent sweep of vision, foresaw that Athens' greatness could come only as a result of radical changes. He therefore allied himself with the reform, or popular party, and in 493 B. C. was elected first archon. It is to be noted at the start that Aristides was of noble birth and that his cautious policy bound to him friends and supporters who stood by him alike during prosperity and reverses. Themistocles lacked ties of social position and the degree of support which often accompanies these; while his love of self-exaltation often estranged him from his acquired followers.

Upon election to the first office of the land, Themistocles determined to give Athens, four miles inland, the advantages of a coast town. To this end he connected her with Piraeus, a harbor later to be incorporated with the great city as its commercial center.

After the battle of Marathon, Themistocles looked ahead and foresaw another struggle with Persia. The Great King would be weakest on sea, and so Athens needed a navy that she might attack her enemy in the most vulnerable place. The greater portion of the Athenians rejoiced in deliverance from a dreaded foe, and were too deeply absorbed by immediate interests to take thought for future conflicts which might beset their country. Themistocles realized that he must proceed diplomatically indeed if he would accomplish his purpose and provide ample defense for the state. The masses would have regarded it as folly to equip a navy against an invasion, imminent only in the mind of Themistocles. To gain their support he pointed out the inadequacies of Athenian defense against her neighbors, and filled his townsmen with hope of gaining importance in their immediate vicinity.

It was one thing to win popular approval to the scheme of building up a navy, and quite another to find means for providing the 200 triremes regarded by Themistocles as essential. But he who had mapped out a plan bold enough to bring ultimate supremacy to his country was not lacking in resources for carrying it out: Athens was poor, and to have proposed taxation as a means of acquiring a fleet would have defeated the cause at the start. So Themistocles bethought him of the silver mines of Laurium, located on the southeastern extremity of Attica. These mines belonged to the state and had been let out to capitalists, who paid a low per cent on their profits for a chance to work them. According to the spirit of Athenian democracy, state possessions were held as the property of the people, so whatever income accrued from the mines above the annual expense of the state was divided equally among the citizens. A declaration of dividends, so to speak,

was soon to be made among the stockholders of the mines—
namely, the Athenian citizens. Themistocles now concentrated
his efforts upon getting this sum and all future incomes from
the mines set apart for a permanent war fund, to be expended
in the building and maintenance of a fleet. Being led to
believe that they might increase their power in the vicinity—
and probably that they might find opportunity from time to
time to share in plunder—the people consented to this propo-
sition. Filled with fresh enthusiasm for the new plan, the
Athenians imported lumber, erected docks, and created great
industrial activity. So great was the demand for carpenters
and shipbuilders that men of other callings abandoned these
to meet the new need; laborers from other countries hurried
to Athens, and soon a large foreign population swarmed in the
city. Wages rose and industrial life underwent a marked
change.

It was to be expected that the conservative element among
the populace would look with misgivings upon such departure
from accustomed paths. These found a leader in Aristides,
who was elected to succeed Themistocles in 489 B. C.

Aristides was as desirous as anyone of making Athens foremost, but he opposed Themistocles' policy because he believed
that Athens was under the protection of the gods. Under the
wing of Pallas Athena the city had come into being; her wisdom and care had thus far guided the state, and to stake all
on a fleet was to question the power of the goddess, in whose
favor alone prosperity was to be found. So far the state had
rested on a stable foundation. Men of landed property had
formed the bulwark of the nation; now, apparently, these were
to be replaced by seamen. Foreigners were flocking in, and
while Athens prided herself on her wide hospitality to strangers of whatever land, yet a large influx at once would be
attended with danger, since these newcomers had different
traditions and beliefs. Such were the arguments put forth
by Aristides and his followers to thwart the measures of the
reform party. Between the conservatives, holding to the old,
and the progressive party, standing for the new, a vigorous
contest waged. Fortunately the rising generation saw in
Themistocles the embodiment of their hopes. When party

feeling grew so high that a vote on ostracism was demanded, Aristides was sent into exile.

It is always to be remembered that no dishonor attached to ostracism; it was merely a means of being temporarily free from one of two rival leaders. No man commanded deeper respect than Aristides, but in hindering the plans of the reform party his presence was regarded as undesirable.

Now Themistocles was given free sway. Inspired by his ambitions, wealthy citizens vied with one another in equipping triremes for the Athenian navy. Athenian youths practised with the oar. The fleet came to take first place in the minds of the people.

Even now Themistocles foresaw need of the long walls which later connected Athens with Piraeus, but for these he must wait.

Presently the much dreaded incursion of the Persians occurred. Themistocles anticipated the difficulty he was sure to meet when he should attempt to persuade the people to leave their city and trust to the fleet, and the Delphian oracle was instructed to advise them to trust in their wooden walls— interpreted by the great leader to mean their ships. Having transferred the government to Salamis, Themistocles forced the allies to open the greatest naval engagement of antiquity. When the war was over and all returned to Athens, he per- suaded the Athenians to give their new city wider compass— thus providing for the country population which in time of war might be protected; and he urged the necessity for walls of defense.

While taking these important steps for the advantage of the city, Themistocles often antagonized the people. He desired constant recognition of his ability and sought con- tinually to exalt himself. This attitude was particularly obnoxious to the Greeks and made him many enemies. More- over, he was scarcely willing to wait for natural growth, anxious as he was for the immediate supremacy of Athens. He incurred the lasting hatred of the Spartans by opposing measures involving them, and they persistently endeavored to bring about his ruin.

Aristides, meanwhile, had returned not long after his

exile. Upon the invasions of the Persian all political exiles were invited to return. Aristides hastened to his countrymen, finding them on board their ships in the bay of Salamis. Making his way to Themistocles, he offered him his hand and assured him that the only question now in dispute between them was which could be of greater service to his country.

After the war he was depended upon and trusted as before, called to act as judge in disputes, and soon asked to organize the Confederacy of Delos—a diplomatic task for which Themistocles would have been utterly unfitted.

It shortly became apparent that if Themistocles continued as leader a breach must come with Sparta; so, weary of his self-exaltation, a popular vote ostracised him. Cimon was given command of the fleet and at home the counsel of Aristides was followed. He, however, soon retired from public life and died in 466 B. C.

Of Themistocles somewhat more remains to be said. Curtius remarks that "he was endowed with great gifts for saving his country in time of danger, but unadapted for directing it in times of peace; he lacked a sense of legal order, respect for the rights of others, and openness of purpose."

Exiled from country, he journeyed from one Greek state to another. The wrath of Sparta still pursued him. Having gained some evidence of his acquaintance with the plot of Pausanias, the Laconians persisted until they compelled Athens to summon him to answer to a charge of treason. Thereupon he took refuge at the court of Xerxes, where he died.

It is difficult to overestimate the services of Themistocles to Athens, for her greatness resulted in the long run because of adherence to the policy he first outlined. Jealousy inherent with the Greeks often caused them to undervalue their leaders, and there is no doubt but that the later years of Themistocles were embittered by what he considered the ingratitude of his countrymen.

CIMON.

More companionable than Aristides the Just, or Themistocles, the far-seeing statesman, was Cimon, who in 470 B. C. took command of the Delian fleet. He was the son of Miltiades and was a natural born leader. For nine years he commanded expeditions against Persia in the eastern Aegean and returned home to find himself in high favor. He dispensed wide hospitality, provided shady promenades, undertook the adornment of Athens, and gained the good will of the people generally. As a leader, however, he could not take Themistocles' broad view, and held too closely to the old order of things. Especially he thought it necessary to maintain peaceful relations with Sparta.

The reform, or popular party, since the exile of Themistocles had been comparatively inactive. They now found a leader in Pericles. This party brought charges of corruption against Cimon, but on these he was heard and acquitted. Soon after followed the earthquake at Sparta and the helot revolt. We have seen the outcome of the Athenian expedition, led by Cimon, to the relief of Sparta, and have noted that its failure, or rather, its dismissal, was the occasion for Cimon's ostracism, in 459 B. C. Five years later he was recalled upon the request of Pericles, who wanted peace with Sparta and felt that Cimon alone could negotiate it.

It would seem that there was probably some understanding between these two leaders to the effect that Cimon should not interfere in domestic matters nor Pericles in foreign affairs. Accordingly, Cimon was reinstated as commander of the fleet. Having made a five years' truce with Sparta, he started to the relief of Egypt, but dying on the way, was brought back to his native city and buried with great honor.

While Cimon played an important *rôle* in Athenian politics for many years, he cannot be ranked with either of these men. In foreign affairs he was influenced by the policy of Aristides, although at home he inaugurated some measures that were later successfully carried out by Pericles.

PERICLES.

Pericles belonged to an old noble family. While his bearing was that of an aristocrat, he early allied himself with the popular party.

He received a particularly thorough education, and as a youth came under the influence of Anaxagoras, the philosopher.

Throughout his life he was a thoughtful, serious man, never mingling in social gatherings, holding himself aloof from various sorts of amusements. He did not move easily among the common people, but he commanded the respect of all. When, on rare occasions, he made public addresses, audiences were deeply impressed by what he said. Other Athenian statesmen were more popular; some were better loved; but no other was trusted with so many functions of government for such an extended time. For thirty years Pericles practically directed affairs in Athens, and although he had plenty of enemies, and was even criticised at times by his own adherents, nevertheless the fact remains that in a democracy where he might have been dismisssed at any time, he continued in control, thus proving that he was acceptable to the majority of the people.

He adopted the general plan for promoting Athenian greatness as originally conceived by Themistocles. Cimon was the leader when Pericles first entered public life; and by his hospitality and genial manner held the favor of the masses. Pericles and his friends went quietly to work to acquire a following. Cimon's habit of conducting foreign affairs without consulting home authorities was challenged by Pericles, but Cimon satisfied all charges brought against him.

Throughout his early public life Pericles proceeded cautiously. He knew that ostracism would ruin his plans for Athens, and for this reason he worked mainly through others. Understanding the two obstacles which hampered pure democracy in Athens, Pericles brought forward two measures to remedy the situation: the paying of jurors and others employed in government service, and providing popular courts to hear cases hitherto tried before the Areopagus.

The Greeks fully appreciated the necessity of amusements for the complete development of the individual, and the drama supplied these largely for the Athenians. Comedy especially served somewhat the ends of a modern journal, since it fearlessly attacked social customs and even assailed particular individuals. Tragedy had its birth in religious worship. Pericles believed that the poorest citizen should share the advantages which the plays offered, and he secured the passage of a law entitling any citizen to the price of admission and of the mid-day meal upon application to the common treasury. Plays were given during the week of religious celebration each spring and fall, and in this way no Athenian was shut out from them for lack of money. In regard to this very wholesome measure it must be remembered that attendance upon these festivals was not only a pleasure, but a religious duty as well, and otherwise the poor would have continued to be excluded from participation in a national celebration. Above all things Pericles hoped to develop an empire wherein all men—not merely some few fortunate ones—should be cultured and enlightened. As the state festivals were in themselves educative, he believed that none should be debarred from attendance because of poverty.

At last Pericles felt sufficiently well established to come forward in his own right, no longer carrying out his purposes through the mediation of others. His extended plan for the adornment of Athens will be considered later. Years of peace allowed him opportunity to promulgate means for making Athens splendid above all other cities.

We get some conception of the various trusts confided in this leader when we find him in control, almost without check, of the finances of the state; bringing forward laws that were usually passed without serious objection; having charge of the public festivals; managing the affairs of the Delian Confederacy—in short, in this land of supposed democracy, directing the government both at home and abroad;—well-nigh embodying within himself the government of Athens.

Pericles fully understood that Athens' strength must remain in her fleet, and at this time she possessed at least 300 ships, capable of transporting 60,000 soldiers. The allies were kept as quiet and contented as any Greek control could have kept them and their annual tax was light.

The later years of Pericles were checkered with troubles and disappointments. Death robbed him of those he cared for, and circumstances estranged him from some of his earlier followers. His personal life was above reproach, and he was never accused of taking a bribe. Had he lived longer, it is quite possible that he would have guided the state through

the civil war that now overtook Greece and brought Athens out
victorious. To bring his countrymen to their best was his
first care, and at no other period in Greek history do we find
the masses so enlightened and intelligent. To be sure, in his
addresses we must realize that he portrayed his townsmen as
he wished them to be rather than as they were—very much as
our orators today in lauding the sterling worth of our citizens speak of the best among them rather than the worst.
Nevertheless, the Age of Pericles stands out in all ages as most
brilliant in Greek annals, and probably unexcelled in art and
intellectual attainment by any subsequent period in any land.

THE PIRAEUS OR HARBOR OF ATHENS (RESTORED).

CHAPTER XI.

PEACE AND PROSPERITY IN ATHENS.

During the thirteen years of peace which followed the Thirty Years' Truce, material prosperity reached a height before unknown in Athens. At home the great interest centered around the beautifying of the city; abroad, a safe and remunerative commerce was built up.

Cimon had begun the improvement of the city. A commander of the fleet for nine years, he had found ample opportunity to take rich booty, and this he expended lavishly at home. He planted promenades of plane-trees—especially appreciated in Attica, where shade was rare. He erected porticoes and colonnades in the market place, and laid even the foundations for the Parthenon. At his direction Phidias executed the great statue of Pallas Athena, placed upon the acropolis, whence her spear could be seen by sailors far out at sea.

Pericles continued and extended the plan of his predecessor. The funds of the state growing low, the treasury of Delos was drawn upon, as we have seen. To understand the agitation concerning such use of it, we must try to get in mind the Greek attitude of mind towards public buildings, particularly temples of worship.

The dwellings of the early Greeks were always simple and unostentatious. Upon public buildings, then, utmost care was expended. Art was the noblest accomplishment known, and hence was employed in the service of the gods. Athena was the patron deity of Athens, and embellishment of the acropolis was an offering to her.

"Athens had enforced yearly payment of this money and she continued to receive it; but she did not spend it all on the equipment of ships and the wages of crews. She could put by a considerable sum every year without neglecting her duty as protectress of the Greeks. The surplus was and remained the property of the League and not that of Athens alone. If, however, a portion of it was spent in embellishing the temple of the tutelar deity of the League and the citadel of Athens, which was her abode, was this diverting the funds from their rightful object? In pronouncing our verdict on this conduct we must consider it from the point of view of the ancients. Art was a matter of religion to the Greeks. It has been frequently pointed out that in early times their dwelling-houses were simple and that splendor was confined to their public buildings. We can go further than this and say that almost all their public buildings were temples. They did not even build fine town-halls.   Pericles used the funds of the League, and with them erected buildings destined for the services of religion and statues of the gods. The members of the League could not well complain of the money being spent in this way." [1]

The Parthenon was the noblest monument erected to the glory of Pallas Athena. Cimon had conceived the idea of building this great temple. Pericles continued the plan and secured the services of Phidias to superintend its construction. Since producing the colossal statue of Athena, Phidias had been away in Elis directing the work of several gifted artists, all absorbed in making splendid the sacred grove wherein the great games were held.

Greek architecture will be considered at another time. We may note here that the Parthenon was built in simple Doric style. The wonderful work on the pediments had historical significance, and was probably in a great measure the work of Phidias alone. The scene on the eastern pediment represented the birth of Athena, as she sprang one day in full armour from the head of Zeus; on the western pediment the contest between Athena and Poseidon was shown, as they strove each for the honor of naming the city. Within the Parthenon was placed the costly statue of the goddess, executed by Phidias. The flesh was of ivory, the drapery of pure gold,—by ingenious skill put on in such a fashion that it could be removed. Costly statues, like this one, or like the famous statue of Zeus, by the same artist, have not come down to us, and we know them only from descriptions left by contemporaries.

For more than seven hundred years this temple stood sacred

[1] Holm: History of Greece, II., 264.

to the worship of Athena, about 450 A. D. it became a Christian church. In 1687 the Venetians bombarded Athens and a bomb destroyed the central portion of the Parthenon. Early in the nineteenth century the sculptures were removed and taken to England. These were not mere reliefs but entire figures. Purchased for the British Museum, they form an important part of surviving Greek art as preserved in England.

Cimon had fortified the acropolis by walls. Since the erection of the Long Walls—connecting Athens with Piraeus—these were no longer necessary. Instead, a magnificent approach was made, with entrance gates flanked on either side by small temples. Many smaller temples and statues of various deities were placed on the acropolis. Pericles also erected the Odeum, or Concert Hall, used for religious purposes; songs and recitations were rendered here. Various other improvements were undertaken. Aqueducts and drainage conduits were made in different parts of the city, while along the harbor of Piraeus wharves and warehouses were constructed.

With this outburst of art came marked intellectual activity. Tragedy and comedy, philosophy and poetry, reached highest development. Since all forms of Greek literature are reserved for future consideration, we pass on to the foreign relations of Athens during the years of peace.

Naturally, extended peace would quickly call forth response in the field of commercial activity. The Athenian Empire embraced practically all important industrial centers and trade ports. The wealthiest, most cultured cities of the Mediterranean were thus accessible to Athenian merchants. We must remember that the Delian allies, making up the greater part of Athens' empire, reached along the northern coast of Thrace and the shores of Asia Minor, included the islands of the Aegean, and westward, encompassed settlements in Italy and Sicily. Articles from any of these distant realms might be procured in Athenian markets for little more than they cost in their native localities. The wharves of Piraeus teemed with life and commercial activity; ships plied back and forth between this harbor and widely scattered sea-ports. The Athenians were not oppressed by taxes. Rich revenues came in consequence of their trade. Neither were the merchantmen burdened by excessive duties; in reality they paid but a low rate for protection of the greatest Greek state.

Certain laws governed the regulation of exports. We learned in the beginning that Attica was not rich in production of grain, nor indeed of any agricultural product. From the very nature of her supremacy, she could not feel absolute security in her outlying possessions for any considerable length of time. Hence it was essential that indispensable things, such as corn, flax, and oil, be exported only when the home demand had been satisfied. Special laws governed the sale of grain—for this was the greatest anxiety of the Greeks in times of disturbance. Within Hellas merchants were allowed to ask but *one* obol a measure above the buying price; and officers were appointed by the state to regulate the grain supply. Speculation in grain would have been severely punished. "For the merchant was, like all other members of the community, above all to be a citizen of the state, and to fulfill his duties as such. He committed a crime if he wished to take advantage of the difficulties of the state and to speculate for his own gain upon the wants of his fellow citizens."

"Athens was rich as well as beautiful. Her harbor-town, the Piraeus, was gay with shipping, the sheds were crowded with boats and about the quays thronged slaves lading and unlading; merchants chaffering their wares and passengers embarking for distant ports. The products of Attica were everywhere in demand, for nowhere else could metal work, lamps and earthenware be had so cheap and so good. Attic ware traveled to all the coasts of the Mediterranean—jars for oil, and wine, and water; mixing-bowls; there was scarcely an event connected with life or death in which vases did not play some part. In return, Athens brought timber and fruit, rare wines from distant islands, incense from Lyris, dates from Phœnicia, carpets from Carthage and papyrus from Egypt. Every country sent of its best to Athens, and the customs and market-dues flowed into the treasury, and seemed a never-failing source of wealth in those golden days of Athenian prosperity."

CHAPTER XII.

CAUSES OF THE PELOPONNESIAN WAR.

We now come to a study of the civil war which for nearly twenty-eight years divided Greek against Greek, caused great suffering at home as well as among the fighting ranks, and led ultimately to the downfall of Athens. For this period we are fortunate in possessing a history of the war, written by Thucydides, himself an Athenian. He took a prominent part in the politics of his day and during early years of the war commanded a detachment of troops. For some military blunder he was dismissed from service and exiled. This gave him opportunity to study the war from different standpoints, although, to be sure, his sympathies were with his countrymen. The early councils he himself attended; those held later, as well as others convened in various parts of Greece, he heard of from persons who had been present. As a result we have a detailed account of the war, of the causes which brought it about, and incidentally much concerning Greek institutions and Athenian life is included.

Since this history of Thucydides far transcends anything written later upon the subject, citations will be made from it freely. The style of the book is simple, straightforward and moderate. Thucydides explains his reasons for writing his history in this way:

"Thucydides, an Athenian, wrote the history of the war in which the Peloponnesians and the Athenians fought against one another. He began to write when they first took up arms, believing that it would be great and memorable above any previous war. For he argued that both states were then at the full height of their military power, and he saw the rest of the Hellenes either siding or intending to side with one or the other of them. No movement ever stirred Hellas more deeply than this; it was shared by many of the barbarians and might be said to affect the world at large.

"And though men will always judge any war in which they

are actually fighting to be the greatest at the time. but, after it is over, revert to the admiration of some other which has preceded, still the Peloponnesus, if estimated by the actual facts. will certainly prove to have been the greatest ever known. . . .

"The greatest achievement of former times was the Persian war; yet even this was speedily decided in two battles by sea and two by land. But the Peloponnesian war was a protracted struggle, and attended by calamities such as Hellas had never known within a like period of time. Never were so many cities captured and depopulated—some by the barbarians, others by Hellenes themselves fighting against one another. Never were exile and slaughter more frequent, whether in the war or brought about by civil strife. There were earthquakes unparalleled in their extent and fury, and eclipses of the sun more numerous than are recorded to have happened in any former age; there were also in some places great droughts, causing famines, and lastly, the plagues, which did immense harm and destroyed numbers of the people. All these calamities fell upon Hellas simultaneously with the war, which began when the Athenians and the Peloponnesians violated the Thirty Years' Truce." [1]

The real cause of the war was growing jealousy of the Athenian Empire, on the part of Sparta and her allies. The incidents that directly led to open hostilities might indeed have caused war between two states, but only the deep-seated dissatisfaction of having seen their state far eclipsed by the more brilliant one in the north can account for the prolonged and bitter struggle that ensued. Always keeping this deep jealousy in mind, let us turn to the events which terminated the Thirty Years' Truce before half that time had expired.

We have seen how each Greek state sent out colonies, largely for purposes of trade. Corinth established a chain of sea-ports for this purpose and among them was Corcyra. This colony early manifested an independent attitude toward the mother country. As her navy grew in strength, she became more rebellious. She soon planted a colony—Epidamnus—of her own, farther north. In this latter city a quarrel broke out between the oligarchs and the people. Such quarrels, we have seen, were frequent in Greece. The democratic element proved

[1] Citations from Jowett's Trans., Book I, 1; 1, 22, 23.

the stronger and drove the aristocratic leaders from the settlement. These exiles continued to harass their townsmen within the walls, and at last the people of Epidamnus appealed to Corcyra for aid. This was refused them. Thereupon they turned to Corinth—as leader of both cities. The Corinthians were only too glad to have a pretext for making trouble with their arrogant colony, and hastened to send a fleet to the relief of the harassed town. When the Corcyreans heard of this interference on the part of Corinth, they were greatly enraged and dispatched a fleet to take home the oligarchal exiles and restore them to power. A battle was fought between the Corinthians and the Corcyreans outside the harbor of Epidamnus, and to the utter humiliation of the mother-city, Corinth was defeated. At once the Corinthians set to work to equip a fleet strong enough to restore them in the eyes of Greece; and now it was time for the Corcyreans to take thought, for they had no such resources at hand as had the older city. In casting about for an alliance which might come to them in a crisis, the Corcyreans determined to seek permission of Athens to join the Delian League—thus to come under the protection of the strong Athenian fleet. When this intention became known at Corinth, ambassadors were hurried to Athens to restrain the citizens from interfering in what might be termed a family quarrel, or, if Athens wished to take a hand in the fight, let her help Corinth.

It was generally felt throughout Greece that a struggle for leadership was now imminent between the two great states, and smaller states ranged on one side or the other by express or tacit alliances. A meeting was called in Athens and before the citizens thus assembled, the delegates from Corinth and Corcyra were heard.

The Corcyreans had hitherto pursued a selfish policy in international matters. They had refused to fight for Greece when the Persian king imperiled the cause of freedom, and they had avoided any entanglement in the affairs of the Confederacy of Delos. For this reason they could not well refer to the past, but to the future. By rousing Athens to her coming need of their support, they tried to enlist her navy in their present trouble. Having explained their situation and stated their request—a desired alliance with Athens,—the Corcyrean orator went on to say:

"To you at this moment the request which we are making offers a glorious opportunity. In the first place, you will assist the oppressed and not the oppressors; secondly, you will admit us to your alliance at a time when our dearest interests are at stake, and will lay up a treasure of gratitude in our memories which will have the most abiding of all records. Lastly, we have a navy greater than any but your own.

"And if anyone thinks that the war in which our services may be needed will never arrive, he is mistaken. He does not see that the Laconians, fearing the growth of your empire, are eager to take up arms, and that the Corinthians, who are your enemies, are all-powerful with them. They begin with us, but they will go on to you, that we may not stand united against them in the bond of a common enmity; they will not miss the chance of weakening us and strengthening themselves. And it is our business to strike first, we offering and you accepting an alliance, and to forestall their designs instead of waiting to counteract them. Corcyra, besides offering many other advantages, is conveniently situated for the coast voyage to Italy and Sicily; it stands in the way of any fleet coming from Thrace to the Peloponnesus, and can protect also a fleet on its way to Sicily. One word more, which is the sum of all we have to say, and should convince you that you must not abandon us. Hellas has only three considerable navies: there is yours, and there is ours, and there is the Corinthian. Now, if the Corinthians get hold of ours, and you allow the two to become one, you will have to fight against the united navies of Corcyra and the Peloponnesus. But if you make us your allies, you will have our navy in addition to your own ranged on your side in the impending conflict."[2]

Then the Corinthians were allowed to state their side of the case. They recalled the self-centered policy heretofore showed by Corcyra—her attitude toward the mother-city, her selfish commercial customs. Corinth, it was said, had never interfered in difficulties occurring between Athens and her allies, and she held that Athens should hold herself aloof from the complicated relationship now existing between Corinth and Corcyra.

The Athenians decided to make a defensive treaty with

[2]Citations from Jowett's Trans., Book I, 33.

Corcyra, by which the two states mutually promised to aid one
another if an attack were made on either: "For they knew
that in any case the war with the Peloponnesus was inevitable,
and they had no mind to let Corcyra and her fleet fall into
the hands of the Corinthians."

Athens sent ten triremes to cruise in the waters off Epidamnus, instructing them to take part in the struggle only if
Corcyra should be in danger.

A battle was soon waged between the new fleet fitted out
by Corinth and the ships mustered by Corcyra. The Corinthians came out ahead, since they sunk or disabled some seventy
ships belonging to the Corcyreans, and took nearly 1,000
prisoners. However, at this juncture a re-enforcing fleet
appeared from Athens, and being told that this would attack
them only if they continued to battle with the Corcyreans, the
Corinthian navy set sail for home. Both sides claimed victory—the one because they had disabled the enemy; the other
because they were left before surrender. Advantage thus
in a measure attended the Corcyreans, and the Athenian fleet
sailed home.

This was the first direct cause of the Peloponnesian war—
Corinth, an ally of Sparta, resenting the fact that Athens
violated the general truce to interfere with her colonies.

The second cause was not long in making its appearance.
Potidaea had been originally a Corinthian colony, but later
joined the Delian League. Athens feared that a revolt in
Potidaea might imperil all Chalcidice, and ordered the colony
to lower its walls and send home the Corinthian officials dwelling in the town. The king of Macedonia had meanwhile
made a treaty with Corinth and he urged the colony to refuse
these requirements made by Athens. Thus sustained, Potidaea
revolted, and Sparta promised to invade Attica if the town
was attacked. Athens laid siege to the rebellious ally and
the Corinthians used their utmost powers to rouse Sparta to the
situation. The Laconians were always slow to act, and while
their business was war, they entered upon it with hesitancy.
Sparta summoned a meeting of her allies in 432 B. C., however, and her policy in Greek affairs was criticised by a
Corinthian ambassador. Because the general course of Sparta
is so truly characterized, the following lines are quoted from
this Corinthian's address, as preserved by Thucydides:

"The spirit of trust, Laconians, which animates your own political and social life, makes you distrust others who like ourselves have something unpleasant to say, and this temper of mind, though favorable to moderation, too often leaves you in ignorance of what is going on outside your own country. Time after time we have warned you of the mischief which the Athenians would do us, but instead of taking our words to heart, you chose to suspect that we only spoke from interested motives. If the crimes which they are committing against Hellas were being done in a corner, then you would be ignorant, and we should have to inform you of them; but now, what need of many words? Some of us, as you see, have been already enslaved; they are at this moment intriguing against others, notably against allies of ours; and long ago they had made all their preparations in expectation of war. And the blame of all this rests upon you; for you originally allowed them to fortify their city after the Persian War, and afterwards to build their Long Walls; and to this time you have gone on defrauding of liberty their unfortunate subjects, and are now beginning to take it away from your allies. For the true enslaver of a people is he who can put an end to their slavery but has no care about it; and all the more if he be reputed to be the champion of liberty in Hellas. And so we have met at last, but with what difficulty! and even now we have no definite object.

"Of all Hellenes, Laconians, you are the only people who never do anything; on the approach of an enemy you are content to defend yourselves against him, not by acts but intentions, and seek to overthrow him, not in infancy but in the fullness of his strength. How came you to be considered safe? That reputation of yours was never justified by facts. We all know that the Persian made his way from the ends of the earth against Peloponnesus before you encountered him in a worthy manner; and now you are blind to the doings of the Athenians, who are not at a distance, as he was, but close at hand. Instead of attacking your enemy you wait to be attacked.

"But here let your procrastination end; send an army at once into Attica and assist your allies, especially the Potidaeans, to whom your word is pledged. Take heed then: you have inherited from your fathers the leadership of the Peloponnesus,—see that her greatness suffers no diminution at your hand." [3]

It is well to dwell at length upon the situation of the two great states on the eve of the Peloponnesian war. The same conditions never again prevailed in Hellas, and it is important to emphasize them. The principles for which Athens stood were far nobler than those of Sparta. The glorious era just ending for Athens had resulted largely because of her democratic ideas. No better characterization of the Athenians during the empire remains than that presented by a Corinthian legate who went to Sparta to enlist help for his state at this time. He said:

"You have never considered what manner of men are those Athenians with whom you will have to fight, and how utterly unlike yourselves. They are revolutionary, equally quick in the conception and in the execution of any new plan; while you are conservative—careful only to keep what you have, originating nothing and not acting even when action is most necessary. They are bold beyond their strength; they run risks which prudence would condemn; and in the midst of misfortune they are full of hope.

"Whereas it is your nature, though strong, to act feebly; when your plans are most prudent, to distrust them, and when calamities come upon you, to think that you will never be delivered from them. They are impetuous, and you are dilatory; they are always abroad and you are always at home. For they hope to gain something by leaving their homes; but you are afraid that any new enterprise may imperil what you already have. When conquerors, they pursue their victory to the utmost; when defeated, they fall back the least. Their bodies they devote to their country as though they belonged to other men; their true self is their mind, which is most truly their own when employed in her service. With them alone, to hope is to have, for they lose not a moment in the execution of an idea. This is the life-long task, full of danger and toil, which they are always imposing upon themselves. None enjoy their good things less, because they are always seeking for more. To do their duty is their only

[3] Citations from Jowett's Trans., Book I, 68-71.

Venus de Milo—the Louvre.

holiday, and they deem the quiet of inaction to be as disagree-able as the most tiresome business. If a man should say of them in a word that they were born neither to have peace themselves nor to allow peace to other men, he would simply speak the truth." [4]

It so happened that while these Corinthian legates were pleading their cause with the Laconians, certain Athenian citizens were sojourning in Sparta. These appeared before the assembled people and attempted to justify the policy hitherto pursued by their state. Speaking of the empire, so greatly derided by their opponents, one of them said: "That empire was not acquired by force; but you would not stay and make an end of the barbarians, and the allies asked us to be their leader. The subsequent development of our power was originally forced upon us by circumstances; fear was our first motive; afterwards ambition, and then interest stepped in.

An empire was offered to us; can you wonder that, acting as human nature always will, we accepted it and refused to give it up again, constrained by three all-powerful motives—ambition, fear, interest. We are not the first who have aspired to rule; the world has ever held that the weaker must be kept down by the stronger. And we think we are worthy of power; and there was a time when you thought so, too; but now when you mean expediency you talk about justice." [5]

After the various ambassadors and strangers had been heard, the Spartans held a secret session and decided to make war, but they felt that their allies should be consulted before decided measures were taken, and adjourned to call a general assembly of all the states friendly to them. These in turn voted to end the truce and invade Attica; however, since time was needed for preparation, Sparta made delays by sending messengers to Athens to make various requests. When one was granted, another was forthcoming. Finally Sparta asked that Athens give up her empire. At this juncture Pericles addressed his assembled townsmen. He said: "For some time past the designs of the Laconians have been clear enough, and they are still clearer now. The treaty says that when differences arise the two parties shall refer them to arbitration, and in the meantime both are to retain what they

[4]Citations from Jowett's Trans., Book I, 70. [5]Ibid, Book I. 75-76.

II—22

have. But for arbitration they never ask; and when it is
offered by us, they refuse it. They want to redress their
grievances by arms and not by arguments, and now they come
to us, using language no longer of expostulation, but of command. They tell us to quit Potidaea, to leave Aegina independent, and to rescind the degree respecting the Megarians.
These last ambassadors go further still, and announce that we
must give the Hellenes independence. I would have none of
you imagine that we will be fighting for a small matter if
we refuse to annul the Megarian degree, of which they make
so much, telling us that its revocation would prevent war.
If you yield to them in a small matter, they will think that
you are afraid, and will immediately dictate some more oppressive condition; but if you are firm, you will prove to them
that they must treat you as their equal. Wherefore make up
your minds once for all, either to give way while you are still
unharmed, or, if we are going to war, as in my judgment
is best, then in no plea, small or great, to give way at all; we
will not condescend to possess our own in fear. Any claim,
the smallest as well as the greatest, imposed on a neighbor
and an equal when there as been no legal award, can mean
nothing but slavery." [6]

Pericles then proceeded to compare the resources at the
command of either state and to show the Athenians that they
had everything in their favor in resisting these affronts offered
by Sparta. After some deliberation it seemed useless to
attempt any peaceful adjustment of their difficulties, and six
months after the engagement before Potidaea, Thebes, a
Spartan ally, opened the war.

[6]Citations from Jowett's Trans., Book I, 141.

CHAPTER XIII.

PELOPONNESIAN WAR TO THE DEATH OF PERICLES.

Details of wars are no longer given extended attention, save by the student of military tactics. In dwelling at length upon the events which characterized this struggle and others which followed as a result of it, we are concerned, not with the campaigns and battles, but with that critical period in Greece when democracy and oligarchy—government by the people and government by the few—came into a conflict so bitter that it meant effectual check for one or the other. The administration of the war in general is consequently important, and for that reason we divide the whole struggle into two very unequal periods—the period when Athenian policy was dictated by Pericles, and second, administration after his death. For the present, then, let us give attention to the conduct of those early years immediately succeeding the violation of the truce.

In 431 B. C. two Plataean citizens agreed to betray their city, once belonging to Boeotia, now an ally of Athens, into the hands of Thebes. In the dead of night a band of 300 Thebans entered the city gates, which opened to them. Instead of making massacre, however, they proclaimed loudly that all who would come over to the side of Thebes would be spared. In consternation, being unable to estimate the number of invaders, the citizens felt obliged to offer allegiance and quiet fell again upon the disturbed town. Under cover of the night, however, the Plataeans rallied and before dawn made a sally upon their invaders, killing some, putting others to flight, and taking 180 prisoners. In the morning it was learned that a larger force was approaching from Thebes. These were notified that unless they turned back the 180 prisoners would be put to death. Thus constrained, they gave up the attack. Misguided ones in Plataea insisted that the prisoners be killed, and in spite of the promise given, this was done. When news of the raid reached Athens, all Boeotians in the city, whether residents or visitors, were at once seized and held as hostages.

Thebes was an ally of Sparta and this unwarranted attack

was practically an aggressive move on the part of the Peloponnesian state, and was regarded as the first event of the war.

War had not been general for some years in Greece, and in all the leading states there was an enthusiastic war-party. The young men were particularly anxious for a chance to try their mettle and win laurels as had their fathers before them. A few lesser states remained neutral; the more important espoused the cause of Athens or of Sparta. Sparta had the support of all the Peloponnesian peoples, save the Argives and Achaeans; in central Greece she was aided by Megara, Phocis Locria, Boeotia, and Corinth. Although others joined later, these were her strong allies.

Athens was helped by Chios, Lesbos, Plataea, her naval empire—which included the cities of Asia Minor, and the islands of the Aegeans. Thucydides notes that "the feeling of mankind was strongly on the side of the Spartans; for they professed to be the liberators of Hellas. Cities and individuals were urged to assist them to the utmost, both by word and deed, and where a man could not hope to be present, there it seemed to him that all things were at a stand. For the general indignation against the Athenians was intense: some were longing to be delivered from them; others fearful of falling under their sway." [1]

Sparta was strong on land; Athens was supreme on the sea. Pericles felt that all was now at stake and determined to spend his forces sparingly. For this reason he abandoned any protracted land fighting, and commanded the country people to leave their farms and take refuge within the city walls—thus making no attempt to guard the unprotected country from attack. On the other hand, the fleet was equipped for action and soon began its work of ravaging the Peloponnesian coast.

In 431 B. C. the Spartans made their first invasion of Attica. When the country people, within the walls of Athens, beheld their buildings in flames and their crops laid waste, while no effort was made to stay the invaders, murmurs arose, but these were silenced by the assurances of Pericles. After the Laconians had laid waste the unprotected districts, they withdrew, and the army of each ally returned home.

[1] Thucydides: II. 36-47.

At the time the Athenians set aside 1,000 talents, to be used only in an extremity; 100 triremes were also held in reserve for a possible sea attack upon Athens. In the fall Pericles led an army into Megara, the fleet returning from the Peloponnesus to assist in devastating the country.

During the following winter a service was held for those Athenians who had fallen in the war. The bones of the dead soldiers were interred without the city walls and appropriate ceremonies were observed. It was on this occasion that Pericles made his famous speech, preserved to us in spirit at least by Thucydides, who was present. Having opened his oration appropriately, Pericles said: "Before I praise the dead, I should like to point out by what principles of action we rose to power, and under what institutions and through what manner of life our empire became great. For I conceive that such thoughts are not unsuited to the occasion, and that this assembly of citizens and strangers may profitably listen to them." Without quoting Pericles' address at length, the following significant sentences have been extracted, pertaining as they do to Athenian development.

"Our form of government does not enter into rivalry with the institutions of others. We do not copy our neighbors, but are an example to them.

"We have not forgotten to provide for our weary spirits many relaxations from toil; we have regular games and sacrifices throughout the year; at home the stage of our life is refined; and the delight which we daily feel in all these things helps to banish melancholy.

"We are lovers of the beautiful, yet simple in our tastes, and we cultivate the mind without loss of manliness. Wealth we employ, not for talk and ostentation, but where there is a real use for it. To avow poverty with us is no disgrace; the sole disgrace is in doing nothing to avoid it.

"To sum up: I say that Athens is the school of Hellas and that the individual Athenian in his own person seems to have the power of adapting himself to the most varied forms of action with the utmost versatility of grace. This is no passing and idle word, but truth and fact; and the assertion is verified by the position to which these qualities have raised the state.   For we have compelled every land and every sea to open a path for our valor, and have everywhere planted eternal memorials of our friendship and of our enmity.

"Such is the city for whose sake these men nobly fought and died; they could not bear the thought that she should be taken from them; and every one of us who survive should gladly toil in her behalf.

"I speak not of that in which their remains are laid, but of that in which their glory survives, and is proclaimed always and on every fitting occasion, both in word and deed. For the whole earth is the sepulchre of famous men; not only are they commemorated by columns and inscriptions in their own country, but in foreign lands there dwells also an unwritten memorial of them, graven not on stone but in the hearts of men.

"The dead have been honorably interred and it remains only that their children should be maintained at the public charge until they are grown up; this is the solid prize with which, as with a garland, Athens covers her sons living and dead, after a struggle like theirs."

The next summer the Peloponnesian army made its second invasion into Attica, while the Athenian fleet ravaged the southern coast, as before. While the country population was sheltered within the city, the Great Plague broke out in Athens.

The acropolis was four and one-half miles distant from Piraeus, or the harbor, and the Long Walls diverged from Athens proper, including quite an area within them. Nevertheless, there had been no adequate provision for so many strangers, and they had taken refuge in the temples, under cover of the fortifications—anywhere and everywhere. During the summer of 430 B. C. this pestilence—known as the Great Plague—appeared to come from Egypt, and manifested itself first in the harbor. It was highly contagious and affected most bitterly those who had no fixed homes. Men in perfect health were seized in a moment, and soon there were none to care for the living or bury the dead. The fever was so intense that those who recovered often lost their minds. "Most appalling was the despondency which seized upon any one who felt himself sickening; for he instantly abandoned his mind to despair and instead of holding out, absolutely threw away his chance of life."

In their misery the people turned against Pericles, whose policy, they declared, had brought upon them all their miseries. He had favored the war in the beginning; he had commanded them to remain in the city and strike no blow at the enemy in their very midst, laying waste their farms. He was evidently to be blamed.

Thereupon Pericles called an assembly of the citizens and addressed them in this way: "I was expecting this outburst of indignation; the causes of it are not unknown to me. And I have summoned an assembly that I may remind you of your resolutions, and reprove you for your inconsiderate rage against me, and want of fortitúde in misfortune. In my judgment it would be better for individuals themselves that the citizens should suffer and the state flourish than that the citizens should flourish and the state suffer.

"I allow that for men who are in prosperity and free to choose. it is great folly to make war. But when they must either submit and at once surrender independence, or strike and be free, then he who shuns and not he who meets the danger is deserving blame. For my own part. I am the same man and stand where I did. But you are changed; for you have been drawn by misfortune to recall the consent which you gave when you were yet unhurt, and to think that my advice was wrong because your own characters are weak.

"As to your sufferings in the war, if you fear that they may be very great and after all fruitless, I have shown you already over and over again that such a fear is groundless. If you are still unsatisfied I will indicate one element of your superiority which appears to have escaped you, although it nearly touches your imperial greatness. I, too, have never mentioned it before, nor would I now, because the claim may seem too arrogant, if I did not see that you are unusually depressed. You think that your empire is confined to your allies, but I say that of the two divisions of the world accessible to man, the land and the sea, there is one of which you are absolute masters, and have, or may have, the dominion to any extent which you please. Neither the Great King nor any nation on earth can hinder a navy like yours from penetrating wheresoever you choose to sail. When we reflect on this great power, houses and lands, of which the loss seems so dreadful to you, are as nothing. They are only the gardens of the house, the superfluous ornament of wealth; and you may be sure that if you cling to our freedom and preserve that, we shall soon enough recover all the rest. But if we are the servants of others, we shall be sure to lose not only freedom, but all that freedom gives.

"The resolution in favor of war was your own as much as mine. What if the enemy has come and done what he was certain to do when you refused to yield? What, too, if the plague followed? That was an unexpected blow, but one might have foreseen all the rest. I am aware that your hatred of me is aggravated by it. But how unjustly, unless to me you also ascribe the credit of any extraordinary success which may befall you. The visitations of heaven should be borne with resignation; the sufferings inflicted by an enemy with manliness. This has always been the spirit of Athens, and should not die out of you.   For the greatest states and the greatest men, when misfortunes come, are the least depressed in spirit and the most resolute in action." [2]

Pericles lived two years and six months after the war opened. It was left for later years to show the excellence of his judgment and the wisdom of his administration. In the words of Thucydides: "For he has told the Athenians that if they would be patient and would attend to their navy and not seek to enlarge their dominions while the war was going on, nor imperil the existence of the city, they would be victorious; *but they did all that he told them not to do,* and in matters which seemingly had nothing to do with the war, from motives of private ambition and private interest, they adopted a policy which had disastrous effects in respect both of themselves and of their allies; their measures, had they been successful, would only have brought honor and profit to individuals, and when unsuccessful, crippled the city in the conduct of the war." [3]

[2]Thucydides: II, 60-65.   [3]Ibid., II, 65.

CHAPTER XIV.

To the Fall of Athens.

After the death of Pericles there was such rivalry among Athenian leaders that the welfare of the state was often made subservient to the ambition of individuals. Pericles had adhered strictly to a well defined policy: namely, to place a commercial blockade on Peloponnesian ports, make no attempt to hazard a land battle, but to stake all on an invincible fleet. In course of time this was bound to wear out the southern state and compel it to yield. It is quite possible that some other policy, as faithfully carried out, might have proven equally effective, but the difficulty was that a course hitherto followed was now abandoned while no other clearly defined plan took its place. Each leader influenced the people to support his individual plan. Sometimes these schemes had for their purpose the crippling of Spartan allies, sometimes to attempts to increase the Athenian empire at the peril of the whole state. Each year, with few exceptions, the Peloponnesian forces invaded central Greece. In 428 Lesbos revolted from the Athenian empire. The following year this island was recovered, but Athens lost a brave little ally when Plataea fell to the share of Sparta. In 426 B. C. the plague broke out again, and perhaps for this reason Attica was spared an invasion that year. The Spartan army appeared the next year, only to be quickly recalled when the Athenians fortified a stronghold in their very midst. Demosthenes, an Athenian general, persuaded those in command with him to establish a fort at Pylos. So successfully was the campaign at this point conducted that a Spartan army was finally obliged to capitulate.

The same year war broke out in Sicily. Athens eagerly consented to aid one of the contending factions, desirous as she was of extending her commercial interests westward.

In 423 B. C. a year's truce was declared. Both sides were tired of war. Sparta was particularly weary of expending her resources in the interest of Corinth. Cleon headed the war party in Athens; Brasidas led the war party in Sparta. It would have been well-nigh impossible to obtain lasting peace while these generals lived. In 422 B. C. Cleon carried the war into Thrace. Both leaders were killed during the campaign and the next year peace was made. Nicias was leader of the Athenian peace party, and the peace-treaty is generally known by his name. It was stipulated that peace should be maintained for fifty years. With important exceptions, each side was to relinquish territory gained during ten years of fight. Boeotia, Megara and Corinth were dissatisfied with the conditions, but as a matter of fact the peace lasted about seven years.

Thus far we have found that Athens maintained her supremacy on the seas. Both states had been exhausted by a costly war, but as yet the imperial power of Athens was unimpaired. From this time forward, however, we shall find a change coming over Athenian affairs, and a little later, a decline of power.

Alcibiades, a brilliant young noble, had been gaining influence among the Athenians; by lavish display of wealth he secured quite a following among the people. By daring escapades and reckless adventure, he soon became popular with the young men of his locality. He had been in favor of a Spartan alliance at first, but finding no opportunity to distinguish himself with the party espousing that cause, he changed around directly and supported the popular party. Alcibiades believed the chances to distinguish one's self were greater in time of war than during years of peace, so he set himself to work to break the truce. Hyperbolus led the democratic faction. Hoping to secure the exile of Alcibiades, he called for a vote of ostracism in 417 B. C. This resulted, quite to the amazement of Hyperbolus, in his own exile. This was the last time the vote of ostracism was taken in Athens. It had been designed to rid the city of one of two rival leaders in times of stress; now there were three striving for first place: Nicias, of the peace party; Hyperbolus, leader of the popular party, and Alcibiades, eager for a renewal of war. Where three or more leaders were involved, ostracism would be ineffectual, and henceforth it was abandoned.

In 416 B. C. an attack was made on Melos, an island once

a member of the Delian League, but long since independent. She had done no injury to Athens and the demand that she tear down her walls and become subservient to the imperial state was refused. Thereupon an expedition was directed against the island, her citizens killed and her women and children sold into slavery. This unwarranted action showed that Athens had become too greedy for imperial power to hold herself any longer to the just measures she had long required of others. Many a thinking Athenian saw only just retribution for this shameless deed in the misfortunes that now overtook his state.

THE SICILIAN EXPEDITION.

We have noted that Athens interfered in Sicilian matters in 425 B. C., with some notion of benefiting herself commercially. The Greeks of Sicily soon settled their differences among themselves and Athens was excluded. Now, in 416 B. C., similar disturbances beset the island and Segesta asked aid of the Athenian fleet, agreeing to bear all expenses of the expedition. When the ambassadors came before the assembled Athenians to enlist their aid, speeches were made by the Athenians both for and against the undertaking. Nicias, always conservative, was anxious to perpetuate the peace; Alcibiades, mindful only of his personal desires and ambitions, wished to embark on the campaign against Syracuse. In urging against it, Nicias said: "I believe the war to be impolitic and ill-timed. I tell you that in going to Sicily you are leaving many enemies behind you, and seem to be bent on bringing new ones hither. You are perhaps relying upon the treaty recently made, which if you remain quiet may retain the name of treaty. But if you meet with any serious reverse, your enemies will be upon you in a moment, for the agreement was originally extracted from them by pressure of misfortune, and the discredit of it fell to them and not to us. In the treaty itself there are many disputed points and very powerful cities, too, persist in rejecting it. Some of these are at open war with us already.

"Sicily is a populous and distant country, over which, if we are victorious, we shall hardly be able to maintain our dominion. And how foolish it is to attack a land which no conquest can secure, while he who fails to conquer will not be where he was before.   We must remember that we have only just recovered in some measure from a great plague and a great war and are beginning to make up our losses in men and money.   The Sicilians have their own country. Let them manage their own concerns. Let us have no more allies such as ours have too often been, whom we are expected to assist when they are in misfortune, but to whom we ourselves when in need may look in vain." [1]

Alcibiades spoke next and in an enthusiastic appeal to the people led them to believe that great glory awaited them in the west and that this was an opportunity not to be rejected. Accordingly, they asked Nicias what equipment he would need to prosecute such a campaign. Thinking to get the best of them there, Nicias named large supplies, numerous ships and men as requisites for such a distant objective point. To his chagrin his requirements were instantly granted and he was instructed to undertake the expedition as speedily as possible.

Thucydides describes the embarking of the fleet for Sicily with characteristic vividness.

"About the middle of summer (415 B. C.) the expedition started for Sicily. Early in the morning of the day appointed for their departure, the Athenians and such of their allies as had already joined them went down to the Piraeus and began to man the ships. The entire population of Athens accompanied them, citizens and strangers alike. The citizens came to take farewell, one of an acquaintance, another of a kinsman, another of a son; the crowd as they passed along were full of hope and full of tears; hope of conquering Sicily, tears because they doubted whether they would ever see their friends again, when they thought of the long journey on which they were sending them. At the moment of parting the danger was nearer; and terrors, which had never occurred to them when they were voting the expedition, now entered into their souls. Nevertheless, their spirits revived at the sight of the armament in all its strength and of the abundant provision which had been made. The strangers and the rest of the multitude came out of curiosity, desiring to witness an enterprise of which the greatness exceeded belief.

[1]Thucydides: VI, 10-14.

"No armament so magnificent or costly had ever been sent out by any Hellenic power.   Never had a greater expedition been sent to a foreign land; never was there an enterprise in which the hope of future success seemed to be better justified by actual power.

"When the ships were manned and everything required for the voyage had been placed on board, silence was proclaimed by the sound of the trumpet, and all with one voice before setting sail offered up the customary prayers; these were recited, not in each ship, but by a single herald, the whole fleet accompanying him.   On every deck both officers and men made libations of wine from vessels of gold and silver. The multitude of citizens and other well-wishers who were looking on from the land joined in the prayer.   The crews raised the Paean, and when the libations were completed, put to sea.   After sailing out for some distance in single file, the ships raced one another as far as Aeginia." [2]

The night before the expedition embarked, a sacrilege had been perpetrated in Athens.   The Hermae, statues of Hermes which served as guide posts, and which were venerated after the manner of shrines, had been mutilated throughout the town.   Since many persons would have been of necessity required to destroy so many, the people were incensed at the evidence of ill-wishers in their very midst.   They instantly accused Alcibiades, since he was the only one who was believed daring enough to commit such an outrage.   He was dismissed, however, and allowed to depart with the fleet.

It was left for the commanding generals to plan the campaign.   Soon it was disclosed that Segesta had no means of complying with her agreement to pay the expenses of the expedition.   Nicias recommended thereupon that the fleet return home.   Another general advised that they make a sudden attack upon Syracuse, which city, unprepared, might possibly be taken.   Alcibiades urged that they rouse the various allies of Syracuse to abandon her and come over to the side of Athens.   This plan was followed, to the destruction of the whole expedition.   It gave Syracuse time to fortify herself, and however the Sicilians might war among themselves, their commercial supremacy in the west demanded that they keep clear of Athenian dominance.

[2]Thucydides : VI, 30-32.

Alcibiades meantime was apprehended by a vessel dispatched to bring him back to Athens, to stand trial for muti-
lating the Hermae.   He apparently submitted but soon effected
an escape to Sparta, where he offered to give his services now
against his country.   He advised the Spartans to fortify a
place in the neighborhood of Athens and to aid the Syracusans
against the Athenian fleet.

For two years an intermittent struggle went on between
the fleet and the states of Sicily.   Nothing decisive happened
on either side.   Athens won some battles, but Nicias, who
commanded, was a timid general and never followed up his
victories.   The Athenians had become despised enemies.
They grew disheartened and fought indifferently.   Finally in
413 B. C. they made a final stand.   They waged a naval
engagement which was to terminate the wearisome struggle.
On shore the army watched the fight with intense excitement.
It was a desperate battle, waged by men who had been some
time from home, who had become accustomed to defeat. and
who lacked a general who might have, even to the end, inspired
his soldiers with confidence.

"No previous engagement had been so fierce and obsti-
nate.   Great was the eagerness with which the men on both
sides rushed upon their enemies whenever the word of command was given, and keen was the contest between pilots as
they manoeuvered one against another.   Many vessels meeting—and never did so many fight in so small a space, for the
two fleets together numbered nearly 200—they were seldom
able to strike in the regular manner, because they had no
opportunity of first retiring or breaking the line; they generally fouled one another as ship dashed against ship in the
hurry of flight or pursuit.

"The crash of so many ships dashing against each other
took away the wits of the sailors and made it impossible for
them to hear the boatswains, whose voices in both fleets rose
high as they gave directions to the rowers, or cheered them
on in the excitement of the struggle.

"The fortune of the battle varied. and it was impossible
that the spectators on the shore should all receive the same
impression of it. Being quite close and having different points
of view, they would some of them see their own ships vic-

terious; their courage would then revive, and they would earnestly call upon the gods not to take from them their only hope of deliverance. But others, who saw their ships worsted, cried and shrieked aloud, and were by the sight alone more utterly unnerved than the defeated combatants themselves.

And while the strife hung in the balance you might hear in the Athenian army at once lamentations, shouting, cries of victory or defeat, and all the various sounds which are wrung from a great host in extremity of danger. At length the Syracusans and their allies after a protracted struggle put the Athenians to flight, and triumphantly drove them to land. Never had there been a greater panic in an Athenian army than at that moment. After the rout of the fleet they knew they had no hope of saving themselves by land unless events took some extraordinary turn." [3]

Surrender was at length the only course open, and a great number of prisoners were taken. In order that they might be guarded, they were put in a great stone quarry.

"Those who were imprisoned in the quarries were at the beginning of their captivity harshly treated by the Syracusans. There were great numbers of them and they were crowded in a deep and narrow place. At first the sun by day was scorching and suffocating, for they had no roof over their heads, while the autumn nights were cold, and the extremes of temperature engendered violent disorders. During eight months they were allowed only about one-half pint of water and one pint of food a day. Every kind of misery which could befall man in such a place befell them. At length the Syracusans sold them, with the exception of the Athenians and of any Sicilian or Italian Greeks who had aided them in the war. The whole number of the public prisoners is not accurately known, but they were not less than 7,000.

"Of all the Hellenic actions which took place in this war, or indeed of all Hellenic actions which are on record, this was the greatest—the most glorious to the victors, the most ruinous to the vanquished; for they were utterly and at all points defeated, and their sufferings were prodigious. Fleet and army perished from the face of the earth; nothing was saved, and of the many who went forth, few returned home.

"Thus ended the Sicilian expedition." [4]

[3] Thucydides: VII, 70-72. [4] Ibid.: VII, 87.

When news of the defeat reached Athens, it was some time before it was credited. It meant total defeat, loss on every hand—for all knew that their enemies would be at once upon them. The greatest navy ever sent out by Athens had been lost; the youth of her land had fallen before the Sicilians; the dream of westward empire was gone, and with what complete destruction!

After a moment's agony the Athenians recovered themselves and prepared for the last struggle. The money which had been set aside the first year of the war was now brought out and expended for a new navy.

While Athens was trying with heroic effort to rise again under her misfortunes, a thrill of grateful joy spread through Hellas. Spartan, Persian, Delian allies—all felt that their time had come.

Wearying of Sparta, Alcibiades had offered his services to the king of Persia. Now Sparta made an alliance with Persia, ceding back to the Persian king all that had ever been his. Thus she proved that Athens alone possessed true patriotism for the cause of Greece; Sparta gave full evidence of her selfish policy on this occasion, as she invariably did whenever opportunity offered.

One after another the allies broke from Athens; battles were waged and the Athenians were sometimes successful. But the opposition had become too strong and Athenian losses had been too great. At last, in 404 B. C., Athens was obliged to make peace on most humiliating terms; her long walls were to be torn down; with the exception of twelve ships, she gave up her fleet; henceforth she was to become subservient to Sparta in every particular.

Thus fell the empire of Athens, and thus ended the glorious era of Athenian supremacy—sacrificed to the weakness of her citizens, who became blind to the needs of their country, and to the selfishness of leaders who no longer put the interests of the state before their own personal ambitions.

Corinth urged that the city of Athens be razed to the ground, but to such lengths Sparta would not go. Pointing out the noble service she had done all Greece in the critical war with Persia, Sparta dismantled her walls and left her prostrate—a democracy, to be ruled now by an oligarchy.

CHAPTER XV.

Spartan Supremacy.

In 404 B. C. Athens yielded to Sparta and in consequence her walls were demolished, her fleet placed at the disposal of the southern state, and her political exiles allowed to return. Sparta had gone into the Peloponnesian war in the beginning to espouse the cause of Hellas, and to champion Greek independence. This position had brought to her side various states desiring most of all to be free, and before the end of the struggle it brought her the Delian allies, weary of the rule of Athens.

When peace was made, however, it soon was apparent that Sparta intended to perpetuate a Greek empire, substituting her rule for that of Athens. A military general, called a *harmost,* with a garrison, was stationed in each town. A Committee of Ten was uniformly entrusted with the government, and in case of opposition on the part of the people, Spartan troops were on hand to support the aristocratic government.

We can only follow briefly the course of events in Athens. In a public assembly it was proposed by an oligarchal sympathizer that thirty citizens be chosen to revise the constitution. When a burst of protest met this demand, Lysander, the Spartan general to whom Athens had capitulated, appeared before the meeting and reminded the Athenians that they were wholly in his power. Thereupon some left the meeting, and without further opposition thirty men—some of them returned exiles, all of them belonging to the oligarchal party—were chosen to remodel the Athenian constitution. Instead of doing so, however, they suspended all popular meetings, courts and institutions, substituting their own rule for that of the people. Having brought control into their own hands, they began to arrest leaders of the democracy; next, wealthy democrats, whose possessions were craved by impoverished oligarchal supporters. To satisfy the latter, prominent democrats were put to death without trial.

II—23

Soon occurred what is known as the "disarming of the citizens." All Athenians were commanded to gather at various places in the city on a specified day, in full armour. Three thousand who were approved as staunch friends of Spartan rule were allowed to retain their weapons; the arms of the rest were confiscated and the stores in the acropolis placed under guard.

Elated with their success, the Thirty—known as the Thirty Tyrants—decreed that none but the 3,000 approved citizens could longer live in Athens—the remainder being compelled to seek homes elsewhere. Such extreme measures were bound to be followed by a corresponding reaction. Other cities were suffering from the high-handed rule of Lysander. Thebes, the old enemy of Athens, was one of these, and offered to receive the Athenian exiles who now thronged out of the city.

Soon after, a little company of these men sallied forth from Thebes and took possession of a dismantled fort in Attica. Here they were joined by other loyal friends. Presently they felt strong enough to seize the harbor of Piraeus. In a battle fought in the streets of the city the democratic adherents defeated the oligarchal faction. These in turn were obliged to flee and called loudly to Sparta for aid. Lysander was no longer in favor, even at home; and King Pausanias was sent to settle Athenian difficulties. He was a broadminded Greek who hated tyranny. Under his protection the Athenians re-established their constitution in September, 403 B. C., and once again a democracy ruled in Athens.

It is now necessary to turn to developments in western Asia.

Upon the death of Darius, in 404 B. C., his oldest son, Artaxerxes, ascended the Persian throne. A younger son, known as Cyrus the Younger, desired the throne for himself, and to this end stirred up the citizens of Asia Minor and Greece to aid him. Eleven thousand Greeks were organized under his command and marched with him to meet King Artaxerxes. At the battle of Cunaxa, near the site of ancient Babylon, Cyrus was killed and his Greek army left without a commander in a hostile country.

At this juncture Xenophon, an Athenian, came forward from the ranks and offered to lead the army home. After many experiences they finally reached the sea. Xenophon has left us an account of this famous Retreat of the Ten Thousand in his Anabasis.

The immediate result of Greek interference in this case was to bring on war between Sparta and Persia. It was natural that Artaxerxes should revenge himself for the direct attack against him on the part of cities recently ceded to him by Sparta. In the war that followed, Persia sought an alliance with Athens, which state now found herself arrayed against her ancient enemy, Sparta.

Conon, the Athenian commander, defeated the Spartan fleet in a battle fought in 394 B. C. at Cnidus. This victory gave Athens once more supremacy upon the seas. The next year Conon rebuilt the long walls at Athens, and many of the old allies, displeased with Sparta's policy, voluntarily returned to the protection of Athens. Thus we see the possibility of a new Athenian empire.

After several years of fighting, some of the Greek states urged Artaxerxes to restore peace in Hellas. In 386 B. C., therefore, the "King's Peace" was made. It stipulated that: "King Artaxerxes thinks it just that the cities in Asia Minor and the islands of Clazomenae and Cyprus shall belong to him. Further, that all the other Greek cities, small and great, shall be independent, except Lemos, Inbros, and Scyros, which are to belong to Athens as of old.

"Should any refuse to accept this peace, I, Artaxerxes, will make war on them, with the help of those who are of my mind, both by land and sea, with ships and with money."

The more important result of the Greek invasion of Asia under Cyrus the Younger was to show the Greeks the weakness of the Persian state, and the great resources of her territory. For long years after the Greeks felt that they could hold their own with the Persians should they press eastward, but only under Alexander the Great was this ambition of the Greeks realized.

ASCENDENCY OF THEBES.

The history of Thebes reaches back to legendary times. When Europa was lured away on the back of a snow-white bull and carried across the sea, King Agenor, the father, blamed his eldest son for having left the child alone. Distracted with grief, he commanded the youth to set out upon a search for the maiden and to return only when he had found her. After years of fruitless search, Cadmus finally consulted the Delphian oracle as to what he should do; whereupon he was instructed to follow a cow which would appear before him, and to found a city on the site where it should lie down to rest. A snow-white cow soon led the way and stopped to rest in a fruitful plain of Boeotia. Cadmus sent his slaves to fetch water from a nearby spring, guarded, so it turned out, by a terrible monster. Cadmus fought the beast and slew him. Under these circumstances Pallas Athena spoke to him, commanding him to sow the ground with the monster's teeth. No sooner had these fallen upon the earth than soldiers in full armour sprang up from the freshly turned soil. Falling upon one another, all were killed but five, who made peace with Cadmus, and from these heroes the great Theban families were proud to trace their origin.

The later life of Cadmus was clouded with sorrows, and these seemed to omen ill for the prosperity of the city he had founded—Thebes, fairest city of Boeotia.

Thebes took no enviable part in the early affairs of Hellas. When the Persian king invaded the land and threatened the freedom of all Hellas, Thebes welcomed him and espoused his cause. Later she pursued a course with Plataea, a town in her own state, which drove the Plataeans to cast in their fortunes with Athens. On the eve of the Peloponnesian war, when Athenian and Spartan allies were but waiting a signal to strike, it was Thebes that made a midnight raid on Plataea and precipitated the struggle. Her usual policy might be characterized as narrow and short-sighted; often ungenerous in her own affairs, and never loyal to the cause of Hellas and Hellenic nationality.

Sparta, it is true, was selfish, yet Sparta was not lacking in fidelity to the state. In face of a common foe, Sparta could forget her personal enmities and fight for the cause of Hellas. Thebes failed even to do this. Only during one period did she come to greatness, and that was under the inspiration of two strong and vigorous men—one, a statesman; the other, a general.

A patriotic party grew up in Thebes during the early part of the fourth century before Christ. Sparta's policy with the states of Greece after the Peloponnesian war was such as to rouse whatever patriotic feeling there might be in the land. There was enmity between Thebes and Sparta, and in 382 B. C., while a Spartan army was on its way north, it was learned that the citadel of Thebes was left temporarily unguarded during a religious festival. This information coming to the Spartan general, he seized the citadel before the citizens were aware of any danger. The attack was wholly unwarranted and provoked intense hatred of the southern state. However, a Spartan garrison was stationed in Thebes and for two or three years Spartan rule was maintained within the city.

Some of the prominent men left the town when it fell under Laconian control, and these formed a nucleus for fugitive Thebans, rallying with a hope of regaining their freedom. In 379 B. C. a counter attack was made upon the garrison while the officers were entertained at a banquet. Theban rule was restored, and naturally, war followed with Sparta.

At this particular time Thebes was fortunate in having a clear-headed statesman, Epaminondas. He can be compared to Pericles in personal character and noble qualities. He was the noblest man who ever became prominent in Thebes, so far as records enable us to judge. At the same time Pelopidas, an efficient general, came forth. Strange to relate, these two men were able to agree upon a plan for the state and to carry it out harmoniously.

Sparta was ill-prepared to make war at this time; signs of weakness were already visible in her state. The number of Spartans had been greatly diminished during the past fifty years, and the old time vigour of the state had largely spent itself.

In the battle of Leuctra, Sparta was defeated. This gave opportunity for a Theban army to march upon the very frontiers of Sparta—something no army had thus far dared to do.

Athens had worked with Thebes against Sparta so long as Sparta continued to be the stronger state. Now when Thebes asserted herself and threatened the very freedom of Laconia, Athens could no longer afford to remain indifferent to the rising state. She herself had hopes of re-establishing her earlier empire and it would not do to have a rival state in her own vicinity. Thus Athens and Thebes came into direct conflict. Within a few years Thebes cleared the seas of Athenian vessels and proved herself supreme on land as well. Nevertheless, Theban greatness was possible only under powerful leadership and when one leader fell first, and soon the other, Thebes was compelled to make peace, and the years of her pride were gone.

In speaking of the failure of Thebes to produce a united Greece, one writer says: "The supremacy of Thebes had failed to create a national state for Greece, just as the supremacy of Sparta and that of Athens had failed before. The Greeks had, it is true, been able to develop a city-state with local self-government, far in advance of the oriental system of government. But they did not possess the capacity to organize their cities into a single state, based upon their common community. Their various leagues failed, because under the predominance of one city the rights of the others were disregarded. Athens had ruled with despotic authority over her subjects. With all their love of liberty springing from their own self-interests, the Greeks failed to recognize that other essential principle of good government, the respect for a higher law based upon the common welfare."

VASE OF HIERO.

The Founding of Thebes.

"When now Agenor had his daughter lost,
He sent his son to search on every coast,
And sternly bid him to his arms restore
The darling maid, or see his face no more,
But live in exile in a foreign clime;
Thus was the father pious to a crime.

The restless youth searched all the world around;
But how can Jove in his amours be found?
When, tired at length with unsuccessful toil,
To shun his angry sire and native soil,
He goes a suppliant to the Delphic dame;
There asks the god what new appointed home
Should end his wanderings, and his toil relieve.

The Delphic oracle thus answer give:
'Behold among the fields a lonely cow,
Unworn with yokes, unbroken to the plough;
Mark well the place where first she lays her down,
There measure out thy walls, and build thy town;
And from the guide Boeotia call the land,
In which the destined walls and town shall stand.'

No sooner had he left the dark abode,
Big with the promise of the Delphic god,
When in the fields the fatal cow he viewed,
Nor galled with yokes, nor worn with servitude;
Her gently at a distance he pursued,
And, as he walked aloof, in silence prayed
To the great power whose counsels he obeyed.
Her way through Panope she took,
And now, Cephisus, crossed thy silver brook,
When to the heavens her spacious front she raised,
And bellowed thrice, then backward turned her gaze
On those behind, till on the destined place
She stopped, and couched amid the rising grass.

Cadmus salutes the soil, and gladly hails
The new-found mountains and the nameless vales,
And thanks the gods, and turns about his eye
To see his new dominions round him lie;

Then sends his servants to a neighboring grove
For living streams, a sacrifice to Jove.
O'er the wide plain there rose a shady wood
Of aged trees, in its dark basin stood
A bushy thicket, pathless and unworn,
O'er run with brambles, and perplexed with thorn;
Amidst the brake a hollow den was found,
With rocks and shelving arches vaunted round.

 Deep in the dreary den, concealed from day,
Sacred to Mars, a mighty dragon lay,
Bloated with poison to a monstrous size;
Fire broke in flashes when he glanced his eyes;
His towering crest was glorious to behold,
His shoulders and his sides were scaled with gold;
Three tongues he branished when he charged his foes,
His teeth stood jaggy in three dreadful rows.

 The Tyrians in the den for water sought,
And with their urns explored the hollow vault;
From side to side their empy urns rebound,
And rouse the sleeping serpent with the sound.

The Tyrians drop their vessels in the fright,
All pale and trembling at the hideous sight.
Spire above spire upreared in air he stood,
And gazing round him overlooked the wood,
Then floating on the ground in circles rolled,
Then leaped upon them in a mighty fold.

And now the scorching sun was mounted high,
In all its luster to the noonday sky,
When, anxious for his friends and filled with cares,
To search the woods the impatient chief prepares.

Soon as the youth approached the fatal place,
He saw his servants breathless on the grass,
The scaley form amid their corpses he viewed,
Basking at ease and feasting in their blood.
'Such friends,' he cries, ' deserved a longer date,
But Cadmus will revenge, or share their fate.'

Then Pallas swift descending from the skies,
Pallas the guardian of the bold and wise,

Bids him plough up the field and scatter round
The dragon's teeth o'er all the furrowed ground;
Then tells the youth how to his wonderings eyes
Embattled armies from the field shall rise.

He sows the teeth at Pallas' command,
And flings the future people from his hand;
And clods grew warm, and crumble where he sows,
And now the pointed spears advance in rows;
Now nodding plumes appear, and shiny crests,
Now the broad shoulders and the rising breasts;
O'er all the field the glittering harvest swarms,
A growing host, a crop of men and arms.

Cadmus, surprised and startled at the sight
Of his new foes, prepares himself for fight;
When one cried out: 'Forbear, fond man, forbear,
To mingle in a blind, promiscuous war.'
This said, he struck his brother to the ground,
Himself expiring by another's wound;
Nor did the third his conquest long survive
Dying ere scarce he had began to live.

The dire example ran through all the field,
Till heaps of brothers were by brothers killed;
The furrows swam in blood, and only five
Of all the vast increase were left alive.
Each one, at Pallas' command
Let fall the guiltless weapon from his hand,
And with the rest a peaceful treaty makes,
Whom Cadmus as his friends and partners takes.

So founds the city on the promised earth,
And gives his new Boeotian empire birth.
Here Cadmus reigned; and now one would have guessed
The royal founder in his exile blessed;
Long did he live within his new abodes,
Allied by marriage to the deathless gods;
But no frail man, however great or high,
Can be concluded blessed before he dies."
—*Ovid: Metamorphoses, Bk. III, 1-195, Addison's trans.*

CHAPTER XVI.

RISE OF MACEDONIA.

Macedonia originally embraced a somewhat indefinite territory north of Thessaly and Epirus. It fell naturally into five divisions: the basins of three large rivers which took their rise in the mountains on the west, and found their final outlet to the sea through a well-nigh common mouth, an alluvial plain formed by the lower course of these rivers, and lastly, a central plain, surrounded by mountains and accessible only through certain mountain passes.

Mountain ranges traversed the land, and made communication with Greece easier than with the various districts of Macedonia itself. The eastern portion of the country was essentially a lowland; the western portion made up wholly of mountain ranges. Civilization as a matter of course followed the nature of the land. Sturdy mountain tribes established themselves in the west; the broadening influences of open communication were evident in the east.

At the dawn of history the country was populated by Pelasgians who may have migrated thence from Asia Minor. In course of time Hellenic clans penetrated north and made homes in the region. The later Macedonians were the descendants of these two mingled races, and were called by the Hellenes by the name which they gave to all foreigners—*barbarians*.

While the Greek states passed through cycles of oligarchies, democracies, and tyrannies, Macedonia continued under a government similar to that of Homeric Greece. Each tribe was ruled by a chief, who was advised by the elders and influenced in matters of common concern by the will of the fighting men. As in days immortalized by the Homeric poems, each man cultivated his own farm, and there was no slave population.

There was almost incessant war among the various tribes peopling Macedonia, but in course of time one chief—leader of a Hellenic band—checked the power of the other chiefs, and assumed kingship over the country. This position was retained by his family with varying success; sometimes all the tribes were held in control; more often the king retained the allegiance of only part of them. It is significant to note, however, that the Macedonian kings were recognized by the Greeks as Hellenes, and were admitted to contests in which only free born Greeks could participate.

The land theoretically belonged to the king, who gave it out in fiefs to his fighting men. Nevertheless, incursions of mountain tribes into more civilized parts of the country were frequent, and conditions were usually more or less unsettled.

We have seen how the Hellenes planted their settlements on every shore, and established their trading posts at every accessible harbor, and for a long time Macedonia was an inland country, since Greek colonies along the coast practically shut it off from the sea. Conflict first arose between Greeks and Macedonians when the latter tried to recover sea-ports along the eastern shore.

Having no commerce, Macedonia was very poor. When she first became a united country, the kings were obliged to develop mines to obtain means for equipping their armies.

Perdiccas was one of the earliest Macedonian kings to make himself felt in Greece. He reigned during the Peloponnesian war and caused Athens some concern because of his craftiness in opposing or befriending her, as temporarily suited his need. It was left for Philip II to make Macedonia a real power.

"The Macedonians were a vigorous peasant race, keen soldiers and hunters. A man who had not killed his boar could not take a seat at a banquet with the men; those who had never slain an enemy wore a cord round their waist. They respected their kings, but sometimes preferred to follow the princes of the various tribes. The nobility enjoyed great prestige; many nobles joined the king's suite as friends, so as to be first in sharing danger and booty in his campaigns Their manners and customs were rude. The king often had several wives, some of the latter came from still more uncivilized neighboring peoples and brought their manners and customs into Macedonia. Their barbarousness was increased by Bacchic ceremonies and mysteries, some of which may have come

from Thrace. Drinking was universally prevalent. There
is a certain resemblance between the Macedonians and the Ger-
mani at the time of the migration of races; great valor, rude
customs, and love of drinking are found in both. Such were
the people which conquered the Greeks, although under the
leadership of kings who were themselves recognized as Greeks.
The conflict originated in a struggle for supremacy on the
coast of Macedonia and Thrace; thence it penetrated into
Greece." [1]

PHILIP OF MACEDON.

Philip II. of Macedon was born in 382 B. C. His father,
Amyntas II., was on the throne, but affairs were in their
usual unsettled condition. The eastern portion of the land,
being more orderly and. civilized, submitted to the king and
gave him support. The western portion, on the other hand,
composed of mountain tribes, joined with some of their
neighbors and refused to yield allegiance.

When Philip was thirteen years of age, King Amyntas II.
died, leaving his throne to his eldest son, Alexander. The
succession was contested, and half the kingdom favored the
pretender, Pausanias. The faithless mother-queen betrayed
her son and he was killed. The following year an alliance
was made between Thebes and Macedonia. Thirty noble
Macedonian youths were given Thebes as hostages—probably
as security for the payment of tribute levied by Thebes.
Philip, the future king of Macedonia, was one of these, and
nothing could have been more fortunate for him than to have
been taken to Thebes for three years' training. Thebes was
now at the height of her power, and Philip had good opportunity to study politics and military affairs. Before he left
the city, this semi-barbarian prince had become Hellenic in
many of his ideas and sympathies. Especially he admired
the part Epaminondas played in Theban politics, and he learned
much of governmental affairs which was of great assistance
to him later on.

Meantime, the second son of Amyntas II. had seized control of the Macedonian government, and in 364 B. C. Philip

[1]Holm: III.. 206

was recalled to take charge of one of the provinces. War soon broke out with the western tribes, and Perdiccas was killed in the struggle. His infant son was left to receive the crown, and for a while Philip acted as regent for his nephew. The times were not auspicious for a baby-king, however, and Philip presently took the title of king for himself.

He realized that two imperative duties lay before him: first, to unite Macedonia and give the country a strong central government; secondly, to weaken the tribes on the frontiers and extend his borders. For the accomplishment of either of these objects a strong army was necessary, so the new king set himself at once to the task of creating one.

The spirit of warring was inborn with his people, and by simply directing this natural tendency and binding his soldiers to him by promises of rewards and shares of booty, Philip was able to rally the nucleus of a fighting force. He drilled his hardy soldiers according to Greek military tactics, gradually perfected discipline, and added special features of his own.

Overmuch has been made of the Macedonian phalanx, yet it was one strong feature of the army, and we may note its organization. It had been the practice among early peoples to draw their soldiers out in lines, thus to face corresponding lines of the enemy. The Greeks had learned the advantage of massing their men, and Philip's phalanx was only the Greek phalanx with certain added features. The heavy-armed infantry formed in squares—16 men in a file, and 8, 12, or 16 files deep. A squad of soldiers 16 in a file and 16 files deep formed a battalion of 256; four such battalions constituted a taxis, and 16 taxes composed a simple phalanx. By advancing *en masse,* a phalanx made a very effective attack. The usual order of battle array was to station the phalanx in the center with cavalry detachments on either wing. Light infantry were placed in front, in the rear, or on either side, as occasion required. It was customary to employ one-half as many light infantry as there were soldiers in the phalanx, and one-fourth as many horse and irregular soldiers. All were drilled not unlike our soldiers today. Discipline was rigid and severe. While the phalanx enabled Philip to win victories, it was only effective upon level ground. Alexander the Great depended principally upon his cavalry, whose discipline was thought to be perfect.

Having thus organized his forces, Philip proceeded to reduce his country to subjection. Then he determined to convert the fighting force into a permanent standing army.

"A national standing army was a new thing in those days. The world was familiar with armies, national, but not standing, levies of citizens, or the subjects of a king, called out for particular campaigns, and relegated presently to private occupations. Even the most professional of such armies, that of Sparta, was not kept constantly under arms, and took a more soldierly than civic character only through constantly mounting guard over a disaffected population. The world was becoming familiar also with armies, standing, but not national, maintained at various epochs by kings or governments of Persia or Egypt, or by commercial cities like Carthage. Such forces as theirs were difficult to control, devoid of *esprit de corps,* liable to seduction and withal enormously expensive. The citizen army, on the other hand, was either sheer militia, incapable of any but the simplest manoeuvres, or very small in numbers, and in both cases difficult to retain in the field. Philip's new army was to combine the merits of both the civic and the mercenary; its chief constituent was to be a large force, derived from his own subjects, imbued with national spirit, and induced by rewards and prizes of war to make soldiering a profession, and remain long enough with the colors to acquire drill and discipline superior to the best mercenary armies.

"A professional army with a national spirit—that was the new idea; and Philip, equally great in principle and theory, intended to add later a new organization, a new weapon, and new tactics. But neither an army nor a nation is made in a day."[2]

Maintenance for the army and for the government was derived largely from the gold mines of Macedonia. These were developed and made to yield a good annual income, thus enabling the king to extend his plans for the kingdom. Desiring a sea-port, he came into conflict with Athens. His course on this occasion was indicative of his usual craft.

[2]Hogarth: Philip and Alexander, 50.

When Athens expostulated with him for attacking her city, he replied that he had merely acted in her behalf, because the town had recently been unfaithful to the Athenians. As soon as it fell into his hands, all Athenian citizens were summarily expelled from its precincts.

By 353 B. C. Philip was ready to move south. As usual, the Greek states were at swords' points with one another. A sacred war was dividing them and it arose in this way: Thebes accused Phocis of some act of desecration in connection with the Delphian oracle and its sacred ground. A council of the Amphictyonic League inflicted a penalty upon Phocis in consequence, and this she refused to pay. Thebes thereupon declared war, and taking time by the forelock, the Phocians seized the temple; then they announced that all were at liberty to visit the sanctuary as of yore, and that they themselves did not mean to touch its treasure. As the war progressed, however, they found it necessary to melt the ornaments to obtain the means of prosecuting the struggle.

Athens, as we have seen already, was in a fair way to regain her old empire. Having rebuilt her walls, obtained a new fleet, and been voluntarily re-enforced by many of her old allies, it seemed quite possible that she would come again into her earlier power. However, she was unable to treat her allies as equals, and they, too, were Hellenic—sensitive about interferences with their own affairs, and resentful of being ignored in matters involving the common good.

During these years Isocrates often appealed to the Athenians to return to their first constitution and first policy—to abandon their fleet, which he conceived to have caused all their difficulties, and once more take the position in Hellenic affairs which they held before the empire.

"It will be asked why I come forward to speak on the 'safety' of Athens at a time when she has a fleet of more than two hundred triremes; peace on the frontiers; the command of the sea, and numerous allies. It is, in truth, this very persuasion of security which alarms me. The rise and fall, first of Athens, then of Sparta, prove that anxious watchfulness leads to success—arrogance to ruin. Our present prosperity is hollow. We have lost the cities in Thrace, spent great sums on mercenaries, become unpopular in Greece, renewed our enmity with Persia, saved the friends of Thebes and lost our own.   The whole political constitution of Athens is vitiated.   It is on this account that I have given notice of an intention to speak on the 'safety' of Athens. Year by year her course becomes more perilous; and the only hope which I can see for her is in a return to the old paths.   I wish to put before you the characteristics of that elder democracy which Solon founded and which Chleisthenes reconstituted.   You can then choose between it and the present.

"Under that democracy, license was not confounded with freedom.   Office was not yet looked upon as an easier soure of income than private industry.   The people collectively reigned; the rich man, who had leisure, served as a duty.

"I shall be suspected, they say, of desiring an oligarchy. As it is, I have only been urging a return to that old system under which, as every one knows, Athens was greatest.   .   .   . If we go through the chief cities of Hellas, a democratic, not an oligarchal, form of government will be found to have been most frequently prosperous.

"Even our corrupt democracy would seem god-made by the side of the government of the Thirty Tyrants.   It was their doing that the walls of Athens were levelled; the dockyards, which had cost 1,000 talents, were destroyed by contract for three; that 1,500 citizens were put to death untried, and more than 5,000 were banished.

"You may ask why, then, I am dissatisfied with this democracy, seeing that it has been productive of so much good?   I answer that it is not enough to excel the tyrants: we must strive to reach the standard of our ancestors.   No race ought to be better than the Athenians.   As other countries have their special products, Attica has her breed of men; we are of that breed, but at this moment we dishonor it.

"If we go back to the old system we shall get the old results.   Then the Greeks trusted us; the generals can tell you how they hate us now.   Then, the citizens were so educated as to be a terror to invaders and to live comfortably with each other; now, not a man will fight but for pay, and they are more destitute than solvent.   If we imitate our ancestors we shall get rid of our own troubles and save Hellas.

Believing this, I have come forward to urge it; reflect and vote as you think best for Athens." [3]

Unsettled conditions in Greece gave Philip an opportunity which he was prompt to improve. He soon declared himself the protector of the oracle of Apollo. In the war which ensued he was victorious. Then, to weaken Athens, he attacked Olynthus, an earlier ally of the Athenians. When this city appealed to Athens for aid, no particular attention would have been given the matter had it not been for Demosthenes. He espoused the cause of the besieged town, and delivered a series of orations against Philip and his encroachments upon Hellenic soil. While the Athenians realized to a certain extent the force of his warnings, they were no longer able to stand as champions for the cause of Greek independence against the world. It is idle to say that the Greeks understood too late the danger of Macedonian aggression. Had they foreseen the full significance of it from the start they were no longer able to rouse themselves as their ancestors had done in the fullness of young vigour. When Olynthus fell and its citizens to the number of 10,000 were sold into slavery, Demosthenes thundered before Athenian audiences and used every effort to stimulate them to action. But Athens' strength was spent. The orations of Demosthenes well express the sentiments of the lesser faction who saw clearly, if they lacked power to act:

"First, men of Athens, if any one regards without uneasiness the might and dominion of Philip, and imagines that it threatens no danger to the state, or that all his preparations are not against you, I marvel, and would entreat you every one to hear briefly from me the reasons why I am led to form a contrary expectation, and wherefore I deem Philip an enemy; that, if I appear to have the clearer foresight, you may harken to me; if they, who have such confidences and trust in Philip, you may give your adherence to them.

"Thus, then, I reason, Athenians. What did Philip first make himself master of after the peace? Thermopylae and the Phocian state. Well, and how used he his power? He chose to act for the benefit of Thebes, not of Athens. Why so? Because, I conceive, measuring his calculations by ambi-

[3] Trans. Jebb, Attic Orators, II, 206.

II—24

tion, by his desire of universal empire, without regard to peace,
quiet or justice, he saw plainly that to a people of our character and principles, nothing he could offer or give would
induce you for self-interest to sacrifice any of the Greeks to
him.   The Thebans he expected (and events prove him right)
would, in return for the services done them, allow him in
everything else to have his way, and, so far from thwarting
or impeding him, would fight on his side if he required it.
From the same persuasion he befriended lately the Messenians
and Argives, which is the highest panegyric upon you, Athenians; for you are adjudged by these proceedings to be the
only people incapable of betraying for lucre the national rights
of Greece, or bartering your attachment to her for any obligation or benefit.

"Consider.   He desires empire: he conceives you to be
his only opponents.   He has been for some time wronging
you, as his own conscience best informs him, since by
retaining what belongs to you he secures the rest of his
dominion.

"You behold Philip, I say, a dispenser of gifts and promises: pray, if you are wise, what you may never know him
for a cheat and a deceiver.   What do you desire?
Freedom?   Then see you not that Philip's very titles are at
variance therewith?   Every king and despot is a foe to freedom, and antagonistic to laws." [4]

"That Philip, from a mean and humble origin has grown
mighty, that the Greeks are jealous and quarrelling among
themselves, that it was far more wonderful for him to rise
from that insignificance than it would now be, after so many
acquisitions, to conquer what is left; these and similar matters,
which I might dwell upon, I pass over.   But I observe that all
people, beginning with you, have conceded to him a right,
which in former times has been the subject of contest in every
Grecian war.   And what is this?   The right of doing what he
pleases, openly fleecing and pillaging the Greeks, one after
another, attacking and enslaving their cities.   You were at
the head of the Greeks for 73 years, the Laconians for 29;
and the Thebans had some power in these latter times after
the battle of Leuctra.   Yet neither you, my countrymen, nor

[4] Second Philipic.

the Thebans, nor Laconians, were ever licensed by the Greeks to act as you pleased; far otherwise. When you, or rather that Athenians of that time, appeared to be dealing harshly with certain people, all the rest, even such as had no complaint against Athens, thought proper to side with the injured parties in a war against her.   Yet all the faults committed by the Spartans in those thirty years, and by our ancestors in the seventy, are less, men of Athens, than the wrongs which, in the thirteen incomplete years that Philip has been uppermost, he has inflicted on the Greeks: nay, they are scarcely a fraction of these, as may easily be shown in a few words. Olynthus and Methone and Apollonia, and thirty-two cities on the borders of Thrace, I pass over; all which he has so cruelly destroyed that a visitor could hardly tell if they were ever inhabited: and of the Phocians, so considerable a people exterminated, I say nothing. But what is the condition of Thessaly? Has he not taken away her constitutions, and her cities, and established tetrarchies, parcelled her out, not only by cities, but also by provinces, for subjection? Are not the Euboean states governed now by despots, and that in an island near to Thebes and Athens?   And we, the Greek community, seeing and hearing this, instead of sending embassies to one another about it and expressing indignation, are in such a miserable state, so intrenched in our separate towns, that to this day we can attempt nothing that interest nor necessity requires; we cannot combine, or form any association for succor and alliance; we look unconcernedly on the man's growing power, each resolving, methinks, to enjoy the interval that another is destroyed in, not caring or striving for the salvation of Greece: for none can be ignorant that Philip, like some course or attack of fever or other disease, is coming even on those that yet seem very far removed.

Yet the Greeks endure to see all this; methinks they view it as they would a hailstorm, each praying that it may not fall on himself, none trying to prevent it.

"But what has caused the mischief? There must be some cause, some good reason, why the Greeks were so eager for liberty then and now are eager for servitude. There was something, men of Athens, something in the hearts of the multitude then, which there is not now, which overcame the wealth of Persia and maintained a freedom of Greece, and quailed not under any battle by land or sea; the loss whereof has ruined all, and thrown the affairs of Greece into confusion. What was this? Nothing subtle or clever: simply that whoever took money from the aspirants for power, or the corrupters of Greece were universally detested: it was dreadful to be convicted of bribery. But now all such principles have been sold as in open market, and those imported in exchange whereby Greece is ruined and diseased. What are they? Envy where a man gets a bribe; laughter if he confesses it; mercy to the convicted; hatred of those that denounce the crime; all the usual attendants upon corruption. For as to ships and men and revenues and abundance of other materials, all that may be reckoned as constituting national strength— assuredly the Greeks of our day are more fully and perfectly supplied with such advantages than Greeks of the olden time. But they are all rendered useless, unavailable, unprofitable, by the agony of these traffickers." [5]

An embassy was dispatched from Athens to make peace with the northern king. Philip stipulated that each power should retain whatever it held at the moment. Then the crafty king manoeuvred to have himself admitted to the Amphictyonic League, and tried to make friends with Athens. Isocrates favored him, seeing thus a possibility for the long-dreamed-of unity of Greece. But Demosthenes saw nothing but danger ahead if Philip were to place his authority over the land. War broke out again, and both Thebes and Athens were defeated. Philip always preserved a profound respect for Athens, impressed as he had been in his youth by her history and her civilization. Because of this affection for her, he never invaded the city, while Thebes, on the other hand, was harshly treated and was ruled by a Macedonian garrison. Having marched into the Peloponnesus and received the homage of the southern states, Greece lay at last at the feet of Philip II., united under his kingship.

Now a congress of Hellenic states was convened at Corinth, and before delegates from all the leading citizens Philip announced that he would now avenge the insult done to Greece by the invasion of Xerxes. Plans were immediately set on

[5]Third Philippic.

foot preparatory to an Asiatic campaign, but Philip fell at the
hand of an assassin. His work, however, was completed. He
had found Macedonia little more than a geographical name;
he left it a united kingdom. Of its condition when he assumed
the crown we may judge from the following lines attributed
to Alexander, when once addressing his army:

"My father, Philip, found you a roving people, without
fixed habitations and without resources, most of you clad in
the skins of animals, pasturing a few sheep among the mountains, and, to defend these, waging a luckless warfare with
the Illyrians, the Triballans, and the Thracians on your borders. But he gave you the soldier's cloak to replace the skins
and led you down from the mountains into the plains, making
you a worthy match in war against the barbarians on your
frontier, so that you no longer trusted to the security of your
stronghold so much as to your own personal valor for safety.
He made you to dwell in cities and provided you with wholesome laws and institutions. Over these same barbarians, who
before had plundered you and carried off as booty both yourselves and your substance, he made you, instead of underlings,
to be masters and lords."

Philip had found Greece composed of many states, warring continually with each other. He had shown the possibility of a united Greece by incorporating the country into his
original kingdom. He left the completion of the task, however, to his son. Philip accomplished mighty things; it
remained for his son alone to do more. On the other hand,
the works of Alexander would have been impossible without
the pioneering of his father.

Because our knowledge of Philip comes to us largely from
his opponents—from the somewhat exaggerated orations of
Demosthenes—and because Philip left his crown to his still
greater son, his own part has frequently been underestimated.
It is enough to say that without him the brilliant empire
brought into existence by Alexander could not have been
realized at this time.

CHAPTER XVII.

ALEXANDER THE GREAT.

During one of his marches, Philip came one day upon a band of religious enthusiasts, celebrating some festival with wild orgies and songs. He was attracted by an impassioned princess of Epirus, and soon after married her. In 356 B. C. she gave birth to a son—Alexander the Great.

As a boy, Alexander received careful training, Aristotle, the greatest savant of antiquity, being engaged as his instructor. This philosopher was far in advance of his time, and made use of various modern methods. For example, he made collections of birds, plants, and animals, for purposes of study and investigation. When, long years after, we find Alexander collecting rare plants and flowers in distant regions to which his campaigns led him, we may feel sure that the habit resulted from Aristotle's teaching.

The story of the boy Alexander and his favorite horse has become too famous to be passed over without a word.

"When only thirteen years of age, Alexander once saw some horse dealers bringing a beautiful steed before the king. The animal had a white spot on his nose shaped somewhat like the head of an ox, and on this account was named Bucephalus, which means 'ox-head.'

"Philip admired the horse greatly, and bade the grooms try him, to see if his gait was good. One after another mounted, only to be thrown a few minutes later by the fiery, restless steed, which was becoming very much excited. The horse seemed so skittish that Philip finally told the men to lead him away, adding that a man would be foolish to purchase such a useless animal. Alexander then stepped forward and begged permission to try him. His father first made fun of him for asking to mount a horse which none of the grooms could manage, but, as Alexander persisted in his wish, he was finally allowed to make the attempt.

"The young prince then quietly walked up to the excited horse, took the bridle, held it firmly, and began to speak gently and pat the steed's arched neck. After a moment, Alexander led Bucephalus forward a few steps, and then turned him around, for he had noticed that the horse was frightened by his shadow. Then, when the shadow lay where he could not see it, and where it could no longer frighten him, the young man dropped his cloak quietly, and vaulted upon the horse's back. Once more Bucephalus reared, pranced, kicked, and ran; but Alexander sat firmly on his back, spoke to him gently, and, making no effort to hold him in, let him speed across the plain. In a few minutes the horse's wildness was over, and Alexander could ride back to his proud father, sitting upon a steed which obeyed his slightest touch. Philip was so delighted with the coolness, courage, and good horsemanship that Alexander had shown on this occasion, that he made him a present of the steed. Bucephalus became Alexander's favorite mount, and, while he would allow no one else to ride him, he obeyed his master perfectly.

"In one of his battles he lost his faithful steed Bucephalus, which had borne him safely through many a fight. Alexander felt his loss deeply, and not only had a monument built over his remains, but also founded a city nearby, which was called Bucephalus." [1]

Alexander was very fond of the Homeric poems, taking them with him on all his campaigns. They depicted a condition of life similar to that prevailing in certain parts of Macedonia, for while Philip and Alexander rapidly absorbed Greek culture and Greek ideas, their country retained on the whole its primitive civilization. For this reason the young prince understood well the spirit of the great Greek epics, having been accustomed to similar manners and customs in his native land.

As he grew into manhood, Alexander is said to have become very restless lest his father would leave him no worlds to conquer, and we may well imagine that he assumed control of the kingdom with keen delight.

When the report of Philip's death spread through Greece in 336 B. C., the news was received with wild rejoicing. The rule of Macedonia was believed to be at an end, for none imagined that a twenty-year old prince could hold together

[1] Guerber: Story of the Greeks, 229.

Philip's kingdom. Having at his disposal a large, well-disciplined army and an ample treasury, Alexander did not wait for coalitions to form against him, but on the contrary, marched at once into the north to make sure his native kingdom. This quieted, he turned to Greece. Thebes, among other Greek states, had renounced Macedonian rule. Before this city Alexander suddenly appeared. Having captured it, the town was destroyed, with the exception of temples and the home of Pindar, a Theban poet, loved by the young king. In face of this evidence of power all Greece opened her gates to the young conqueror, recognizing him as master and pledging him support and allegiance.

By 334 B. C. Alexander was ready to start out upon the eastern campaign which his father had previously outlined. We have already learned about the strenuous resistance made by Tyre when Alexander demanded that the city gates be opened to him. His persistency in withstanding the defense of the Tyrians gave indication that no obstacle would be sufficient to baffle him.*

In three encounters with the Persian forces, numbering far greater than his own, he was each time victorious. Persia soon lay at his feet. With tireless energy he pressed eastward to India, and south into Egypt. The entire civilized world of antiquity fell before his army and all countries offered homage to the greatest conqueror the world has ever seen.

Not only did Alexander conquer this vast extent of territory, but he planned out its government as well. He founded many cities, several of which were called by his name. Most renowned is the mighty Alexandria in Egypt, standing yet a splendid monument to the greatness of its founder.

At the age of 33 years, Alexander fell a victim to fever and to his own indulgences.

"As a man Alexander possessed remarkable natural endowments—a body of great beauty, agility, and strength, capable of extraordinary feats of endurance; a mind of transcendent genius, of restless activity, of wonderful powers of insight, of broad and comprehensive views, prolific in resources, and unerring in the adjustment of means to ends; a will power such as is rarely given to men, irresistible and untiring; and

*See The Story of Phoenicia.

an emotional nature made up of a strange mixture of generosity and cruelty, of self-control and self-indulgence, of calm repose and furious passion, capable of performing the worst of crimes, and immediately giving way to penitence and remorse.

"As a soldier he has had scarcely a peer in the world's history—a born commander of men, a supreme master of strategy and tactics, equally great in marches, sieges, and battles.

"As a statesman he possessed a cosmopolitan breadth of view. He believed that the state should not be narrowed to the limits of a city or small territory, like that of the Greeks, but should take in all civilized peoples. He showed his broad ideas by favoring the mixture of races, by encouraging a wider commercial intercourse, by patronizing the arts and sciences, by building up new cities as centers for the diffusion of Greek civilization. He adopted, in some respect, higher methods of government than those which had hitherto prevailed in the East. But it remains true that the great world empire which he carved out with the sword fell to pieces almost immediately after his death." [2]

It is difficult to adequately characterize Alexander, rightly called the Great, without seeming to exaggerate his personality and ability. Military leaders of all subsequent ages have found in him their ideal; monarchs ambitious for world-power have emulated his example; hero-worshippers have held him to be worthy of deep admiration.

Effects of Alexander's Conquests.

When we find that the vast empire of Alexander fell to pieces after his death, it seems at first sight that the work of the great conqueror was destroyed. Perdiccas, to whom the dying king gave his signet ring, was unable to hold the wide territory together, and it shortly divided into three natural divisions, each governed by one of Alexander's generals. Syria and Western Asia fell to the share of Seleucus. He founded the city of Antioch, which became his capital and an important center for many years. His sons and descendants—

[2] Morey: Outlines of Ancient History, 236.

the Seleucidae—succeeded him, and maintained a powerful
kingdom for some generations.　Egypt was claimed by Ptol-
emy, who also established his dynasty, and made Alexandria,
newly founded, a seat of learning and culture.　Macedonia,
together with Greece, was apportioned to Cassander, but his
successors proved too weak to hold the kingdom intact.
Strong Greek leagues were formed to oppose them and the
states of Greece remained under the administration of these
leagues, or confederacies—until the interference of Rome.

Thus it is plain that the dream of Alexander to establish a
world-empire was never fully realized in his own life, and
vanished immediately after his death.　Politically, the great
conquests were a failure.　However, from a social standpoint,
it is well-nigh impossible to over-estimate the effects of these
conquests.　Before his time, Hellenic culture had been confined to those parts of the world peopled by Hellenes—that is,
to continental Greece, the cities of Asia Minor and the coasts
and islands of the Aegean sea.　Alexander sought to diffuse
this wonderful civilization throughout the ancient world, and
in this he was largely successful.　As he conquered districts
in Asia and Egypt, he at once laid plans for their administration.　A commander of troops, a collector of taxes, and a
general administrator were placed in new towns, founded for
the very purpose of becoming Greek centers.　Alexander himself is credited with having founded over seventy new cities,
and the same plan was followed by his generals in the portions of his empire which fell to each.　Greeks were induced
to leave the mother country and colonize these new centers.
Schools were built up, theaters were erected, temples arose.
The Greek language was spoken in these cities and Greek art
and Greek ideals were introduced.　Asiatics who had dwelt
before in country districts found it to their advantage to come
into these towns and make their homes.　Hence we find a
mingling of Greeks and Barbarians, Europeans and Asiatics,
such as the world had never before known.　Only two or
three times since the age of Alexander has there been such an
outpouring, such a diffusion of ideas and such a corresponding influx as now occurred.　Greeks migrated to the new cities
in such numbers that the country was drained of its vigour and
enterprise.　Each became a center for spreading Hellenic cul-

ture throughout the East; trade took on unwonted activity, and Asiatic wealth and oriental ideas returned to Europe. The civilization of modern times has come from the blending of East and West—not from Greece alone. And all of this was made possible by the work of Alexander. "He grafted the new West upon the old East, and from this graft sprang the plant of our later civilization." [3]

"Although nothing that Alexander left unfinished at his death was done by another as he himself would have done it, very little that he had done was ever undone. Alexander's own principle and model of civilization, the general scheme of his provincial organization, the channels into which, half-unconsciously, he had directed trade, his types and standards of currency, and the military system of his father and himself, held good until and even beyond the coming of Rome. He did more than any single man to break down that proud division of the world into few Greeks and myriad barbarians, which had stimulated the seed of civilization, but was become a cramping and suffocating influence on the grown plant. He did more than any single man up to his day to make one part of the world known to the other, and, unconsciously enough, so to widen the application of his great teacher's principle of social organization, that little more than three centuries later a church became possible which contained Jews, Greeks, Latins, Parthians and Medes, and the dwellers in Mesopotamia." [4]

There was mutual benefit for the East and West in this mingling of knowledge and civilization. Greece could teach her truer conceptions of life, her wonderful art, her esteem of the beautiful, her literature and philosophy, her games and festivals. But the East also had contributions to make: she had wealth and trade, scientific knowledge and observations, records and traditions antedating the earliest migrations of Hellenes. From a fusion of these ideas came a stimulus. a new incentive to study and investigation which worked for higher learning and broader culture.

Among the centers which became famous for its learning, the greatest was Alexandria, in Egypt. A school, or Museum—so-called because sacred to the Muses—was opened here and

[3]West: Ancient History, 223. [4]Hogarth: Philip and Alexander.

attracted students from all parts of the civilized world. In connection with this school, a library grew up, possessing finally some five hundred thousand manuscripts. A school of philosophy developed here and races and literatures mingled in the city which rivaled Athens in learning, and was far more cosmopolitan. Such centers as this preserved Greek culture for future ages to an extent which would have been impossible had it remained the sole property of Greece. When Christianity tried to eliminate everything "pagan," much learning of the Greeks was cast aside, and later, when the zeal for classical study returned, these cities, founded by Alexander and his successors, were able to supply much which had disappeared in Europe.

"If we consider in its large features what the early Hellenistic period has done for us in literature, we may divide its action into the care and preservation of Hellenic masterpieces and the production of works of its own.

"As regards the former, there can be no doubt that the creation of the great cosmopolitan library at Alexandria and the great trade in books which came thence, were the greatest acts of protection ever done for the greatest literature the world has seen.   Though we have no explicit record telling us the fact, there must have been some regular permission to copy books in the library, and, multiplying them by slave hands, to disperse them by way of trade all over the Greek-speaking world.

"I say, then, that not merely for the preservation, but for the diffusion, of Hellenic literature, the work of Alexander was a permanent education to the whole Greek speaking world.

"Let us now turn to art, and ask, what was the influence of Hellenism upon the nations which it drew within its mighty influence.

"Of the recognized fine arts the two most subtle and subjective were lost to us—music and painting. The hand of time has been against us, and we have only stray fragments which give us not even adequate suggestions. The remains of Greek melodies, of which we understand the notation, are not only to us exceedingly ugly, but so queer and strange that no musician can attempt to restore a single bar, where there is a gap or fracture in the inscription. But let us take up sculpture and architecture.   In recent years we have much fresh evidence of the diffusion of this noble art into the East. The great glory of the museum at Constantinople is the famous tomb of Sidon, which so amazed its discoverers that they called it the tomb of Alexander the Great. That, of course, was absurd. But as to its age there is no doubt. It commemorates in its noble reliefs the conflicts of Macedonians, Greeks and Persians, as was evidently intended to honour the tomb of some companion of Alexander.

"But if the date had not been thus fixed, we should have seen another recurrence of the controversy which rages over every new masterpiece in marble or in bronze which is recovered from the earth or the sea. Is it Hellenic or Hellenistic? Is it of the fourth or the third century before Christ? Can there be any better proof than this, that Hellenism had not only spread a knowledge of, and a taste for, great plastic art throughout the nearer East, but that it also raised up no mean successors to the great men of genius whose work in marble and in bronze has never since been rivalled, not even by all the study and all the resources of modern civilization?

"The case is far simpler with architecture. We may say broadly that the Corinthian style is exclusively Hellenistic and Roman. All the great remains in that style, from the splendours of the Olympian temple at Athens to the colonnades at Palmyra—all are essentially the product of Hellenism." [5]

In view of this wide diffusion of Greece culture, this successful uniting of the world so far as civilization was concerned, we understand the far-reaching effects of Alexander's conquests.

"No single personality, excepting the carpenter's son of Nazareth, has done so much to make the world we live in what it is as Alexander of Macedon. He leveled the terrace upon which European history built. Whatever lay within the range of his conquests contributed its part to form that Mediterranean civilization, which under Rome's administration became the basis of European life." [6]

[5] Mahaffy: Hellenism in Alexander's Empire, 109.
[6] Wheeler: Alexander the Great.

HELLAS.

Land of bards and heroes, hail!
    Land of gods and godlike men,
Thine were hearts that could not quail,—
    Earth was glorious then;
Thine were souls that dared be free:
Power, and fame, and liberty.

Like the infant Hercules,
    Thou didst spring at once to power.
With the energy that frees
    Millions in an hour:
From the wave, the rock, the glen,
Freedom called her chosen then.

What though thousands fought with one,
    Did thy sons draw back in fear?
No—with Aegis like a sun,
    Pallas hovered near;
Wisdom with her diamond shield
Guarded well the fatal field.

Land where every vale and mountain
    Echoes to immortal strains,
Light is round the stream and fountain,
    Light on all thy plains.
Never shall thy glory set;
Thou shalt be our beacon yet.
                   JAMES GATES PERCIVAL.

SOCIAL LIFE IN GREECE

CHAPTER I.

HELLENIC CITIES.

Viewed from our modern standpoint, the cities of ancient Greece were unattractive and inconvenient in their general plan. As in many old towns to be found in the East today, the streets were irregular, narrow, unpaved, undrained, and very dirty. In the later age of Greece we discern some improvement in the towns. Piraeus, the harbor of Athens, was laid out in an orderly way, its streets being at right angles with parks reserved in different parts of the city. Nevertheless, while examples can be cited to the contrary, the important cities of Hellas were those that had been ancient centers—some like Athens, having been peopled in prehistoric times. Such places had no regular plan or order. They were usually provided with a citadel or acropolis—a natural hill. For centuries in Athens the citadel remained a fortified stronghold, within whose shelter the inhabitants gathered in time of danger. When periods of peace settled upon Greece, and especially when an increasing population required the city to expand, a wall was thrown around a wider area, and the acropolis lost its early significance as a fort. It was then adorned by temples erected to the honor of the gods, by statues and public buildings. A similar course was followed in several Greek centers.

Aside from the acropolis, the Hellenic city received little care or attention. The unpaved streets were either dusty or muddy; sewers were unknown, and refuse from the houses was thrown into the highways. Indeed, gutters frequently led from private dwellings into the streets. At night the city was unlighted, and the belated pedestrian had to give quick heed to the cry of warning which preceded a deluge of water or garbage in his very path—for no sidewalks were provided the foot-traveler. At public festival times the authorities required citizens to clean out the streets through which the processions would pass; otherwise no particular attempt was made to keep the highways in condition. In dark alleys and narrow passages where light and fresh air was excluded, the picture of Apollo, god of health, was often painted, with the hope that he would protect dwellers in that section from disease. It is small wonder that when pestilences broke out fearful ravages were made among the population before they could be checked.

The streets were not always named, and the houses were never numbered, so we find citizens describing their residences as near a certain city-gate, fountain or temple. In case a man sought one whose locality was unknown to him, slaves might be obliged to make prolonged search before discovering him.

The Agora.

The real home of the Greek was the *agora,* or market-place. Hither he came not only to do the marketing—although that duty fell to the master of the house, not to his wife—but in the agora he met his acquaintances, heard the news, discussed political questions, and exchanged ideas with his neighbors.

The agora was ordinarily located in the central part of the city. It was an open space surrounded by shops and booths. In the shelter of the shops citizens gathered to sun themselves and escape awhile from the cold winds that occasionally swept down upon Hellas. In cold weather the poor gathered around some public oven—commonly the oven in a baker's shop—to warm themselves, for their houses were unheated.

The trade center, the agora, was also the meeting place for public assemblies. Here the great questions of Greek government were argued and discussed. Policies that worked for the weal or woe of Hellas were outlined, and statesmen here won followers to their projects. In short, the agora was the very heart of the Greek city—the political and commercial center, the arena of the Hellenes. For this reason, those who wished to win or retain public favor often beautified and adorned it. Statues of prominent men were erected; porticoes were built, groves planted and memorials of various kinds scattered here and there in haphazard fashion. A relative of Cimon erected a portico in the agora of Athens, having it decorated with paintings that commemorated events closely interwoven with the past—the battle of Marathon, and mythological exploits. Cimon himself planted clusters of plane-trees to protect the citizens from the hot rays of the summer sun.

The morning hours were most animated in the agora. At noon-day, the heat compelled most to indulge in a siesta, after which the baths were visited. It was time enough to go home when night fell upon the city—there to dine, to entertain or be entertained, to sleep and await the morrow.

Houses.

Public buildings interested the Greek far more than private ones. Greek houses were often small and always plain on the outside. A single door broke the bare aspect of the wall which fronted upon the street. The houses were generally two stories in height and were larger or smaller, according to the needs and means of the family. The wealthy Greek lavished his care upon his country home rather than his city home, so in the city there was not so much difference in the external appearance of the abodes of rich and the moderately comfortable citizens. Owing to the fragile walls and temporary construction of these houses, few remains have been recovered.

Windows were placed in the second story of Greek houses; if in the first, they were placed so high as to merely admit light. A door on the street gave entrance to a hall which led into the important room of the house. This was usually surrounded with pillars and in the center was a court, open to the sky. Sleeping rooms and private apartments opened on this court, and obtained not only light but fresh air from it. The houses were frequently built so closely together that air could not circulate freely between them.

The women's quarters were as a rule in the second story, although during the day, when the men were absent, the court was used as a living room. Here were altars to the gods. In early times here was the hearth where food was prepared. As years went on, the houses of the well-to-do were furnished with kitchens. A *megaron*, or dining hall for men, opened upon the court. This may be compared to the old Saxon *hall*. Here the master of the house banqueted his friends, and here they were entertained after the conclusion of the meal by harpers, songs and dancing.

II—25

Slaves were so cheap that even families in limited circumstances owned one or two, and the wealthy possessed many.

The climate was usually so mild that no artificial heat was deemed necessary, and the only chimney the house possessed was in the kitchen. Even here, no pipe connected the portable stove with the chimney and the smoke had to find an escape as best it might.

Niches were left in the walls for lamps. Torches afforded the sole means of lighting houses in early times; later, it was discovered that wicks placed in olive oil would supply a light, and this discovery led to the invention of various kinds of lamps—some of which remain. At best they gave poor light and in unventilated rooms emitted an unpleasant odor.

Glass for windows was unknown to the ancients. The Greeks closed their windows with rugs or shutters. The floors of the wealthy were covered with rich oriental rugs; those of the poor, with mats woven of rushes, which were used also as beds by the family. In wealthier homes, bedsteads of costly material were common. If made of plain wood, this was concealed by soft coverings which were heaped upon them. Even in Homeric times the beds of the nobles were seemingly comfortable.

> "White-armed Arete spake,
> And bade her maidens in the portico
> Place couches, and upon them lay fair rugs
> Of purple dye, and tapestry on these,
> And for the outer covering shaggy cloaks.
> Forth from the hall they issued, torch in hand;
> And when with speed the ample bed was made,
> They came and summoned thus the chief to rest:
> ' Rise, stranger, go to rest; thy bed is made.' "[1]

In this case, over all the woolen coverings, fur coats or mantles were thrown. In later times, mattresses filled with wool or feathers were laid upon the beds. If a Greek were wealthy and fond of fine furniture, his bedstead might be inlaid with precious metals, and be covered with softest coverlets.

---

[1] Odyssey.

There was by no means such a variety of articles of furniture as we have today, but the beauty and perfection of workmanship upon articles they did possess was remarkable. Tables were common. These were lower than those ordinarily in use now. Instead of sitting around a table at meal time, members of the family, or guests, if the master entertained, reclined on couches and were waited upon by slaves who served from the tables and supplied each guest. The custom of reclining at meals was probably confined to the wealthy. The busy people, whether in town or country, no doubt sat around a table and ate their meals much as they do today.

Chairs were common articles of furniture. Some of these were mere stools, having no backs. Others were provided with arms and backs as well. Frequently great skill was shown in the carving upon the legs of the chairs. Chests were needed in every well ordered household. These were elaborately decorated and were numerous in the homes of the wealthy. In them the bedding, linen and clothing were stored.

Mirrors such as we have today were unknown, but the Greeks made others of highly polished metal—gold, silver, or bronze. These were carefully protected lest their highly polished surfaces be scratched or injured.

Vases and jars of all kinds and descriptions were in evidence. Vases were used for purely ornamental purposes, or, being supplied with stoppers, were used to contain unguents and oil. It is from paintings found upon these vases that we learn much concerning Greek life. Costumes, bridal processions, women in all kinds of employment, drinking scenes, banquets and warriors were all depicted by the vase painters. Many of these antique vases have been recovered and are to be seen today in the great museums of Europe.

Jars were even more essential. They were used to store water, oil, and all kinds of provisions. In early times they were made of earthenware. Later they were sometimes made of bronze, iron, and other metals, but the common jars were still of clay. Beautiful paintings often adorn even the humblest vessels. The Greeks loved beauty, and whatever articles they produced were designed to please the eye. Quite naturally it came about, then, that the jar which held wine or honey was ornamented until of itself it was decorative, and

added to the beauty of the house.   It would be difficult to
exaggerate the service these jars and clay vessels rendered in
the ordinary household.   No running water was supplied to
each house, and for drinking purposes slaves went each day
to the fountains or springs and brought pure water for the
family.   Cisterns were usually built in connection with each
establishment, so rain water was preserved for general purposes.   Pure water was kept in covered clay jars, and by
radiation was cooled for drinking purposes.

Some kitchen utensils have been found.   The kettles and
vessels for cooking are not unlike those used today.   They
seem crude in comparison with our convenient utensils, and
were possessed in very small numbers as compared with those
to be found in all modern kitchens.   To be sure, many articles
of food were uncooked in antiquity.   Fruit was used in abundance, little meat was eaten, and bread was baked at a common
oven.   Wine was the usual beverage, and thus the amount of
cooking required was comparatively small.

The walls of the houses were not very substantial and to
protect them a coat of stucco was put on, both inside and outside.   The court was the most attractive part of the house.
In wealthy residences the pillars were often pleasingly decorated, rich tapestries hung between adjoining rooms, and made
the place cheery by their gay colors; ornamental jars stood
here and there, and often a fountain played in the center of
the court, while plants and flowers added to the pleasant
aspect.   Less care was bestowed upon the other rooms, for
the court was as important to the home as the agora to the
city.   Mosaic floors were often laid here, some of them especially ingenious and attractive.   These, however, came as a
result of foreign influence.

Lack of room in town made it impossible for the house to
have spacious grounds around it.   The wealthy maintained
elaborate country places.   More than ten thousand houses
were contained in Athens within a city-wall measuring only
five miles in circumference.   This meant that they must be
crowded close together.   In Homeric times, however, bards
sang of the pleasant grounds surrounding the homes of the
nobility.

"Without the palace-court, and near the gate,
A spacious garden of four acres lay.
A hedge enclosed it round, and lofty trees
Flourished in generous growth within,—the pear
And the pomegranate, and the apple-tree
With its fair fruitage, and the luscious fig
And olive always green."[2]

Increasing populations and crowded cities forced the wealthy out to the suburbs, and the poorer people, living an out-of-door life so characteristic of the Greeks, thrived very well in towns. At least, we know that the Greeks were an especially healthy race, in spite of their lack of sanitary conditions and their poorly ventilated houses.

[2]Odyssey.

VASE PAINTING.

CHAPTER II.

WEARING APPAREL.

The climate of Greece was mild, and it naturally followed that clothing worn by the Hellenes was simple. From the earliest to the latest times two garments constituted the principal part of one's wardrobe, and these with some differences of shape and adjustment were worn by both men and women. The first was called the *chiton*—a kind of tunic or shirt. This was open on one side, closed on the other, was long or short according to the period or the needs of the wearer, was closely belted in at the waist, and generally sleeveless. Some modification of this garment was worn by most Hellenes throughout Greek history. The other garment, called the *himation*, was a robe or mantle, worn over the chiton. The himation was in fact an oblong piece of heavy material, and its character was given to it by the way it was thrown over the body of the wearer. It was draped gracefully over the shoulder, hung in loose folds, and presented the pleasing appearance made familiar to us by numerous Greek paintings and statues.

The Greeks of early times naturally did not dress entirely like their descendants who lived in the Age of Pericles, although they dressed similarly. However, the differences came about chiefly from changes in these two garments, the chiton and himation. In Homeric times the chiton was long. When it inconvenienced the wearer, it was drawn up above the belt and left to blouse over it. Again, in this period the chiton was ordinarily made of linen. Later, wool was found to be the more satisfactory material, especially since sheep were extensively raised in Greece, while flax was grown only in a limited supply. The himation was usually made of wool. The difference between the garments worn by rich and poor came to be chiefly a difference of quality in the material used. The poor had to content themselves with coarse woolen chitons, and often did not wear the himation, except on holiday occasions. The wealthy procured the finest, softest wool for their clothing, and always wore the himation when they went abroad.

While women commonly wore these garments also, their chitons and himations—or peplos—were more ample. Either one could be drawn up around the head. The robe donned by wealthy women fell in graceful folds, falling from the waist with loose drapery. The women succeeded in bringing greater individuality into their costumes than the men, and while the garments of men were generally white—unless their employment compelled them to don dark colors, the women wore a variety of hues.

A military cape, called the *chlamys,* was in favor among the soldiers, and among others like hunters, whose interests frequently led them into colder regions. Other garments were sometimes added, as need required.

Foot gear was by no means as essential to the Greeks as to us today. Sandals were commonly worn by both men and women. They were mere soles held in place by straps and were removed upon entering the house. However, many wore nothing whatever upon their feet. Socrates prided himself upon having served in two campaigns with nothing upon his feet, although soldiers usually found it advantageous to wear heavy shoes upon the march. Stockings were never worn in Greece, although the leg was sometimes wrapped with bandages if exposure were great.

As foot gear was worn or not, according as one desired, so also was the case with head-coverings. They were by no means regarded as essential. Caps were often in vogue; felt hats were worn by those subject to exposure. Certain peculiarities of shape indicated special callings. Women as a rule drew their peplos around their heads when they went abroad.

Jewelry was always popular in Greece, but in later times we do not find men affecting the barbaric splendor which characterized the Mycenaean age. Rings were worn by men everywhere, usually combining the seal. They commonly carried some kind of a cane. Women delighted in many kinds of jewelry, and various ornaments were worn by them. The diadem and fillet were especially attractive. Necklaces, bracelets, earrings, chains, and rings were worn by women of means. Nevertheless, the moderation which the Greek dearly loved,

the desire that harmony should prevail and no feature of a
thing detract from its pleasing entirety, barred any such display
of jewelry as was made, for example, by the Egyptians.

Garments were woven by women in early times, and even
later, when trade with all the ancient world brought costly
stuffs from other lands, much of the material used by the Greek
family was made at home. In Homeric times this was altogether the case.

"And he had fifty handmaids in the house, and some grind
the yellow grain on the millstone, and others weave webs and
turn the yarn as they sit, restless as the leaves of the tall
poplar tree; and the soft olive oil drops off that linen so closely
is it woven. For as the Phaeacian men are skilled beyond all
others in driving a swift ship upon the deep, even so are the
women the most cunning at the loom, for Athena hath given
them notable wisdom in all fair handiwork and cunning wit." [1]

Even the royal ladies spent their time largely with the
loom:

> " She drew near
> To Helen, in the palace, weaving there
> An ample web, a shining double-robe,
> Whereon were many conflicts fairly wrought,
> Endured by the horse-taming sons of Troy
> And brazen-mailed Achaians for her sake
> Upon the field of Mars." [2]

Likewise, Andromache busied herself with weaving while
Hector fought the Greeks:

> " She sat
> In a recess of those magnificent halls,
> And wove a twofold web of brilliant hues,
> On which were scattered flowers of rare device." [3]

Hesiod addressed himself to the common people in his
Works and Days, instructing them to fortify against the
dampness and the cold:

"Even then, as I bid you, clothe yourself in a defense for
your body, a soft cloak and a frock reaching to the ground;

[1] Odyssey: Butcher & Lang trans., 133.
[2] Iliad: Bryant's trans., Bk. III, 157. [3] Ibid., XXII, 541.

and into a scant warp weave an abundant woof; this cast around you that your hairs may not shiver, nor bristle, raised erect about your body. And about your feet bind suitable sandals of the hide of an ox slaughtered with your might, having covered them thick within with felt. Then, when the season of cold is come, stitch together with the sinew of an ox the skins of first-born kids, that so upon your back you may throw a shelter from the rain; and on the head above keep a well-wrought felt hat, that you may not get your ears drenched. For bleak both is the morn, when the north wind falls upon one, and in the morning over the earth from the starry heaven a wheat-bringing mist is spread above the tillage of the rich." [4]

Paintings upon numerous Greek vases enable us to study many details of Greek costume. Women reveled in bright hues and brought a multitude of trifling changes into their apparel, in spite of a certain uniformity which characterized their dress.

"We know very little about the colour and pattern of the dresses. The clothing worn by men, or, at any rate, those of the lower classes who laboured in the workshop or in the field, was certainly dark, either of the natural colour of the wool or dyed brown, grey, etc. Otherwise the commonest colour for the chiton and himation was white, and, as such garments naturally soon got dirty, they were often sent to the fuller, who washed them and gave them fresh brightness by means of pipeclay and similar methods. On festive occasions gaily-coloured dresses were usually worn, and then even simple people indulged in the luxury of bright colour; though, as a rule, to display this in ordinary, every-day life was regarded in the better ages of Greek antiquity as a mark of vanity or characteristic of a dandy. Naturally, women were more inclined to bright hues, and they were especially fond of saffron-coloured dresses, and also of materials with coloured borders and rich designs. Generally speaking, we may infer from the works of art that bright colour and rich ornamentation were most popular in the oldest period, and afterwards again in the epoch of declining taste; while the classic period

[4] Hesiod: Works and Days, Banks, 104.

made but a sparing use of either.   The older vase pictures almost always represent materials with coloured patterns, either purely ornamental designs, or with representations of figures.   Sometimes whole scenes full of figures in coloured embroidery were part of the dress, and this was sometimes arranged in rows, like the decorations on pots in ancient art.

Purely ornamental patterns are also very common, and show great variety, but very seldom good designs.   Checks and diamonds were especially popular.

"As the fashion in dress changed, so did the use of materials with patterns; for garments worn at religious ceremonies, or by actors, the coloured embroidery was retained; but in ordinary life the men, and even women, gradually discarded it, or at any rate reduced it to moderate proportions compared with the rich fulness of ornament in the older fashion, which almost concealed the real colour of the dress.   This is especially noticeable in the chiton when it falls in free folds, while the old-fashioned chiton, which had very few folds, bore bolder designs.   It is also the case with the himation, which even in the classic period, when it no longer fell stiff and straight over the back, but was drawn round the body in plentiful drapery, was often richly adorned with embroidery.

The fashion of the better period shows its classic sense of beauty in forming chiton and cloak from materials of one colour, and merely introducing ornaments at the seams and edges, and these such as are of special beauty and noble simplicity."

Fans and parasols were popular with women of the upper classes, being carried by slaves for their convenience and use. However, such articles of mere fancy and luxury in no way entered into the national dress.   Simplicity, harmony, moderation, were characteristics much loved by the Greeks as a whole, and their costumes were controlled by them in a great measure, as a natural result.

CHAPTER III.

Meals and Food in Ancient Greece.

In early times the Hellenes were limited by the natural supply of their country to comparatively few articles of food. Later, when their out-posts were established for purposes of trade on every shore, the delicacies of many lands were brought thither.

In the Homeric period, breads and meat were the staple foods. The flesh of cattle, sheep and goats was roasted over fires, a portion offered as a sacrifice to the gods and the remainder divided among the family or the guests. Fish was eaten, but only in the absence of meat. It did not become a popular dish until later. Cakes of barley or wheat meal were made, and wine was the usual beverage, being mixed with twice its amount of water. When milk was used, it was almost invariably the milk of sheep or goats; cow's milk appears to have been drunk very seldom, if ever.

Three meals were served in Homeric days: early breakfast, dinner at midday, and supper at sunset or in the evening. In this period the various members of the family, or the guests, sat around a common table, or sat each by the side of a small table. This custom later gave way to that of reclining upon couches, while slaves served from low tables.

The Homeric poems give several glimpses of meals, their preparation and the manner of serving. The Iliad, portraying camp-life, gives scenes from soldiers' out-door meals: the Odyssey, picturing domestic life, and years of peace, describes regular customs of settled communities. Both have to do with the nobility and upper classes, and the common people are introduced but to show their ignorance, their need of guidance and their dependence upon their betters. We may be sure that they lived in a very primitive way indeed.

These two scenes from the Iliad convey some idea of Homeric meals:

" When the prayers
Were ended, and the salted meal was flung,
Backward they turned the necks of the fat beeves,
And cut their throats, and flayed the carcasses,
And hewed away the thighs, and covered them
With caul in double folds; and over this
They laid raw fragments of the other parts.
O'er all the aged priest poured dark wine,
And burned them on dry wood.   A band of youths
With five-pronged spits, beside him, thrust these through
The entrails, which they laid among the flames.
And when the thighs were all consumed, and next
The entrails tasted, all the rest was carved
From the hot coals.   This task performed, they made
The banquet ready.   All became its guests
And all were welcome to the equal feast.
And when their thirst and hunger were allayed,
Boys crowned the ample urns with wreaths, and served
The wine to all, and poured libations forth." [1]

The second citation describes merely a slight refreshment
offered Greek warriors in Nestor's tent:

" Now when they reached the tent of Neleus' son,
The warriors in the chariot set their feet
Upon the nourishing earth.
                      Hecamede, bright of hair,
Prepared for them a mingled draught; the maid,
A daughter of the great Arsinous, came
From Tenedos with Nestor, when the town
Was ravaged by Achilles, and the Greeks
Gave her to Nestor, chosen from the rest
For him, as wisest of their counsellors.
First she drew forth a table fairly wrought,
Of polished surface, and with steel-blue feet,
And on it placed a brazen tray which bore
A thirst-provoking onion, honeycomb,
And sacred meal of wheat.   Near these she set
A noble beaker which the ancient chief
Had brought from home, embossed with studs of gold.

[1] Iliad: Bryant. Bk. I. 574.

Four were its handles, and each handle showed
Two golden turtles feeding, while below
Two others formed the base.   Another hand
Could scarce have raised that beaker from its place,
But Nestor lifted it with ease.   The maid,
Fair as a goddess, mingled Pramnian wine,
And grated o'er it, with a rasp of brass,
A goat's-milk cheese, and, sprinkling the white flour
Upon it, bade them drink." [2]

Two scenes from the Odyssey throw some light upon prevailing customs.   The first describes a simple repast; the second enumerates various trees and plants cultivated in a garden.

"Then a handmaid bare water for the washing of hands in a goodly golden ewer, and poured it forth over a silver basin to wash withal, and drew to their side a polished table. And a grave dame bare wheaten bread and set it by them, and laid on the board many dainties, giving freely of such things as she had by her.   And a carver lifted and placed by them platters of divers kinds of flesh, and nigh them he set golden bowls, and a henchman walked to and fro pouring out to them the wine." [3]

"And without the courtyard hard by the door is a great garden, of four ploughgates, and a hedge runs round on either side.   And there grow tall trees blossoming, pear trees, and pomegranates, and apple trees with bright fruit, and sweet figs and olives in their bloom.   The fruit of these trees never perisheth, neither faileth, winter or summer, enduring through all the year.   Evermore the west wind blowing brings some fruit to birth and ripens others.   Pear upon pear waxes old, and apple on apple, yea, and cluster ripens upon cluster of the grape, and fig upon fig.   There, too, hath he a fruitful vineyard planted, whereof the one part is being dried by the heat, a sunny spot on level ground, while other grapes men are gathering, and yet others they are treading in the wine-press.   In the foremost row are unripe grapes that cast the blossoms, and others there be that are growing black to vintaging.   There, too, skirting the farthest line, are all manner of garden beds,

²Iliad., Bk. XI, 757. ³Odyssey: Butcher & Lang, 30.

planted trimly, that are perpetually fresh, and therein are two fountains of water, whereof one scatters its stream all about the garden, and the other runs over against it beneath the threshold of the courtyard, and issues by the lofty house, and thence did the townsfolk draw water." [4]

This last description is of a garden on an island, where imagination could be given freer play. Nevertheless, the poet naturally placed within it fruits which were known and enjoyed by the people generally.

The Athenians were moderate in their enjoyment of food, as in everything else. While some of their neighbors indulged too heartily in wine and made gluttons of themselves—notably the Thessalians, Corinthians, and Boeotians—the Athenians were known to be temperate in their eating and drinking.

The Athenian partook of a light breakfast, luncheon at noon, and a heavy meal at sundown, or night. The fare of the poor man was simple indeed. His breakfast consisted of a barley-cake dipped in wine, and a few dried figs. The noon-day meal was light, and at night some vegetables, honey, and wine were eaten. Meat among the poor of ancient Greece, as among the Greek peasants today, was a rarity. On special occasions they had the flesh of sheep or goats; beef was very uncommon among them.

Fish became a favorite dish in Hellas. Herrings and sardines were common; mussels, turtles and oysters were available, but were bought only by the well-to-do. Game was plentiful. Hare, deer, wild duck, geese, quail and blackbirds were to be found in abundance. Fruits were used in greater quantities in later times. Several trees grown today were not yet cultivated to yield fruit of pleasant taste.

While many vegetables common today were unknown in ancient Greece, quite a variety were raised. Spinach, lettuce, cabbage, peas, beans, radishes, onions, leeks and garlic were cultivated. Parsley and thyme grew wild, and mushrooms were likewise procurable.

The wealthy Athenian did not lack for delectable dishes. Nuts, brought from Asia Minor, were found upon his table. Walnuts and almonds were favorites and were served before wine was passed, because they created a thirst. Dates were

---

[4] Odyssey: Butcher & Lang, 134.

also imported from Western Asia. Grapes were converted into raisins, and choice figs and olives were native.

The bakers enjoyed a lucrative business in Greece. Many kinds of bread were sold. Rolls were sprinkled with poppy seed, or the seed of the flax or sesame. An officer examined the markets daily to see that no loaves under-weight were offered for sale.

Honey was used where we today use sugar, and whatever sweet cakes the Hellenes prepared were made of it. The honey of Hymettus was noted for its superior quality. The poets sang of its sweetness, and well-appointed tables served it to the guests. Even today, the inhabitants of Greece delight in Hymettus honey, and inn-keepers offer small jars of it to favored guests.

Olive oil filled the place of butter. Bread was dipped in the oil, which was used bountifully in the food. Butter never gained much favor with the ancient Greeks. Cheese was used extensively.

Although wine was the sole drink—for water was scarcely ever served with meals—the Hellenes as a rule were not intemperate. It was ordinarily mixed with twice its quantity of water. It was put up in goatskins or in earthen jars, and pitch was put in to preserve it. Tourists today object to the wine in Greece because pitch is still used by the people of that country to keep it from spoiling.

If a Greek had no guests, he dined at night with his family. In this case the meal was quickly over. During the classical age men made use of the opportunity which dinner offered to enjoy the society of their fellowmen. They either entertained others or were themselves invited guests elsewhere. Public dinners were often given where each shared the expense of the meal, which was served by caterers. Or again, one man would offer his house, and the rest who made up the company, either sent portions of the meal, or more commonly, paid each a part of the cost. These dinners were never so elaborate as those given by wealthy and fastidious men, who vied with each other in serving elaborate menus. Cooks demanded good compensation, and rare and unusual dishes were highly prized. However, the Greeks never went to such lengths in this regard as the Romans, who exceeded all reason in their extravagances at the banquet.

The Greek banquet and the symposium will be considered in connection with Greek diversions. The customs there prevailing were unlike those of every-day life in the family.

We may note, so far as table service is concerned, that people ate with their fingers, wiping them on bits of bread, afterwards tossed upon the floor, to be eaten by the dogs, or swept up at the close of the meal. Spoons were few and forks were employed only by the servants in the kitchen in preparing food for the table. Dishes seen on the tables of the rich were often costly, being of gold or silver and handsomely decorated. Silver beakers were provided for the wine.

In Homeric times the goblets or beakers for holding wine were highly prized. Several incidents are to be found in the Iliad showing how much the Greeks prized their drinking cups. Warriors took them with them on their campaigns. In connection with the scene laid in Nestor's tent, recently quoted, we find that he had brought a beaker with him to Troy. Here again:

> " Entering his tent, Achilles raised the lid
> Of a fair coffer, beautifully wrought,
> Which silver-footed Thetis placed on board
> His bark, and filled with tunics, cloaks well lined,
> And fleecy carpets. *There he also kept*
> *A goblet richly chased,* from which no lip
> Of man, save his, might drink the dark red wine,
> Nor wine be poured to any god save Jove,
> The mighty Father." [5]

Because salt was offered to the gods with every meal, the salt cellar was an important dish among the ancient Greeks. Instead of using some simple dish, today deemed suitable, the most elaborate receptacle on the table was the one containing salt. Most beautiful silver dishes, often richly ornamented, have been found. These give evidence to the reverence of the Hellenes for the gods, whom they believed to share each repast with them. Libations of wine were also made the Mighty Ones at meal time.

Slave help was available everywhere, and meals were served by slave girls or boys. They removed the sandals of

[5] Iliad. Bk. XVI, 278.

guests and bathed their feet; they poured water from ewers over the hands before and after the meal.   They prepared the food, frequently, and served it to the family.

The Greeks were always very hospitable and none were turned hungry from their doors.

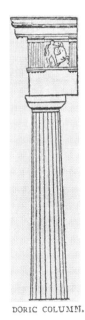

DORIC COLUMN.

CHAPTER IV.

WOMEN IN ANCIENT GREECE.

Girls in ancient Greece were not given any special schooling. The girl was brought up by her mother to take a future
place as mistress of her husband's household, so whatever
training was regarded as essential for such a *rôle* was given
her. Physical exercise was understood to be necessary for
both girls and boys.

In Homeric times, women and girls mingled freely in the
society of men. A wife was obtained by making presents to
the father of some maiden deemed desirable. To win favor,
a man must be well developed physically and mentally alert.
Homeric women were deeply respected, and maintained a
strong influence over their sons and husbands.

"Readers of the Iliad and the Odyssey will find depicted
there, amid all the barbarity of an age of rapine and war,
relations between men and women so tender, faithful and
beautiful, that they may almost stand as universal types of
the ultimate human ideal. Such, for example, is the relation
between Odysseus and Penelope, the wife waiting year by
year for the husband whose fate is unknown, wooed in vain
by suitors who waste her substance and wear her life.

"Such, again, is the relation between Hector and Andromache, as described in the well-known scene of the Iliad,
where the wife comes out with her babe to take leave of the
husband on his way to battle. 'It were better for me,' she
cries, 'to go down to the grave if I lose thee; for never will
any comfort be mine, when once thou, even thou, hast met
thy fate, but only sorrow.   Thou art to me father
and lady mother, yea, and brother, even as thou art my goodly
husband. Come, now, have pity, and abide here upon the
tower, lest thou make thy child an orphan and thy wife a
widow.' Hector answers with the plea of honour. He cannot
draw back, but he foresees defeat; and in his anticipation of
the future nothing is so bitter as the fate he fears for his wife.
'Yet doth the conquest of the Trojans hereafter not so much

trouble me, neither Hekabe's own, neither King Priam's, neither my brethren's, the many and brave that shall fall in the dust before their foemen, as doth thine anguish in the day when some mail-clad Achaian shall lead thee weeping and rob thee of the light of freedom.

'But me in death may the heaped-up earth be covering, ere I hear thy crying and thy carrying into captivity.' " [1]

Secure in their high social position, the Homeric women mingled freely with their maids in performing the household duties. For example, we may note the scene in the Odyssey where Nausicaa goes with her maids to do the household washing.

> "I pray, dear father, give command to make
> A chariot ready for me, with high sides
> And sturdy wheels, to bear to the river-brink,
> There to be cleansed, the costly robes that now
> Lie soiled.
>
> Now when they reached the river's pleasant brink,
> Where lavers had been hollowed out to last
> Perpetually, and freely through them flowed
> Pure water that might cleanse the foulest stains,
> They took the garments out and flung them down
> In the dark water, and with hasty feet
> Trampled them there in frolic rivalry." [2]

Mistress and maids wove the fabrics from which the tunics and robes were made, as well as tapestries to adorn the walls.

> "Her mother sat
> Beside the hearth with her attendant maids,
> And turned the distaff loaded with a fleece
> Dyed in sea-purple.
> "Go quickly through the palace till thou find
> My mother where she sits beside the hearth,
> Leaning against a column in its blaze,
> And twisting threads, a marvel to behold,
> Of bright sea-purple, while her maidens sit
> Behind her." [3]

[1] The Greek View of Life: Dickinson, 157. [2] Odyssey, Bk. VI. 75; 110.
[3] Ibid.. 68-70; 384-388.

With the passing of Homeric civilization, we find a general decline of the fresh, spontaneous life. For some generations woman's social position was high, but during the classic period, in Athens, at least, women were kept in seclusion. Contact with Asia doubtless had much to do with it, for countries more remote from Asiatic influences than Attica continued to allow considerable freedom to the women.

The Athenian girls were usually poorly educated. They were kept under close supervision before their marriage, which came early. Girls fifteen years of age and even younger were married. From fifteen to twenty years it was considered suitable for them to marry. Only on great state occasions were they allowed to appear in public. They sometimes had religious duties which brought them out of their accustomed retirement. As a rule, a man did not see his bride until he was married, for marriage alliances were arranged between the parents of the bride and groom. A dowry was given with the bride, and since the amount of the dowry could be stipulated by the father of the groom, this supplied quite an incentive to a man to wed.

"It was the father who arranged with the bride's father or guardian all the preliminaries, such as the kind and the amount of the dowry, the value and extent of the trousseau and other personal belongings she was to bring with her, and other matters, all of a strictly business nature. The arrangement was looked upon as a contract, with securities given, and as such the betrothal was called 'the act of giving security'—for which the presence of witnesses, but not of the betrothed, was necessary. The bride's guardian had complete control over her fate; he was said 'to give her away,' and thus the expression 'given away' is used of a married woman in the *Anabasis*. Legally, the bride was a mere chattel, passively submitting to the disposition of her friends. Of her, the verb 'marry' is always used in the passive.

"This system, prosaic and unromantic as it seems, in which pecuniary and social advantage was considered above the personal inclination of the parties most concerned, was designed to be an aid to the growth and power of the state. Marriage was entered into in order that a new family circle might be formed to perpetuate the worship of the gods of home and state, and that the ties between citizens and commonwealth might be strengthened through well-trained and loyal children. The system produced many happy unions, and not infrequently furnished inspiring examples of devotion between husband and wife or parents and children." [4]

Winter was the time when most Greek marriages were solemnized, the month which corresponded to the last half of January and the first of February was sacred to Hera, goddess of marriage. The full of the moon was regarded as opportune, and great care was taken to do whatever might propitiate the Mighty Ones. The various ceremonies connected with the wedding were on this account strictly observed.

On the wedding morn, both bride and groom bathed in water brought by relatives from some sacred spring. Then the bride was arrayed in her finery by her young friends, and crowned with a wreath. The groom dressed in festive garb, and went to the house of the bride, where guests were gathered in honor of the occasion. As they entered, each was presented with a sesame cake—made of ground sesame seed mixed with honey. This has been called the "prototype of the modern fruit cake used at weddings."

When all the friends were gathered, the bride's father offered a sacrifice to the gods. Then a banquet was served, including portions of the sacrificed animal. Another sesame cake was passed.

This was one of the few occasions upon which women feasted with men. The bride, with her veil closely drawn, sat with some of her friends. Toward evening the mother gave her daughter to the groom, who took her to his home in the wedding chariot. Only among the very poor people did the bride walk upon this occasion. The friends who had witnessed the wedding ceremonies accompanied the procession as it passed through the street, singing appropriate songs. The mother of the bride walked in the procession, carrying the bridal torches, lighted from the fire on the paternal hearth, that the fire in the new home might be brought thence.

At the door of the groom's home the mother showered the couple with confetti, this symbolizing the blessings which would be showered upon them through life. The house was

[4]Life of the Ancient Greeks : Gulick, 120.

decorated in honor of the bride, and the wedding pair were led to the nuptial chamber, while friends sang wedding songs. Now for the first time the groom saw the bride unveiled.

After a day or two the wedded pair received their friends at their home, the bride being now unveiled. Presents were brought and the groom made presents to his wife. Another sacrifice was offered and a second banquet served, thus ending the wedding festival.

While the married woman possessed rather more freedom than she had enjoyed as a girl, yet in Athens her life was very secluded. She could not go from the house without her husband's permission and then must always be accompanied by a slave. She never attended her husband's banquets nor mingled with his friends. Her life was bounded by her household duties, and having passed from the father's to the husband's care, she had no legal status.

Divorce was much more easily obtained by the husband than by the wife. He might simply dismiss her, returning her dowry and supplying perhaps some income to her. On the other hand, she had to bring complaint before an archon, and even then it was difficult for her to be released from her marriage obligations. In case of separation, the children remained with the father.

Many women busied themselves with household cares and lived very contented lives. They were not fitted by their education to be companions to their husbands or to share in the problems that beset the men. Nevertheless, some cases of generous-hearted men, who themselves educated and trained their wives to take a broader view of life, are on record. These must necessarily be regarded as exceptional. The children had to be cared for during infancy, the meals of the family must be supervised, the housewife must assist in weaving clothing for the family, and such tasks filled the lives of the vast majority of Athenian women. As a result, women ceased to hold the deferential attention of men so characteristic of Homeric days.

"Nothing more profoundly distinguishes the Hellenic from the modern view of life than the estimate in which women were held by the Greeks. Their opinion on this point was partly the cause and partly the effect of that preponderance of the idea of the State, and from which it followed naturally enough that marriage should be regarded as a means of producing healthy and efficient citizens.

"The modern conception that the marriage relation is a matter of private concern, and that any individual has a right to wed whom and when he will, was one altogether alien to the Greeks. In ancient Greece, as far as our knowledge goes, there was little or no romance connected with the marriage tie. In Athens we know that marriages were commonly arranged by the father, much as they are in modern France, on grounds of age, property connection and the like, and without any regard for the inclination of the parties concerned." [5]

Pericles, in his Funeral Oration, said: "If I am to speak of womanly virtues to those of you who will henceforth be widows, let me sum them up in one short admonition: To a woman not to show more weakness than is natural to her sex is a great glory, and not to be talked about for good or for evil among men." Similar sentiments are to be found among the writings of the classic period. "War, politics, and public speaking are the sphere of man; that of woman is to keep house, to stay at home and to receive and tend her husband."

Yet this condition called forth expostulation, even when it was most encouraged. Aristophanes satirized the part women played and the conservative way in which they adhered to old customs:

"They dip their wool in hot water according to the ancient plan, all of them without exception, and never make the slightest innovation. They sit and cook, as of old. They carry upon their heads, as of old. They conduct the Themophorias, as of old. They wear out their husbands, as of old. They buy sweets, as of old. They take their wine neat, as of old."

One of Euripides' characters voiced sentiments that many women must have felt in classic Athens:

"Of all things that have life and sense we women are most wretched. For we are compelled to buy with gold a husband who is also—worst of all!—the master of our person. And on his character, good or bad, our whole fate depends. For divorce is regarded as a disgrace to a woman and she cannot

[5]Greek View of Life, 154.

repudiate her husband.   Then coming as she does into the
midst of manners and customs strange to her, she would need
the gift of divination—unless she has been taught at home
how best to manage her husband.   And if we manage so well
that he remains faithful to us, and does not break away, we
may think ourselves fortunate; if not, there is nothing for it
but death.   A man when he is vexed at home can go out and
find relief among his friends or acquaintances; but we women
have none to look to but him." [6]

Women in other parts of Greece, notably Sparta, did not
lead this secluded existence, so general in Attica.   Following
a different course, Sparta produced more renowned mothers
than Athens, and Spartan wives exercised a greater influence
over their husbands than did their northern sisters.   While
Athenians respected the chastity of their wives, they found
them dull companions and neglected them to find their diversions elsewhere.

[6]Medea: Euripides.

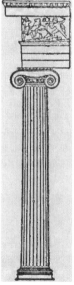

IONIC COLUMN.

CHAPTER V.

CHILDHOOD AND EARLY EDUCATION.

Children were very much desired in Greece. By them alone could the family name and the worship of the gods be perpetuated. No greater calamity could befall a Hellene than to be left childless in his old age. Daughters were welcome, to be sure, but great rejoicing accompanied the birth of a son. He could take his father's place in serving the state, in handing down the family name, and in strengthening his tribe.

A fillet of wool upon the door of a house announced the birth of a girl; an olive wreath proclaimed the birth of a son and heir. In either case, two important ceremonies were observed—one five days after birth, the other, five days later still. The Greeks, like many other primitive people, regarded the mother and those who had attended her at the birth of the child as requiring purification. This was accomplished five days after the event, by running around the hearth several times, in the presence of guests. By the family hearth dwelt the family gods, and this ceremony was thought to place the child under their immediate care and protection. After this religious ceremony a feast was made for those gathered, and upon this occasion shell-fish were always served.

Ten days after the birth of the child, friends were bidden to celebrate the "name-day." Now the father, before the witnesses gathered, took the child in his arms, thus acknowledging it as his own. He thereupon gave it a name. The oldest son was often given the name of his paternal grandfather. A custom more frequently resorted to in Sparta than Athens allowed the father to refuse to acknowledge a child, in which case it was exposed—left in a basket before some temple or in some public place. Babes thus exposed were generally taken by those who brought them up for purposes of profit. The singing girls who entertained guests at banquets were supplied by various men or women who obtained children in this way, trained them until they became quite proficient in music and dancing, and hired them out for feasts and entertainments.

After the father named his child and by acknowledging it signified his intention of rearing it, a sacrifice was made and a bountiful feast followed. Friends brought gifts, especially such as might protect the infant from "evil-eye," so dreaded by parents.

During the first seven years both girls and boys were left together under the mother's care. Even in humble homes a nurse was employed to look after their wants and assist the mother. Many toys have been represented by vase-artists, painting them in the hands of children who played quite as children have done in all ages.

"The Greek baby had his rattle, the little girl had her pets, and her doll made of painted clay or wax, often with movable hands and feet. Baby-houses, toy dishes, tables, wagons, and animals were as interesting then as now. Sometimes the older boys made their own carts and hitched to them dogs or goats. For older children, too, there were the swing, the ball, the whipping-top, the hoop. Many games resembled those played today: hide-and-seek, tug of war, ducks and drakes, and blind man's buff, or the ' bronze fly,' in which the boy who was 'it' was struck with whips by the others until he caught one of them. Another amusement among the street gamins, not so innocent, was to catch a beetle, tie a string to it, and so control its flight. Jackstones, played with knuckle bones, 'pitching pennies,' played with bronze coins, and hopping with one foot on a greased wine-skin, were other favorites, the last being a sport indulged in by grown people at the Dionysiac festival of the Anthesteria." [1]

When boys reached seven years of age, they were taken from the care of their mothers and placed under charge of a "pedagogue," whose duty it was to accompany them to and from school, to the play grounds, in short, wherever they went. This pedagogue was usually an old slave who might be ignorant so far as any book knowledge was concerned, but he was supposed to be able to teach his young charge how to conduct himself and to protect him from harmful influences.

A certain amount of school training was given to all Greek boys. They received gymnastic training, were taught to read and write, and had some instruction in music, which also

[1] Life of the Ancient Greeks; Gulick, 76.

included poetry. Schools attended by the poorer children were often held out of doors with no pretense of equipment. Those attended by children from wealthy families, however, were held indoors and furnished with benches. They wrote on wooden tablets covered with wax, with a metallic stencil. Copies were made for them, and under guidance of the teacher's hand they learned to shape the letters. Portions of the Homeric poems were memorized, and in various ways they learned to read and write. The gymnastic training was given in special open fields, reserved in various parts of the city. Here, under the direction of a master, boys learned to wrestle, box, run, jump, throw the discus, cast the spear. After energetic exercises of this kind they took a plunge in water, which was also provided nearby, that they might learn to swim. Athletic sports were very popular in Greece and were connected with nearly all public celebrations and festivals. For this reason children were given physical training from their earliest years. The Greeks believed that the body should be perfectly developed, and every grace of motion and freedom of bodily activity was theirs.

Boys of wealthy families were given military training; they had their mock battles and encounters, supervised by some competent person, who saw to it that a general idea of military tactics was grasped by these young soldiers.

Music was taught the youth of Greece, for it was necessary that each man be able to accompany himself upon the harp. The harp or lute was the most popular instrument in Hellas. The flute was brought in from Asia Minor. Some see in the story of the musical contest between Apollo on the lute and Pan upon the flute, under the care of King Midas, a symbolized contest between the music of Greece and of Asia Minor. Not only were instruments themselves studied, but the poems which accompanied the music were carefully examined, that the meaning of the poet should be clearly understood. Music was deemed one means of expression by the Greeks, who classed it thus with the arts—painting, sculpture, dancing, and the drama.

Speaking of the Greeks, Plutarch says: "Their instruction in music and verse was not less carefully attended to than their habits of grace and good breeding in conversation. And

their very songs had a life and spirit in them that inflamed
and possessed men's minds with an enthusiasm and ardor for
action; the style of them was plain and without affectation;
the subject always serious and moral; most usually, it was in
praise of such men as had died in defense of their country, or
in derision of those that had been cowards; the former they
declared happy and glorified; the life of the latter they
described as most miserable and abject. There were also
vaunts of what they would do and boasts of what they had
done, varying with the various ages; as, for example, they
had three choirs in their solemn festivals, the first of the old
men, the second of the young men, and the last of the children;
the old men began thus:

> We once were young and brave and strong;
> The young men answered them, singing
> And we're so now, come on and try:
> The children came last and said:
> But we'll be strongest bye and bye.

Indeed, if we shall take the pains to consider their compositions, and the airs on the flute to which they marched when
going to battle, we shall find that Terpander and Pindar had
reason to say that music and valour were allied." [2]

Such being the importance attached to music, it was natural that the children should have been given elementary
instruction in it.

The teachers of elementary schools depended for their
remuneration upon fees paid by parents at the close of the
term. These were likely to have been in proportion to the
ability of the teachers. Most of them were poorly paid.
There was no long vacation, such as is common at the present
day, but holidays were many. Indeed, the Greeks believed in
plenty of diversion and celebrated all holidays with games and
feastings. Since school was not held on these days, no long
recess was essential as it is today among serious people of the
present who find time for but few holidays and limited diversion throughout the year.

[2]Plutarch: Lycurgus.

Parents who desired advanced training for their sons, placed them under the special instruction of some noted teacher or philosopher. Plato had quite a following of young men, as did his successor and pupil, Aristotle. Other men of less note taught the youth of Athens, in groves or gardens apart from the turmoil of busy life.

For the vast majority of Greeks the simple instruction supplied by the elementary schools sufficed, although, to be sure, the dramas and national games supplemented higher education in a large measure.

Girls may have attended elementary schools, but they were left largely to their nurses and mothers, learning whatever these could teach and giving most of their time to matters of purely domestic concern.

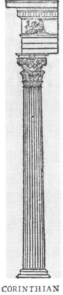

CORINTHIAN
COLUMN.

CHAPTER VI.

THE CITIZEN'S CAREER.

When an Athenian youth reached his eighteenth birthday he became of age, and was presented by his father or guardian for membership in the tribe or phratry. He swore: "Never to disgrace his holy arms, never to forsake his comrade in the ranks, but to fight for the holy temples and the common welfare, alone or with others; to leave his country, not in a worse, but in a better state than he found it; to obey the magistrates and the laws, and defend them against attack; finally, to hold in honour the religion of his country." He was then enrolled in the deme to which his family belonged.

It was an important occasion in the life of an Athenian youth when his entrance upon manhood was thus acknowledged. A banquet was given by him to his companions just before, and afterwards his guardian offered a sacrifice in the company of the phratry, who then were served portions of the sacrificed meat. The hair of the young man, allowed to grow long in his boyhood, was cut, and he donned the citizen's apparel. Yet even now he could not at once undertake the duties of a citizen, for he, in company with other youths of his age, was placed under the care of a man who drilled young men in military tactics for one year. Then a review was held, the candidates going through their drills and manoeuvres. Those who evinced skill upon this occasion were presented by the State with a shield and spear, and were sent to do garrison duty on the frontiers for another year. At the expiration of this they were enrolled as active citizens. Those among them who possessed an income often enlisted in the regular cavalry.

The daily exercise at the gymnasia ("exercise grounds") was not abandoned by the youth who had completed his schooling. Indeed, Greeks took daily exercise throughout their lives. The two most popular exercise grounds in Athens were the Academy and the Lyceum. Because these were favorite

haunts of men, philosophers founded schools under the shadow
of each, so that these names today suggest, not grounds for
the physical development of men, but schools where they
received advanced mental discipline.

When the young Athenian had completed his year of garrison service, he had to decide what course he would follow for
the remainder of his life. The Greek believed that his life
belonged to the State, and if he were compelled to earn a
living, he was in a measure bound—not free. For this reason
the Greeks scorned labor, which was relegated to slaves and
the lowest classes. To be sure, great wealth accrued to individuals and to the State from commercial undertakings, but
these were either managed on such a gigantic scale that they
brought honor rather than contempt, or else the citizen worked
indirectly through servants. It is important to keep in mind
this Greek attitude toward labor, and especially to remember
why such an attitude was taken. It is not to be thought for
a moment that the Greeks were idle people—far from it.
But the State was the first concern, and individual interests
were lost sight of, that the State might be best served. We
shall find that many Greeks fell away from this lofty conception, and thought first of their own plans, but this did not
change the national regard for the State, which was earnestly
taught the young and inculcated into the masses by orator,
philosopher and dramatist. If a man were to be free to
serve the State, he must not at the same time be absorbed
with the consuming question of earning a living; hence artisans and trades people were looked down upon by the independent Greek, who received a good yearly income from his
property if he lived in Athens, or who made his wants few
and lived frugally as did the Laconian at Sparta. The noble
youth, nurtured in such ideas, had to decide in what capacity
he would serve the State.

Civic duties were manifold. All citizens above thirty
years of age were eligible to serve on the Boulé, or Council of
500. The members of this council were exempt from military
service, and were entitled to a front seat at the theatre. After
the entrance of Pericles upon public life, all officers of the
State received some remuneration. Members of this council
were paid a little more than fifteen cents a day, but it is to be

remembered that money had far greater purchasing powers than now.

The public could attend meetings of the Boulé, held daily, as a general thing, but were shut off from the body of law-makers by a railing. Once elected to the council, it was not difficult to keep the office indefinitely.

The ecclesia, or public assembly, was supposed to be made up of all citizens above eighteen years of age, but we have just seen that military training and garrison service detained youths until their twentieth year and, as a matter of fact, only a part of the people as a rule attended the meetings.

One might also serve in the department of the judiciary, as a juror. About 6,000 jurors were engaged constantly in Athens, serving in ten courts, while 1,000 acted as substitutes. Five hundred and one sat each day in each of the ten courts of the city, listening to cases brought before them. As a rule, older men, having had some experience, were chosen for this purpose.

Plaintiff and defendant pleaded each his own case before the court. It came to be the custom for one unused to the business of the court room to get another to write his plea, which he memorized and delivered before the court. This demand for writers of pleas gave rise to the Sophists, a so-called school of philosophers, who took money for their services and who espoused either side of a question with equal readiness, as did the dialecticians of the Middle Ages. Their methods were held in contempt by contemporary schools of philosophy.

Later yet, advocates were permitted to aid one who par-tially presented his own case. These were allowed to speak with the permission of the court, and were understood to receive no compensation for their services. It is evident that the place of the modern lawyer was taken by these Greek advocates.

When both sides had been heard, and equal time was allowed to both, the jurors voted at once upon the matter of conviction or acquittal, without any conference among them-selves. Two jars were provided, one for conviction, the other for acquittal, and each tossed his ballot into one or the other. This method did not allow of sufficient secrecy, so after a

ACROPOLIS AND TEMPLE OF JUPITER.

time this following method took its place: two bronze discs were supplied each juror. One had a solid cylindrical axis running through it, the other a similar axis but hollow. When the pleas were ended, the jurors cast the disc they wished counted into the 'deciding' urn, while the other was thrown into another jar. The discs with solid axes signified acquittal, but when the ends of the axis were covered by the fingers the two were so similar that the spectator could not tell how any individual had voted.

Like all officers, jurors were paid a trifling sum, which allowed one to live in Athens, and this sum was drawn daily, at the close of the session.

If a young Athenian did not care to serve the State in any of these ways, he might enter upon the career of a soldier. This was at all times deemed a most honorable calling and was generally popular in Greece. The cavalry was the portion of land service in favor with the sons of wealthy families, although the Greeks never depended to any great extent upon their cavalry in time of danger. The infantry bore the brunt of the land battles. Service upon the seas was thought desirable—especially during the period of Athenian Empire, when opportunity for obtaining rich booty was frequent.

"Even in time of peace, there was abundant occupation in the military and naval service for all classes of citizens. In Athens five hundred men were necessary to guard the dockyards and arsenals, fifty kept watch at the Acropolis, which, however, was probably not otherwise fortified, and some sixteen hundred maintained order in the city and the country districts, particularly on the border; besides these, two thousand men served in garrisons throughout the various cities and islands belonging to the Athenian empire." [1]

[1] Life of the Ancient Greeks: Gulick, 205.

CHAPTER VII.

AMUSEMENTS AND PASTIMES.

The Greeks found much of their diversion in the market-place, meeting friends and acquaintances, discussing state affairs, and matters of local interest. To be sure, this was business and was done during business hours, but the Greeks, like men of today, found much satisfaction and pleasure in the actual affairs of life. The gymnasiums afforded meeting places for citizens, and here they occupied their time with what they deemed as important as mental training—the development of the body. A beautiful soul, dwelling in a beautiful body, was the Greek ideal, and from his childhood the Hellene took daily exercise in order to strengthen and develop every muscle. As a result, the Greek nation of antiquity produced the most perfect specimens of humankind the world has ever seen.

After exertion of whatever nature, the public baths were daily visited. Private houses were not, as today, furnished with every convenience for the bath. Had such been the case, with his particular nature and disposition, the Hellene would have preferred to mingle with his townsmen during the hours of day. Some considerable period each day was spent at the baths, and here again men met and exchanged ideas. While all these interests—the agora, the gymnasia, and the bath—were absorbing to the Greek, yet none could be called mere pastimes. Each had its earnest, serious aspect, which was not lost sight of.

When night fell upon Hellas, the Athenian loved to bring his friends around him, that he might enjoy their conversation in a lighter vein, their wit and quick repartee. The banquet, followed by the symposium, gave best opportunity to do so, and it came about that men of accomplishment seldom dined with their families. They either entertained their friends, or were themselves guests at the home of another; or the feasting club, to which many belonged, met for a feast of less private character.

Invitations were usually given verbally. An Athenian either summoned his guests personally, sent his slave, or secured the assistance of a friend for this purpose. Nor was there any established custom about bidding them long in advance. Dinner invitations might be given the very morning of the feast. For more formal affairs, a day or two usually intervened.

As the simplicity of earlier days gave way before increasing wealth and demand for delectable dishes, professional cooks were required. These soon grew to be essential to the banquet. The cook brought his assistants with him, aided in planning the feast and prepared new and attractive features for the dinner. Sometimes he even brought with him dishes sufficient for the occasion, these being rented in the market. In short, the place held today by city caterers was filled in ancient Greece by these professional cooks.

One bidden to a feast was always at liberty to bring along his friends if he chose to do so. Strangers were welcome and friends not infrequently dropped in if it were known that the master entertained. Upon arrival, sandals were removed, usually by slaves accompanying each guest, to assist him and attend him home. After the feet had been cleansed from the dust of the street, the feasters gathered in the dining hall. Here they reclined upon couches, resting upon the left arm, while the right was free to take the food. Water was poured over the hands by slaves, after which small tables loaded with tempting dishes were brought in and placed before each guest.

In matter of service, the dinner was not unlike the usual dinner, already described. At the conclusion of the meal, the guests often sang a paean to the accompaniment of the flute.

Now followed the symposium, or the drinking. While slaves mixed the wine, nuts, cakes and other things to provoke thirst were passed around. Garlands were brought for the adornment of each guest, and scented ointments were brought for anointing the hair and beard. A master of the wine was appointed, corresponding to our toastmasters. He decided how much water should be mixed with the wine, and made the rules to govern the drinking for the evening. Any violation of his rules was punishable by forfeits—comical tasks given the violator. Sometimes the wine was to be quaffed at a single draught; indeed, some wine goblets were made in a cornucopia shape, which compelled one to empty them before returning them to the table.

The master of ceremonies proposed toasts, which were readily responded to by the guests. Every Greek was able to entertain by song, to quote from the lyric poets, to tell a good story. Naturally, then, these symposiums were often the occasions for brilliant display of wit and mental agility.

Between the toasts the feasters were entertained by conversation and hilarity in early times, but later professional performers were brought in to entertain them. Flute girls, singing girls, dancing girls, girls who went through acrobatic feats, came before the revellers to make the hours pass gaily. Some of these performers were very accomplished, and the most difficult feats done today by acrobats appear to have been well known in Greece.

Dancing was enjoyed by the Hellenes, but it was generally individual. Dancing of men and women together was impossible under the social conditions which kept them entirely separated in their hours of leisure.

In addition to these hired artists, it grew to be the custom for men who might be compared to court jesters, or clowns, to visit houses where banquets were in progress, for the purpose of sharing a bountiful meal without expense, compensating in a measure by their entertainment. So far as they have come down to us, their jokes were tiresome and dull. They came sometimes in numbers and disturbed the evening by their loud laughter and noisy jests. For some reason they seem to have been tolerated, although the better element found them disagreeable.

The conservative Greeks objected to the change that came over the banquet and symposium by the rapid increase of wealth and luxury. It was felt that these social gatherings were far more dignified and beneficial when the feasters used their own, rather than hired, wits for their entertainment. The older men liked to discuss such general subjects as love, hate, envy, friendship and the like. By questions and replies many bright ideas were called forth in course of an evening. Naturally such an even course was interrupted by the noise

of wandering jesters and by the hilarity which often occurred because of the presence of the dancing girls. However, the remonstrances of the few availed little against the wishes of the idle and the young for any new diversion.

When at last the feasters departed, they often disturbed the sleepers of the city by their noisy disputes and songs on the highway. Their slaves were usually needed to assist them in reaching their homes. Nevertheless, Plato relates in his Symposium how Socrates spent the night discussing questions at such a gathering in Athens, and when the dawn of morning found most of the guests overcome with wine, he departed from the house and went to the agora, as composed and unwearied for the duties of the day as though he had spent the night at home.

DRINKING SONG.

Observe when Mother Earth is dry,
She drinks the droppings of the sky;
And then the dewy cordial gives
To every thirsty plant that lives.
The vapours, which at evening weep,
Are beverage to the swelling deep;
And when the rosy sun appears,
He drinks the ocean's misty tears.
The moon, too, quaffs her paly stream
Of lustre, from the solar beam.
Then, hence with all your sober thinking!
Since Nature's holy law is drinking;
I'll make the laws of nature mine,
And pledge the universe in wine.

Anacreon. Moore's trans.

CHAPTER VIII.

LABOR AND TRADE.

The Greek scorn of labor was unknown in Homeric times. Kings cultivated land in periods of peace, and personally supervised the work done upon their farms. Slaves were few during this remote age, for wars had not given numbers of captives to the victors. The poor people were attached to lords, who themselves shared in the labor on their lands. Noble ladies engaged their time in spinning and weaving, and even the gods were conceived as occupied in a variety of ways. Athena was regarded as the most expert spinner, and whoever among the people excelled in this art was believed to be under her special protection. Vulcan, the smith god, possessed rare cunning in the forging of armor. During this simple age skillful labor was praised by song. The beauty of wine goblets, the carving upon plates and other receptacles for food, the fine workmanship displayed in armour and weapons of defense, all testify to the exalted position of clever workmanship.

This attitude, however, underwent a complete change in the later Hellenic period. That he might retain the respect of his fellow men and attain as nearly as possible to his own ideals, a Hellene scorned to take money from others in turn for service done. This testified to a dependence upon them. Moreover, he wished to develop his body in accordance with Greek ideals of beauty. Constant exertion necessary in manual labor tended to destroy bodily beauty, and those who thus occupied themselves were scorned by the Greeks of the upper classes.

"A beautiful soul, housed in a beautiful body, and supplied with all the external advantages necessary to produce and perpetuate such a combination—that is the Greek conception of well-being; and it is because labour with the hands or at the desk distorts or impairs the body, and the petty cares of a calling pursued for bread pervert the soul, that so strong a contempt was felt by the Greeks for manual labor and trade.

'The arts that are called mechanical,' says Xenophon, 'are also, and naturally enough, held in bad repute in our cities. For they spoil the bodies of workers and superintendents alike, compelling them to live sedentary indoor lives, and in some cases even to pass their days by the fire. And as their bodies become effeminate, so do their souls also grow less robust. Besides this, in such trades one has no leisure to devote to the care of one's friends or of one's city. So that those who engage in them are thought to be bad backers of their friends and bad defenders of their country.'

"In a similar spirit Plato asserts that a life of drudgery disfigures the body and mars and enervates the soul; while Aristotle defines a mechanical trade as one which 'renders the body and soul or intellect of free persons unfit for the exercise and practice of virtue;' and denies to the artisan not merely the proper excellence of man, but any excellence of any kind, on the plea that his occupation and status is unnatural, and that he misses even that reflex of human virtue which a slave derives from his intimate connection with his master.

"If, then, the artisan was excluded from the citizenship in some of the Greek states, and, even in the most democratic of them, never altogether threw off the stigma of inferiority attaching to his trade, the reason was that the life he was compelled to lead was incompatible with the Greek conception of excellence." [1]

Statesmen frequently called attention to the great resources which accrued to the state because of the extensive commerce of Hellas; laws were passed in Attica allowing artisans and trades-people to take part in governmental affairs, and a law of Athens made it an offense to reproach a man in public for his humble vocation. All these efforts, however, failed to diminish to any marked extent the contempt popularly felt toward the working classes.

"The work of the handicraftsmen was designated by them with the word *mechanical,* a word indicating a contempt that cannot be expressed in the translation. This word expressed the full scorn felt by the free citizen living on his own fortune, and devoting all his intellectual and physical powers to the State—of the gentleman, in fact—for the man with the

[1]Greek View of Life, 126.

horny hand, who toiled in his workshop to earn his daily bread. This reproach of 'mechanical' was never aimed at the rich owner of a number of slaves, who worked for his benefit; a factory owner need not take part in the work himself, but had his overseers to attend to that; it was the little man who had no other hands to work for him, and who wielded the hammer himself, or who worked the cloth in the fuller's shop, whom they looked down on. In vain wise lawgivers tried to call the attention of the citizens to the blessing of handicraft, and the honourable nature of this occupation; in vain the democrats gave political equality to artisans by permitting them to vote and speak in the Assembly of the people along with the other citizens. There were some states in which an important part of the prosperity depended on handicrafts, and there a more moderate view gradually made way, but, generally speaking, the contempt for handicraft remained and continued, the rather as even philosophers regarded it as but a necessary evil. Doubtless they recognized the usefulness of handicrafts, but still they maintained that work of this kind in the workshop, near the hot furnace or in the gloomy room, was not suited to a free citizen, and that the effort of gaining money which was connected with it was injurious to the mind, and made it coarse and uncultivated." [2]

Agriculture remained an honorable employment. Slaves performed the menial part of the work, and the owner merely superintended the whole. The religion of the Greeks dignified agriculture—or, at least, recognized it as an occupation worthy of men. Demeter, goddess of the harvest, was loved, and the god of wine was celebrated by national festivities. Indeed, the Greek drama had its birth in the worship of Dionysus.

Owing to the nature of the land in Greece, some was much better suited to farming than others. Grains were grown in the plains, and olive groves and vineyards covered the hillsides. Grain was never raised in sufficient quantities for home consumption; olive oil was extensively made and exported. Owing to the great demand for honey, which supplied the place of sugar, bees were raised in large numbers.

[2] Home Life of the Ancient Greeks. 499.

Herding was an important occupation. Sheep-raising was extensively carried on, and cattle-raising had been common since Homeric days, when the value of an ox was taken as the standard of all values. Lack of pasturage often compelled herders to drive their cattle long distances, and interstate regulations sometimes allowed pasturage to be used by those outside their own borders.

The tools and implements of Hellas were always primitive. The plough was little more than a stick which scratched the soil. Farmers sowed and reaped and gathered into storehouses in the most enlightened ages of Greece quite as they had done in the age of Hesiod, who instructed them in his Works as to how their various duties should be performed. While we study Greek life as it developed in the cities—the culture-centers—yet the fact remains that the masses of Hellenes spent their lives in the rural districts of Greece, and the peasants who tilled the soil and passed uneventful years amid their vineyards, grain fields and olive groves, made up a staple and very important part of the population.

> " When, Atlas-born, the Pleiad stars arise
> Before the sun above the dawning skies,
> ' Tis time to reap ; and when at sunrise now
> They sink beneath the west, ' tis time to plough.
> Know too they set, immerged into the sun,
> While Forty days entire their circle run,
> And with the lapse of the revolving year,
> When sharpened is the sickle, re-appear,
> Law of the fields and known to every swain,
> Who turns the fallow soil beside the main ;
> Or who, remote from billowy ocean's gales,
> Tills the rich glebe of inland-winding vales.
>
> A house, a ploughing steer, a maid be thine,
> Not wife, but purchased slave, to tend thy kine.
> Within, let all fit implements abound,
> Lest with refused entreaty, wandering round
> Thy wants still press, the season glide away,
> And thou with scanted labor mourn the day.

Thy task defer not till the morn arise,
Or the third sun th' unfinished work surprise,
The sluggish man shall ne'er his garners fill,
Nor he that still delays, and lingers still;
Zeal speeds the work; the loiterer at his cost
Wrestles with damage, and his pains are lost.

Improve the season: to the plough apply
Both thou and thine, and toil in wet and dry:
Haste to the field with break of glowing morn,
That so thy grounds may wave with thickening corn.
In spring upturn the glebe; nor spare the toil
In summer days to break afresh the soil:
It shall not mock thy hopes: then freely sow
The fallow field, whilst light the mould below;
The fallow field bids muttered curses flee,
And gathers happy children round thy knee.

I warn thee now the season's rigor meet
With soft-napped cloak, and tunic to the feet.
Wrap in the cloak thy body, tempest-proof,
If on scant warp thou weave a plenteous woof.

Bleak is the morn, when blows the north from high;
Oft when the dawnlight paints the starry sky,
A misty cloud suspended hovers o'er
Heaven's blessed earth, and wafts its wheaten store,
Drained from the living streams: aloof in air
The whirling winds the buoyant vapor bear,
Resolved at eve in rain or gusty cold,
As by the north the troubled rack is rolled.

Hesiod: Elton's trans.

Sons of the poor usually followed the trade of the father. Those engaged in the same trade lived ordinarily near one another. Thus a portion of a street would be known as the district of the boxmakers, the jewelers, and the like.

Greeks were not taxed on their trade, but foreigners who

came to live and ply their trades in Hellas paid a tax to the
government for this privilege.   Piraeus, the harbor of Athens,
was populated to quite an extent by these foreigners who took
up their abode and were allowed to become naturalized citizens.

Most artisans attained great skill in their work.   The
bakers were famous for the many kinds of bread they made,
fashioning it often in a diversity of forms—figures of men
and animals.   They made a variety of cakes, sweetening them
with the rich honey of Hymettus.

Tanners and shoemakers—the two workers in leather were
often combined—were compelled to pursue their callings outside the city limits, since the odor of the leather was objectionable.   Potters manufactured their jars and urns and sold
them in the market booths.   The same was true of various
artisans, who made the articles they sold in the bazaars.

Jewelers attained great skill in the cutting of stones.
"Gems cut as intaglios or as cameos were used in signet rings,
earrings, and necklaces; the principal stones were agate, ame-
thyst, chalcedony, and carnelian, and specimens in European
museums today still testify to the wonderful skill and taste of
the artists who carved them.   More common than these were
gold and silver ornaments.   Gold was brought from the East
and from Thrace, and fashioned by goldsmiths into small
objects for personal wear.   Silver was more plentiful than
gold, though its relative value to gold was much greater than
it is today.   The silver mines at Laurium were productive
throughout the fifth century, and jewelers were able to use
silver not only for personal ornaments, but also for vases, large
mirrors, lamp-stands, and similar articles."[3]

Fullers and dyers, carpenters, masons, cabinetmakers, potters, armour-makers—all drove a thriving business.   Their
wares were needed and in spite of the social disadvantages to
which they were placed, they gave eager attention to their
work and accumulated property.   In Greece we have to distinguish between the men of commerce and the petty tradesmen, for these differences counted for more than they do
today.   The wholesale merchant ordinarily owned his merchant boat, which imported and exported his goods.   Loaded
with the products of Greece, his vessel plied along the harbors,

[3]Life of Ancient Greeks, 230.

stopping at favorable ports and holding a sort of fair; buying in turn what things were demanded at home, and continuing a voyage after this fashion until all was ready for the home port. Men who carried on business on such a scale as this, often leaving the entire management of their affairs, to say nothing of its details, to others, came not at all under the social bane which hampered tradesmen. Athens was made up to a large extent of men whose wealth had been similarly made.

Opposed to these we may place the small retail merchant, who bought where he could, in such small quantities as he was able, and who had the reputation of having two or three prices for the same article. The Greeks felt that it was impossible for such a man to prosper and not to take advantage of his fellow men. They thought that the petty trafficking to which he was constantly subjected must of necessity narrow his vision and warp his mind. They saw that he was by no means free to serve the State, and hence they argued that his manner of living was incompatible with the highest good.

Bankers had their tables of exchange in the market place with the trades people. Their business was to exchange money, to examine and decide upon the worth of coins, and to make loans. They resorted to many devices which won them hard reputations. One grudge held against them was that they took advantage of one's distress to exact high rates of interest. Men frequently wanted to borrow money to enable them to undertake commercial ventures, where some chance of failure was apparent. Because they took such risks, bankers charged as high as 33 1/3 and even 50 per cent for the use of their money. Nevertheless, in commercial centers these money changers were needed and in many cases gave immediate relief to those carrying heavy financial obligations.

From all that we know about the early Greeks, it is plain that a study of trade and commerce does not bring us to the heart of the people nor in contact with the characteristic Greek life.

CHAPTER IX.

Worship and Religious Festivals.

No people ever possessed a religion which was more completely the expression of the popular mind than the ancient Greeks. No spiritual law-giver promulgated the tenets of their faith; no body of priests instructed the individual as to what he should believe and what he should reject. Just as Greek art was the expression of a people developing under certain conditions and surroundings, so was the Greek religion in the truest sense original and spontaneous.

Today we are able to separate the religion of a nation from its political and industrial life for purposes of study. Indeed, it is in fact something quite apart from these. The men who mold the religious thought of the age are entirely a different body of men than those who control the great industrial movements of a nation or who guide its political progress. This modern condition would have been inconceivable to the ancient Greek. To him the unknown power that rules the world was not thought of as the attribute of one World-Spirit, but as divided among many gods. Like all primitive men, his conception of these gods was often crude and material, yet it included much that was exalted and noble. The Mighty Ones whom he called into being to explain the natural world around him shared every experience of life with him, accompanied him at home and abroad, moved unseen at every festival, and symbolically partook of every meal.

By the will and protection of the gods the State prospered. Should their favor be withdrawn, destruction was certain. They were not beings to be feared; rather, they were unseen companions who blessed the good and punished the wrong-doer. They were not spirits to judge severely of a mortal when death removed him from earth. They themselves shared passions, desires, ambitions common to men, and so understood them. The gods were immortal, mighty, just, mindful of their people and responsive to prayer and worship. No undertaking was begun without a sacrifice to them, no triumph was conceivable in their absence.

The Greeks were constantly reminded of the gods in the home and in public places. Awaking, the master of the house saw the image of the gods of marriage, who blessed his marriage alliance and caused his house to prosper. Passing into the living room of his house, the family hearth appeared, blessed by Hestia, goddess of the domestic hearth. Here sacrifices were offered upon any special occasion in the household, and here strangers were protected and welcomed. When he left his home and merged into the street, Hermae greeted him at every turn, for posts crowned by the carved head of Hermes served as guide posts. Statues of Athena, Zeus and other deities adorned the acropolis. Even the market-place was frequently beautified by statues of the Mighty Ones. Temples and shrines were everywhere, and no priest was essential to the sacrifice. Domestic and foreign affairs, the State, the home, the family—all needed the care and protection of the mighty gods, and life apart from them was not conceived. To be sure, men did not sit down and reason all this out, in a cool, argumentative way. It had been the belief of their fathers and from infancy they had heard it, and it was the natural conception for men to hold.

In the Story of Greek Mythology we have learned about the various deities worshipped by the Hellenes, and have seen how these beings were originally brought into existence to explain natural phenomena. We are concerned now with the various acts of worship observed in consequence of such beliefs, and with the great national religious festivals.

In the home, sacrifices were made before and after marriage, after the birth of a child, before a journey to be undertaken by some member of the family, and when any unusual event occurred. Libations of wine and offerings of salt were made at every meal.

No one who had offended the gods by unrighteous acts could approach the Mighty Ones, and lest one might have offended unawares, purification was necessary. Before marriage, both bride and groom bathed in water from a sacred spring, that they might purify themselves before the union. After birth of a child, the mother purified herself by passing around the domestic hearth, in this instance purified by fire. In case of death, a jar of water from some sacred spring was placed outside the house, so that any who visited the house or came in contact with the dead might wash the hands in the lustral water. Death was regarded as especially objectionable to the gods, and funerals occurred after sunset, that the god of light, riding in the chariot of day, might not be offended by the sight.

In the State, sacrifices were similarly made before great enterprises were undertaken. This was true from earliest times. For example, before going into battle Agamemnon and his soldiers offered sacrifices: "And they did sacrifice, each man to one of the everlasting gods, praying for escape from death and the tumult of battle. But Agamemnon, king of men, slew a fat bull of five years to most mighty Kronion, and called the elders, the princes of the Achaian host. .
Then they stood around the bull and took the barley meal, and Agamemnon made his prayer in their midst and said: 'Zeus most glorious, most great god of the storm cloud, that dwellest in the heavens, vouchsafe that the sun set not upon us, nor in the darkness come near until I have laid low upon the earth Priam's palace smirched with smoke, and burnt the doorways thereof with consuming fire, and rent on Hector's breast his doublet, cleft with the blade; and about him full many of his comrades, prone in the dust, bite the earth.' "

So in later days of Greece, when the Athenian empire was at the height of its power—soon to fall because of the short-sightedness of selfish, unscrupulous men—Thucydides tells of the sacrifices that preceded the embarking of the Athenian fleet to Sicily.[1] In a like manner we find offerings to the gods made on all great public occasions, when their aid was especially implored.

Religious festivals were often connected with agriculture—with sowing and reaping. A yearly festival was held in honor of Demeter, Mother-Earth, on whose bosom ripened the grain. Various conceptions were held of Demeter at different periods. She was goddess of the harvest, taught men how to reap and sow and make the earth productive. In every village men made merry at the harvest home. All were welcome and song and dance filled the joyous hours.

[1] See Account of Sicilian Expedition.

"Now look, this road holds holiday today:
For banded brethren solemnize a feast
To richly-dight Demeter, thanking her
For her good gifts: since with no grudging hand
Hath the boon goddess filled the wheaten floors.
So come. The way, the day, is thine as mine:
Try we our woodcraft—each may learn from each.

Say, ye who dwell upon Parnassian peaks,
Nymphs of Castalia, did old Chiron e'er
Set before Heracles a cup so brave
In Pholus' cavern—did as nectarous draughts
Cause that Anapian shepherd, in whose hand
Rocks were as pebbles, Polypheme the strong,
Featly to foot it o'er the cottage lawns,—
As, ladies, ye bid flow that day for us
All by Demeter's shrine at harvest-home?
Beside whose corn stacks may I oft again
Plant my broad fan: while she stands by and smiles,
Poppies and corn-sheaves on each laden arm."

The yearly festival was less important than the one held
every fourth year. This, like the annual celebration. occurred
from the 9th to the 13th of October. Married women had
some special ceremonies, holding in memory the loss of
Persephone and her restoration.

To Ceres chief her annual rites be paid,
On the green turf, beneath a fragrant shade,
When winter ends, and spring serenely shines,
Then fat the lambs, then mellow are the wines,
Then sweet are slumbers on the flowery ground,
Then with thick shades are lofty mountains crown'd.
Let all the hinds bend low at Ceres' shrine;
Mix honey sweet, for her, with milk and mellow wine;
Thrice lead the victim the new fruits around,
And Ceres call, and choral hymns resound:
Presume not, swains, the ripen'd grain to reap,
Till crown'd with oak in antic dance ye leap,
Invoking Ceres, and in solemn lays,
Exalt your rural queen's immortal praise.

                                    Virgil: Pitt's trans.

One of the most imposing festivals held in Attica was the Panathenaea. It commemorated, according to some Greek writers, the part taken by Athena in uniting the various tribes of Attica into one state. If not instituted by Theseus, he at least gave prominence to the occasion. The early significance of the festival was lost sight of, and the Panathenaea in reality was a celebration held in honor of the patron deity of Athens, under whose wise direction and guidance the city prospered. Some time previous to the festival, maidens were chosen from the noblest families to weave a gorgeous robe for the statue of the goddess, which stood in the temple on the acropolis. Embroidery in rich designs covered the sacred peplos. On the day of the festival it was carried through the streets, while a procession of all the people accompanied it to the temple. Old men carried olive branches in their hands, and young men bore arms. Women carried baskets on their heads, loaded with all kinds of choice viands for the sacrifice.

After this part of the celebration, athletic games were held. These were participated in only by Athenians, and the prizes awarded were jars of pure olive oil. Some of the vessels given as prizes have been preserved. On one side is usually painted the mythological contest between Poseidon and Athena, when they contended for the honor of naming the city; on the reverse side is pictured some scene in the particular festival in which the victor participated.

Metal workers and other artisans kept the Hephaestia, in honor of their patron, Hephaestus, or Vulcan. The feast of Hera was celebrated by married women. All Greece paid honor to Dionysus. Especially were the Athenians ardent in keeping the Greater and Lesser Dionysia. The drama originated in the dance and songs given in honor of the god of wine. One festival was held in the spring, when the first thrill of life was manifest in nature, and another in the autumn, when their grapes were gathered.

The Greeks were very responsive to the changing seasons. Each locality had its special deity whom it particularly honored, and, as a result, festivals were held in villages, in the country, and in various cities at different times of year. Such celebrations were important in the national religion and formed one bond of union among the inhabitants of a disunited country.

CHAPTER X.

Spartan Life.

Any consideration of Greek life which left out of account the peculiar social organization of Sparta would be incomplete. Spartan and Athenian life stand over against one another, each throwing the other into marked relief. We have discussed at length the various social institutions of Athens, and have dwelt upon her manner of life, her special civilization, because they were the best that Greece produced. Sometimes it has been said that the history of Greece is the history of Athens. This is no doubt leaving out much that is important, and yet, the greatest attainments in the realm of arts and letters were realized in Athens, and the policy of Athens towards other States was, generally speaking, nobler and broader than that exercised by any other Hellenic state. However, Sparta developed a particular social condition, unparalleled in all time.

The Dorians, who founded Sparta, brought with them many customs, to which they adhered throughout their existence as a body politic. They were a sturdy mountain race, caring for nothing but war. When they migrated into the Peloponnesus they drove out the earlier possessors of the land, and appropriated the fertile valley region for themselves. In course of time they annexed territory round about them, compelling the captives taken in war to till the soil. The earlier land owners who surrendered to them were allowed to settle new farms somewhat remote from Sparta, and to keep a local administration under general supervision of the Spartans.

After the Spartans had become a settled people, they did not pass through the various stages of political revolution general in Greece. On the other hand, they retained two kings. and in the main the form of government with which they started. This does not imply that the power of the people and the administrators underwent no modifications as years passed by. Such a thing would have been impossible even in conservative Sparta, but while states around experienced repeated political vicissitudes, Sparta remained practically unchanged. Nor was that all. Having been warlike in their mountain home, the Spartans retained their military disposition. Much that Plato pictured in his ideal state was actually true in Sparta. Marriage was considered from the standpoint of future generations. Babes who were crippled or deformed, or even deemed too weak to become vigorous citizens, were exposed upon the hills to die. Boys were taken from their parents at an early age and educated by the state. Girls were given physical training which might prepare them for their duties in later years. Mothers sent their sons forth to battle gladly and grieved only if they proved unworthy on the field of battle. If brought home dead, having fallen while nobly fighting, Spartan mothers rejoiced, nor mourned for those who had acquitted themselves so well. Spartan husbands and fathers scorned work of any kind, unless indeed it pertained to the life of a soldier. They dined at the public mess, kept themselves severely disciplined in feats of endurance, and indulged in little or no family life. Their duty was to defend their country, and it was their glory that Sparta's walls were her citizens.

Money was despised. For internal trade, iron coin was used. So cumbersome was it that an ox team would have been required to draw much of it around, and no one could easily secrete it. Any remunerative employment was forbidden citizens. Trade, commerce and labor of artisans were left to slaves. Houses were barren of comforts and even the temples were simple and unostentatious.

This austerity, so absolute, so unyielding, was not conducive to noblest development of the human mind. Genius must have something to feed upon, and rarely do the most gifted come from surroundings shorn of every beauty. In Sparta we find no splendid architectural structures, no sublime statuary, no literary monuments to stand unmatched through fast succeeding centuries. The tender sentiments and emotions had no opportunity to develop, and without them the soul of a people is lacking.

"Sparta was a great military camp, and the Spartans had, as a rule, no other occupation than that of serving as soldiers

when they were required to do so.   The Spartans are
one of the few examples of what a State can perform, which
has one aim, the preservation of existing institutions, and pur-
sues it with wisdom and energy.   It was a one-sided idea of
life, yet it proved of great service to Greece.   Sparta certainly
possessed hardly anything of what makes Greece of importance
for all time, that is, of art or of science.   But, in the first
place, it helped much to make Greece feared, and thus worked
for her preservation.   And secondly, but for Sparta the athletic exercises of the Greeks would probably never have existed.
Sparta appears to have given the Olympian games that impulse
which did so much for the welfare of Greece.   And who would
care to contest the assertion that without the Olympian games
we should never have had Greek sculpture?

"Finally, we must do her justice in another direction.   It
is true that Spartan education and Spartan government were
a mere training-school, but what were the means which were
employed?   They appealed to the noble and generous side of
human nature, to simplicity of life, self-control, respect for
natural and social superiors, and obedience to the higher powers in the widest sense of the word; all this was the rule in
Sparta, and it was strictly carried out in practice.   It is not
too much to say that some bright lights would be wanting in
the moral picture of Greece if Sparta had not existed." [1]

[1]Holm: Hist. of Greece, V. I, 183, 184.

VASE PAINTING.

GREEK LITERATURE.

CHAPTER XI.

BEGINNINGS OF GREEK LITERATURE.

The Greeks were ardent lovers of beauty. Beauty of bodily form they glorified in sculpture; beauty of architecture, in their temples; beauty of thought, in their literature; beauty of speech and vocal expression was manifest in the subtlety of their tongue. "Do nothing too much," was one of their maxims; do nothing too little; do each thing just enough; do not over-accentuate one part nor allow details to claim attention at the expense of the whole. All this was implied in the favorite saying: "Do nothing too much."

This characteristic of the Hellenes in worshipping the beautiful is apparent in their literature, some knowledge of which should be acquired by even the general reader. Not only is much pleasure to be thus derived, but Hellenic writings have greatly influenced the literature of subsequent peoples, and have continued to be a source of inspiration to poets and writers of all ages. Comparatively few may read these masterpieces in the original, but while translations fail to convey the same impressions, they nevertheless give some conception of the Greek mentality.

Literature of ancient Greece had its beginnings in remote ages, culminated in the palmy days of Athenian supremacy, and gradually declined with decaying Hellas. It is possible for us to consider only the more important literary epochs, and to characterize the productions of the most brilliant Hellenic writers.

Among primitive peoples the first literary productions ordinarily are composed in adoration of deities. After these religious hymns come songs of heroes and their deeds. The skill of the fighter, the prowess of the hunter, pillages of bold adventurers—these are likely to appeal to semi-civilized peoples, and these were the themes of wandering bards who brought messages from distant lands in an age lacking all means of rapid communication. If today all modern methods of communication were temporarily destroyed—if the world should suddenly find itself bereft of telegraph, postal systems, newspapers, printing, steam ships, steam cars, and other vehicles of rapid transit, we can imagine how welcome would be the stranger bringing word of distant lands.

In early Greece, minstrels, or bards, journeyed from shore to shore, singing thrilling tales of deeds to the accompaniment of harps. In course of time, the tales of these harpers fell largely into two classes: those which continued to be sung to musical accompaniment, and those which were merely recited. The first were especially rhythmical, and became known as lyrics; the second were narrative tales, and were called *epe*, or spoken verses. These early songs were gathered up by long succeeding poets, who wove them into poems, still preserved, and into many, doubtless, which have been entirely lost.

The function of the ancient Hellenic minstrel was important indeed. Again and again in the Homeric poems we find reference to the bard who gave spirit to the feast and beguiled the idle hours of Homeric princes. In the scene vividly drawn in the home of Penelope, where her suitors arrogantly banquet, to the ruin of her fortune, the bard has his place.

> " Silent all
> They sat and listened to the illustrious bard,
> Who sang of the calamitous return
> Of the Greek host from Troy, at the command
> Of Pallas. From her chamber o'er the hall
> The daughter of Icarius, the sage queen
> Penelope, had heard the heavenly strain,
> And knew its theme."

Take again the description of the banquet given by the mighty Alcinous for Ulysses, who had taken refuge at his court:

> " Then make fast the oars
> Beside the benches, leave them there, and come
> Into our palace and partake in haste
> A feast which I will liberally spread
> For all of you. This I command the youths;
> But you, ye sceptred princes, come at once
> To my fair palace, that we there may pay

The honours due our guest; let none refuse.
Call also the divine Demodocus,
The bard, on whom a deity bestowed
In ample measure the sweet gift of song,
Delightful when the spirit prompts the lay.

And when their thirst and hunger were allayed,
The Muse inspired the bard to sing the praise
Of heroes; 'twas a song whose fame had reached
To the high heaven, a story of the strife
Between Ulysses and Achilles, son
Of Peleus, wrangling at a solemn feast
Made for the gods. They strove with angry words,
And Agamemnon, king of men, rejoiced
To hear the noblest of the Achaian host
Contending; for all this had been foretold
To him in sacred Pythia by the voice
Of Phoebus, when the monarch to inquire
At the oracle had crossed the rock which formed
Its threshold. Then began the train of woes
Which at the will of sovereign Jupiter
Befell the sons of Ilium and of Greece.
      So sang renowned Demodocus."

As old Greek bards beguiled the hours of early Hellenes, so did Saxon minstrels entertain their lords with deeds of Beowulf, and Frankish warriors listened later with delight to the exploits of the Mediaeval Roland.

Roughly speaking, we may indicate the period of the Greek epic as preceding 800 B. C. Because the epics sing generally of heroes, the measure in which they were written has been called "heroic." Greatest of Greek epics are the Iliad and the Odyssey. The Iliad with its rapid sweep and dramatic force, and the Odyssey with its picturesque touches and scenes from wandering and from domestic life, remain today the most remarkable masterpieces of all time. Since these poems have already been considered at length, we may turn to the works of Hesiod, belonging to a somewhat later period.

Whereas the Homeric epics were in all probability produced in Asia Minor, Hesiod composed his poems in Boeotia.

Little is definitely known of this writer, and some have been tempted to say that his poems, like the Homeric masterpieces, were really the productions of many poets. Nevertheless, it would seem that there is no good reason to discredit the few facts ordinarily accepted concerning Hesiod. It would appear that his parents migrated from Asia Minor to Continental Greece, settling in Boeotia, near Mt. Hymettus. Here the poet was born and, while a youth, tended his father's flocks. Finally, according to legendary lore, the Muses, whose abode was on this mountain, inspired him to compose the epics now attributed to him.

As has been noted, the metre of the epic has been called "heroic," because the epos generally recounted exploits of heroes; Hesiod, however, used the measure for narrating simple deeds and homely maxims. While the Homeric poems were composed for the entertainment of nobles, Hesiod wrote for the instruction and edification of the common folk While the Homeric epics extolled the mighty gods and godlike men, Hesiod portrayed the simple people, their work, their life and cares.

Two poems are supposed to be the work of Hesiod: *The Theogony* and *Works and Days*. The first is made up of legends and folklore pertaining to the gods, as prevalent among the peasants of Boeotia. *Works and Days* is composed largely of maxims, experiences and beliefs pertaining to the everyday life of the common people. The homely truths and beliefs embodied in these poems were ill suited to the grandeur of heroic verse, but the art of writing prose was yet unknown, and hence the inspired writer was compelled to give his sentiments the only form of expression known to him.

As literary compositions, Hesiod's poems cannot be ranked with the Homeric masterpieces. Nevertheless, we would have been deprived of a vast store of information regarding primitive Greek life and customs had these works not survived.

The *Theogony*, or *Origin of the Gods*, comprises 1,022 lines. It has deep interest for the student of Greek religion. Many myths and legends clustering around the Greek divinities have been preserved to us in this poem alone.

Works and Days, containing 828 lines, is made up of three parts: The first division includes a series of counsels given

by the poet to his brother, Perses. It appears that difficulty
had arisen between the brothers regarding their inheritance.
Perses had taken the lion's share, and was yet dissatisfied.
Hesiod's advice to him forms the first section of the epic.
The second division contains rules for the aid and guidance
of farmers and sailors. Tillers of the soil are instructed
when to reap and when to sow; how to tame their oxen, and
how to tend their vines. Sailors are instructed how to make
boats and how to propel them. The third division of the
poem, called the Calendar, or Days, enumerates days which
are lucky for various undertakings and those whereupon ill
fortune is supposed to befall the misguided one who risks his
luck. Incidentally other interesting bits of current belief and
practice crept into the poems. We know, for example, the
very climate in which Hesiod lived from his counsels to those
who dwelt in it. He never had a good word for the damp
chill of his native land.

> "Ascra, in winter vile, most villainous
> In summer, and at no time glorious."

"Alexander the Great once said that Homer was reading
for kings, Hesiod for peasants. This contrast reflects the
difference both in the environment out of which the two found-
ers of the epic sprung, and also the purpose of the two poets.
The Homeric poems were perfected in Ionia, where life was
eager and bustling, occupied with adventures of the sea and in
constant contact with travellers from strange lands; where,
too, the stories of the Trojan war were sung by wandering
minstrels. Life in Boeotia offered a striking contrast. Not
only were the Boeotians less imaginative than the Ionians, but
their daily routine of agricultural and pastoral labors was
unbroken by stormy adventures of the present or thrilling
tales of the past. Hesiod, besides, seems to scorn the romances
of Homer, and aims rather to tell the plain, homely truths of
the farm to narrating the glowing pictures of the heroic age." [1]

[1] Capps: From Homer to Theocritus.

THE DAYS.

A decent heed thy slaves enjoin to pay,
And well observe each Jove-appointed day.
The thirtieth of the moon inspect with care,
Each monthly task, and every ration share
To every slave; and choose the hour that draws
Th' assembled people to the pleaded cause.
Lo! these the days appointed from above
By the deep counsels of all sapient Jove.
Of each new morn, the rolling year around,
The first, the fourth, the seventh, are prosperous found.
Phoebus, the seventh, from mild Latona born,
The golden-sworded god, beheld the morn.
The eighth, nor less the ninth, with favoring skies,
Speeds of th' increasing month each rustic enterprise;
And on the eleventh let thy flocks be shorn,
And on the twelfth be reaped thy laughing corn;
Both days are good, yet is the twelfth confessed
More fortunate, with fairer omen blessed.
On this the air-suspended spider spreads,
In the full moon, his fine and self-spun threads;
And the wise emmet, tracking dark the plain,
Heaps provident the store of gathering grain.
On this let careful woman's nimble hand
Throw first the shuttle, and the web expand.
On the thirteenth forebear to sow the grain,
But then the plant shall not be set in vain.
The sixteenth profitless to plants is deemed;
Auspicious to the birth of man esteemed;
But to the virgin shall unprosperous prove,
Then born to light, or joined in wedded love.
So to the birth of girls with adverse ray
The sixth appears an unpropitious day;
This day keen railleries, loves, deluding lies,
And love tales bland and whispered secrecies.
The tenth propitious lends its natal ray
To men, to gentle minds the fourteenth day.
Tame the shy sheep on this auspicious morn,
And ox of flexible hoof and twisted horn;

The sharp-toothed dog and patient mule command,
And gently bring them to thy mastering hand.
The fourth and twenty-fourth, no grief shall prey
Within thy breast, for holy either day.
Fourth of the moon, lead home thy blooming bride,
And be the fittest auguries descried.
Beware the fifth, with horror fraught and woe;
'Tis said the Furies walk their round below.
Avenging the dread oath, who awful birth
From Discord rose, to scourge the perjured earth.
On the smooth threshing floor the seventeenth morn
Observant throw the sheaves of sacred corn;
For chamber furniture the lumber hew
And blocks for ships with shaping axe subdue.
The fourth upon the stocks thy vessels lay
Soon with light keel to skim the watery way.
The nineteenth mark among the better days,
When passes to fervor of noon-tide blaze.
Harmless the ninth; 'tis good to plant the earth,
And fortunate each male and female birth.
Few know the twenty-ninth, nor heed the rules
To broach their casks, and yoke their steers and mules,
And fleet-hoofed steeds, and on dark ocean's way
Launch the oared galley; few will trust the day.
Pierce on the fourth thy casks; the fourteenth prize
As holy; and when morning paints the skies
The twenty-fourth is best (few this have known);
But worst of days of which the careful heed
Each human enterprise will favoring speed:
Others there are, which intermediate fall,
Marked with no auspice, and unomened all:
And these will some, and those will others praise,
But few are versed in mysteries of days.
In this a stepmother's stern hate we prove,
In that the mildness of a mother's love.
O fortunate the man! O blessed is he,
Who skilled in these, fulfills his ministry;
He, to whose note the auguries are given,
No rite transgressed, and void of blame to Heaven."

—Elton's trans.

Finally, we may note that the age of the Greek epic brought forth the Homeric Hymns. These belong to a period somewhat later than that of Hesiod. Thirty-three hymns survive, and they were apparently written to preface epic poems. Composed in honor of some religious festival, each praises the power of a favorite deity. The following, the twenty-ninth, a hymn of praise to Athena, has been freely translated by Shelley:

> " I sing the glorious Power with azure eyes,
>   Athenian Pallas! tameless, chaste, and wise,
>   Tritogenia, town-preserving maid,
>   Revered and mighty; from his awful head
>   Whom Jove brought forth, in warlike armour dressed,
>   Golden, all radiant! wonder strange possessed
>   The everlasting gods that shape to see,
>   Shaking a javelin keen, impetuously
>   Rush from the crest of aegis-bearing Jove;
>   Fearfully heaven was shaken, and did move
>   Beneath the might of the Carulean-eyed;
>   Earth dreadfully resounded, far and wide;
>   And, lifted from its depths, the sea swelled high
>   In purple billows; the tide suddenly
>   Stood still, and great Hyperion's son long time
>   Checked his swift steeds, till where she stood sublime,
>   Pallas from her immortal shoulders threw
>   The arms divine; wise Jove rejoiced to view.
>   Child of the aegis-bearer, hail to thee!
>   Nor thine nor others' praise shall unremembered be."

THE GREEK EPIC.

All important nations have passed through the *epic* period
—that period wherein heroism and hero-deeds appeal to them
more forcefully than any other manifestation of human greatness. Beowulf is the epic of the Viking; as a remnant of
early Saxon literature it is invaluable to us today, since it
pictures the life of a young and vigorous race. The story of
Samson contains elements of the epic, and no doubt such a
tale was once related after the fashion of other early epics. The
Iliad and the Odyssey are the masterly epics of ancient Greece
and have been loved by readers of all subsequent ages.

From remote times the struggle which is still waged on
the border between Europe and Asia has been carried on.
Sometimes Europe has forced itself into Asia; sometimes the
Asiatic has taken his revenge by forcing himself into Europe.
The geographical boundaries are not now, nor have they ever
been well defined. The first clashing of arms is legendary
and is related in the Iliad.

"Listen to the Iliad singing the first and clearest note of
the conflict which lasted while Greece lasted, lasts to this day.
Paris of legend, Xerxes of history, came against the West;
Agamemnon of legend, Alexander of history, went against the
East; it is all one theme, making a world-epos, one in Universal History, one in the human heart. Here, as elsewhere, the
heart-beat and the world-beat make one music, heard still in
all true poetry, heard most distinctly, if not most profoundly,
in this earliest Book of Literature."

The story has to do with gods and mortals—as any student
of early Greek history would expect. To the ancient Greek it
would have been inconceivable that the fortunes of men could
be shaped apart from the will of the immortals. Jealousies

437

among the deities themselves became potent forces; in a struggle which divided two mighty peoples the gods themselves were divided.

Helen, the beautiful wife of King Menelaus, is enticed away from her home, her country and her friends by Paris, who takes her to his father's court. Supporters of the outraged king flock to his cause by tens of thousands to march against the Trojans, drawn inadvertently into a terrible war. Here again the attitude of the early Greek must be kept in mind. Since the sacrifice of many was involved in this cause, it is evident that the call seemed imperative; the loss of Helen signified national loss; her restoration implied national vindication. In modern times nations have been embroiled in war for injuries inflicted upon a countryman. Sometimes injury done a citizen implies insult to the country to which he belongs. Thus the early Greeks felt a restoration of Helen necessary for the maintenance of national honor, at home and abroad.

In the last year of the Trojan war occurred an estrangement between Achilles, the daring hero, and Agamemnon, supreme in authority. The mighty king dishonored the one who for brave deeds and dauntless courage had won deep admiration of his fellow men. Achilles accordingly withdrew from the military activities of the Greeks and for awhile the question at stake was: could the Greeks take Troy without the help of their favorite hero. This they proved unable to accomplish.

The first book of the Iliad relates the quarrel between the chieftains which led to the withdrawal of Achilles from the army; the doubt in the mind of Agamemnon as to whether the Greeks will fight without their hero is dispelled in the second book, where the muster is given by ships. The third book has to do particularly with the beautiful Helen—who she was and for what she stood to the ones called to arms in **her** behalf. Suddenly two nations, long engaged in hostilities, agree to end all by a duel and a compromise: Paris and Menelaus will fight a duel and Helen shall fall to the share of the victor while all the rest agree to make peace. Nevertheless, this solution which for the moment seemed so possible is soon shown to be quite inadequate. This is a struggle between two races and cannot be made a personal question nor be settled in a personal way.

Much is made by the poet of the interposition of the gods, and in the fifth book it is plain that the Greeks are contending with the deities who are espousing the cause of the Trojans;

then the gods agree to stand aloof and let mortals decide the issue by battle.

Hector is the great Trojan figure. Unwillingly, whether he will or no, he is drawn into a war with which he feels small sympathy. Patriot that he is, he cannot keep out of a conflict which includes his father, his brothers and his countrymen. His is a most difficult position; one feels that Troy can never fall while Hector lives.

Owning himself defeated in his project of taking Troy without the help of Achilles, Agamemnon takes counsel of his supporters; he is so discouraged that he urges the Greeks to return home. Nestor and other staunch Greeks hold firmly to the cause for which all have suffered such untold woe; they scorn to give up what has been begun. Gifts are sent by Agamemnon to Achilles and the chieftain offers such amends as he can for the long estrangement.

From the ninth to the eighteenth book the story of the terrible battle is recounted; now the Greeks are successful—now the Trojans carry all before them. The death of Patroclus brings sorrow and remorse to Achilles who vows to avenge his death by taking the life of Hector.

The description of the armor made by Vulcan for Achilles to protect him in his furious onslaught is remarkable. From the devices on the shield one may learn much of the social conditions prevailing in Homeric times. Arrayed in his god-wrought armor, the hero goes forth, kills his adversary and then stoops to petty revenge by doing insult to the Trojan's dead body. For this injury the immortals are themselves incensed. The story ends with the pathetic scene of the Trojan king in sorrow and bitterest grief, entreating Achilles to deliver to surviving ones the dead Hector's body; Achilles is moved to pity, and in the peace that settles over the camp when the grief-stricken Trojans are allowed to administer the last rites to Hector, the poem closes.

The parting between Hector and Andromache is unsurpassed in all literature and holds an enduring place in the heart of every lover of Homeric lore. Finally, the whole poem is a storehouse of mythology from which Greek and Latin writers found the inspiration for their songs. Aeschylus said that his plays were but crumbs that fell from Homer's banquet and poets of every age have acknowledged the debt they owe to the early bard.

The Quarrel of Achilles and Agamemnon.

The mighty monarch, Agamemnon, rose,
His dark soul fill'd with fury, and his eyes
Flashing like flames of fire; on Calchas first
A with'ring glance he cast, and thus he spoke:
" Prophet of ill, thou never speak'st to me
But words of evil omen; for thy soul
Delights to augur ill, but aught of good
Thou never yet hast promis'd, nor perform'd.
And now among the Greeks thou spread'st abroad
Thy lying prophecies, that all these ills
Come from the Far-destroyer [Apollo], for that I
Refus'd the ransom of my lovely prize,
And that I rather chose herself to keep,
To me not less than Clytemnestra dear,
My virgin-wedded wife; nor less adorn'd
In gifts of form, of feature, or of mind.
Yet, if it must be so, I give her back;
I wish my people's safety, not their death.
But seek me out forthwith some other spoil,
Lest empty-handed I alone appear
Of all the Greeks; for this would ill beseem;
And how I lose my present share, ye see."
To whom Achilles, swift of foot, replied:
·"Haughtiest of men, and greediest of the prey,
How shall our valiant Greeks for thee seek out
Some other spoil? No common fund have we
Of hoarded treasures; what our arms have won
From captur'd towns, has been already shar'd.
Nor can we now resume th' apportion'd spoil.
Restore the maid, obedient to the God.
And if Heav'n will that we the strong-built walls
Of Troy should raze, our warriors will to thee
A threefold, fourfold recompense assign."
To whom the monarch Agamemnon thus:
"Think not, Achilles, valiant though thou art
In fight, and godlike, to defraud me thus;
Thou shalt not so persuade me, nor o'erreach.
Think'st thou to keep thy portion of the spoil
While I with empty hands sit humbly down?

The bright-ey'd girl thou bid'st me to restore;
If then the valiant Greeks for me seek out
Some other spoil, some compensation just,
'Tis well: if not, I with my own right hand
Will from some other chief, from thee perchance,
Or Ajax, or Ulysses, wrest his prey;
And woe to him, on whomso'er I call.
But this for future counsel we remit:
Haste we then now our dark-ribb'd bark to launch,
Muster a fitting crew, and place on board
The sacred hecatomb; then last embark
The fair Chryseis; and in chief command
Let some one of our councillors be plac'd,
Ajax, Ulysses, or Idomeneus,
Or thou, the most ambitious of them all,
That so our rites may soothe the angry God."
    To whom Achilles thus with scornful glance:
"Oh, cloth'd in shamelessness, oh, sordid soul,
How canst thou hope that any Greek for thee
Will brave the toils of travel or of war?
Well dost thou know that 'twas no feud of mine
With Troy's brave sons that brought me here in arms;
They never did me wrong; they never drove
My cattle, or my horses; never sought
In Phthia's fertile, life-sustaining fields
To waste the crops; for wide between us lay
The shadowy mountains and the roaring sea.
With thee, O void of shame, with thee we sail'd,
For Menelaus, and for thee, ingrate,
Just retribution to exact from Troy.
All this hast thou forgotten, or despis'd:
And threat'nest now to wrest from me the prize
I labor'd hard to win, and Greeks bestow'd.
Nor does my portion ever equal thine,
When on some populous town our troops have made
Successful war; in the contentious fight
The larger portion of the toil is mine;
But when the day of distribution comes,
Thine is the richest spoil; while I, forsooth,
Must be too well content to bear on board
Some paltry prize for all my warlike toil.
To Phthia now I go; so better far

II—29

To steer my homeward course, and leave thee here,
Dishonored as thou art, nor like, I deem,
To fill thy coffers with the spoils of war."
   Whom answer'd Agamemnon, King of men:
"Fly then, if such thy mind.   I ask thee not
On mine account to stay; others there are
Will guard my honor and avenge my cause:
And chief of all, the Lord of counsel, Jove.
Of all the Heav'n-born Kings, thou art the man
I hate the most; for thou delight'st in nought
But war and strife: thy prowess I allow;
Yet this, remember, is the gift of Heav'n.
Return then, with thy vessels, if thou wilt,
And with thy followers, home; and lord it there
Over thy Myrmidons.   I heed thee not.
I care not for thy fury.   Hear my threat:
Since Phœbus wrests Chryseis from my arms,
In mine own ships, and with mine own good crew,
Her I send forth; and, in her stead, I mean,
Ev'n from thy tent, myself, to bear thy prize,
The fair Briseis: that henceforth thou know
How far I am thy master; and that, taught
By thine example, others too may fear
To rival me, and brave me to my face."
   Thus while he spake, Achilles chaf'd with rage;
And in his manly breast his heart was torn
With thoughts conflicting—whether from his side
To draw his mighty sword, and thrusting by
Th' assembled throng, to kill th' insulting King;
Or school his soul, and keep his anger down.
But while in mind and spirit thus he mused,
And half unsheath'd his sword, from Heav'n came down
Minerva, sent by Juno, white-arm'd Queen,
Whose love and care both chiefs alike enjoy'd.
She stood behind, and by the yellow hair
She held the son of Peleus, visible
To him alone, by all the rest unseen.
Achilles, wond'ring, turn'd, and straight he knew
The blue-eyed Pallas; awful was her glance;
Whom thus the chief with winged words address'd:
   "Why com'st thou, child of ægis-bearing Jove?
To see the arrogance of Atreus' son?

But this I say, and will make good my words,
This insolence may cost him soon his life."
  To whom the blue-ey'd Goddess thus replied:
"From heav'n I came, to curb, if thou wilt hear,
Thy fury, sent by Juno, white-arm'd Queen,
Whose love and care ye both alike enjoy.
Cease, then, these broils, and draw not thus thy sword.
In words, indeed, assail him as thou wilt.
But this I promise, and will make it good,
The time shall come, when for his insolence
A threefold compensation shall be thine,
Only be sway'd by me, and curb thy wrath."
  Whom answer'd thus Achilles, swift of foot:
"Goddess, I needs must yield to your commands,
Indignant though I be—for so 'tis best;
Who hears the Gods, of them his pray'rs are heard."
  He said: and on the silver hilt he stay'd
His pow'rful hand, and flung his mighty sword
Back to its scabbard, to Minerva's word
Obedient; she her heav'nward course pursued
To join th' Immortals in th' abode of Jove.
But Peleus' son, with undiminish'd wrath,
Atrides thus with bitter words address'd:
  "Thou sot, with eye of dog, and heart of deer,
Who never dar'st to lead in armed fight
Th' assembled host, nor with a chosen few
To man the secret ambush—to thy fears
Apparent death—no doubt 'tis easier far,
Girt with thy troops, to plunder of his right
Whoe'er may venture to oppose thy will.
A tyrant King, because thou rul'st o'er slaves.
Were it not so, this insult were thy last.
But this I say, and with an oath confirm,
By this my royal staff, which never more
Shall put forth leaf nor spray, since first it left
Upon the mountain-side its parent stem,
Nor blossom more; since all around the axe
Hath lopp'd both leaf and bark, and now 'tis borne
Emblem of justice, by the sons of Greece.
Who guard the sacred ministry of law
Before the face of Jove! a mighty oath!
The time shall come, when all the sons of Greece

Shall mourn Achilles' loss ; and thou the while,
Heart-rent, shalt be all-impotent to aid,
When by the warrior-slayer Hector's hand
Many shall fall ; and then thy soul shall mourn
The slight on Grecia's bravest warrior cast.''

Thus spoke Pelides ; and upon the ground
He cast his staff, with golden studs emboss'd,
And took his seat ; on th' other side, in wrath,
Atrides burn'd ; but Nestor interpos'd ;
Nestor, the leader of the Pylian host,
The smooth-tongued chief, from whose persuasive lips
Sweeter than honey flowed the stream of speech.

HELEN AT THE SCÆAN GATE.

THE beauty of Helen, "divine one of women," was the primary cause of the Trojan war. Paris, the somewhat effeminate son of Priam, King of Troy, who had been hospitably entertained by her husband, Menelaus, King of Sparta, persuaded her to elope with him. Priam, when called upon to restore her, refused. Thereupon Agamemnon, the brother of Menelaus, and King of Argos, summoned all the kings of the Achaians to avenge the wrong by an expedition against Troy. The bravest and best of the warlike race willingly united for the purpose, and prosecuted the ten years' siege. Through all this time Helen's beauty does not fade, and the Odyssey shows her restored to her former home. As to the moral aspects of her career Homer is remarkably silent.

In Book III. the Achaians and the Trojans gather in the plain before Ilium, ready to fight, but it is agreed that Menelaus and Paris shall

decide the contest in single combat. Helen is then invited to the
Scæan Gate, where Priam and the Trojan elders are to witness the
fight. Our extract is taken from Cowper's version:

Iris, ambassadress of heaven, the while
To Helen came. Laodice she seem'd,
Loveliest of all the daughters of the house
Of Priam, wedded to Antenor's son,
King Helicaon. Her she found within.
An ample web magnificent she wove,
Inwrought with numerous conflicts for her sake
Beneath the hands of Mars, endured by Greeks
Mail-arm'd, and Trojans of equestrian fame.
Swift Iris at her side, her thus addressed,

Haste, dearest nymph! a wondrous sight behold!
Greeks, brazen-mail'd, and Trojans steed-renown'd,
So lately on the cruel work of Mars
Intent and hot for mutual havoc, sit
Silent; the war hath paused, and on his shield
Each leans, his long spear planted at his side.
Paris and Menelaus, warriors bold,
With quivering lances shall contend for thee,
And thou art his who conquers; his forever.

So saying, the goddess into Helen's soul
Sweetest desire infused to see again
Her former lord, her parents, and her home.
At once o'ermantled with her snowy veil
She started forth, and as she went let fall
A tender tear; not unaccompanied
She went, but by two maidens of her train
Attended, Æthra, Pittheus' daughter fair,
And soft-eyed Clymene. Their hasty steps
Convey'd them quickly to the Scæan Gate.
There Priam, Panthoüs, Clytius, Lampus sat,
Thymœtes, Hicetaon, branch of Mars,
Antenor and Ucalegon the wise,
All elders of the people; warriors erst,
But idle now through age, yet of a voice
Still indefatigable as the fly's [the cicada],
Which perched among the boughs sends forth at noon
Through all the grove his slender ditty sweet.
Such sat those Trojan leaders on the tower,

Who, soon as Helen on the steps they saw,
In accents quick, but whispered, thus remark'd:
    Trojans and Grecians wage, with fair excuse.
Long war for so much beauty.   Oh, how like
In feature to the Goddesses above!
Pernicious loveliness!   Ah, hence away,
Resistless as thou art and all divine,
Nor leave a curse to us, nor to our sons.

HECTOR AND ANDROMACHE.

HOMER, while giving superiority to the Achaians, does justice to the Trojans. The loyal, valiant Hector and his loving wife Andromache, with infant child, are shown in one of the finest passages of the Iliad. The battle in the plain was going against the Trojans, and Hector at last returned to Troy to request the women to go in solemn procession to the temples to ask aid of the gods. Then he sought an interview with Andromache, but found her not. He was told that she had gone to the walls to see the fight. The following passage, describing their meeting, was translated by Charles Kingsley.

So spoke the stewardess: but Hector rushed
From the house, the same way back, down stately streets,
Through the broad city, to the Scaian gates,
Whereby he must go forth toward the plain.
There running toward him came Andromache,
His ample-dowered wife, Eetion's child,—
Eetion the great-hearted, he who dwelt

In Thebé under Placos, and the woods
Of Placos, ruling over Kilic men.
His daughter wedded Hector brazen-helmed,
And met him then; and with her came a maid,
Who bore in arms a playful-hearted babe,
An infant still, akin to some fair star,
Only and well-loved child of Hector's house,
Whom he had named Scamandrios, but the rest
Astyanax, because his sire alone
Upheld the weal of Ilion the holy.
He smiled in silence, looking on his child:
But she stood close to him, with many tears,
And hung upon his hand, and spoke, and called him.
    " My hero, thy great heart will wear thee out:
Thou pitiest not thine infant child, nor me,
The hapless, soon to be thy widow;
The Greeks will slay thee, falling one and all
Upon thee: but to me were sweeter far,
Having lost thee, to die; no cheer to me
Will come thenceforth, if thou shouldst meet thy fate;
Woes only: mother have I none, nor sire.
For that my sire divine Achilles slew,
And wasted utterly the pleasant homes
Of Kilic folk in Thebé lofty-walled,
And slew Eetion with the sword; yet spared
To strip the dead: awe kept his soul from that.
Therefore he burned him in his graven arms,
And heaped a mound above him; and around,
The damsels of the ægis-holding Zeus,
The nymphs who haunt the upland, planted elms.
And seven brothers bred with me in the halls,
All in one day went down to Hades there;
For all of them swift-foot Achilles slew
Beside the lazy kine and snow-white sheep,
And her, my mother, who of late was queen
Beneath the woods of Placos, he brought here
Among his other spoils; yet set her free
Again, receiving ransom rich and great.
But Artemis, whose bow is all her joy,
Smote her to death within her father's halls.
Hector! so thou art father to me now,
Mother, and brother, and husband fair and strong!

Oh, come now, pity me, and stay thou here
Upon the tower, nor make thy child an orphan
And me thy wife a widow; range the men
Here by the fig-tree, where the city lies
Lowest, and where the wall can well be scaled;
For here three times the best have tried the assault
Round either Ajax, and Idomeneus,
And round the Atridai both, and Tydeus' son,
Whether some cunning seer taught the craft,
Or their own spirit stirred and drove them on."
Then spake tall Hector, with the glancing helm:
   "All this I too have watched, my wife; yet much
I hold in dread the scorn of Trojan men
And Trojan women with their trailing shawls,
If, like a coward, I should skulk from war.
Beside, I have no lust to stay; I have learnt
Aye to be bold, and lead the van of fight,
To win my father, and myself, a name.
For well I know, at heart and in my thought,
The day will come when Ilios the holy
Shall lie in heaps, and Priam, and the folk
Of ashen-speared Priam, perish all.
But yet no woe to come to Trojan men,
Nor even to Hecabe, nor Priam king,
Nor to my brothers, who shall roll in dust,
Many and fair, beneath the strokes of foes,
So moves me, as doth thine, when thou shalt go
Weeping, led off by some brass-harnessed Greek,
Robbed of the daylight of thy liberty,
To weave in Argos at another's loom,
Or bear the water of Messeis home,
Or Hypereia, with unseemly toils,
While heavy doom constrains thee, and perchance
The folk may say, who see thy tears run down,
'This was the wife of Hector, best in fight
At Ilium, of horse-taming Trojan men.'
So will they say perchance; while unto thee
New grief will come, for such a husband's loss,
Who might have warded off the day of thrall.
But may the soil be heaped above my corpse
Before I hear thy shriek and see thy shame!"
   He spoke, and stretched his arms to take the child,

But back the child upon his nurse's breast
Shrunk crying, frightened at his father's looks,
Fearing the brass and crest of horse's hair
Which waved above the helmet terribly.
Then out that father dear and mother laughed,
And glorious Hector took the helmet off,
And laid it gleaming on the ground, and kissed
His darling child and danced him in his arms;
And spoke in prayer to Zeus, and all the gods:
"Zeus, and ye other gods, O grant that this
My child, like me, may grow the champion here
As good in strength, and rule with might in Troy
That men may say, ' The boy is better far
Than was his sire,' when he returns from war,
Bearing a gory harness, having slain
A foeman, and his mother's heart rejoice."
Thus saying, on the hands of his dear wife
He laid the child ; and she received him back
In fragrant bosom, smiling through her tears.

Priam Begs the Body of his Son Hector.

HOMER represents Achilles as roused to savage fury to revenge the death of his friend Patroclus. Hector, when dying at his hands, requests that his body be restored to his parents, but the young hero passionately refuses. The gods, however, interpose, and after a few days his goddess-mother, Thetis, induces him to relent. By the same agency Priam is instructed to go secretly to the camp of the Achaians and beg from Achilles the body of his son. The god Hermes directs Priam on his sad journey.

The following extract is taken from Sir John Herschell's translation of the Iliad in hexameter verse. The contrast is emphasized between the aged king, subdued by manifold sorrows, and the fierce youth, whose passion had been roused to its utmost intensity by the loss of his friend. Touched by the reference to his father and moved by the hoary head of the suppliant, he yields, yet he must do it in his own way. His anger rises when Priam shows impatience.

Hermes thus: and away to the lofty realms of Olympus,
Darted and disappeared. From the car then Priam dismounted,
And while Idæus remained in the court behind, in attendance,
Holding the horses and mules, at once to the tent of Achilles
Passed. The belov'd of Zeus he found within, who was seated,
Musing in mournful thought, and apart stood rang'd his atten-
    dants.
Alcimus, scion of Mars, alone, and Automedon near him,
Minist'ring stood. The table remained undrawn; for but newly
Food and drink had he ta'en, and his joyless meal had concluded.
All unperceived by these the monarch came, and, approaching,
Flung himself down at his feet and embraced the knees of
    Achilles,
Kissing those dread and murderous hands which had slaughtered
    his children.
As when some conscience-stricken wretch, just fresh from a mur-
    der,
Flies to a foreign land, and in some conspicuous mansion
Refuge claims, its inmates aghast behold his arrival:
Such the dismayed surprise of Achilles, Priam beholding,
Such the amaze of those around, as they looked at each other,
While at his feet illustrious Priam preferred his petition:
    "Godlike Achilles! look upon me, and think of thy father,
Far away, on the threshold of age, and broken by sorrow:

Fancy thou seest him feeble, oppressed by the neighbors around
    him,
No protector at hand, no saviour from war and destruction.
Yet when he hears his son still lives, fresh joy in his bosom
Springs, and the hope day after day renewed, to behold thee,
Victor from Troy, restored to his arms and strong to avenge
    him.
Wretched beyond all mortals am I, whose sons were the bravest
Troy's wide realm hath beheld—and of these not one have I left
    me.
Fifty were mine when first the Greeks our city assaulted.
Nineteen to one fair queen were born, the noblest and dearest,
All the rest to the beauteous wives who dwell in my palace.
Ares insatiate hath swept them off—so brave and so many.
Hector, my only hope, ourselves' and our city's defender,
Him hast thou slain, contending bravely in arms for his country.
'Tis for his sake that thus I come to the ships of the Grecians,
Begging his corpse at thy feet, and a priceless ransom I bring
    thee.
Have respect for the Gods, O Achilles! pity my mis'ry!
Think of thy father, my equal in birth, inferior in sorrows.
Have I not borne what no dweller on earth before me hath suf-
    fered?
Have I not pressed to my lips the hand that slaughtered my
    children?"
  Tears to the eyes of Achilles rose at the thought of his father.
Laying his hand on the old man's arm he gently removed him.
Sad recollections o'ercame them both—one, weeping for Hector
Unrestrainedly, sank on the earth at the feet of Achilles.
He on his part for his father wept—then grief for Patroclus
Prompted his tears: and groaning arose and sobs through the
    chamber.
  Godlike Achilles, soon as his burst of emotion was over,
And his strong heart and frame, relieved, had resumed their com-
    posure,
Rose from his seat, and, extending his hand, the suppliant monarch
Raised: for his hoary head and beard much moved his compas-
    sion.
Then, in consoling words and in gentlest accents, addressed him:
"O most unhappy! grievous indeed are the woes thou hast suf-
    fered!
How couldst thou dare alone to approach the ships of the Grecians?

How endure to confront the man who so many and valiant
Sons of thine hath destroyed?   Is the heart within thee of iron?
Rise now and take thy seat.   For some brief time let oblivion
Cover our griefs and a respite afford, be they never so bitter.
Little avails to chill the heart with woe and complaining.
Such is the fate of man.   By the Gods above is he destined
Ever in sorrow to live, while themselves from care are exempted.
Fast by the threshold of Zeus two urns are ever established;
Evil gifts from one he bestows, and good from the other.
Who by the Thunderer's hand is supplied from both, in his for-
    tunes
Good comes mingled with ill: now joys, now sorrows await him.
Who from the evil alone his cup must fill, for misfortune
Stands forth a mark.   Destruction hunts him down to devour him:
Through the fair earth he wanders, by Gods rejected and mortals.
Thus upon Peleus ev'n from his birth were show'red by th' Im-
    mortals,
Blessings beyond the common lot.   With pow'r and with riches
Gifted, over the Myrmidon race they gave him dominion,
And to a mortal prince an immortal bride was united;
Yet was his happiness dashed in this, that sons were denied
    him,
Sons to succeed to their father's throne, and rule in his palace.
One he begat—myself; short-liv'd, nor doomed to survive him;
Nor am I nigh, to sustain his age; but, far from my country,
Linger at Troy, to thee and thy race a scourge and affliction.
Thou too wert blest, so fame reports, with extended dominion.
All fair Lesbos and Makar's seats embrace to the northward,
Southward to Phrygia's utmost bounds, to the Hellespont west-
    ward,
Wealth, and a noble array of sons by the Gods were accorded:
But since the dwellers in heav'n these dire afflictions have sent
    thee,
Bloodshed and war unceasing thy city's walls have surrounded;
Therefore endure, nor ceaseless thus let sorrow consume thee:
Naught can avail this bitter regret for thy son.   Thou canst never
Back recall him to life, nor escape such woes as await thee."
    Ended Achilles; and thus the godlike Priam responded:
"Bid me not, favored of Heav'n, arise; so long as my Hector
Lies in thy tent unransomed.   O grant these eyes to behold him,
Once more my own.   Accept those costly gifts that I bring thee,
Price of his lov'd remains.   Thy gains enjoy, and, departing,

Hence to thy home return; and complete the grace thou hast
    shown me,
Sending me forth, to behold the light of day, from thy presence."
  Then with a gathering frown thus spake swift-footed Achilles:
" Anger me not, old man ! 'Tis not for the sake of thy ransom—
'Tis to the ancient sea-god's daughter, the mother that bore me,
Bearing the orders of Zeus himself, that I yield up thy Hector.
This is Heav'n's act. For, Priam, I know, and thou canst not
    conceal it,
One of the Gods must have brought thee safe to the ships of the
    Grecians.
None would have dared—no mortal man, in youth and in vigor,
Could have succeeded in entering our camp and eluding our out-
    posts;
Nor could a mortal arm, from without, my gates have unfastened,
Therefore, old man ! beware, lest thou change my pity to anger;
Lest, though a suppliant here in my tent, I fail to respect thee;
Lest, in despite of Zeus' commands, I do thee a mischief."
Thus he spake: and the old man feared, and rose at his bidding

PRIAM KISSING THE HAND OF ACHILLES.

ODYSSEUS WEEPS AT THE SONG OF DEMODOCUS.

THE ODYSSEY.

It was once supposed that the two epics, the Iliad and the Odyssey, were the product of one great genius who shone forth from the obscure dawn of early Greek civilization. This opinion is no longer accepted by scholars. Both poems, no doubt, were composed by several singers whose ballads and songs were gradually blended into the two epics known to us. Having for hundreds of years no permanent written form, they were given a variety of renderings by bards living in different parts of the country. Even after the epics were preserved in writing they were edited and re-edited until it is often impossible today to distinguish between the early and later portions of the poems.

The Odyssey was probably composed at least two hundred years after the Iliad. It appears to have developed in Greece itself, while the Iliad was known first in Asia Minor. Although in general a similar social life is portrayed in both poems, nevertheless there are indications of an advancing sense of moral obligation, of a more settled life, of a growing intelligence, in the Odyssey.

After the fall of Troy the gods were angry with Ulysses and for ten years baffled his efforts to regain his home in Ithica. Almost twenty years before the beginning of the story related in the Odyssey, he had set sail with the Ithicans to espouse the cause of Menelaus. After the burning of Troy he started back, with the other surviving Greeks, to his native land; buffeted about at the caprice of the immortals, he passed

454

through weary years of disheartening experiences. However, possessing a love of adventure and dauntless courage, he gained much by his very mishaps.

The Odyssey opens with the late weeks of wandering, in the tenth year after the burning of Troy. Received hospitably by Alcinous, Odysseus is led to recount the happenings of recent years. In following his story, related at a banquet given in his honor, we are able to follow the events of his homeward journey. He tells of his escape from the Sirens, of his encounter with the one-eyed giant Polyphemus; of his visit to the island of Aeolus, god of winds, and of the favor shown him by Aeolus in giving into his keeping all adverse winds, upon departure from the magic island. The adventure with Circe, the visit to Hades, the loss of his companions—all these he recounted to his eager listeners.

Meanwhile, Penelope, the patient, faithful wife, awaited the return of her lord. Pressed by suitors who would persuade her that Ulysses could never more return, she long delayed them by agreeing to choose among them when the web she was weaving should be finished. That the fatal day might not arrive, each night she unraveled the labor of the day. Year after year her suitors wasted her substance; year after year Penelope hoped in vain for the return of Odysseus.

Disguising himself as a beggar, Ulysses discovers the insolence of the suitors and plans dire revenge. With some difficulty he is able to persuade Penelope of his identity and is restored to wife and kingdom.

THE SONG OF THE SIRENS.

Thus were my comrades of their several charge
Admonished; and the well-built ship meanwhile
Cut lightly through the waves, and neared the marge
Of that fell coast, the Sister-Sirens' isle.
Anon the wind slept, and for many a mile
Some god in silence hushed the marble mere.
Forthwith our men the canvas furl, and pile
Safe in the hollow ship their naval gear,
Lean to their oars, and whiten the blue waters clear.

Then did I haste to sever with iron keen
In morsels a great roll of wax, which lay

Stored in the hollow ship, and in between
My strong palms pressed and chafed it every way.
Soon the wax warmed, for the great Lord of Day,
Hyperion's offspring, the imperial Sun,
Came to my succor with his burning ray,
So when the mass with heat was nigh to run,
I filled my comrades' ears, in order, one by one.

Then did they bind me by the hands and feet
Upright against the mast with cordage strong,
And each again retiring to his seat
Smote the calm sea with furrows white and long.
We, lightly drifting the blue waves among,
Soon in our course such interval attain
As that the ear might catch the Sirens' song,
Nor did the swift ship moving through the main
Escape them, while they sang this sweet soul-piercing strain:

"Hither, Odysseus, great Achaian name,
Turn thy swift keel and listen to our lay;
Since never pilgrim near these regions came
In black ship, on the azure field astray,
But heard our sweet voice ere he sailed away,
And in his joy passed on, with ampler mind.
We know what labors were in ancient day
Wrought in wide Troia, as the gods assigned;
We know from land to land all toils of all mankind."

While their sweet music took my spirit thus,
I with drawn brows made signal for release;
But Perimedes and Eurylochus
Bind me yet faster and the cords increase,
Nor for my passion would the seamen cease
Their rowing. When no more the Sirens' song
Thrilled the deep air, and on my soul came peace,
My trusty mariners unsealed ere long
Their ears, and from my limbs unwound the cordage strong.

NAUSICAA AND ODYSSEUS.

NAUSICAA is the loveliest female creation of Homer, the type of
innocent, princely maidenhood. She was the daughter of Alcinous,
king of the Phæacians, on whose island of Scheria shipwrecked Odys-

seus was washed ashore. According to the primitive usage, she took
the lead in household duties. Expecting soon to be married, she goes,
accompanied by her maidens, to a lonely stream near the beach to wash
the household linen. After their task is done, they bathe and play
until Odysseus, who had been sleeping in a rude shelter, is roused from
his deep slumbers. The meeting of the sea-worn hero and the bright
princess is here given, as translated by P. S. Worsley.

So when they came to the fair-flowing river,
  Which feeds good lavatories all the year,
Fitted to cleanse all sullied robes soever,
  They from the wain the mules unharnessed there,
  And chased them, free to crop their juicy fare
By the swift river, on the margent green;
  Then to the waters dark the vestments bare,
And in the stream-filled trenches stamped them clean,
Urging the welcome toil with emulation keen.

Which, having washed and cleansed, they spread before
  The sunbeams on the beach, where most did lie
Thick pebbles, by the sea-wave washed ashore.
  So having left them in the heat to dry,
  They to the bath went down, and by-and-by,
Rubbed with rich oil, their mid-day meal essay,
  Couched on green turf, the river rolling nigh;
And thence, unveiling, they rise up to play,
While the white-armed Nausicaa leads the choral lay.

But when she thought to yoke the mules and fold
  The raiment, then Athene cast to wake
Odysseus, that the maid he might behold
  Ere she returned, and following in her wake
  To the Phæacian town her guidance take.
Just then by a false aim she flung the ball
  Far in the swirling river:—the maidens brake
Into a long loud scream, whose echoing call
Odysseus roused. . . . .

Then from the olive-brake Odysseus came,
  And from the forest, all around him spread,
Snapped a young shoot, thick-leaved, to veil his shame—
  And as a lion on the mountains bred,
  With rain and wind and hunger hard bested,
Goes, trusting in his strength, his eyes on fire,
II—30

Against the sheep and oxen making head,
Or rending the wild deer; yea, fierce desire
Drives him in quest of ravin, stung with the famine-fire,

Even a house well-builded to essay—
  So to the fair-haired maidens would have gone
Odysseus—such sore need upon him lay—
  Though naked, his dire anguish to make known,
  But terror seized them when his form was shown,
Squalid with brine; and divers ways they fled,
  Hurrying along the bending banks. Alone
Stood firm Alcinous' child. Athene fed
Her soul with strength, and freed her tender limbs from dread.

Him she stood fronting, while within his heart
  Pondered Odysseus whether now to press
The virgin-knees and all his prayer impart,
  Or if aloof he should the maid address
  With gesture mild and voice of tenderness.
Seemed best her spirit from afar to prove
  With gesture mild and voice of tenderness,
Lest the knees clasping he should anger move.
He in a smooth-set speech to gain her heart thus strove:—

"Queen, hear me—art thou of the earth or skies?
  If of the deities in heaven that dwell,
To Artemis, the child of Zeus, in size
  And form and beauty I thee liken well—
  Or if of mortals who on earth excel,
Thrice fortunate thy mother and thy sire!
  Thrice fortunate thy brothers! Haply swell
Their hearts when they behold in fair attire
Such scion of their house threading the mazy choir

But he more fortunate than all beside,
  Who with rich gifts contending shall prevail
To win thy hand and lead thee home a bride.
  No mortal form did ever these eyes hail,
  How amiable soever, but would fail,
Or man or woman, to compare with thee;
  Yea, as I gaze, much wonder makes me pale.
Lady, I reverence thee, and fear to touch
Thy knees—yet wounding griefs assail me overmuch.

But yester-even, on the twentieth day,
   I was delivered from the wine-dark deep.
Me all that time the waves and storms affray,
   While from Ogygia's isle I onward sweep.
   Now fortune hurls me hither—perchance to weep.
It cannot be the gods will hold their hand.
   O queen, have mercy! To thee first I creep,
Broken with sorrow, and thy help demand,
No mortal else I know inhabiting this land.—

Show me the city, and some shred bestow
   To shield my nakedness, if aught thou hast;
And unto thee the heavenly gods make flow
   Whate'er of happiness thy mind forecast,
   Husband and home and spirit-union fast!
Since naught is lovelier on the earth than this,
   When in the house one-minded to the last
Dwell man and wife—a pain to foes, I wis,
And joy to friends—but most themselves know their own bliss."

To whom Nausicaa, the white-armed, replied:
   "Stranger, who seemest neither vile nor vain,
Zeus both to good and evil doth divide
   Wealth as he listeth. He perchance this pain
   Appointed; thou thy sorrow must sustain.
But, since thou comest to our land and state,
   Nor succor shalt thou lack, nor welcome fain,
Raiment, nor any comfort, small or great,
Such as doth aye behoove on suppliant wretch to wait.

Now to the city will I guidance give,
   And in thy ears unfold this people's name.
Know the Phæacians in this land do live—
   My father is Alcinous, first in fame,
   Large-hearted, who the regal power doth claim,
And sways the sceptre of Phæacia's might."
   She spake, and to her maidens cried: "For shame!
How then hath one man's form put you to flight!
Deem ye a wretch like this some trampler down of right?

That mortal is not living, nor can be,
   Who brings us sword and fire. Far off we dwell,

Loved by the gods, and zoned by the deep sea;
   Nor can men hitherward their barks impel.
   Now comes this wanderer—let us treat him well;
All strangers and all poor by Zeus are sent,
   And love can make a little gift excel.
Come, to this stranger food and drink present,
And in wind-sheltered stream lave ye his limbs sore spent."

Thereat they standing each to other cried,
   Then to wind-sheltered stream Odysseus brave
Led, and a robe and tunic at his side
   Placed, and the golden cruse of oil they gave,
   And bade him wash there, in the river's wave.
   . . . . Divine Odysseus there
In the clean stream dissolved the sea-scurf, rolled
   In flakes about his shoulders, loins and hair;
   Then rubbed his skin with oil, and donned with care
The raiment.   And behold! Athene shed
   New grace, and made him ampler and more fair,
Hued like the hyacinth his locks dispread,
Streaming in loose array from his thrice-glorious head.

ULYSSES AND PENELOPE.

PENELOPE, at the bidding of her son Telemachus, had retired from the hall before the entrance of the disguised Odysseus, and remained in the women's apartments till after the slaughter of the suitors. She was fast asleep when the old nurse came to tell her that Odysseus was come, and had slain the disturbers of her peace. Penelope wavers in mind, but enters the hall and sits down afar off. Telemachus wonders at her coldness and reproves her. But Odysseus smiles and bids all prepare as for a wedding, and himself takes a bath. The following extract is from the translation by W. Cowper, who uses the more familiar Latin form of the hero's name.

    And now Ulysses saw himself attired
    Royally once again in his own house.
    Then Pallas over all his features shed
    Superior beauty, dignified his form
    With added amplitude, and pour'd his curls
    Like hyacinthine flowers down from his brows.

As when some artist by Minerva made
And Vulcan wise to execute all tasks
Ingenious, borders silver with a wreath
Of gold, accomplishing a graceful work,
Such grace the Goddess o'er his ample chest
Copious diffused, and o'er his manly brows.
He, godlike, stepping from the bath, resumed
His former seat magnificent, and sat
Opposite to the Queen, to whom he said:
  "Penelope, the gods to thee have given
Of all thy sex, the most obdurate heart.
Another wife lives not who could endure
Such distance from her husband new-return'd
To his own country, in the twentieth year,
After such hardship. But prepare me, nurse,
A bed, for solitary I must sleep,
Since she is iron, and feels not for me."
  Him answered then prudent Penelope:
"I neither magnify thee, sir, nor yet
Depreciate thee, nor is my wonder such
As hurries me at once into thy arms,
Though my remembrance perfectly retains,
Such as he was, Ulysses, when he sail'd
On board his bark from Ithaca.—Go, nurse,
Prepare his bed, but not within the walls
Of his own chamber built with his own hands.
Spread it without, and spread it well with warm
Mantles, with fleeces, and with richest rugs."
  So spake she, proving him, and, not untouch'd
With anger at that word, thus he replied:
"Penelope, that order grates my ear.
Who hath displaced my bed? The task were hard
Even to an artist; other than a god
None might with ease remove it; as for man,
It might defy the stoutest in his prime
Of youth, to heave it to a different spot,
For in that bed elaborate, a sign.
A special sign consists; I was myself
The artificer; I fashion'd it alone.
Within the court a leafy olive grew
Lofty, luxuriant, pillar-like in girth.
Around this tree I built, with massy stones

Cemented close, my chamber, roof'd it o'er,
And hung the glutinated portals on.
I lopp'd the ample foliage and the boughs,
And severing near the root its solid bole,
Smooth'd all the rugged stump with skillful hand,
And wrought it to a pedestal well squared
And modell'd by the line.   I wimbled, next,
The frame throughout, and from the olive-stump
Beginning, fashioned the whole bed above
Till all was finish'd, plated o'er with gold,
With silver and with ivory, and beneath
Close interlaced with purple cordage strong.
Such sign I give thee.   But if still it stand
Unmoved, or if some other, severing sheer
The olive from its bottom, have displaced
My bed—that matter is best known to thee."
    He ceased; she, conscious of the sign so plain,
Given by Ulysses, heard with fluttering heart
And faltering knees that proof.   Weeping she ran
Direct towards him, threw her arms around
The hero, kissed his forehead, and replied:
    " Ah! My Ulysses! pardon me—frown not—
Thou who at other times hast ever shown
Superior wisdom.   All our griefs have flow'd
From the Gods' will; they envied us the bliss
Of undivided union sweet enjoyed
Through life, from early youth to latest age.
No.   Be not angry now; pardon the fault
That I embraced thee not as soon as seen,
For horror hath not ceased to overwhelm
My soul, lest some false alien should perchance
Beguile me, for our house draws numerous such.
Jove's daughter, Argive Helen, ne'er had given
Free entertainment to a stranger's love,
Had she foreknown that the heroic sons
Of Greece would bring her to her home again.
But heaven incited her to that offence,
Who never, else, had even in her thought
Harbor'd the foul enormity, from which
Originated even our distress.
But now, since evident thou hast described
Our bed, which never mortal yet beheld,

Ourselves except and Actoris, my own
Attendant, given me when I left my home
By good Icarius, and who kept the door,
Though hard to be convinced, at last I yield."
   So saying, she awaken'd in his soul
Pity and grief; and folding in his arms
His blameless consort beautiful, he wept.
Welcome as land appears to those who swim.
Whose gallant bark Neptune with rolling waves
And stormy winds hath sunk in the wide sea,
A mariner or two perchance escape
The foamy flood, and swimming reach the land,
Weary indeed, and with incrusted brine
All rough, but oh, how glad to climb the coast;
So welcome in her eyes Ulysses seem'd,
Around whose neck winding her snowy arms,
She clung as she would loose him never more.

HESIOD.

ETWEEN Homer and Hesiod, the other great poet of the prehistoric period, there is a marvellous contrast. Though both use the same hexameter verse, they agree in little else. Homer is concerned with the exploits and adventures of kings and chiefs, with courts and camps, and treats all aspects of Achaian and Trojan life by land and sea as these are necessary to his song. But of himself he makes no mention, nor gives a hint directly. Far different is the father of didactic poetry.

Hesiod probably lived some generations later than the father of the epic. He treats of agriculture and the humble life of tillers of the soil. His verse, if genuine throughout, tells much of his personal history. Of Æolian descent, he was born at Ascra in Bœotia, and pastured his sheep on the slopes of Helicon. Inspired by the Muses, at an early age he won the prize in a contest of song in funeral games at Chalcis, and dedicated it to Apollo. But his elder brother's injustice deprived him of a share of his father's property; he settled at Orchomenos, where he lived a bachelor and woman-hater. According to some accounts his speadthrift brother sank into distress and begged and received his aid. To his brother he addressed his chief poem, "Works and Days," calling him "most foolish Perses." The contents of the poem are praises of industry and justice, proverbial rules for behavior, advice on husbandry and trade, a description of winter, and a farmer's calendar, with a list of lucky and unlucky days; but besides this homely stuff, the poet tells of the five ages of the world—the golden, silver, bronze, heroic, and finally the iron age, in which he himself was fated to live and suffer. The heroic age, here arbitrarily thrust in, relates to the men of the Trojan war, and this fact seems to bring Hesiod to a later time than Homer. The truly poetical part of this miscellaneous poem is the myth of Prometheus and Pandora, the Greek version of the Fall of Man.

The second work ascribed to Hesiod is the "Theogony," an attempt to reduce to system the conflicting popular notions of the creation of the world and the genealogy of the gods and heroes. Herodotus gives credit for the accepted system to both Homer and Hesiod, probably meaning that the Greeks of later times looked to both authors for instruction on the relative places of the numerous personages of mythology. Some critics, ancient as well as modern, regard the "Theogony" as of different authorship from the "Works and Days." A third poem, much shorter, called the "Shield of Hercules," is also attributed to Hesiod. It relates an adventure of Hercules, but is chiefly occupied with a description of his shield, thus appearing to attempt rivalry with Homer's description of the shield of Achilles.

PANDORA.

(From "The Works and Days.")

THE food of man in deep concealment lies,
The angry Gods have veil'd it from our eyes.
Else had one day bestow'd sufficient cheer,
And, though inactive, fed thee through the year.
Then had the laboring ox foregone the soil,
And patient mules had found relief from toil.
But Jove conceal'd our food, incens'd at heart,
Since mock'd by wise Prometheus' wily art.
Sore ills to man devised the Heavenly Sire,
And hid the shining element of fire.
Prometheus then, benevolent of soul,
In hollow reed the spark recovering stole,
Cheering to man, and mock'd the God, whose gaze
Serene rejoices in the lightning's rays.
"O son of Japhet!" with indignant heart

Spake the Cloud-gatherer, "O unmatch'd in art!
Exultest thou in this the flame retriev'd,
And dost thou triumph in the God deceiv'd?
But thou, with the posterity of man,
Shalt rue the fraud whence mightier ills began:
I will send evil for thy stealthy fire,
Evil, which all shall love, and all admire."

    Thus spoke the Sire, whom Heaven and Earth obey,
And bade the Fire-God mould his plastic clay;
Inbreathe the human voice within her breast,
With firm-strung nerves th' elastic limbs invest.
Her aspect fair as Goddesses above,
A virgin's likeness with the brows of love.
He bade Minerva teach the skill that dyes
The web with colors as the shuttle flies:
He call'd the magic of love's charming queen
To breathe around a witchery of mien,
Then plant the rankling stings of keen desire,
And cares that trick the limbs with prank'd attire;
Bade Hermes last impart the craft refin'd
Of thievish manners and a shameless mind.

    He gives command, the inferior powers obey,
The crippled artist moulds the temper'd clay:
A maid's coy image rose at Jove's behest;
Minerva clasp'd the zone, diffus'd the vest,
Adored Persuasion and the Graces young
Her taper'd limbs with golden jewels hung;
Round her smooth brow the beauteous-tressed Hours
A garland twin'd of Spring's purpureal flowers;
The whole attire Minerva's graceful art
Dispos'd, adjusted, form'd to every part;
And last the winged herald of the skies,
Slayer of Argus, gave the gift of lies;
Gave trickish manners, honeyed words instill'd,
As he, that rolls the deep'ning thunder, will'd:
Then, by the winged messenger of Heaven,
The name PANDORA to the maid was given:
For all the Gods conferred a gifted grace
To crown this mischief of the mortal race.
The Sire commands the winged herald bear
The finish'd nymph, th' inextricable snare:
To Epimetheus was the present brought;

Prometheus' warning vanish'd from his thought,
That he disdain each offering from the skies,
And straight restore, lest ill to man arise.
But he received, and conscious knew too late
Th' insidious gift, and felt the curse of fate.
   On earth, of yore, the sons of men abode
From evil free and labor's galling load:
Free from diseases, that, with racking rage,
Precipitate the pale decline of age.
Now swift the days of manhood haste away,
And misery's pressure turns the temples gray.
The Woman's hands an ample casket bear;
She lifts the lid—she scatters ills in air.
Hope sole remain'd within, nor took her flight,—
Beneath the vessel's verge conceal'd from light.
Issued the rest, in quick dispersion hurl'd,
And woes innumerous roam'd the breathing world:
With ills the land is full, with ills the sea,
Diseases haunt our frail humanity;
Self-wandering through the noon, the night, they glide,
Voiceless—a voice the power all-wise denied:
Know then this awful truth—it is not given
To elude the wisdom of omniscient Heaven.

THE BATTLE OF ZEUS AND THE TITANS.
(From the Theogony.)

ALL on that day roused infinite the war,
Female and male; the Titan deities,
The gods from Cronus sprang, and those whom Zeus
From subterranean gloom released to light:
Terrible, strong, of force enormous; burst
A hundred arms from all their shoulders huge:
From all their shoulders fifty heads upsprang
O'er limbs of sinewy mould. They then arrayed
Against the Titans in fell combat stood,
And in their nervous grasp wielded aloft
Precipitous rocks. On the other side alert
The Titan phalanx closed: then hands of strength
Joined prowess, and displayed the works of war.
Tremendous then the immeasurable sea
Roared: earth resounded: the wide heaven throughout
Groaned shattering: from its base Olympus vast

Reeled to the violence of the gods: the shock
Of deep concussion rocked the dark abyss
Remote of Tartarus: the shrilling din
Of hollow tramplings and strong battle-strokes,
And measureless uproar of wild pursuit.
So they reciprocal their weapons hurled
Groan-scattering, and the shout of either host
Burst in exhorting ardor to the stars
Of heaven: with mighty war-cries either host
Encountering closed.

              Nor longer then did Zeus
Curb his full power, but instant in his soul
There grew dilated strength, and it was filled
With his omnipotence.   At once he loosed
His whole of might, and put forth all the god.
The vaulted sky, the mount Olympian flashed
With his continual presence, for he passed
Incessant forth, and scattered fires on fires.
Hurled from his hardy grasp the lightnings flew
Reiterated swift: the whirling flash
Cast sacred splendor, and the thunderbolt
Fell: roared around the nurture-yielding earth
In conflagration; for on every side
The immensity of forests crackling blazed:
Yea, the broad earth burned red, the streams that mix
With ocean and the deserts of the sea.
Round and around the Titan brood of earth
Rolled the hot vapor on its fiery surge.
The liquid heat air's pure expanse divine
Suffused: the radiance keen of quivering flame
That shot from writhen lightnings, each dim orb,
Strong though they were, intolerable smote,
And scorched their blasted vision: through the void
Of Erebus the preternatural glare
Spread mingling fire with darkness.   But to see
With human eye and hear with the ear of man
Had been as if midway the spacious heaven
Hurtling with earth shocked—e'en as nether earth
Crashed from the centre, and the wreck of heaven
Fell ruinous from high.   So vast the din
When, gods encountering gods, the clang of arms
Commingled, and the tumult roared from heaven.

CHAPTER XII.

THE GREEK LYRIC.

The age of the Greek epic and the age of the lyric were not two sharply defined eras, clearly set off and separated from each other. Such is not the course of development in any literature; rather, the two forms of writing overlapped. While heroic verses were yet widely written, some lyrics appeared, and later, when the epic was declining and the lyric held first place, epics were nevertheless produced.

Great changes had taken place in Greece since the birth of the Homeric poems. Tribes no longer served a chieftain in time of war, and during times of peace tilled the soil. Political revolutions had resulted in various forms of government—oligarchal, democratic and tyrannical. The masses had grown to think for themselves, and more than this, to act for themselves. Along with changed political conditions came social progress. Hellenic colonists extended commerce and brought the products of the east to semi-barbarous Hellas. With these advances in political and social life came progress in literature, which still held to the form of verse.

During tribal days the poet had been content to sing the praises of his king, or of some popular hero. With democratic triumph, however, he gave expression to his own feelings and emotions. And herein we find the difference between the epic and lyric: the epic narrates heroic deeds—the exploits of others; the lyric is personal, and indicates the emotions of the composer.

The word lyric is apparently derived from the word *lyre*, and its close association shows plainly that lyrics were originally sung to the accompaniment of music. If we seek for the beginnings of the Greek lyrics, they are to be found in early wedding chants, dirges, and folk-songs.

It is possible to divide Greek lyrics into (1) elegiacs, (2) iambics, and (3) melics. The first two are named from their metre; the third from its melody. All expressed the poet's own emotions, and all were originally sung to musical accompaniments.

Whether *elegy* came from one Armenian word meaning *flute,* or from another meaning *mournful,* is uncertain. Its theme was not restricted as it later came to be. With the Greeks its subject might range "from war to political philosophy—from moral advice to the pleasures of life."

The first great name to follow Homer was that of Pindar, but the intervening period was spanned by a long series of lyrists, from whom mere fragments alone remain.

Callinus of Ephesus was the first known elegiac poet. The following war-song is attributed to him:

" How long will ye slumber? when will ye take heart
   And fear the reproach of your neighbors at hand?
   Fie! comrades, to think ye have peace for your part,
   Whilst the sword and the arrow are wasting our land!

   Shame!—grasp the shield close! cover well the bold breast,
   Aloft raise the spear as ye march on the foe!
   With no thought of retreat,—with no terror confessed,
   Hurl your last dart in dying, or strike your last blow.

   Oh, 'tis noble and glorious to fight for our all,
   For our country,—our children,—the wives of our love!
   Death comes not the sooner; no soldier shall fall,
   Ere his thread is spun out by the Sisters above.

   Once to die is man's doom; rush, rush to the fight!
   He cannot escape, though his blood were Jove's own;
   For awhile let him cheat the shrill arrow by flight;
   Fate will catch him at last in his chamber alone!

   Unlamented he dies; unregretted. Not so
   When, the tower of his country, in death falls the brave;
   Thrice hallowed his name amongst all high or low,
   As with blessings alive, so with tears in the grave."

Tyrtaeus was a Laconian, and wrote war-songs for the Spartan soldiers. This snatch of an old battle song remains from him:

> " Ye men of Sparta bold,
>   Worthy your sires of old,
>   On the left the shield advance,
>   In the right hand poise the lance,
>   Your dear lives sparing not ;—
>   For such of yore the Spartan's lot ! "

A longer martial song, "How Glorious Fall the Valiant," also remains. It has been commented that while Callinus addresses himself to the actual occasion, showing all to be in danger and exhorting his men to stand or fall as heroes, Tyrtaeus calls to mind some vague patriotism; he gives fresh expression to old maxims instead of concentrating his vigour upon immediate issues. Callinus wrote about 700 B. C.; Tyrtaeus during the second Messenian war—630-600 B. C.

How Glorious Fall the Valiant.

How glorious fall the valiant, sword in hand,
In front of battle for their native land!
But oh! what ills await the wretch that yields,
A recreant outcast from his country's fields!
The mother whom he loves shall quit her home,
An aged father at his side shall roam;
His little ones shall weeping with him go,
And a young wife participate his woe;
While scorned and scowled upon by every face,
They pine for food, and beg from place to place.

Stain of his breed! dishonoring manhood's form,
All ills shall cleave to him: affliction's storm
Shall blind him wandering in the vale of years,
Till, lost to all but ignominious fears,
He shall not blush to leave a recreant's name,
And children, like himself, inured to shame.
But we will drain the life-blood where we stand,

To save our children.—Fight ye side by side,
And serried close, ye men of youthful pride,
Disdaining fear, and deeming light the cost
Of life itself in glorious battle lost.

Leave not our sires to stem the unequal fight,
Whose limbs are nerved no more with buoyant might;
Nor, lagging backward, let the younger breast
Permit the man of age—a sight unblest—
To welter in the combat's foremost thrust,
His hoary head dishevelled in the dust,
And venerable bosom bleeding bare.
But youth's fair form, though fallen, is ever fair,
And beautiful in death the boy appears
The hero boy, that dies in blooming years:
In man's regret he lives, and woman's tears;
More sacred than in life, and lovelier far,
For having perished in the front of war."
                              —*Thom. Campbell's trans.*

Contemporaneous with these elegists, Mimnermus of Asia
Minor composed his verses.   He sang of love rather than war.
His poem on Youth and Love is best remembered:

" What were life, and where its pleasure,
          Golden Venus, wert thou flown!
Ne'er may I omit the pleasure
          Given to man by thee alone,—
          Honied gifts and secret love,
          Joys all other joys above! "

Mimnermus is said to have composed a long poem in praise
of his sweetheart, Nanno, but no part of it has come down to
us.   A soft, luxuriant strain pervades his poems. breathing of
indolent Ionic life, while fast o'ertaking age impresses him in
a melancholy sort of way.

Two lyrists to make politics the burden of their songs were
Solon of Attica and Theognis of Megara.   Solon's verses gave
expression to his wholesome ideas of politics and government.
He was in sympathy with the trend of affairs during his active

life, and this feeling of agreement and harmony is apparent in his poems. Theognis, on the other hand, was a supporter of the oligarchal party, which was at length driven from the city. His property, with that of his political adherents, was confiscated and his life ruined by reverses of fortune. It followed naturally enough that his lyrics were colored by these unhappy experiences, and bitterness toward the masses crept into them. This for example:

To a Statesman.

"Join with the world; adopt with every man
His party views, his temper, and his plan;
Strive to avoid offense, study to please,
Like the sagacious inmate of the seas
That now accommodating color brings,
Conforming to the rock to which he clings,
With every change of place changing his hue;
—The model for a statesman such as you."

Another bit, entitled "Theognis' Prayer," gives evidence of no very lofty mood:

"May Jove assist me to discharge the debt
Of kindness to my friends, and grant me yet
A further boon—revenge upon my foes!
With these accomplished, I could gladly close
My term of life—a fair requital made;
My friends rewarded, and my wrongs repaid,
Gratitude and revenge, before I die
Might make me deemed almost a deity."

One more will suffice:

"With kine and horses, Cyrnus! we proceed
By reasonable rules, and choose a breed
For profit and increase at any price;
Of a sound stock, with no defect or vice.
But in the daily matches that we make,
The price is everything; for money's sake
Men marry: women are in marriage given:

The churl or ruffian that in wealth has thriven
May match his offspring with the proudest race;
Thus everything is mixed, noble and base!
If then in outward manner, form and mind
You find us a degraded, motley kind,
Wonder no more, my friend! The cause is plain,
And to lament the consequence is bain."

Iambic poetry, taking its name from its measure, was the form of expression frequently given to satire and lampoon. Its rhythm was produced by alternating long and short syllables. Greatest of the iambic lyrists was Archilochus of Paros. On the battlefield he one day cast away his shield.

"That shield some Samian decks, which 'gainst the grain
   I left—fair, flawless shield!—beside the wood.
Well! let it go! I and my purse remain;
   Tomorrow's bullskin may be just as good."

Archilochus was popular among the Greeks and the following lines give evidence of a noble soul:

"Tossed on a sea of troubles, Soul, my Soul,
   Thyself do thou control;
And to the weapons of advancing foes
   A stubborn breast oppose;
Undaunted 'mid the hostile might
Of squadrons burning for the fight.

Thine be no boasting when the victor's crown
   Wins thee deserved renown;
Thine no dejected sorrow, when defeat
   Would urge a base retreat:
Rejoice in joyous things—nor overmuch
   Let Grief thy bosom touch
Midst evil, and still bear in mind
How changeful are the ways of humankind."

Simonides of Amorgus wrote iambic verse. His longest poem was a satire directed against the women of his day. His grandson, a gentler spirit, was better known and loved.

Melic poetry, sung to the accompaniment of the lyre, and the development of music went hand in hand. The Greek lyre was originally a four-stringed instrument, and the few notes producible upon it made its music monotonous in the extreme. In the eighth century before Christ, Terpander invented a seven-stringed lyre, and music immediately made rapid advance. Along with it, melic poetry gained favor.

Melic poetry fell into two classes: Aeolian lyrics, which were written for one voice only, and Dorian choral songs, composed for choruses, singing as they danced. Greatest of Aeolian singers was Sappho, who lived, as did Alcaeus, on the island of Lesbos. Here indeed the Aeolian verse had its birth. A school for the instruction of young maidens, singing to the cithera, or lyre, was here founded and taught by Sappho.

SAPPHO.

All womanhood expressed in one great soul,
   Her love, her hope, her trust, and her desire,
A single instance of a mighty whole,
   Revealed in character of living fire.

Shall it be said the whole is incomplete,
   The woman's only—not the master's power?
Nay, owning both, she does forever speak
   As with the freshness of her June-time flower.
         —*Mary M. Adams: Sonnets and Songs.*

The character of Sappho has been basely maligned. It would appear that she was a lovely, passionate woman, who loved intensely and voiced her feeling in verse. In her own land she was honored, and long after her death, her memory was fondly cherished. It remained for later ages to misinterpret her passion, and to weave stories wholly to her discredit, until today her name is frequently used as synonymous with sensuality.

Lines written by Sappho concerning her little daughter have been rendered in English in this way:

"I have a child, a lovely one,
  In beauty like the golden sun,
  Or like sweet flowers of earliest bloom:
And Cleris is her name, for whom
I Lydia's treasures, were they mine,
  Would glad resign."

The following lines have been offered as translation for one of her fragments:

To a Maiden.

"Of foliage and flowers love-laden,
  Twine wreathes for thy flowing hair,
With thine own soft fingers, maiden,
  Weave garlands of parsley fair.
For flowers are sweet, and the Graces
  On suppliants wreathed with, may
Look down from their heavenly places,
  But turn from the crownless away."

One of Sappho's fragments, literally translated, would read in this manner: "Evening, thou that bringest all that bright morning scattered; thou bringest the sheep, the goat, the child back to her mother." This has been rendered by modern poets in a variety of ways:

"Hesperus brings all things back
  Which the daylight made us lack;
  Brings the sheep and goats to rest,
  Brings the baby to the breast."

Or again:

"O Evening, thou who bringest everything
  That the bright, glaring day has scattered wide,
The sheep thou bringest, and thou bring'st the goat,
  The child thou bringest to his mother's side."

The loss of Sappho's poetry is deeply to be deplored. "So perfect in the smallest fragments that we muse in a sad rapture of astonishment to think what the complete poems must have been. Of all the poets of the world, of all the illustrious artists of all literature, Sappho is the one whose every word has a peculiar and unmistakable perfume, a seal of absolute perfection and inimitable grace."

Alcaeus lived contemporaneously with Sappho, about 600 B. C. Of his writings, also, only fragments remain, and it is not possible to adequately estimate his work from these bits. Horace imitated his style in certain of his odes, which fact alone would give evidence of his genius. A fragment on Winter has been rendered thus:

> " The rain of Zeus descends, and from high heaven
>   A storm is driven;
> And on the running water-brooks the cold
>   Lays icy hold:
> Then up! beat down the winter; make the fire
>   Blaze high and higher;
> Mix wine as sweet as honey of the bee
>   Abundantly;
> Then drink with comfortable wool around
>   Your temples bound.
> We must not yield our hearts to woe, or wear
>   With wasting care;
> For grief will profit us no whit, my friend,
>   Nor nothing mend;
> But this is our best medicine, with wine fraught
>   To cast out thought."

Anacreon also wrote in the Aeolian style. He lived in Teos, Asia Minor. His compositions held high favor, and shortly there arose a host of imitators, whose poems have been called Anacreontics. These were long attributed to Anacreon, but it is now generally accepted as probable that they were produced by later writers.

THE WISER PART.—ODE VIII.

> " I care not for the idle state
> Of Persia's king, the rich, the great;
> I envy not the monarch's throne
> Nor wish the treasured gold my own.
> But oh! be mine the rosy wreath,

Its freshness o'er my brow to breathe;
Be mine the rich perfumes that flow,
To cool and scent my locks of snow.
Today I'll haste to quaff my wine,
As if tomorrow ne'er would shine;
But if tomorrow comes, why then—
I'll haste to quaff my wine again.
And thus while all our days are bright,
Nor time has dimmed their bloomy light,
Let us the festal hours beguile
With mantling cup and cordial smile;
And shed from each new bowl of wine
The richest drop on Bacchus' shrine.
For Death may come, with brow unpleasant,
May come, when least we wish him present,
And beckon to the sable shore,
And grimly bid us—drink no more!"

It remains to speak of choral melic poetry—songs written for choruses, and accompanied by the dance. Chorales were composed for a variety of occasions: processionals, hymns to deities, songs honoring brave men, and odes commemorating victories in athletic contests at the national festivals. Alcman was one of the earliest composers of choral songs. He lived about the middle of the seventh century. Many fragments have come down to us from him; the following literal translation gives evidence of his appreciation of nature: "The peaks of the mountains and the ravines are sleeping, the capes and the torrents, the leaves and all creeping things that the dark earth nourishes, the beasts of the mountains and the race of bees, and the monsters in the depths of the dark seas; the tribes of long-winged birds are asleep."

Arion of Lesbos made an innovation,—a musical dialogue between the leader and the chorus, and in this we find the beginnings of the Greek chorus, so prominent in Greek tragedy.

Greatest of choral lyrists was Pindar of Thebes. In the story of Hellas we have found that Alexander the Great, two hundred years after the poet's age, spared his home when destroying Thebes. Pindar was a noble, and held naturally to the conservative, the aristocratic order of things. However, he was broad enough to take a wide view of life, and was a poet of all Hellas and for all Hellenes. His wide popularity was due, without doubt, to his triumphal odes, which made him indispensable at the great national festivals. We still possess many songs of victory composed in honor of those who bore away the laurel and palm, the parsley and pine, from the four great festivals of ancient Greece. These odes are splendid, the more because Pindar never stooped to mere fulsome flattery, but in dignified strains he mentioned the ancient family of the victor, did honor to the winner's town and wove into the ode some legend or mythological tale connected with the locality of the winner or his house. · All these odes have interest, not only for their artistic value and poetic strains, but for the historical significance as well. The following lines comprised the third ode, and were written in commemoration of an Isthmian victory:

Strophe.

" The man, by fortune raised, that holds
    Unflushed with pride his blameless course,
Though glory's wreath his front enfolds,
    Or wealth with power hath blessed his stores,
His country's praise to deathless fame shall give.
    Yet but from thee th' exalted virtues flow,
All-bounteous Jove! and they that know,
And fear thy laws, rejoice and live;
    While he that walks sin's wandering way,
    Ends not in bliss the changeful day.

Antistrophe.

Reward awaits the virtuous dead;
    The brave command the grateful lyre;
For then th' applauding Graces lead,
    And swell the loud triumphal choir.
Fortune on proud Melissus hath bestowed
    The two-fold boon, that glads his manly breast;—
    First in the cirque his waving crest
With Isthmian wreaths exalting glowed;
    Now through the Lion's vale the name
    Of Thebes his herald's shout proclaim.

EPODE.

Him master of the equestrian race
   Proclaim; his deeds no kindred name disgrace:
   His grandsire's fame, 'mong charioteers of old,
   Cleonymus, all tongues have told;
Told how from Labdacus, with affluence
His mother's sires in happier days
   The car quadrigal proudly drove.
   But Time, as rolling seasons onward move,
His alternating hand on all things lays.
The sons of gods alone nor chance nor change can wound."

   —Written in honor of Melissus who won the chariot race.

"Pindar was of all the poets of his time the best fitted by birth, training and genius to do justice to such subjects as the great religious festivals offered him. An aristocrat through and through, he makes the nobility of family and the proud traditions of race stand out in bold relief. Closely connected himself with the worship of Apollo at Delphi, he keeps the religious aspect of the festivals in the foreground, not permitting the mere athletic side to overshadow all else. Keenly alive to the grander and more imposing aspects of external nature, he never lets us forget the splendid scenes through which his subject leads him. And finally, with his superb genius as a poet and his marvellous mastery of musical and choral technique, he produced poems which are perfect as works of art. The Greeks counted him their greatest lyric poet." [1]

[1]Capps: Homer to Theocritus, p. 175.

DESCRIPTION OF ILLUSTRATIONS

IN PART II.

JOPPA GATE—JERUSALEM.

The city of Jerusalem at present, as in Bible times, is enclosed by a high wall. At intervals in the wall gates are placed, giving entrance and exit to the throng that press back and forth. The Joppa Gate is most important, it giving access to the long road which connects Joppa with Jerusalem. During the day the gates are open. At night they are closed and he who would enter must come through the "needle's eye," which is a small gate placed in the larger one. A camel can squeeze through with difficulty, hence the expression in the time of Christ that it is as difficult for a rich man to attain heaven as for a camel to pass through the "needle's eye."

CHRISTIAN STREET—JERUSALEM.

This is the bazaar district as seen at present in Jerusalem. Observe the various nationalities shown in the picture. Here the tourist comes to buy his souvenirs from the Mohammedan, Armenian, or Hebrew who own the bazaars and form the greater part of the permanent population; truly in the narrow street is depicted the present motley life in the Holy City.

JERUSALEM FROM THE MOUNT OF OLIVES.

The city of Jerusalem does not look like our American cities. It is divided into four sections, the Mohammedans occupying the northeast portion; the Christians, the northwest; the Armenians, the southwest; the Jews, the southeast. In modern times quite a city has grown up outside the city walls. Taken altogether, within and without, the population is estimated at 57,000; 42,000 being Jews. The Mount of Olives lies east of the city and is now crowned by a Greek church. In the time of Christ it was covered with vineyards and olive groves.

THE SEA OF GALILEE.

We would probably call this a lake rather than a sea. In the time of Christ it was settled almost all the way around the shore, nine towns being located upon it. Today, as then, fishermen dwell upon its waters and cast their nets for fish. The water is frequently quiet but may be lashed into fury by winds from the north in an incredibly short time.

THE DEAD SEA.

This is the lowest spot on the earth's surface, lying 1,300 feet below sea level. The water is very dense, so that it is impossible for one to sink in it or even wade out waist-deep. From the Mount of Olives it may be seen in the clear light of day seeming to be but three or four miles distant, whereas it is in reality eighteen miles away. The vapor from the surface of the sea can be seen from far distant points constantly rising as from a great caldron.

Hera.

Hera was the Queen of Heaven. She was the wife of Zeus and the mother of Hebe, Ares and Hephaestus. Very beautiful herself, she was thought to be jealous of the beauty of others. She presided over marriage and the birth of children.

Poseidon.

Poseidon was god of the sea. Brother of Zeus and Pluto, he was thought to be envious of Zeus' dominion and to be ever encroaching upon the land. Thus did early people explain the action of the waves against the shore. Poseidon is generally shown in art with a trident in his hand. His home was in the caves of ocean.

Athena.

Athena was goddess of wisdom. She alone of all the Greek deities never committed a foolish act. She entered into a contest with Poseidon for the naming of Athens. Zeus declared that the one who should make the most useful gift to the city should have this honor. Poseidon struck the ground and the horse sprang forth. Athena thrust her spear into the earth and the olive tree came forth. With its grateful shade, its nourishing oil and fruit, this was considered the greater gift and she called the city by her one name—Athens.

Niobe.

Niobe had seven sons and seven daughters. Leto had two children, Apollo and Artemis. She was so proud of her twins that she made boast of their accomplishments, whereupon Niobe laughed her to scorn. In revenge, Leto commanded Apollo to slay Niobe's seven sons and Artemis to slay her daughters. In art Niobe is shown trying to save her last daughter, whereupon the gods, in pity for her grief, changed both into stone. The myth has been interpreted to explain an aspect of nature, the sons being darkness whom the shafts of light put to flight.

Venus de Milo.

Venus, or *Aphrodite*, was goddess of beauty. It was said that she had been born one day of the ocean wave, as it broke in gleaming whiteness off the coraled rocks. Favorite among the Greeks, she was frequently represented in art. This statue, so generally known today, was dug up in modern times on the island of Melos, in the Aegean Sea. Both arms were gone and what their position was no one knows. In spite of this defect, the statue is surpassingly beautiful and is now preserved in the Louvre.

The Acropolis and Temple of Jupiter.

This is the hill in the city of Athens upon which the first settlement was made in prehistoric times. Primitive people located here for the sake of protection; later, the hill became a sort of fort where they might take refuge in times of disquietude. Finally when it was no longer needed for this purpose, the Greeks placed upon it their finest temples and buildings, these being sacred to the divinities which had given prosperity and peace to Athens. There may be seen today, as indicated in the picture, all that remains of the temple of Jupiter and ruins of other once magnificent temples.

Study Guide Book Two

Palestine

"Two great currents of thought and influence flow out of the past. United, they determine to a great extent the character of that which today is called 'civilization.' Hellenism contributed the elements of philosophy, art and political organization, and the canons of scientific thought; but this fair stream, abounding in so much that stimulated human progress was pitiably destitute in that which is the basis of higher good. This was religion. Rising farther back in human history there came from the barren hills of Canaan that other current which furnished those absolute essentials to the highest civilization—religion, ethics, and the elements of the laws which regulate the relations of man to man and to his God.

". . . The Hebrews first taught man that the supreme goal of life is righteousness. Consequently they are the great ethical teachers of humanity. Hand in hand with ethics went its objective expression—law. Today the elements of Hebrew legislation have become the bone and marrow of the world's greatest legal systems. In grappling with the social problems of their age, the enlightened Hebrew prophets, priests and wise men deduced social laws which are as applicable today as they were twenty-five hundred years ago. Therefore for the student of religion, law and social science Hebrew history possesses pre-eminence with no other. It also furnishes the historical background without which the literature and thought of the Old Testament is only half intelligible." –Kent

I. Hebrew Manners and Customs

1. Certain benefits befell the Hebrews through contact with the Canaanites. What were they? 2:7

2. Under what circumstances did the simplicity of early years give way to luxury? 2:8

3. Were the Hebrews builders? 2:9

4. Who built their famous temple?

5. What additional light has been thrown upon their history by recent excavation? 2:46

6. Read Whittier's beautiful poem on Palestine. 2:viii

II. Hebrew Literature

The great literature of the world all have their distinctive character, and the comparison of their differences adds greatly to one's enjoyment of them. Even the most casual reader recognizes that the Old Testament has a style which is different from that of English literature. A discerning reader will see a difference between the Old Testament books and those of the New Testament. A partial explanation of this difference is found in the Hebrew language.

There was but one connective in Hebrew, vav, and its meaning was quite indefinite, says Gardiner in The Bible as English Literature: "In the King James Version it is translated indifferently, and, but, or so, and sometimes incorrectly, when. Thus we get the constant succession of ands which are so familiar a characteristic of Biblical style."

These were but two tenses in the Hebrew verb, and these did not express time. One indicated action going on, whether in the past, present or future, and the other represented action completed in the past, present or future. There were no potential or subjunctive moods. These limitations of language result in a limitation of logic. While few literatures express single ideas with greater emotional and imaginative force than the Hebrew, there is an almost complete absence of the philosophical writing which connects one idea with another.

1. What Hebrew writings are known to have been lost? 2:12

2. In what way may Hebrew poetry be classified? 2:13

3. Many kinds of odes, elegies, songs, etc. are included in the Psalms. Note some of them. 2:16

4. Was the Song of Solomon written by him? 2:21, 61

5. What does it teach? 2:22

6. The Book of Job is a drama. Read what is said of it in chapter 16, p. 23

7. What well-known musical production tells part of the story?

8. What biblical book contains much folklore? 2:32

9. The Book of Ruth is an exquisite idyl. Read what is said of it, p. 35, and then turn to p. 48 and read the entire story.

10. For what purpose was the Book of Jonah probably written? 2:36

11. What is meant by Wisdom literature? 2:39

12. Compare the essay on Friendship, contained in Ecclesiasticus, 41, with essays by Bacon, Cicero and Emerson on the same theme.

BOOKS FOR ADDITIONAL READING

Home Life in All Lands by Morris
The House by Brevier
Study of Child Life by Washburne
Semitic Origins by Barton
Hebrew Religion to the Establishment of Judaism by Addis
The Religion of the Old Testament by Karl Marti
Historical Geography of the Holy Land by George Adams Smith Armstrong
History of the People of Israel by Cornill
Short History of the Hebrew by Ottley
History of the Hebrew People by Kent (2 volumes)
Social Life of the Hebrews by Edward Day
Modern Reader's Bible by Ed Moulton
Life and Literature of the Ancient Hebrews by Lyman Abbott Houghton
Short Introduction to Literature of the Bible by Richard Moulton
Literary Study of the Bible by Richard Moulton
Out-of-Doors in the Holy Land by Henry Van Dyke

I. Greek Mythology

The whole body of legends which these early people developed to account for the origin and the progress of the world, with all the lore which came to gather around their divinities, we call mythology. The stories which we call myths, and which make up the literature we call mythology, were not the imaginings of poets and dreamers, but they were the explanations devised by grown people, in the childhood age of the world, to account for the mysteries of nature. As ages passed, and the real significance of natural phenomena was better comprehended, stories expanded to meet the expanding ideas, or the stories told in the same way meant more to those who told them.

Greek mythology is of more interest to us than that of any other nation because of the beauty of the stories themselves; because these stories have been the inspiration of so much of our literature and art; and because they have been a potent influence in shaping the very language we speak.

For our practical age, when even the studies of our children are closely scrutinized to make sure that they will prove directly useful in future years, perhaps there is nothing more urgently needed than something which shall lift us out of the sordid world in which we live and stimulate our imaginations. A study of the beautiful is the surest means of accomplishing this end–whether the beautiful in art, literature or nature. If we seek the beautiful in thought and fancy, we can do no better than to wander with the early Greeks in the realm of nature myths, where each moving branch or flower suggested the presence of divinity. After all, it was not an unwholesome notion that every fountain contained a nymph who might overhear anything amiss that was said; that each tree was the home of a dryad and so should not ruthlessly be destroyed. Ancient Greece was a beautiful land and the Greeks loved beauty. They developed the most beautiful language the world has known, and their fancies were clothed in this beautiful language. The beauty of nature laid strong hold of them, while for the most part discordant aspects passed by, unheeded. It is well for those of us who are taxed by the strenuous life of moderns to turn aside now and then, and wander with the child-like Greeks in their simple world of fancy. Rested by their simplicity, refreshed by their glorious conceptions, we cannot fail to bring back some of the beauty, some of the simplicity to enhance our own surroundings and make keener our perceptions of nature's varied moods.

1. How can we explain the nature myths that grew up among the Greeks in early times? 2:78-82

2. For what reasons is some acquaintance with Greek Mythology essential for all educated people? 2:82

3. Is it true that people today need to have their imaginations stimulated?

4. Memorize if possible the quotation from Ruskin on 2:84-85. It contains wholesome truths for us all.

5. How did the Greeks account for the existence of the world? 2:86

6. The early Greeks looked back to a Golden Age; we of today look forward to one. Compare our conceptions of a Golden Age with theirs. 2:92

7. Why has the story of Prometheus appealed to poets of all ages? 2:95

8. Read Longfellow's beautiful poem. 2:98

9. Compare the Greek version of the Deluge myth with that of the Hebrews and Babylonians. 2:99

II. Greek Deities

1. What was the attitudes of the early Greeks toward

their divinities?   2:100

2. Read the story of Iris, whose presence was made known by the rainbow in the sky. 2:110

3. Athena, Goddess of Wisdom, was the most perfect conception of Greek divinity. Read what is said of her. 2:115

4. Why was the owl supposed to be sacred to her? 2:121

5. Compare the two explanations offered for the changing of the seasons. 2:124, 159

6. What was the mythical origin of the hyacinth? 2:124 The laurel? 2:125 The sunflower? 2:126 The myrrh tree?   2:125

7. What was the oracle of Delphi? 2:128. Find Delphi on the map.

8. What is the story of Artemis, Diana and Endymion?   2:132 Keats and other poets have immortalized the theme.

9. How came it about that a certain hill in Athens was called the Areopagus? 2:136

10. Vulcan possessed great skill in metal work. Read the description of the shield he was accredited of having made for Achilles, related by Homer.

11. How did the early Hellenes account for the origin of Aphrodite, Goddess of Beauty? Remember the story when the spray gleams some day on the rocks and catch some faint conception of the subtle Greek imagination.

12. What is the symbolic meaning of the Psyche myth? 2:147

13. What truth does Lowell's "Finding of the Lyre" convey? 2:153

14. Who were the Fates? 2: 157

15. How did the Hellenes account for their mythical creatures, the dolphins? 2:164

16. What was the origin of the Greek drama? 2:167

17. Note how well Keats carries out the spirit of the festivals celebrated in honor of the wine-god in his poem. 2:167

18. Read the description of Poseidon's (Neptune') dwelling in the sea and note that it was no more

wonderful–not very different–than the grottoes and ocean caves seen today in marine gardens, for example, off the Pacific coast.

19. Read the myths of the sirens, 2:176, and see how naturally they arose in the early days.

20. Compare the spirit of the poem "To the Winds" with the stories of the wind deities.　2:182

21. How did the expression, "the halycon days," come into being?　2:187

22. Our word tantalize had what origin?　2:192

23. Who was the greatest musician of mythical lore? 2:195

24. What do we mean by Nemesis?　2:204

25. Who was the Old Man of the Sea?　2: 220

26. Where are the Atlas Mountains?　The story of Atlas is told 2:221, 180.

III. Stories for Children

Note: Most children love imaginative stories and enjoy

mythological tales as well as fairy stories. It is urged that they be made familiar with old Greek myths in early years, in which case they will generally retain them for future remembrance.

1. The Golden Age, 2:91
2. The Story of Echo 2:106
3. Arachne the Spinner 2:118
4. The Apple of Discord 2:141
5. The Golden Touch 2:164
6. Pan and Apollo 2:169
7. Perseus and the Gorgons 2:178
8. Aurora and Tithonus 2:183
9. The Bag of Winds 2:185
10. All stories of Hercules 2:206

Many other stories are available and more can easily be adapted to young listeners. They will bear repeating again and again and will soon become popular if not at first appreciated.

IV. Mythology in Art

1. How was Zeus represented in Greek Art 2:104

2. Why was Cupid given the form so well known to us? 2:144

3. Study the Psyche myth in connection with the beautiful modern painting, "Psyche at Nature's Mirror." 2:144

4. Hermes–Mercury–is a well known figure in bronze. Why is he thus shown? 2:148

5. There are several conceptions of the Fates in painting. Try to find them.

6. Who was Aurora and how is she generally represented. 2:183

7. How did the Greeks represent Sleep? 2:178

It is most helpful to accumulate copies of the old mythological beings. They are available in inexpensive prints which are useful indeed. Some familiarity with famous statues and paintings acquired in this way will make visits to art galleries far more pleasurable.

V. Greek Literature

1. Which form of literature, prose or poetry, as a rule finds first expression among a people? 2:429

2. What was the function of the early bards? 2:429 Why do they no longer survive?

3. For what audience did Hesiod write? 2:464

4. What is meant by lyric poetry? 2:469

5. What service was rendered melic poetry by Terpander? 2:475

6. What was the true character of the Greek Sappho? 2:475

7. Who was Pindar, and why did Alexander the Great spare his home in the destruction of Thebes? 2:478

BOOKS FOR FURTHER READING:

Manual of Mythology by Murray
Myths of Greece and Rome by Guerber
Classic Myths by Gayley
The Mythology of Greece and Rome by Fairbanks-Appleton
Classical Mythology by D'Ooge
Tanglewood Tales by Hawthorne
Wonder Book by Hawthorne
Greek Gods, Heroes and Men by Harding
Favorite Greek Myths by Hyde
Gods and Heroes by Francillon
Mythology in Marble by Bell
Classic Myths in Art by Addison

VI. Political and Social Life of Greece

For you must know that of all the peoples that have ever lived the Greeks were the greatest, the keenest-witted, the most intelligent, the most artistic. There was nothing they did not see to know, or if they did not know it they divined it. They had the noblest and most perfect language ever invented by any nation; and not only that: they had the most to say, and said it better than any other race of men that ever lived. Others took lumps of stone and modelled and chipped and hammered them into rude likenesses of human figures and faces; the Greeks took the snowy marble and made it live, filling it with heavenly grace, charged every limb with mysterious force, and did everything but make the marble talk. Others built great pyramids and labyrinths and systems of artificial irrigation, or filled their land with mummies and sphinxes; the Greeks with the wand of enchantment made their glorious shrines and dwelling-places for their gods, their porticoes and marketplaces, their theatres and colonnades, rise all over their cities and filled them with a varied throng of folk eager to inquire, to learn, to study political life, to buy and sell, to teach and to worship. Finally the Greeks gave the world the most perfect poems and dramas, . . . and the most eloquent discourses that we can ever hope to have."
–Prof. Jas. A. Harrison

The early Greeks possessed a quick appreciation of beauty and a rare sense of proportion –qualities stimulated by nature of the land wherein they dwelt. Because they were thus gifted, the people as a whole attained more nearly to perfection in whatever they attempted than have other nations. The most perfect language so far evolved is the Greek language; the noblest literature, the Greek literature. The finest specimens of sculpture are those which remain to us of Greek execution; the greatest philosophers the world has yet produced have been Greek philosophers. In the domain of civil life the Greeks strove for equality, and they tried many experiments in government which we may still study with profit.

"They had faults in abundance, and a great part of their history is the history of discord and violence. But in the midst of these evils we shall meet with instances of the most striking goodness; and while the vices of the Greeks belonged to other ancient nations, their good points raised them in many respects above all the rest of mankind. No other race ever did so many different things as well as the Greeks. They were the first people who thought of finding out the truth and the reason in everything. Busy men in our own day take pleasure in what remains of Greek poetry and history, and artists know that they can never make anything more beautiful than what is left of Greek sculpture. Men will always be interested in ancient Greece, not only because the Greeks were so bright and so clever themselves, but because so many things which we value most in our own life, such as the desire for knowledge, the power of speaking eloquently, and the arts of music and painting, have come down to us from the Greeks."

Since the civilization we possess has been inherited largely from the Greeks, and our debt to them is greater than to any other people, it is natural that we should wish to know by what successive steps these children of the Aryan race, these first scientific inquirers after truth, came into an understanding of the world around them; how they organized themselves into little states, and attained to a superior degree of civilization. We can only hope to consider the general development of their race, establishing certain landmarks which shall serve to guide all our subsequent study of this ancient people. The importance of our subject, however, cannot be too often called to mind, for without some understanding of Greek history it is not possible to comprehend modern civilization. Among the Greeks modern civilization had its beginnings.

The Land of Greece

The early people whom we call Greeks never called themselves by that name. They believed that they were descended from an illustrious ancestor Hellen, and taking his name, they called themselves Hellenes and their country Hellas. By the time authentic history begins they were established not only in the little country we know as Greece, but upon the islands of the Aegean Sea, along the western coast of Asia Minor and the shores of Italy. Wherever Hellenes lived there was Helas, and although continental Greece may be regarded as their especial home, they set no limits to their territory.

The following outlined reading has been prepared to aid the general reader and the beginner in historical study to acquire readily some familiarity with these ancient people and the civilization they evolved.

VII. Prehistoric Greece

1. Study the map of Greece until its principal divisions are clearly in mind. Note its general topography and its island-dotted seas.

2. What noted German in recent times discovered what is supposed to have been the site of ancient Troy? 2: 236

3. For what reason has the prehistoric civilization of Greece become known as Mycenaean civilization? 2:241

4. What motives prompted early peoples to settle on hilltops? 2:241

5. What is now believed as to the origin of the Iliad and the Odyssey? 2:88, 247

6. What is the general theme of the Iliad? The Odyssey? 2:248

7. What armor was worn by a Homeric hero? 2:252

8. How were women occupied in this remote age? 2:260

9. Read of the quarrel between Achilles and Agememnon. 2:440

10. The parting between Hector and Andromache is one of the most beautiful passages in all literature. 2:446

11. The Odyssey recounts the various experiences of Ulysses in his homeward voyage from Troy. How did he and his followers pass the sirens? 2:455

12. Read the selection in which the interview between Nausicaa and Ulysses is recounted. 2:456

Note: The Iliad and Odyssey are perhaps the greatest of

all literary productions. They are available today in both prose and poetical English versions. Some acquaintance with them will prove very enjoyable. It is especially urged that children be encouraged to browse among their store-houses of tales at will.

VIII. Political Life in Greece

1. Why should the history of the ancient Greeks appeal particularly to us today? 2:227-28

2. What sources have we for knowledge of these people? 2:262

3. What was the Spartan idea of a state? How closely did the Spartans adhere to this conception? 2:272

4. Do you understand what was the acropolis of Athens? 2:275

5. What did the word tyrant signify originally? 2:285

6. Why was it impossible for the Greeks to develop large states? 2:288

7. Physical conditions tended to separate the Greeks. What tended to unify them? 2:289

8. How do you account for the victory of Marathon? 2:295

9. Why does the story of the defense of Thermopylae inspire us even yet? 2:297

10. What were Percles' hopes for Athens? 2:305

11. Note that Athens was at its greatest during the truce that preceded the Peloponnesian War. 2:318

12. What brought about this great civil war in Greece? 2:322

13. What was Pericles' policy for the conduct of the war? 2:332

14. How can we account for the Great Plague that broke out in Athens in 438 B.C.? 2:334

15. Read what is quoted from Percles' speech at the Memorial Services held at the close of the first year of the war. 333 Portions of this may fittingly be compared to Lincoln's speech at Gettysburg.

16. What was the Sicilian Expedition? 2:339 Read Thucydides' masterly description of its fate. 2:342

17. Note that with the failure of this Expedition,

Athens fell rapidly from power. 2:344

18. What did Philip of Macedon do for Greece? 2:356

19. Alexander the Great is one of the foremost characters in all history. Note how much he accomplished before his death at thirty-three years of age. 2:366

20. By the Hellenizing of the East is meant the diffusion of Greek learning and culture, made possible by Alexander's conquests. This was their most important result. 2:369

IX. Social Life

1. Compare our cities of today with those in ancient Greece. 2:375

2. Which were regarded as of greater importance: public or private buildings? 2:377

3. How were Greek houses lighted? 2:378

4. Where was the real home of the Greek? 2:376

5. What garments were worn generally by the Hellenes? 2:382